The Friend

The Friend

ALAN BRAY

The University of Chicago Press
Chicago and London

Alan Bray was Honorary Research Fellow in Birkbeck College, University of London, and co-convenor of the Seminar on Society, Belief, and Culture in the Early Modern World. He also wrote *Homosexuality in Renaissance England*.

The University of Chicago Press, Chicago 60637
The University of Chicago Press, Ltd., London
© 2003 by The University of Chicago
All rights reserved. Published 2003
Printed in the United States of America

12 11 10 09 08 07 06 05 04 03   1 2 3 4 5

ISBN: 0-226-07180-4 (cloth)

Portions of the book appeared previously in the following publications: "The Body of the Friend: Continuity and Change in Masculine Friendship in the Seventeenth Century," with Michael Rey, in *English Masculinities, 1600–1800*, edited by Tim Hitchcock and Michèle Cohen (London: Longman, 1999); "Homosexuality and the Signs of Male Friendship in Elizabethan England," *History Workshop Journal* 29 (1990): 1–19 (used by permission of Oxford University Press), reprinted in *Queering the Renaissance*, edited by Jonathan Goldberg (Durham, NC: Duke University Press, 1994); "Friendship, the Family, and Liturgy: A Rite for Blessing Friendship in Traditional Christianity," *Theology and Sexuality* 13 (2000): 15–33 (used by permission of Sheffield Academic Press Ltd.), reprinted in *Celebrating Christian Marriage*, edited by Adrian Thatcher (Edinburgh: T&T Clark, 2001); "Why Is It That Management Seems to Have No History?" *Reason in Practice: The Journal of Philosophy of Management* 1, no. 1 (2001): 21–25; "Medieval Blessing," *Lesbian and Gay Christians* 57 (2000).

Library of Congress Cataloging-in-Publication Data

Bray, Alan.
    The friend / Alan Bray.
        p. cm.
    Includes bibliographical references and index.
    ISBN 0-226-07180-4 (cloth : alk. paper)
    1. Male friendship—England—History. 2. Homosexuality, Male—England—History. I. Title.
    BJ1533.F8 B755 2003
    177'.62'09—dc21

2003002464

⊗The paper used in this publication meets the minimum requirements of the American National Standard for Information Sciences—Permanence of Paper for Printed Library Materials, ANSI Z39.48-1992.

To the memory of my beloved parents, Elsie and Jack Bray

In Paradisum deducant eos angeli:
in eorum adventu suscipiant martyres,
et perducant eos in civitatem sanctam Ierusalem.

JOHNSON. "Why, Madam, strictly speaking, he is right. All friendship is preferring the interest of a friend, to the neglect, or, perhaps, against the interest of others; so that an old Greek said, 'He that has *friends* has no *friend.*' Now Christianity recommends universal benevolence, to consider all men as our brethren, which is contrary to the virtue of friendship, as described by the ancient philosophers. Surely, Madam, your sect must approve of this; for, you call all men *friends.*" MRS. KNOWLES. "We are commanded to do good to all men, 'but especially to them who are of the household of Faith.'" JOHNSON. "Well, Madam. The household of Faith is wide enough." MRS. KNOWLES. "But, Doctor, our Saviour had twelve Apostles, yet there was *one* whom he *loved.* John was called 'the disciple whom JESUS loved.'" JOHNSON. (with eyes sparkling benignantly) "Very well, indeed, Madam. You have said very well." BOSWELL. "A fine application. Pray, Sir, had you ever thought of it?" JOHNSON. "I had not, Sir."

From this pleasing subject, he, I know not how or why, made a sudden transition to one upon which he was a violent aggressor; for he said, "I am willing to love all mankind, *except an American.*"

—James Boswell, *Boswell's Life of Johnson*

***

He who loves his Enemies betrays his Friends;
This surely is not what Jesus intends.

—William Blake, *The Everlasting Gospel*

***

Even the friend may sometime become a foe;
Even the foe may sometime become a friend;
Remembering this, bear enmity to none.

—Tibetan proverb told to Sir Charles Bell

***

Friendship is far more tragic than love. It lasts longer.

—Oscar Wilde, "A Few Maxims for the Instruction of the Over-Educated"

CONTENTS

EDITOR'S NOTE

When Alan Bray died on 25 November 2001, he left this book in typescript. The typescript was complete. He had reviewed it thoroughly and entered only a dozen marginal corrections.

Alan Bray did not have time to prepare the citation apparatus, the notes and the bibliography, in the style of the University of Chicago Press. For example, almost every citation to a printed book lacked necessary information, and the cumulative bibliography was organized idiosyncratically. Because I had reviewed the manuscript before its acceptance, and because I had corresponded with Alan about his last revisions of it, it fell to me to help the press prepare the manuscript for publication.

Our overriding desire has been to respect Alan's wishes as we could read them from the typescript. If we have rewritten most notes, reconstructed the whole list of works cited, and corrected some faults in the body, we have not tampered either with the book's argument or with its voice.

Despite my best efforts, I may well have introduced or approved errors while redoing the manuscript. I apologize for these to Alan Bray and to his readers—but to Alan first of all.

Mark D. Jordan, Emory University

This book began in the chapel of a Cambridge college. Nearly twenty years ago, I visited Cambridge to give a lecture. As I was finishing breakfast in college the morning after my lecture, I was joined by my host Jonathan Walters, then a graduate student in the university. We walked to the chapel of Christ's College, where we looked at the seventeenth-century monument by the communion table that marks the burial in the same tomb of John Finch and Thomas Baines. "What," I was asked, "do you make of this?" This book is a long-delayed reply to that question.

It is a book, as will become apparent, about ethics; but it is also the work of a historian, and it may puzzle and then anger scholars in both ethics and history. Others may recognize in its terms a question and a possibility that had already begun to form in their minds: that at least is my hope. With this in view, I set out to explain in this introduction why I have written this book—and why it may matter. That morning walk in Cambridge is of a kind with other moments that have shaped the book. These have rarely been in the setting of the academic seminar room or the university library. The last such moment was the walk across the Norfolk countryside to Wiveton Parish Church, where at last I saw—all at once—what it was that had impelled the book forward.

But on that morning in Cambridge, the walk to Wiveton Parish Church lay many years ahead, and my difficulty in answering the question lay in grasping that what I was seeing in the chapel of Christ's College was near the far shore of a continent that by the end of the seventeenth century already stretched back across more than half a millennium. Later at the suggestion of the Oxford historian Diarmaid MacCulloch, I visited Merton College chapel to see the great memorial brass that at the turn of the fourteenth century was placed above the tomb of John Bloxham and John Whytton, standing side by side under canopies. I realized then that I had found the perspective I was looking for: that and the scale of the task that now faced me. The result was the silence of the years that followed and this book.

Like many of the works of history that I would seek to equal, it is a story, with a beginning, a middle, and an end. Its subject is the distinctive place friendship occupied in traditional society. What I mean by "traditional society" I shall come to shortly. My book extends from the opening of the year 1000, as Europe acquired a shape that was to become its enduring form in the centuries that followed. It pursues its account into the eighteenth and nineteenth centuries, until the forms of society that it follows seem finally to fade from view under the civil society of the eighteenth century. Whether indeed they do fade is a question I will return to. What I think is not to be gainsaid is that, in the centuries after the opening of that second millennium, the bonds of friendship—between individuals and between groups— would become part of the sinews of an expanding and increasingly confident culture.

From the viewpoint of the modern world, that traditional society seems far away (and long ago). Friendship is now certainly a comforting relation and a good one perhaps, but understood to be essentially private—"just" friends. Yet the present turning point in late modern culture can be described, I think, as a crisis of friendship; and if this book is more than the account of a past world, it is because I am convinced that history allows us to interrogate the uncertain ethics of this crisis. Herein lie my motives for writing this book.

The principal difference between the friendship of the modern world and the friendship I describe in this book is that, in the traditional culture that it explores, friendship was significant in a public sphere. In modern civil society friendship has not been perceived to be a public matter, or more precisely *ought* not to be so. Yet increasingly it is. Feminism was perhaps the first sign of that change, together with the corresponding suspicions and the crisis in masculinity that have accompanied it. But its most contested form in western Europe and North America has concerned the claims of homosexual friendship to constitute a family, claims that have had the effect of radically putting at issue a view of the family (and its place in what is assumed to be traditional religious belief). This book is likely to be perceived as addressing those claims. In part, that would be right. In part, it is to misunderstand it, perhaps gravely.

Let me explain. Certainly this book will explore that "traditional family," and may appear to find its academic context in the writings of other historians on that subject. But how clear *is* that academic context? This question came increasingly to occupy me as I attempted to master the many writings by historians on the history of the family. It began to bear on me how little those writings seemed to cohere, to add up. It was as if a piece was missing. That curious impression would play a subsequent part in shaping this book—through what at first seemed a stray detail. I noticed that one of the most influential early academic works on the history of the family, Peter Laslett's *World We Have Lost*, appeared first not as an academic publication but in a series of broadcasts by the British Broadcasting Corporation in the spring of 1960. Why? I pursued the question to the volumes of the *Listener* in the stacks of the London Library: it was to be a second crucial moment. The yellowing pages of the *Listener* contained the text of Laslett's broadcasts, and I heard again his broadcast voice as he moved to his conclusion. An attack on the Soviet Union and the regimes of Eastern Europe. I had found my missing piece.

Laslett's broadcasts pointed me toward the realization that the polemics among historians on the "history of the family" was a proxy for the political tensions of the postwar years. What was at issue was not only the friendship created by kinship in the past. It was also the proper scope for friendship between individuals and groups in Britain as it emerged into the postwar welfare state, and in a United States that would never forget Roosevelt's New Deal.

The twentieth-century writings on the history of the family were dominated by two hostile camps that appeared to divide sharply over the role to be assigned to the conjugal family of mother, father, and children. One stressed the modernity of that unit and saw it emerging in the sixteenth century from a wider frame of "extended" kinship relations. This was a view identified with Marxist historians and with other historians who were ultimately influenced by them without necessarily sharing their political program. The opposed school, identified rather with the contending claims of economic individualism, argued on the same ground (and, in their account, crucially in England) that there is no effective kin group to be identified, at any point as far back as the records take us, beyond that conjugal unit of mother, father, and children: that the extended family of the other camp was a myth.

These opposing views of history are something that I deal with at much greater length in the afterword to this book, with its technical and academic detail: a guide to the pipes and plumbing that lie concealed beneath the surface of this book. My concern here is something broader: despite the differences between them, both of these schools nevertheless shared the assumption that the conjugal family *is* the interpretative crux for any history of the

family. Characteristically each has avoided the slippery definitional questions by diminishing, on a priori grounds, the relevance of other potentially
competing definitions of the family, when they have pushed themselves into
historical accounts: in the one case describing them as a recidivist "feudalism," in the other as only an extension of "natural" kinship.

The fraught nature of this underlying political context was to make other
historians understandably wary of being drawn into this loaded debate. Its
inadequate parameters began to become apparent to them, and they began
to explore other potential definitions of the family, in terms of households
other than the conjugal household or in terms of other kinds of kinship
formed (as marriage is) by ritual and promise. Their work remained cautiously presented within alternative frames of reference, with an understand-
able reticence to point to the moral in this respect. It is now nearly twenty
years since that reticence broke, and a steady stream of academic studies has
begun the task of providing a more complex and objective account of the
history of kinship and the family, a development to which this book contributes. Its distinctive viewpoint is that of the equivocal ethics in the friendship that kinship could create, between individuals and groups who might
otherwise be hostile.

In that sense this book both substantiates and interrogates the defense
of a "traditional" family that has figured in the at times bitterly contested
debate over the family and its claims. But the manner in which it does so
was marked to a radical degree by another moment such as my visit to Cambridge (or my reading the *Listener*). It took place in a hospital room looking
out onto a garden in Paris, where in 1993 I visited and said farewell to my
friend and colleague Michel Rey, shortly before his death.

Michel Rey was a student of Jean-Louis Flandrin at the University of
Paris. In 1987 I heard Michel give a lecture in Amsterdam, entitled "The
Body of My Friend." The lecture was only an outline, and his early death
left his doctoral thesis uncompleted and his loss keenly felt by many. I say
more of his thesis in the afterword, but in the years that followed that lecture Michel and I often discussed the history of friendship, and after his
death the sense that I should follow his work began to grow on me. There
is much in this book he would not have liked—I can hear his voice now—
but let no one be in doubt how much this is his book as well as mine. I
marked this in print by publishing an earlier version of what is now the
fourth chapter of this book ("The Body of the Friend") in our joint names
as a tribute to his memory, seeking to complete that lecture that I heard in
1987 as he might have done had he lived.

But Michel Rey stands also for so many others. His death was a part of those waves of dying friends that so many knew during the years of the AIDS crisis. It was an experience that would leave many profoundly changed. Friends and family. Nurses and doctors. Priests, neighbors, visitors. People who simply saw and heard. That change would manifest itself only slowly, but it would be deep and lasting. For many the world would never be the same again. It would touch me also, perhaps one of the most defining contexts that would shape this book. Out of it would come a readiness to see in the past ways perhaps of transcending—with integrity on all sides—the looming confrontation that is still with us between Christianity and homosexuality without the damaging conflict on which it seems bent. In this sense, then, this book revisits the ethical ground first essayed in John Boswell's *Christianity, Social Tolerance, and Homosexuality*, in the greatly changed world that now prevails nearly a quarter of a century later.

I shall return later to the implications of this ethical terrain, but the point I want to make here is something more concrete and immediate. It is about the tomb monuments of friends buried together in ecclesiastical settings that punctuate the argument of this book. They are perhaps its most startling evidence, certainly its most graphic. The point here is not, of course, the common burial. A common burial might reduce the burial fees required, and the later movement of remains meant that, in some sense, many if not most burials were in the end burials with others. But why these joint *monuments*? Why their eloquent imagery of friendship? Why at times is the imagery startlingly reminiscent of a marriage?

One of the questions this book pursues is why these tomb monuments have played so little part in our understanding of the past, noticed (if at all) by antiquaries in the past or by a few modern historians. But the question I propose to pursue here is more direct and personal. It is why *I* pursued these monuments.

Modern social historians are more likely to be found in university libraries or county record offices than haunting the transepts of the English cathedrals or a country church after Divine Service (although it was not always so). In retrospect, I think I was seeking among the tombs of the dead those lost friends; I would not let them go: and, with the guiding hand of scholarship and the eye of a historian, against all expectations I found such friendship there in these monuments. With it I was able to come back with the story I had also found, the story that constitutes this book.

Let me now return to that book I wrote nearly twenty years ago: my *Homosexuality in Renaissance England*. Its origin lay in the degree to which, as it seemed to me, the exotic language of "sodomy" could be suspended in sixteenth- and seventeenth-century England from the physical intimacy that appeared to pervade its culture: this seemed like the detective story where the clue was that the dog did *not* bark. This book is in a sense the second volume to that study, some twenty years on: if the one turned on how that intimacy was not understood, this turns rather on how it was. But to expect that the rhetoric of that intimacy could be invoked today in support of a polemical debate is to misunderstand both intimacy and this book.

The account I give is cast in unrelentingly historical terms until I come to the chapter "Friendship and Modernity." My task as a historian is to let the past speak in its own terms, not to appropriate it to those of the contemporary world. Only in this late chapter, as the account I give begins to enter the world in which I live, do I step forward in my own voice and say what I believe the story to be. Many readers will find this frustrating. Rightly they will apprehend my account in contexts they know and understand. Given the fraught contemporary issues it articulates, such readers are likely to feel frustrated that its author stays so unrelentingly in the past—until these late pages. Scholarship demands this, but I shall not hide behind its claim: for I hope for more. Readers of this book can and will appropriate the past for themselves, if I stick to my job of presenting the past first in its own terms. Could it be that that very appropriation might prelude a resolution of the conflict between homosexual people and the Christian church today? Could that common space they find themselves occupying in the past mark out a space they might with integrity occupy together today?

But there is another—and more hard-edged—historical reason why the ethics of friendship that come into view through the analysis of this book cannot be appropriated by any one side in a polemical debate today. They emerge slowly in this book as it probes the rhetorical gestures of friendship that it follows. Let me therefore, with these expectations in mind, at the onset say directly what I believe those ethics to have been, for the ethics those gestures articulated were designed to negotiate uncertainties about friendship, which is not an unreserved good. Indeed it could be a great evil, as it could be a great good. What I have sought to convey is the conviction at the heart of these cultural practices that the ethics of friendship operated persuasively only in a larger frame of reference that lay *outside* the good of the individuals for whom the friendship was made. To pose the historical question in terms of the essential good or ill of sexuality therefore, the question that has come to dominate the corresponding modern debates, operates necessarily by contrast *within* the friendship. The inability to conceive of relationships in other than sexual terms says something of contemporary poverty; or, to put the point more precisely, the effect of a shaping concern with sexuality is precisely to obscure that wider frame.

This is not to say that such an ethical praxis must exclude the erotic. The ethics of friendship in the world I describe began with the concrete and the actual, and the only way to exclude anything would be by abandoning that starting point. That hard-edged world included the potential for the erotic, as it included much else, with a potential for good (and ill) alike: self-advancement, the equivocal love for the familiar and the same; but also a capacity to love, and a desire to give, and above all a traditional Christian faith that took it as axiomatic that the point of religion—what it did for a living—was that it was an instrument by which neighbors, kin, and friends could succeed in living in peace with each other.

Such ethics are likely to puzzle, even anger, those for whom the question of sexuality is central; this will be so not only within the world of academic historians, and for similar reasons. Let me therefore, if I may, recall another of those revealing moments. It drove home to me how angry those angry people are likely to be. In July 2001 I lifted the wraps on my book during a lecture in Newman House, by St. Stephen's Green in Dublin. Newman House was where John Henry Newman established the Catholic University of Ireland as its first rector. My lecture told why Newman was buried in the same grave as his friend Father Ambrose St. John. The day before the lecture I appeared on Irish breakfast TV. My expectations that this would be a relaxed chat evaporated when—within seconds of the cameras starting—the interviewer asked me, "Is it true that half the priests in Ireland are homosexual?" To this day I cannot fathom how he thought I, on my first visit to Dublin, might know the answer to such a question; but clearly a bumpy road lay ahead.

In the weeks that followed, the response to that lecture echoed across Europe, from Dublin to Vienna; and the positive nature of the reaction demonstrated to me that many were ready to pick up the opportunity that my book would offer and that my lecture anticipated. But it also demonstrated the capacity for what I would say in this book to puzzle and then anger.

It will puzzle and anger those historians for whom sexuality is the element that radically separates marriage in their eyes from other kinds of kinship formed by promise and ritual—however they may differ on its historical perspective. It will puzzle and anger those contending political factions who regard the wrongs and rights of sexuality as synonymous with what rightly constitutes a "family"—however bitterly they are divided over the conclusions to be drawn. As each party reaches out (as it thinks) to vanquish its opponents, this history asks, not whether they have found the right answer, but whether they have found the right question. This history provides an escape from this impending conflict by widening its terms.

Here lies the rationale for the earlier warning I made, that to read this book within the narrow terms of a debate as to whether homosexual friendship constitutes a family would be to misunderstand it, perhaps gravely. The ethics it deals with overflow that question. To widen the terms of this debate as I attempt to do in this book is to see it within a broader contemporary crisis in the ethics of friendship, the signs of which have been the diverse loyalties of identity, region, culture, or language that have come to mark the pluralism of the late modern world, of which sexuality has been one, but only one, strand. In the eighteenth-century Enlightenment, the philosopher Immanuel Kant placed the moral basis of friendship in an undifferentiated moral benevolence. Kant's axiom has lost its sharpness in a world as determinedly diverse as the late twentieth century. A response to the crumbling of confidence in that view was Jacques Derrida's *Politics of Friendship* (published in 1994 as *Politiques de l'amitié*). When I read Derrida's book, I realized that he was asking at root the same questions that I was pursuing in this book. In the traditional cultures I describe, friendship was ultimately inalienable from the particular loyalties in which it was begun, as in the contemporary world on which Derrida reflects. The ethical uncertainties of that stance were pivotal in the ethics of the world I have described. There is, of course, no return now to the friendship of traditional society, but the ethics of friendship have an archaeology, if I may put it that way, that can be recovered; and if this book in some measure helps to explain and find ways of transcending the ethical problems raised by friendship in a diverse world, it will have served its purpose.

One last defining moment, which touches on the perilous breadth of this book. The delightful room of Dr. Wendy Bracewell is in the School of Slavonic and East European Studies in the University of London: in a Georgian terrace house perched high above Russell Square. Dr. Bracewell had told me of her work on ritual brotherhood in the *triplex confinium* of the Balkans, and I had come to tea to discuss how it might relate to my own work on ritual brotherhood in the Latin West. That memorable visit came at a time when I was finding it difficult to persuade some that the subject even existed as a coherent field, let alone what its parameters might be. Dr. Bracewell fully grasped what I was talking about. To her and to her colleagues it was indeed a coherent field (and familiar ground). But more, I had wondered whether there was a Latin rite for the sworn friendship of ritual brotherhood (as well as the Greek and Slavonic rites edited by John Boswell shortly before his death). Dr. Bracewell simply took down from the shelf the Latin *Ordo ad fratres faciendum* (the Catholic rite for "making brothers") that a Dominican scholar had published in a journal in Croatia thirty years before.

What I came to see in that rite was (as I argue in the course of this book) crucially as much a contrast with what I had seen in the Latin West as its counterpart. The contrast that places the friendship I describe in this book is wider than the contrast between England's culture and its close neighbors in France or even Italy. Indeed, the account I give of families and friends does not differ markedly from the account given of them by historians of France and Italy. The contrast that allows one to see the distinctive nature of the response to friendship within these cultures, from outside as it were, lies rather in a wider view that comprehends the two halves of Europe and that corresponds to the dividing line in the political structure of Europe that is emerging as the boundaries created by Communism melt. This line running across Europe follows almost exactly the rift that opened up in Europe a thousand years before in the middle of the eleventh century, between its Greek (and Slavonic) half and its Latin West: between the philosophical and ethical world of Rome and that of Byzantium.

The scope of this book is likely to seem reckless, if not perverse, to many professional historians, and not only in this expansive contrast between the two halves of Europe. Its timescale also extends perilously across the traditional boundaries dividing "medieval" history from that of the "Renaissance" and modernity. The coherence of that timescale turns on the term "traditional society," which I undertook earlier in this introduction to defend and maintain: by which I mean the forms of friendship (and in that sense "social" life) that subsisted from at least the beginning of the eleventh century until the end of the seventeenth, when it appears to be succeeded by the friendship of civil society, that universal benevolence of Immanuel Kant. Dr. Johnson's altercation with the Quaker lady in the epigraph marks that transition. The adherents of Dr. Johnson's initial opinion would get the better of the argument.

This is not to say that over this immense period of time the social outline of friendship between individuals and groups remained unchanged, but the changes occurred slowly. One of the arguments of this book is that these changes were affected by religious and political upheavals less than the polemics of those upheavals might suggest. What one sees is often rather a process of adaptation or even one of change revitalizing rather than undermining traditional practices. Hence the timescale I have essayed. A shorter timescale would have obscured this long interaction between change and continuity.

The term "traditional religion" is less of a problem. The term "traditional society," as I use it, is also the justification for its counterpart in "traditional religion" although I am well aware that I am taking the term out of the hands of polemicists (especially in the United States) who have seized the term as a party label. I make no apologies for returning to its owners a term that can only make sense in terms of a historical study.

A far greater practical difficulty is left for me in the scale of a study that traverses close to a thousand years. The focus of this book on a single country—England and what can be gleaned from England's presence among its neighbors—is in part an attempt to keep a study of this scale within coherent bounds. It is also, however, something more. Its precise cultural context helps focus those nagging, troublesome details that do not quite fit this past culture's account of itself. The danger of the broad generalized synthesis that I have sought to avoid is not only that it can miss those significant details: it can also collude with the strategies of denial and displacement toward which they point, a point that emerges only gradually as the book proceeds.

There is also a more practical reason for focusing on England. England uniquely failed in the sixteenth century to share in the dramatic transformation in the status of marriage that occurred elsewhere, in Catholic and Reformed countries alike, a peculiarity that left England with a recognizably medieval pattern of kinship, painted in a breadth of sources historians associate with the sixteenth or seventeenth century. England's development in this respect would not prove in time to be fundamentally different from those of its immediate neighbors, but these changes took place in England later and provide the historian with an extraordinarily clear vantage point to view a timescale as great as the one I have essayed. This book is not about marriage, but it is about the equivocal ethics of friendship with which marriage and kinship were inextricably entwined in traditional society. Could the same be true in England of friendship as it was of marriage? To this I must also add the desire of an Englishman to write about his own country and its common people.

A more rough-edged question will also be asked about the scope of this book, by readers outside the academy as much as within it. Am I writing about friendship or about *masculine* friendship? Curiously, this question is more difficult to answer, because friendship has been no less asymmetrical than gender itself. There is no more revealing question about the friendship of traditional society than to ask how it encompassed women. Their absence in some of the sources for its history, at first marginal, becomes tangible and eventually central: but it does so, first, as the troubling silence between the lines. This is not to say that evidence for women's friendship is lacking. This book will follow Valerie Traub's seminal work on female friendship and will be followed soon after by that of Martha Vicinus, and the kind of sources to which one can turn will be apparent from their works. But what struck me as lacking, in the search I made, is the distinctive evidence that I follow in this book: the formal and objective character that friendship could possess that could overlap with the character of kinship. Before the seventeenth century I could not find it. Time may well show that I was not looking in the right place, but as the reader will see, I decided to stay with this curious difficulty and to persist in interrogating it until a possible answer presented itself.

In the seventeenth century and beyond, I can bring women more clearly into the historical practices that I have followed, and I do so in the critical chapter 6, in which I draw together the threads of this book across its history: indeed the diary of Anne Lister becomes the vantage point for that final questioning look back into the past. My hope in weighting my evidence this way in that chapter is this. In his book on modern Catholicism, Mark Jordan has argued that the anxieties of a (male) clerical agenda have silently stood in the way of ethics, and this may be true. I would add that the problem, it seems to me, has been inadequate scholarship, not conspiracy (and a response that has remained trapped within the same terms). But if this is the actual problem, then telling the history of women's friendship is one of the ways of breaking that silence: and that is why I accord it a shaping, final place that arguably transcends its place in the surviving evidence—measured simply in the number of references.

My first task is to let the traditional culture that I describe speak for itself about friendship, in its own diverse voices, however strange, unpalatable, or incoherent they may seem; and it does so in men's voices and about male concerns: women enter the picture—apparently—only at its margins. Only as the inconsistencies in this culture's account of itself—those troubling details that do not quite fit—come into view am I entitled to assume the role of a reluctant protagonist and intervene. To do otherwise would be unjust. For if this book has a conclusion beyond the pressing ethical questions that it may indirectly touch—that is, a conclusion within the story itself—it is that there has never been a time when male intimacy was possible in a space untouched by power and politics, however much that was desired or rhetorically projected. But that is emphatically not to deny the reality of that desire or the stature at times even of its failures. For women it may have been different, in that silence between the lines.

Because I want first to let the past speak for itself, I have begun my account with one of the few sources available to the historian that, in part at least, deliberately and self-consciously was designed to convey a message to an unimaginable future. As I do so, I need to put aside the shaping moments

CHAPTER 1

Wedded Brother

Then David made this lament . . .
"O Jonathan, in your death I am stricken,
I am desolate for you, Jonathan my brother."

In 1913 the Turkish workmen who were restoring the Arap Camii, the
Mosque of the Arabs, in Istanbul broke through its wooden floor and uncovered below it paving and tombstones. The startled workmen were gaz-
ing at the paving of what five centuries before had been the church of the
Dominican friars in the bustling village of Galata, across the Golden Horn,
within sight of the towers and palaces of ancient Byzantium. One of the
tombstones they uncovered that day can now be seen in the archaeological
museum in modern Istanbul and sets out for me in graphic form the question that I have sought to pursue and answer in this book (see fig. 1).[1]

The tombstone is more than seven feet long and is made of gray white
marble streaked with blue and pink veins. Part of the inscription at the top
of the monument, once identifying it, was obliterated probably during the
reconstruction of the church as a mosque; but the opening words—"HIC
JACET" [Here lies]—are still clearly visible and announce that the monument once lay horizontal above the tomb or sarcophagus below it, in what
must have been a prominent setting in the crowded church. A small card
placed by the museum beside the tombstone identifies it for the visitor as
that of two English knights who died near Galata at the end of the fourteenth century, and below the inscription are depicted the shields carrying
their armorial bearings, together with their helmets and the extravagant
crests and mantlings that accompany them.

The design on the tombstone is likely to make even the casual visitor
pause, for in the engraver's arrangement the helmets of the two men seem

Figure 1
The shared tombstone of Sir William Neville and Sir John Clanvowe,
who died a few days apart in 1391 and were buried in Istanbul.

as if about to kiss. One might conclude that this is a trick of their appearance to a modern viewer—for it is at eye level that the visors meet—were it not for the arrangement of the shields below them. A heraldic device is not a realistic depiction; it is a kind of code (like a modern road sign), but here that code is transgressed by the shields below; for the inclination of the shield on the viewer's left is reversed and heraldically incorrect. There is, however, a singular precedent for this (and from the same period) in the stalls of the Knights of the Garter in St. George's Chapel, Windsor, where the heraldic shields on one side of the choir were inclined incorrectly in the same direction as the shield on the left on this tombstone, so that all the shields above the stalls corresponded to the posture of the knights who had once sat below them, as they had turned to gaze toward the high altar. The tilting of the shields toward each other on the tombstone at Galata would then correspond, by the same device, to the bodies of the two knights that were laid below—turned not toward the altar but toward each other.[2]

The presentation of the two helmets in profile corresponds here to the stylized depiction of a kiss, and the arrangement of the two overlapping shields below to that of an embrace. Fourteenth-century culture recognized more than one kind of kiss, of ascending significance: a touching of the shoulders with an inclination of the heads, a kiss on the cheek, and a kiss on the mouth. The last, which brings the eyes into contact and exchanges the breath and saliva, was the most momentous and is evidently the kiss indicated here. Although the precise meaning that gesture held in the fourteenth century will probably escape a modern viewer, it is a sufficiently universal symbol to hold the visitor's attention. The modern visitor would be correspondingly more surprised, even incredulous, if he or she could then read the coats of arms within these shields through the eyes of the inhabitants of the fourteenth century, who (as has been said) could read a coat of arms for the most part more easily than they could a letter. The arrangement given to the arms of these two men in the church of the Dominican friars is that of a married couple.

The two shields are divided in half, left side from the right, and in each half a whole coat of arms is shown. In this arrangement the left side of the shield (from the viewpoint of the viewer)—the dexter half—is the more honorable and by convention bore the arms of the husband, while the right, or sinister, half bore those of the wife. The technical term is "impalement," and by the end of the fourteenth century it was an established device for presenting the arms of a married couple. The impaled arms of Thomas, Lord Camoys, and his wife Elizabeth Mortimer on their monumental brass in the

church in the Sussex village of Trotton are an example from the same period, which one can set by the impaled arms from the church in Galata.[3]

In modern terms, the apparently marital imagery of the tombstone is inexplicable, although the context for its imagery of an embrace and a kiss is
initially easier to explain than its imagery of a marriage. The kiss depicted
here points to a ritual act that would have been familiar in any Latin church
in the fourteenth century, including that of the Dominican friars in Galata.
After the priest's consecration of the elements in the mass, he would take
the peace of God as it were from the altar and pass it to the deacon in the
form of a "kiss of peace"—the *osculum pacis*—from whom it would pass
among those present, each receiving God's peace from their neighbors and,
in return, passing it on to others. The liturgical reference and the ecclesiastical setting of the tomb suggest an intriguing question, however improbable it may sound in the twentieth century, that might go some way toward
explaining its marital imagery. Could what I am seeing, at the conclusion of
the friendship that this tombstone marks so publicly, be the counterpart in
stone to a liturgical act that marked its beginning?

Despite the setting in Byzantium, this tombstone is not a counterpart to
the Greek liturgy of the *adelphopoiesis* (literally a rite "for the making of brothers" or "sisters").[4] The inscription on the tombstone is not in Greek but in
Latin, and the Dominican church in Galata was a Latin church. Galata lay
outside Byzantium and was an enclave for foreigners, principally the
Genoese: a cutting from the West planted by the Bosporus. If the context
for the iconography of this tomb is a liturgical one—and if that goes some
way toward explaining its marital imagery—then that context is distinctively Western.

These possibilities are strengthened by a student studying heraldry in
the 1450s called Richard Strangways, whose notes attribute to two knights
an armorial arrangement of precisely the kind shown on this tombstone: on
the grounds that they were "sworn" brothers.

> There were ii knights, and their lineage is yet in Spain, and there fell so great
> love betwixt them that they were sworn brothers, and that one of them bore
> his arms with a bend; and for the great love that his sworn brother had to
> him he forsook his own arms and said he would bear his brother's arms and
> took the same arms, saying that he laid the bend up on the left side: and her-
> alds considered the great love betwixt them and granted thereto.[5]

The word "sworn" implies a ritual of some kind; that this was the essence of
the matter is indicated nicely by the addition Strangways made to his note.

As one can see from the manuscript in the British Library, when he came to the term for the second time, he nodded and first wrote only "brothyr," then carefully added to it the word "sworn," above the line—an addition that emphasizes that what made the impalement appropriate was not merely that they were brothers but that an *oath* had made them such.

Although the word "sworn" implies a ritual of some kind, it does not necessarily imply a ritual act in *church*; but two pieces of evidence suggest that that was indeed what Strangways had in mind. One is a passage in the romance of *Amys and Amylion*, the story of two sworn brothers that was still popular in Strangways's fifteenth century. Virtually every European language has had a version of the tale (including English), but Strangways's culture also knew a popular Latin version that presented the two friends as Christian saints and was evidently written by a churchman. In the course of this version, the king's steward Ardericus seeks a sworn brother of his own and does so with the injunction that the oath of fidelity be sworn "super sanctorum reliquias" [on relics of the saints]. The point is that the place where one might expect to find the relics of saints would be at the altar of a church.[6]

The second piece of evidence that a church was thought to be an appropriate setting for such a ritual is the implication of a compact made in France a few years before Strangways wrote his note, between two English esquires in the army of Henry V, called Nicholas Molyneux and John Winter. The document confirming the compact between them employs terms that are close parallels to those that were used in Strangways's notes. Their compact was one that made them sworn "freres darmes" [brothers in arms], and it records with careful and telling precision that their compact was made on 12 July 1421 in the *church* of St. Martin at Harfleur: "en leglise de Saint Martin de Harefleu."[7] Is the context for the tomb monument in the church of the Dominican friars at Galata a similar ritual oath in church? The ritual kiss depicted on their tomb figures runs like a thread through the stories of sworn brothers like Amys and Amylion. The promises of fidelity that Amys and Amylion exchange are preceded by the public (and binding) exchange of the kiss before witnesses. A ritual kiss also marks the sworn brotherhood of Guy and his sworn brother Tirry in the romance *Guy of Warwick;* and when the chronicler Henry of Huntingdon recounted the ritual brotherhood of the English king Edmund Ironside and Cnut in 1016, he simply says, "osculum pacis invicem datum est" [they exchanged the kiss of peace].[8]

Who then were these two men who were laid together by their friends in the same tomb in the church at Galata for the long last sleep of death? The inscription identifying the tomb is divided into two fields by a vertical line, which presumably corresponds to the division between the arms on the

[It was also on 17 October that in a village near Constantinople in Greece the life of Sir John Clanvowe, a distinguished knight, came to its close, causing to his companion on the march, Sir William Neville, for whom his love was no less than for himself, such inconsolable sorrow that he never took food again and two days afterward breathed his last, greatly mourned, in the same village. These two knights were men of high repute among the English, gentlemen of mettle and descended from illustrious families.][11]

"Companion on the march" is the translation of "comes in itinere" offered by the two modern editors of the *Westminster Chronicle*, L. C. Hector and Barbara Harvey, and this description of the two men corresponds to the "freres darmes" of Nicholas Molyneux and John Winter's covenant and the formal imagery on the tombstone in Galata. It suggests something more than a mere description of William Neville as John Clanvowe's "companion on the *journey*," as the phrase might have been translated. That accidental sense would miss the formality of the Ciceronian counterpart, of the true friend as a second self, that follows. The "verus amicus" [real friend] of Cicero's *De Amicitia*, "est tamquam alter idem" [is, as it were, another self].[12] More mundanely, the chronicler's grammar makes the same point. The chronicler does not employ the partitive genitive—John Clanvowe is not "one of his companions"—and there were surely other companions with them on such a journey: he is his "comes in itinere." The implication of the carefully formal phrase is that the monks at Westminster knew William Neville and John Clanvowe and the nature of the bond between them. The strength of the term explains something of William Neville's grief, but it is also a further hint of the formal and *public* context for their friendship to which the imagery of their tomb monument insistently points.

The *Westminster Chronicle* is a strong and reliable source: the monks of Westminster were at the hub of power and well informed; and the editors of the chronicle suggest that that otherwise curious phrase "inter Anglicos" [among the English] is attributable to the passage's being taken, in part at least, verbatim from a contemporary newsletter. The surviving tomb monument confirms their death a few days apart in October 1391, and the difference in the precise dates between the tomb monument and the chronicle (or the newsletter on which it drew) were most probably due to the time that elapsed before the newsletter was written (or the tomb constructed). The evidence of the *Westminster Chronicle* and the tangible evidence of the remaining tombstone tell alike the same story: that William Neville died of inconsolable grief a few days after the death of his friend John Clanvowe.

The Visibility of Friendship

That story raises more questions than it answers. Despite the distance in time that separates us from William Neville and John Clanvowe, a great deal is known about their lives, as indeed it is of the lives of Nicholas Molyneux and John Winter, the two esquires in the army of Henry V who became "freres darmes" in the church of St. Martin at Harfleur. I shall return to the details of their lives at several points in the course of this study. The outline of their lives (and that of others like them) eventually explains that marital imagery on the tomb monument in Galata, but lying doggedly in the way is the fundamental and intractable problem in all social history, apparent in that treatise on arms that I quoted earlier and again in the document recording the compact of Nicholas Molyneux and John Winter. It is the beguiling assumption these documents make, that what they are describing is something that needs no explanation for the reader they have in mind.

For the modern reader that is far from being the case. *Why* did the heralds grant these two knights in this treatise on arms—because of their "great love"—the same arrangement of their arms as that of a married couple? Why the *same* arrangement rather than a distinctive one? What was actually indicated—in concrete terms—when the compact of Nicholas Molyneux and John Winter carefully records that it was made "en leglise de Saint Martin de Harefleu"? The simple assumption in both of these documents is that these points are too obvious to need explanation, that their import will be self-evident to the reader. What one comes up against here is the first and fundamental problem shared stoically by all social historians: the historical sources now available to us tend not to be explicit about what—for them—was usual and familiar.

It is for this reason that, before I turn to the detail of the lives of these people, I propose to turn to two sources that exceptionally (and markedly) provide evidence of the normal and familiar form for a rite in Catholic Europe that corresponded to the language used in these documents. Both illuminate the liturgy of which a material trace appears to remain in the tomb monument of William Neville and John Clanvowe; in the one case indirectly, in the other directly. The first of these is the indirect evidence of the *Topographica Hibernica* of Giraldus de Barri (Gerald of Wales). This is not a sober and objective work but a piece of propaganda, intended to justify to its audience in Catholic Europe the invasion of Ireland by the Anglo-Norman army under Henry II in 1171.[13] As evidence concerning Ireland this is hardly wholly reliable, although in the tomb monuments of early medieval Ireland one can apparently see traces of the "sworn" brotherhood of the kind one would see later in the church of the Dominican friars on the tomb monument of William Neville and John Clanvowe. These provide a possible material context for Giraldus's account.

One of these is a fragment of a sepulchral cross from the church at Delgany, in County Wicklow, with the inscription

ŌRDO DICU[L] OCUS [MAEL]ODRAN SAIR

[Pray for Dicul and Maelodran, the wright]

A second is a beautiful inscription on a stone near the entrance to the remains of the church at Termonfechin, in County Louth, about three miles east of Drogheda.

+ OROIT DO OLTAN & DO DUBTHACH DORIGNI IN CAISSEL

[Pray for Ultan and for Dubthach, who made the stone fort.]

The description of Maelodran as "the wright" (that is, "carpenter" or "artisan") implies a distinction from Dicul, with whom he was apparently buried, rather than that they were members of the same family. The same would apply to the description of Dubthach in the second inscription as "who made the stone fort," "dorigni" [made] being singular. But the most striking of these monuments is the great tomb slab from the monastic complex at Glendalough, in County Wicklow, now set by the wall in the chancel of the ruined cathedral there (see fig. 2). The inscription has been damaged by weathering, but can still be read with the aid of the drawing made by the antiquary George Petrie at some point between 1820 and 1830. To each side of the intricate cross set on the stone are its two matching inscriptions.

ŌRDO DIARMAIT

[Pray for Diarmait]

This is on the one side: on the other is

ŌRDO MAC COIS

[Pray for Mac Cois]

Figure 2
Tomb slab from Glendalough Abbey in County Wicklow, Ireland.
(Drawing by George Petrie)

As "Mac Cois" means "son of Cois," the implication is that Diarmait and Mac Cois were not buried together as brothers or as kin in the sense that they were sons of the same father, but presumably as *sworn* brothers. If this is the case, the careful symmetry of the monument anticipates what one sees later in the tomb monument of William Neville and John Clanvowe. The magnificence of the monument—one of the finest sepulchral slabs found from early medieval Ireland—is a corresponding measure of the standing of the relation.[14]

This passage in the *Topographica Hibernica* of Giraldus de Barri also reflects the presence of sworn brotherhood in Ireland—indeed its satirical intentions would not have hit home if it had not been present in Ireland—but a work of propaganda such as this needs particular caution. Its value as historical evidence is its indirect ability to preserve evidence of the values and prejudices of the *audience* that Giraldus was seeking to manipulate. In the course of this work, Giraldus describes a ritual confirming friendship, which its audience could be expected in this way to recognize and value. Or rather, to recognize as debased here by the blood that according to Giraldus follows its treacherously pious beginning among the Irish.

> Inter alia multa artis iniquae figmenta, hoc unum habent tanquam praecipuum argumentum. Sub religionis et pacis obtentu ad sacrum aliquem locum conveniunt, cum eo quem oppetere cupiunt. Primo compaternitatis foedera jungunt: deinde ter circa ecclesiam se invicem portant: postmodum ecclesiam intrantes, coram altari reliquiis sanctorum appositis, sacramentis multifarie praestitis, demum missae celebratione, et orationibus sacerdotum, tanquam desponsatione quadam indissolubiliter foederantur.

Ad ultimum vero, ad majorem amicitiae confirmationem, et quasi ne-
gotii consumationem, sanguinem sponte ad hoc fusum uterque alterius
bibit. Hoc autem de ritu gentilium adhuc habent, qui sanguine in firmandis
foederibus uti solent. O quoties in ipso desponsationis hujus articulo, a viris
sanguinum et dolosis tam dolose et inique funditur sanguis, ut alteruter
penitus maneat exsanguis! O quoties eadem hora et incontinenti vel sequitur
vel praevenit, vel etiam inaudito more sanguinolentum divortium ipsam in-
terrumpit desponsationem.

[Among the many other deceits of their perverse ways, this one is particularly instructive. Under the appearance of piety and peace, they come together in some holy place with the man with whom they are eager to be
united. First they join in covenants of spiritual brotherhood. Then they
carry each other three times around the church. Then going into the church,
before the altar and in the presence of relics of the saints, many oaths are
made. Finally with a celebration of the mass and the prayers of priests, they
are joined indissolubly as if by a betrothal.

But at the end as greater confirmation of their friendship and to conclude
the proceedings, each drinks the other's blood: this they retain from the custom of the pagans, who use blood in the sealing of oaths. How often, at this
very moment of a betrothal, blood is shed by these violent and deceitful men
so deceitfully and perversely that one or the other remains drained of blood!
How often in that very improper hour does a bloody divorce follow, precede or even in an unheard-of-way interrupt the betrothal.][15]

Giraldus's satire first attributes to this ritual all the proprieties to hand
that could confirm the friendship created by ritual kinship; and he does this
so comprehensively that each of the forms of ritual kinship that he knew his
audience would value finds its place. The first is that established by baptism.
These vows, he tells his audience, are vows of *compaternitas. Compaternitas* was
the spiritual brotherhood—what one might call the "godbrotherhood"—
established at baptism between, among others, the sponsors of a child and
its natural parents, relations that figured more significantly as the specifically social consequences of baptism than any subsequent tie to the child.
The second that he invokes is that established by a betrothal. The vows, he
goes on to assure his soon-to-be scandalized audience, are moreover given
the force of a *desponsatio:* an agreement to a marriage. In the twelfth century
a betrothal—a *desponsatio*—might precede the marriage itself by several
years; but when it was solemnized at the church door, where the rite of baptism also began, its binding terms established kinship relations that stood

with those created by marriage or a baptism. In Giraldus's awesome composite the third form of ritual kinship that leaves its trace in this account is the ritual brotherhood of the kind that Nicholas Molyneux and John Winter entered into, created directly by vows of sworn brotherhood and without the symbolic instrumentality of the child or the marriage. The heady mix in Giraldus's description invokes the spiritual brotherhood of *compaternitas*, the binding force of a betrothal, and the liturgical form of sworn brotherhood—a form whose culmination is the Eucharist.

Giraldus then aims his blow. After a beginning that could not have confirmed friendship in more solemn terms, the pagan addition proves disastrous. The blood of the pagan rite stimulates the blood lust of the participants, and the ritual ends not in friendship but in violence and murder. Giraldus's claim "then they carry each other three times around the church" may be a comically distorted form of the kiss of peace: the Irish do not know *how* to exchange the kiss of peace because they do not know *what* it means. The drawing at the opening in the Bodleian manuscript of two men fighting to the death makes Giraldus's point. But the historical evidence the passage contains lies not in what he has to say about the Irish but in the evidence he indirectly preserves of the form of a ritual that he knew his readers in Catholic Europe would recognize and value. The force of Giraldus's satire depends on familiarity with the rituals he is invoking and his audience's acceptance of their legitimacy. The implication of Giraldus's *Topographica Hibernica* is that his readers in Latin Catholic Europe knew that the ceremony of "sworn" brotherhood ended with a celebration of the mass, and this knowledge prepares them to be all the more scandalized by the blood that (according to Giraldus) all too often follows among the Irish.

The same conclusion is the implication of the second of the two sources. It is the direct evidence of a letter addressed on 14 July 1411 to the king of France, Charles VI, by the sons of Duke Louis of Orléans, which the fifteenth-century historian Juvénal des Ursins included in his *Histoire de Charles VI.* It fills out that terse phrase "en leglise de Saint Martin" in the document recording the compact between Nicholas Molyneux and John Winter, also made in France, in the church at Harfleur, almost to the day ten years later on 12 July 1421. In this letter the sons give a detailed description of the rite by which their father Duke Louis had become the ritual "brother" of his cousin Duke Jean of Burgundy on 20 November 1407 when, as in the ritual indirectly implied by Giraldus's account, they had made their communions together before witnesses in a votive mass for this purpose.[16] The ritual as Juvénal des Ursins summarizes it is that

le dimanche vingtiesme jour de novembre monseigneur de Berry, et autres
seigneurs assemblerent lesdits seigneurs d'Orleans et de Bourgongne, ils
oüyrent tous la messe ensemble, et receurent le corps de Nostre Seigneur. Et
prealablement jurerent bon amour et fraternité par ensemble.

[on Sunday the 20th of November the lord de Berry and other lords as-
sembled together, and the said lords of Orléans and of Burgundy heard the
mass together and received the Body of Our Lord; and before doing this
they swore true love and brotherhood together.]

From the viewpoint of the social historian, the unusual value of this letter lies in the stress it places on the customary and familiar nature of the rite
followed in 1407, a point its writers press in their letter because of the in-
famy of the subsequent murder of their father by the servants of Duke Jean.
As they put it, their father and Duke Jean during the ritual in 1407 had made
"plusieurs grandes et solemnelles promesses, *en tel cas accoustumées . . . par especiales convenances sur ce faites*" [many grand and solemn promises *of the kind as are
customary in such a situation . . . by the special conventions recognized in such a matter*].

Both of these pieces of evidence point one, in the first case indirectly and
in the second directly, to the same conclusion: that in the churches of
Catholic Europe from at least the end of the twelfth century until the beginning of the fifteenth, the mass provided a familiar culmination for the
creation of ritual "brothers," a ritual completed in their taking Holy Communion together. Such a liturgical practice should not surprise us. In her
classic study *Corpus Christi: The Eucharist in Late Medieval Culture* Miri Rubin has
described how, in the eleventh and twelfth centuries, the Eucharist was re-
figured as a symbol at the center of the secular world, becoming incorporated into its forms of life, shaping them and in turn being shaped by them.
The ritual evident in these accounts was part of that process.

A ritual like this gave friendship a formal and objective character markedly
different from friendship in modern society. The conventional sources for
liturgical history are unlikely, though, to allow the historian to take these descriptions further. Neither account suggests that a specific office was used;
and if Giraldus's account implies the mass that followed was the betrothal
mass, it would have been that of the Holy Trinity, which was popular and
widely used.[17] The problem of extrapolating from these descriptions—to
an understanding of what this ritual meant for those who took part in it—
is that a practice of the kind described would not leave any direct traces
within the liturgical manuscripts. Are there then guides elsewhere?

The Traces of Friendship

Friendship created by sworn brotherhood left its traces in the world about it. These traces are now only fragments and occasional details that the historian must piece together to reconstruct the mosaic they once composed. But the evidence is there, in the references to sworn friendship scattered across the documents produced as traditional culture went about its business and politics. Let me give an example from the end of the thirteenth century.

In the 1280s the abbey of Oseney, near Oxford, had as its abbot the energetic and forceful William de Sutton who had been the *procurator* [attorney] of the abbey, a character described in its annals as being as prudent as a serpent. One of his primary tasks was to secure the abbey's lands and property against legal challenge, and to this end Abbot William set about the task of organizing into a more effective register the records of the abbey's extensive landholdings. In the course of this we catch a glimpse of two sworn brothers who had come to England two centuries before and who were still remembered by the community at Oseney. Abbot William put his hand to a suitably sonorous opening for his register—enough to make it formidable even to the most intractable of officials—and he found this in a gift of land from two of the followers who had come over to England with the Conqueror, whom he describes as "fratres iurati" [sworn brothers].[18]

> Memorandum quod Robertus de Olleyo & Rogerus de Iuereyo, fratres iurati & per fidem & sacramentum confederati, venerunt ad conquestum Anglie cum rege Willelmo Bastard.

> [It is to be minded that Robert D'Oilly and Roger D'Ivry, sworn brothers and i-confedered and i-bound everich to other by faith and sacrament, came to the conquest of England with King William Bastard.]

The English version I have given is the form in which Abbot William's community at Oseney, nearly two centuries later still mindful of his memorably sonorous opening, translated it in the fifteenth century. ("Sacrament" here is used in the sense of on oath, translating "sacramentum" in the Latin register.)

References to such "sworn" brothers in medieval chronicles grew out of imperatives such as this, at a time when the organization of archives was often rudimentary; and a document had a better chance of being located if it had prudently been copied into a chronicle. Earlier in the twelfth century, the monks of Peterborough Abbey had employed the same tactic as Abbot William when they interpolated a passage into the copy of the *Anglo-Saxon*

Chronicle that was being made for them, following the fire that had destroyed their library in 1116: an interpolation designed to substantiate a charter ostensibly derived from the endowment of Peterborough Abbey in the seventh century, when it was known as Medeshamstede. The claim was spurious, and claims such as this needed respectable clothing. The interpolation begins in the entry for the year 656:

656   Her waes Peada ofslagan. & Wulfere Pending feng to Myrcena rice. On his time waex þet abbodrice Medeshamsteded swiðe rice. þ his broðor hafde ongunnen. Þa luuede se kining hit swiðe for his broðer luuen Peada. & for his wed broðeres luuen Oswi. & for Saxulfes luuen þes abbodes.

[656   In this year Peada was killed, and Wulfhere, son of Penda, succeeded to the kingdom of Mercia. In his time the abbey of Medeshamstede, which his brother Peada had begun, grew very wealthy. The king loved it much for love of his brother Peada, and for love of his sworn brother, Oswy, and for the love of Saxulf, its abbot.]

A twelfth-century interpolation is not reliable evidence for England six centuries earlier, but it is evidence for what constituted, in twelfth-century England, respectable clothing for such a claim.[19]

The chronicles of Edward II's reign are more reliable accounts, including contemporary or near contemporary documents. From these we can establish (as Pierre Chaplais has pointed out) that Edward II was the sworn brother of his friend Piers Gaveston.[20] The chronicle of the civil-war years of Edward's reign in the Cottonian manuscripts is explicit on the point. This is how it describes Edward and Gaveston's first meeting.

[F]ilius regis intuens, in eum tantum protinus amorem iniccit quod cum eo fraternitatis fedus iniit, et pre ceteris mortalibus indissolubile dileccionis vinculum secum elegit et firm[i]ter disposuit innodare.

[When the king's son gazed upon him, he straight away felt so much love that he entered into a covenant of brotherhood with him and chose and firmly resolved to bind himself to him, in an unbreakable bond of love before all men.][21]

Edward's passionate attachment to Gaveston in the years that followed amply bears out all the force of the chronicler's description. The precision of the term "fraternitatis fedus" [covenant of brotherhood] in this account corresponds to the "compaternitatis foedera" [covenants of spiritual brotherhood] that Giraldus invokes and the "fedus amicicie" [covenant of friendship] of the Latin *Amys and Amylion*.[22] The *Vita Edwardi Secundi* is equally explicit about the formal character of their friendship and characterizes it in the language of fraternal adoption.[23] This is taken from the passage that follows an account of Gaveston's murder by Edward's opponents.

> Occiderunt enim magnum comitem quem rex adoptauerat in fratrem, quem rex dilexit ut filium, quem rex habuit in socium et amicum.

> [For they put to death a great earl whom the king had adopted as brother, whom the king loved as a son, whom the king regarded as friend and ally.]

The *Annales Paulini* composed among the cathedral clergy at St. Paul's uses the same term.[24]

> Rex quidem adoptivi fratris sui Petri de Gavastone personam exulare seu honorem ejus minuendum non potuit sustinere.

> [Indeed the king could not bring himself to send his adoptive brother into exile or diminish his honor.]

Edward and Gaveston appear to have become sworn brothers shortly after Gaveston's arrival in England with his father in 1297, probably at some point in 1300 or early in 1301, when the two young men first became involved in Edward I's Scottish wars (as suggested by Pierre Chaplais). The chronicles do not describe the form in which Edward and Gaveston swore their *fraternitatis fedus*, but that of their oaths together in 1307 at the time of Gaveston's first exile (at Edward I's command) employed the Eucharist. In 1307 their oaths are described in the memorandum in the close rolls as having been taken upon the cross of Neit, upon the king's relics, and "sur le cors dieu" [upon God's body], and that description of their oaths in 1307 makes it probable that their earlier oaths also took the eucharistic form that Juvénal des Ursins would later regard as customary. This phrase in the close rolls follows closely the "oath sworn on the precious body of Jesus Christ" of Juvénal des Ursins (and the oaths in Giraldus's account "in the presence of relics of the saints" as well as the oath of brotherhood made "on relics of the saints" in the Latin *Amys and Amylion*).[25]

Gaveston's position close to the king gave him a monopoly of patronage, and the accounts in the chronicles reflect the disruption and resentment this aroused; but the relation of sworn brotherhood itself is treated with cautious respect. The cleric who composed the chronicle of Edward II's reign in the Cottonian manuscripts, for example, profoundly disapproved of Edward II's choice of sworn brother but characterized the relation itself in the same term of personal fidelity—"dileccionis vinculum"—that could be applied to the bond that bound the believer to Christ. In this respect it is typical. The careful respect with which sworn brotherhood is characterized in the chronicles written by ecclesiastics in England from the eleventh to the fourteenth centuries ought in itself to have raised the possibility, if not the likelihood, of a ritual of the kind Giraldus or Juvénal des Ursins portray. A monk of the Benedictine abbey of Jumièges in Normandy characterized it, in similar terms, as within the highest degree of love.[26] Sworn brothers figure as respectfully in the monastic chronicles compiled near Worcester, at Peterborough, at Durham, and at Malmesbury Abbey.[27] But it can be seen throughout the medieval English church: in the writings of a Worcestershire priest[28] and in those of an archdeacon in the diocese of Lincoln,[29] among the Anglo-Saxon canons at Ramsey Abbey[30] as later among the canons of St. Paul's[31] or the Franciscan friars in Carlisle.[32] Chronicles like these were in substantial measure the collective products of the communities and reflected their shared values. The respect they accorded sworn brotherhood was the reason that in Abbot William's estimation the gift of two sworn brothers so memorably provided the sonorous opening to the register of Oseney Abbey.

Across the Latin chronicles written in England from the eleventh to the fourteenth centuries, "fratres iurati" such as these—or described as "confederati," "foederati," "adjurati," "conjurati," or "adoptivi"—make a repeated appearance and correspond to the sworn brothers of the Oseney register or the "wed" or "wedded" brothers of the Anglo-Saxon and vernacular *Brut* chronicles.[33] Terms like this catch the nature of the world this ritual inhabited. A "wed" in Middle English was a pledge or a covenant—the church door was a setting for such "weddings"—and language of this kind recovers a social world constructed in binding oaths and ritual acts made before witnesses, human and divine. The written documents that survive for the historian to study catch that world only fitfully.

The same is true of the second group of sources where sworn brotherhood has left its trace. It had a recurring role in that common stock of stories chanted by petty chapmen, performed by traveling players, danced to at church ales—or shouted as insults—that Tessa Watt has described. These traces lie in characteristics such as mnemonic devices (including the stylized use of sworn brotherhood itself), in the specification of tunes that were never written down, the presence of elements side by side implying performances

to different kinds of audiences, and in the analogues to these stories in folk-
tales collected by ethnographers. Many of these sources were ephemeral,
drawn together by a performer from memory and from a repertoire of recognizable situations and stock phrases, varied to fit the audience of the
moment. But the part that the sworn friendship of traditional society played
in these stories is still visible in the traces it left in the romances, ballads, and
chapbooks and in folk song into the early part of the nineteenth century.[34]
These are not, of course, realistic depictions of social life. They are highly
colored stories of the love between sworn brothers and the testing of the fidelity of their oaths to each other in the most extreme of circumstances, but
they catch the ideals of sworn brotherhood that the written compact of
Nicholas Molyneux and John Winter could invoke for contemporaries.

   Typical of this genre is the ballad *Bewick and Graham.* As one can see from
its incidental details, such as the reference to a psalmbook, it was composed
as a ballad probably toward the end of the sixteenth century. It tells the story
of the love of two sworn brothers—"sworn-brethren will we be"—who are
caught in the mortal dilemma created by the quarrel of their fathers and the
demand from his father that confronts Christy Graham either to kill his
sworn brother or his own father. Christy Graham goes with a heavy heart to
his duty and the unsuspecting welcome of his sworn brother, his "bully" (a
term that in North Country dialect meant both a brother and a friend).

> "O welcome, O welcome, bully Grahame!
>   O man, thou art my dear, welcome!
> O man, thou art my dear, welcome!
>   For I love thee best in Christendom."

> "Away, away, O bully Grahame!
>   And of thy bullyship let me be!
> The day is come I never thought on;
>   Bully, I'm come here to fight with thee."

To resolve his dilemma Christy Graham fights his "bully" Bewick, as he
must; but to remain faithful to their vow, he slays himself when he hears that
he has mortally wounded him.

> "O if this be true, my bully dear,
>   The words that thou dost tell to me,
> The vow I made, and the vow I'll keep;
>   I swear I'll be the first that die."

The dying words of his friend recall the joint burial of William Neville and John Clanvowe.

> "Nay, dig a grave both low and wide,
>   And in it us two pray bury;
> But bury my bully Grahame on the sun-side,
>   For I'm sure he's won the victory."

The ballad ends, like *Romeo and Juliet* from the same period, with the lament of the two fathers over the tragedy their quarrel has caused.[35]

The story of Horn and his "wed brother" Ayol comes from the same genre, as does that of Guy of Warwick and his sworn brother Tirry; but arguably the most popular of all the Middle English romances was the romance of Amys and Amylion, a story of two sworn friends that turns like *Bewick and Graham* on the testing of the "truth" of their friendship.[36] Stories like this drew on a wider culture of oral performance. *Amys and Amylion* is a variant of a folktale that has been collected by ethnographers from India to the Atlantic coast,[37] and the place sworn brotherhood occupied in this largely oral culture is visible in the use evidently made of it to structure the telling of a story. When listening to a ballad or a singer reciting a lay, the audience cannot pause or return to an earlier passage. For the storyteller's narrative to be intelligible, it needs immediacy and structuring elements with which the audience is already familiar. The repetitive tags of traditional storytelling are one way of providing this; another lay in the stock situations they drew on; and the same devices enable the storyteller to extemporize a performance from memory. The contrast between the false friend and the true appears to have been one of these stock situations, and the ready symmetry of two sworn brothers was one of the familiar tags on which storytelling drew.

> Go we now to Yuni again and to Ivor his wed-brother ...
> ... Send after mine son Octa and after one other Ebissa his wed-brother.
> ... hight* come Octa and his wed-brother Ebissa.
> ... and my son Octa and his wed-brother Ebissa.
> ... Octa ... and Ebissa his wed-brother.[38]

> *command

These lines are from a Middle English poem composed around the end of the twelfth century by the poet who describes himself as Layamon (the priest of Ernley in Worcestershire whom I mentioned earlier), but in lines like this one can still hear the voice of the twelfth-century storyteller whose conventions Layamon was drawing on, extemporizing a story and helping his audience to keep up with its narrative by building it around a familiar theme.

The references to sworn brotherhood in courtly poetry such as that of Geoffrey Chaucer or the romance *Athelston* are not necessarily the product of this broadly shared culture, but they provide a guide to how common the phenomenon of sworn brotherhood was. Of course, Chaucer's poems are no more transparent depictions of social life than a ballad like *Bewick and Graham*, but they are social satires, and they would have lost their edge if they had not been placed in fourteenth-century culture. William Neville and John Clanvowe were part of Chaucer's circle, as we know from their presence as witnesses in 1380 to a deed releasing Chaucer from rights of action in the rape case brought against him;[39] and the sworn brotherhood of the two knights in Chaucer's *Knightes Tale* appears to have been one of the anachronisms by which Chaucer translated the ancient Greece of his story into the social conventions of late fourteenth-century England. Sworn brotherhood was not restricted to a chivalric context. Chaucer depicts it as set widely across fourteenth-century society. The *Shipmannes Tale* depicts the sworn brotherhood of a wealthy merchant and a worldly monk. The *Freres Tale* shows that between two minor court officials, one in an archdeacon's court, the other in a sheriff's court. The *Pardoners Tale* depicts sworn brotherhood among a number of peasant farmers. In the *Shipmannes Tale* the vow of sworn brotherhood is set beside vows of religious life and marriage as equal facts of life, and it is difficult to see why Chaucer's social observation should have been less sharp-eyed in the one than in the other.[40]

At this distance it is difficult to say how common sworn brotherhood was in strictly statistical terms, although one indication is given by its repeated appearance around the end of the fourteenth century in the army pay and muster roles that Kenneth McFarlane pointed to some years ago.[41] The question is perhaps easier to answer if posed in terms of how *familiar* the relation was, as the references to "fratres iurati," to "wedded brothers," or to "sworn brothers," from the eleventh to the sixteenth centuries invariably assume that the terms will be readily intelligible to the reader; I know of no occasion before the seventeenth century when any need is shown to explain what these terms mean. An illustration is the note that Richard Strangways made in the 1450s that I quoted earlier. Strangways was the son of a Yorkshire gentleman—heraldry was then part of the education of a gentleman—and he seems to have shared with his tutor a pleasure in making the terms of the art as obscure as possible to the uninitiated. He notes one such term, but the illustration he gives in the course of writing the note—of the two knights who were sworn brothers and that I earlier quoted—was designed to translate the term for him into the familiar sights of his culture, as Chaucer did with the *Knightes Tale*. The author of the Middle English *Story of Genesis and Exodus* similarly used sworn brotherhood to translate the Old Testament into what for him was evidently a contemporary convention.[42] The most telling evidence is perhaps the immense popularity of a story like that of *Amys and Amylion* or the impression one has in late medieval England of hearing, again and again, the same story of sworn friendship tried and tested: among learned courtly knights reading Chaucer, among merchants or their families reading romances, or among peasants in the English countryside listening to a storyteller at a fair or a church ale. One can only make a reasoned guess at the actual incidence of sworn friendship; but of the hold it had on the imagination—on its ability to articulate a world of fantasies and fears—there can scarcely be any doubt.

The vow was the motor of these dreams, and its testing shaped their narrative as much as it shaped those terms like "sworn brother" that the chroniclers employ. In these stories its form is that of an unreserved commitment, personal and all-encompassing.

> On a day the children ware and wight*
> Together were troth-plight
> While they lived in land:
> Both by day and by night,
> In well, woe, wrong, right
> Frerly should they fond,†
> Hold together at every need,
> In well, woe, word, and deed
> While they might stand,
> From that day forward ever mo‡
> Neither fail other for well ne§ woe.[43]

> *prudent and brave   †fairly deal   ‡further   §nor

That is the vow that Amys and Amylion swear. Chaucer is characteristically ironic in the *Knightes Tale* and the *Hous of Fame*, but the terms are the same in each.

> . . . thy brother
> Y-sworn full deep, and each of us till other,
> That never, for to die in the pain,

Till that the death depart shall us twain
Neither of us in love to hinder other,
Ne in none other case, my leve brother;
But that thou shouldest truly further me
In every case, and I shall further thee.
This was thine oath, and mine also, certain.
    . . . I shall never fro thee go
But be thine own sworn brother!
We will meddle us each with other
That no man, be he never so wroth,
Shall have that one of two but both
at once, all beside his leave,
Come we a-morwe or on eve,
Be we cried or still y-rouned.[44]

If these stories are the narrative equivalent to the terms used by the chroniclers, the tomb monument of William Neville and John Clanvowe is their
visual equivalent. The tombs in English churches, like that of Neville and
Clanvowe, of covenanted friends lying in their tombs together as if they had
been husband and wife are traces of the objective character friendship had in
traditional society and represent a third major source of evidence on which
this study draws. They punctuate its argument and its turning points,[45] but
such tombs also reiterate the place that friendship held in traditional Christianity, a characteristic it shared with traditional culture more generally. The
setting of these tombs reinforce the connection that John Bossy has written
about between the friendship of traditional society and the rites, places,
and (perhaps to a lesser extent) persons of Christianity. The impression one
gains of that connection growing after 1000 may be more than a growing
availability of evidence. Layamon's poem characteristically employed the
archaic term "swerd brotheren" [sword brothers], which was removed by
the modernizing scribe who revised the poem in the thirteenth century (the
"Otho" manuscript), evidently regarding swearing brotherhood on a sword
as by then an unintelligible practice.[46] By the early fifteenth century Juvénal
des Ursins evidently regarded a swearing of brotherhood in church as the
customary form at that date. This is probably also the explanation of the
otherwise curious detail in the Latin *Amys and Amylion*, that the two friends
swear their fidelity to each other on a sword "ubi erant sanctorum reliquie"
[where relics of the saints were]: while the modernizing scribe of the "Otho"
manuscript of Layamon's poem has changed the older practice to some-

thing by then more intelligible, the churchman who wrote the Latin version of *Amys and Amylion* appears to have conflated the two.[47]

Tomb monuments to friends buried together are also a powerful corrective to the impression given by the chronicles. Chronicles were typically concerned with the wider public affairs that might touch on the abbeys and cathedrals that produced them. The sworn friendships they describe are overwhelmingly political, and the glimpse one catches of Robert D'Oilly and Roger D'Ivry in the register of Oseney Abbey is unusual in this respect. More typical of the chronicles are sworn friendships like those between Edmund Ironside and the Danish king Cnut in the eleventh century or those of the earls of Northumbria described in the chronicles compiled by the monks at Durham. Political concerns were uppermost in the mind of the monk of Jumièges in Normandy, who I mentioned earlier, when he recorded that Duke Robert of Normandy adopted as brothers two sons of King Ethelred of England before the conquest when they were in exile in Normandy. Sources like this pass without comment over figures like Nicholas Molyneux and John Winter or William Neville and John Clanvowe unless they impinge on wider political concerns, and even less visible from the viewpoint of the chronicles are the sworn brothers lower down the social hierarchy that one glimpses in storytelling and the literary accounts. The common tombs of friends buried together vividly fill that void, and for that reason they will form one of the threads throughout this book. But one might well pause when one turns from the sources for such a history to what historians have already made of the motives that animated it, from within as it were. The conclusions one sees are wildly different—and one might well wonder why. It is the first hint of how difficult is the terrain that lies ahead.

Historians, Friendship—and Ritual

Violence, profit, and love—each of these at different times has variously been suggested as the motive that animated sworn brotherhood. It is deceptively easy to undermine any of these judgments, for the paradox they present is how effectively each is able to nullify the claims of the others.

> [A]rtificial brotherhoods were formed for the purposes of protection, defense, and armed aggression in a disintegrated social order in which the threat of violence and physical force was a real and ever-present danger . . . I suggest that this institution was more frequently found . . . inside state structures characterized by less formal or less "rationalized" relationships

of amity . . . connected with the prevalence of primal forms of social organization in the face of the weakness of effective central state power.[48]

Brotherhood-in-arms, as defined in this contract, was thus a business-
partnership, an insurance against the heaviest financial loss that could befall
a soldier—to be taken alive—and a gamble on survivorship, a kind of rudimentary tontine. The risk of loss was spread and a chance—not a very outside chance—was offered of double gain.[49]

In almost every age and place the ceremony fulfilled what most people today regard as the essence of marriage: a permanent romantic commitment
between two people, witnessed and recognized by the community . . . a personal commitment, as opposed to a religious, political, or family union.[50]

The first of these views is the oldest. It is the characterization of the contemporary American historian Brent D. Shaw, but he is voicing the view of
the English nineteenth-century constitutional historians that, as Pollock
and Maitland put it in 1898, "[s]tep by step, as the power of the State waxes
. . . kindred wanes."[51] Where the friendship created by kinship had obtruded on their accounts, its presence was glossed over as a form of "bastard feudalism" obstructing the onward march of the royal administration.[52]
That onward march—leading in their view to the constitutional settlement
of English history—was the theme of their writings, but their historical
framework was inherited by more recent historians such as Brent D. Shaw
without the political program it had been created to buttress. Kenneth
McFarlane (the author of the second of these judgments) leveled his sights
against that notion of "bastard feudalism," and his writings on William
Neville and John Clanvowe illustrate how wide of the mark is this characterization of sworn brotherhood. Neville and Clanvowe appear to have become sworn brothers soon after January 1373, when Clanvowe joined Neville
in the service of Edward III; and when in 1380 the minority of Richard II
(Edward III's heir) effectively ended, both men were employed by Richard
as part of an extension of the machinery of royal household government to
an extent unparalleled since the reign of Edward II. In 1381 they became
royal chamber knights together and were to act jointly for Richard II in administrative and diplomatic roles and in military campaigns throughout
their careers, counterbalancing the influence of magnates whom Richard II
did not believe he could trust. Both were entrusted with the custody of
strategically important castles: Neville with that of Nottingham, Clanvowe
with that of Haverford. If there was an onward march of the royal admin-

istration of the kind nineteenth-century English historians believed they could trace, two sworn brothers like Neville and Clanvowe were not its unruly opponents: they were part of it. The detailed provisions agreed to by Nicholas Molyneux and John Winter similarly place their motives firmly within their careers together in the armies of Henry V; and later they acted together in administering the affairs of Sir John Fastolf, one of the wealthiest knights in England and the master of the household of the regent of France, the duke of Bedford. Nor does it seem likely that Chaucer assumed that the wealthy merchant and the worldly monk who appear as sworn brothers in the *Shipmannes Tale* had any intention of murdering their neighbors (or each other); and if Edward II had been seeking a sworn brother of the kind Brent D. Shaw conjectures, he would have sought it among the magnates who were threatening him and not in an intimate who could act for him like Piers Gaveston.

The third of these characterizations—love—is that of the historian John Boswell. But does it accord any better with the detailed provisions for the division of profit in the agreement of Nicholas Molyneux and John Winter, analyzed by Kenneth McFarlane in the study from which I quote? William Neville and John Clanvowe were both trained soldiers employed in royal campaigns and may have had a similar agreement, and Edward II and Piers Gaveston seem to have become sworn brothers significantly at the same time as they became involved together in Edward I's Scottish wars. As McFarlane put it in his study of Molyneux and Winter, "Their concern was with loss and gain reckoned without affectation in terms of cash and heritages, and despite a reference to fraternal love the sort of disloyalty one brother-in-arms desired to guard himself against in another was financial fraud . . . Here was more professed love than trust."[53]

Yet these characterizations by Shaw and Boswell point to the weaknesses in McFarlane's conclusion—difficulties that his paper elides. The first is the practicality of keeping the force such men could deploy within civil boundaries. Shaw's characterization however inadequate is, in sober fact, a good deal more accurate a picture of the sworn brotherhoods one sees in the chronicles than McFarlane's. The sworn brotherhood of the dukes of Orléans and Burgundy, which Juvénal des Ursins included in his history, was designed to end the *hostilities* between them, and the stress Juvénal des Ursins places on the customary nature of the ritual is his scandalized commentary on the subsequent murder of the duke of Orléans by a servant of his sworn brother. These two men were attempting to defend themselves from something a great deal more lethal than financial fraud, and a similar attempt to restrain a potential (or actual) enemy characterized the sworn brotherhoods of the earls of Northumberland and the "wedded" brotherhood that—ostensibly—ended the conflict between Edmund Ironside and Cnut. The "emphasis on safety," as Brent D. Shaw put it, was "employed precisely because the men often entered into these relationships . . . out of fear."[54]

McFarlane's study also leaves unexplained the questions brought out in Boswell's view—even when one has rejected Boswell's conclusions. One is the elective nature of sworn brotherhood. Why did William Neville and John Clanvowe or Nicholas Molyneux and John Winter choose to enter into such a bond *with each other*? Why this man rather than another? Molyneux and Winter said in their agreement that they were prompted to become brothers in arms by the desire to augment the love and fraternity *already* growing between them ("Premierement pour acroistre et augmenter lamour et fraternite qui est piera en commencee entre ledit Molyneux & Winter"),[55] and that claim should not be put aside casually, as the detailed provisions they made in their written agreement in the end counted for little. Winter was to misappropriate the money he should have been holding for his brother in arms while Molyneux was still abroad, and the fact came to light when Winter died. Yet when Winter made his will, he still trusted Molyneux— the man whom he had cheated—to be one of his executors; and his trust was not misplaced, for when Molyneux returned to England to recover his assets he provided for a chantry, for masses to be said to release the soul of his friend from purgatory. Does that act correspond to a description of their friendship as a kind of rudimentary tontine—a coldly calculating gamble in which the winner (or rather survivor) takes the stakes? It would be still more improbable, if not grotesque, to attribute such a motive to William Neville, who in the end died with his friend rather than survive without him.

A second uncomfortable difficulty is the evidence for Boswell's consequent view that sworn brotherhood could be a relationship between two men or women that was (or could become) sexual. The fourteenth-century chronicle of the Cistercian abbey of Meaux in Yorkshire—a work of outstanding scholarship—recorded that Edward II "in vitio sodomitico nimium delectabat" [particularly delighted in the vice of sodomy], and Gaveston's modern biographer understandably concludes that it is beyond dispute that Gaveston and Edward's relationship was sexual. This would not, of course, have been countenanced by the church's canon law, but it is unlikely that Edward and Gaveston were unique in this respect. There was a comparable sexual ambiguity about the other forms of ritual kinship that Giraldus's composite account evokes. Church courts disapproved of sexual relations before a betrothal was solemnized at church and did not countenance sexual relations between the spiritual kin, the *commatres* and *compatres*, of *compaternitas*; but the disapproval of sexual relations after a betrothal was widely disregarded, and the particular pleasure of sexual relations with one's *commatres* and *compatres* was a good source of jokes throughout the Middle Ages.[56]

But the element most damagingly missing from Kenneth McFarlane's characterization is the immense popularity of the idealized stories of sworn brotherhood, and necessarily so, as it cannot explain them. The ideals of the romance of Amys and Amylion, of the two knights in Chaucer's *Knightes Tale*, of Horn and his wed brother Ayol, of Christy Graham and his "bully" Bewick—these figure as rhetoric in a popular culture, but they are not lies; and the *personal* commitment they avow in the event more accurately prefigured the outcome of the covenant between Nicholas Molyneux and John Winter than the detailed provisions their compact so carefully made—and in the end so signally failed to secure.

There is no simple solution to the dilemma presented by these mutually contradictory views. This stubbornly remains the case however one juggles with the facts. Could one, for example, relate the ritual I have described in this chapter to sworn brotherhoods of the kind that Shaw conjectured rather than the "business partnerships" envisaged by McFarlane? Was it employed only to *force* men to make peace with each other, when their violent conflict was disrupting good order? The simplicity of the solution is attractive—and preserves the distinction between the two characterizations—but the details belie so neat a distinction. The most obvious of these is that the agreement between Nicholas Molyneux and John Winter was entered into in the *church* of St. Martin at Harfleur, a setting that appears as suitable for sworn brotherhood of the one supposed kind as of the other; and the distinction also requires one to disregard the terms used by both Giraldus and the sons of the murdered Duke Louis of Orléans: in the one case the ritual being described takes place when the two men *desire* to come together—"ad sacrum aliquem locum conveniunt, cum eo quem oppetere cupiunt" [they come together in some holy place with the man with whom they are eager to be united]—and in the other the term they employ is "vraye fraternité et comgagnée d'armes," substantially the same term as the "freres darmes" [brothers in arms] used in the agreement of Nicholas Molyneux and John Winter.

[J]urerent et promirent solennellement vraye fraternité et compagnée d'armes ensemble, par especiales convenances sur ce faites.

[They swore and solemnly promised *true brotherhood and company of arms* together, by the special conventions recognized in such a matter.][57]

The incoherence among these three different estimates of sworn brotherhood is at too radical a level for a simple distinction to rationalize them. It
resides rather in the comfortless fact that all are employing the *same* evidence
to reach radically different conclusions. The same language that one inter-
prets as denoting a voluntary union appears to another as an enforced union.
What one sees as denoting trust, the other sees as fear: one sexuality, the
other violence. These three contradictory characterizations are set up in-
tractably against each other because what each shares with the other is a positivist view of history, that at root the historian's sources are just plain *facts*
and that once the historian has concluded what they are really about he or
she can assemble the reliable sources and dispose of the rest as mere rhetoric—as an exception or something irregular. In such a view there is no place
for the apprehension that the sources may be conceptually difficult, the
traces of practices and experiences that have simply no modern equivalents:
that they are untranslatable into modern terms.[58] Each of these attempted
descriptions leaves behind them the quandary that a detailed and objective
view of the evidence as a whole points insistently to a conclusion that is not
at all easy to grasp: however wildly incompatible these characterizations
may be, they are *all* precise and accurate—if not in demonstrating what
sworn brotherhood was, then at least in demonstrating what it was not.

No careful sifting of reliable from unreliable sources will solve that
quandary. Viewed from outside, the strangeness to the modern eye in the
friendship of traditional society lies in the formal and objective character
that it evidently could possess. The tomb of William Neville and John
Clanvowe is only one particularly vivid illustration of how difficult it is to
translate such terms into modern equivalents, but the problem in doing so
does not lie merely in finding adequate sources: the friendship of traditional
society is difficult to detect within the administrative records left by church
and state, but that silence is not in itself insurmountable. There is no *Liber
de Fraternitate Jurata*, no practitioners' manuals, codes of canon law, or convenient collections of administrative records that comment on friendship
and illustrate its workings. What the historian has is rather a collection of
fragments, preserved in the descriptions of contemporaries and the traces
that the friendship of traditional society left in the documents with which
it recorded its agreements, in the stories it told about friendship, and in the
tombs in which it buried its dead. But these pieces are plentiful and not
difficult to find, and I have argued in this chapter that their provenance was
a customary social world constructed through binding oaths and ritual acts
made before witnesses, human and divine, a world that was widely intelligible across traditional society and associated with the rites, places, and

(perhaps to a lesser extent) the persons of traditional Christianity: apparently as familiar to a merchant or a peasant as to a courtly knight. But a view from outside comes up against its limits when one attempts to explore, from within as it were, the motives that animated friendship. The obstinate diversity in the evidence quickly escapes explanations that are readily intelligible in modern terms, and the mischief that each of these three characterizations so effectively creates for the other two is elegantly illustrative of that fact. The problem does not lie in finding the evidence: the problem is of having too much evidence rather than too little, or rather that the evidence one has taken on its own patently does not cohere, that it will not explain itself. The unseen barrier one comes up against is the evident reticence of this culture to explain how this contradictory evidence does cohere, and simply amassing more data will not provide a way through that barrier.

One needs to ask a different kind of question and perhaps a wider one. Could it be that the need is to interrogate traditional society in a wider historical perspective than the one I (and my predecessors) have taken so far? As England passes into the sixteenth century, an apparently quite different kind of friendship becomes visible and is far more familiar: a noninstrumental friendship, based in affinity, that does not (and should not) obtrude on a wider world of public affairs. With its quite different assumptions, modernity seems to arrive, with a world we can recognize. Does this change provide the access to understanding the culture it apparently replaced? Yes, I think it does, although the answer it provides is not the one that might be expected.

CHAPTER 2

Friend to Sir Philip Sidney

When in disgrace with Fortune and mens eyes,
I all alone beweepe my out-cast state,
And trouble deafe heaven with my bootlesse cries,
And looke upon my selfe and curse my fate.
Wishing me like to one more rich in hope,
Featur'd like him, like him with friends possest,
Desiring this mans art, and that mans skope,
With what I most injoy contented least,
Yet in these thoughts my selfe almost despising,
Haplye I thinke on thee, and then my state,
(Like to the Larke at breake of daye arising)
From sullen earth sings himns at Heavens gate,
For thy sweet love remembred such welth brings,
That then I skorne to change my state with Kings.
—William Shakespeare, sonnet 29

Fulke Greville never built the memorial he had planned for himself and his friend Philip Sidney, by Sidney's tomb in St. Paul's Cathedral, but the tomb monument he intended for them can be recovered from the letter that he sent to his friend John Coke in the autumn of 1615.[1] By any standards, it would have been an impressive sight. Its intended setting was the vast retro-choir of St. Paul's, beneath its clustered piers and the great rose window. The old St. Paul's that Wren's later cathedral replaced was one of the greatest cathedrals in Europe and dominated the skyline of seventeenth-century London. The crowds in St. Paul's at the time were more likely to be there to hear the news than to say their prayers—the indefatigable William Fleetwood had hastened to inform William Cecil of the gossip about the latest appointments to the queen's council that had "occupied Powles all the last week"[2]—but Fulke Greville's intention (as he explained in his letter to John Coke) was to enclose the monument from the crowds milling about it "because ther is or can be no severed Isle ther, my purpose is to encompass the sepulchre round & inclose wth a highe grate of Iron." That "highe grate of Iron" would have corresponded to the protecting railings that still stood around the remnants of the shrine of the seventh-century bishop St. Erkenwald, whose relics had once been venerated there: an apt gesture for the tomb of a hero of the reformed religion that Fulke Greville had depicted in the account he wrote of Philip Sidney's life.[3]

The splendor of the setting was matched by the decoration of the tomb.

> Too deynty large stones of touche delycately porlished, borne up one above an other, by 4 pillers of brass 3 foote & a halfe highe & double guylt. The uppermost worthely his, the nether myne. now because I would not marr the delicacy of the stones, or embose ther lusre, wth adding any thing to cover it. I have devysed a pillar of the same touche, raysed above & yet disjoyned from the tombe, and placed at the upper end of Sr Philips wch shall carry skutchions for his armes, and inscriptions, to be graven uppon it in guilded letters, & in lyke manner at the lower end, marry only halfe the tombe highe, a more humble one to carry myne.

This was also an arrangement that might have been expected of the tomb of a husband and wife. The tomb monument in the nearby choir to Nicholas Bacon, Queen Elizabeth's lord keeper of the great seal, and to his two wives had the same arrangement: a double tomb monument arranged as two beds of stone one above the other, the husband depicted as lying above and his wife below. At first sight, the unabashed marital imagery appears strikingly reminiscent of the tomb monument of William Neville and John Clanvowe—the tomb of the two sworn brothers with which the last chapter opened—and the lives of Fulke Greville and Philip Sidney together at the court of Elizabeth I corresponded to that of Neville and Clanvowe at the court of Richard II. Yet the terms in which Greville and Sidney themselves described their friendship emphatically deny a comparison of this kind. This chapter opens by hearing them speak in their own voices about friendship, as in Sidney's "Two Pastoralls," and listening to these terms, which are likely to be more recognizable to us now than those of the friendship amounting to kinship of two sworn brothers in fourteenth-century England. Friendship is here an essentially private relationship that is necessarily set apart from the commerce and practice of the world, as Shakespeare's boundlessly beautiful sonnet 29 can be read. By the end of the sixteenth century in England, this assertion is everywhere to hand, and it seems to mark a change to a more modern and recognizable world. This chapter is designed to put that wide proposition to the test: by sustaining a close view of the friendships of these two men, which seem to exemplify friendship's terms within a compass as detailed and exquisite as a miniature by Nicholas Hilliard. It is an appealing proposition, no less than the beginnings of modernity and the world in which we live. If these terms are what they appear to be, we have that broad perspective on a history of friendship that seemed to elude us at the end of the last chapter. If they are not, then we need to look more closely and think again.

Friendship in a Pastoral Landscape

"I lived with him and knew him from a child." That was Fulke Greville's claim in his life of Philip Sidney, and it was right.[4] They entered the same school in Shrewsbury on the same day in 1564, and their intimacy as schoolfellows is caught in Greville's boyish scribbling in Sidney's surviving schoolbook.[5] The lives they pursued together at the court of Elizabeth I did not undermine that intimacy: their friendship remained as much a matter of the literary interests they pursued together, or the bed they shared, as matters of state; and when Sidney left England to become governor of Flushing in 1585, it was with Greville that he left his literary papers; and when he died still a young man in the wars in the Low Countries the following year, it was Greville who oversaw the publication of his *Arcadia* in 1590. The intimate nature of their friendship was signaled by the books Sidney left to Greville in his will (and to their common friend Edward Dyer). "For my own part," Greville was to write in his life of Sidney, "I observed, honoured and loved him so much as, with what caution soever I have passed through my days hitherto among the living, yet in him I challenge a kind of freedom even among the dead."[6] In his *Poetical Rapsody* of 1602 Francis Davison included "Two Pastoralls, made by Sir *Philip Sidney*, never yet published *Upon his meeting with his two worthy Friends and fellow-Poets, Sir Edward Dier, and Maister Fulke Greville*." It is the second of these that is printed here.

   In the crisp tones of Elizabethan verse, the three friends are transformed by Sidney's poem into shepherds set in a pastoral landscape and their verses into bucolic songs; and on its surface at least that pastoral landscape corresponds with the precision of a literary metaphor to a friendship among them based on affinity and a shared love of letters, set against the power and

Two Pastoralls, made by Sir *Philip Sid-*
ney, never yet published
Upon his meeting with his two worthy Friends
and fellow-Poets, Sir Edward Dier,
and Maister Fulke Greville . . .

Disprayse of a Courtly life
Walking in bright *Phoebus'* blaze
Where with heate oppreste I was,
I got to a shady wood,
Where greene leaves did newly bud.
And of grasse was plenty dwelling,
Deckt with pyde flowers sweetely smelling.

In this wood a man I met,
On lamenting wholy set:
Rewing change of wonted state,
Whence he was transformed late,
Once to Shepheard's God retayning,
Now in servile Court remayning.

There he wandring, malecontent,
Up and downe perplexed went,
Daring not to tell to mee,
Spake unto a sencelesse tree,
One among the rest electing
These same words, or this effecting:

"My old mates I grieve to see,
Voyde of me in field to bee,
Where we once our lovely sheepe,
Lovingly like friends did keepe,
Oft each other's friendship proving,
Never striving, but in loving.

"But may Love abiding bee
In poore shepheard's base degree?
It belongs to such alone

To whom arte of Love is knowne:
Seely shepheards are not witting
What in art of Love is fitting.

"Nay, what neede the Arte to those,
To whom we our love disclose?
It is to be used then,
When we do but flatter men:
Friendship true in hart assured,
Is by nature's giftes procured.

"Therefore shepheardes wanting skill,
Can Love's duties best fulfill:
Since they know not how to faine,
Nor with Love to cloake Disdaine,
Like the wiser sort, whose learning
Hides their inward will of harming.

"Well was I, while under shade
Ofen Reedes me musicke made,
Striving with my Mates in Song,
Mixing mirth our Songs among,
Greater was that shepheard's treasure,
Then this false, fine, Courtly pleasure.

"Where, how many Creatures be,
So many pufft in mind I see,
Like to *Junoe's* birdes of pride,
Scarce each other can abide,
Friends like to blacke Swannes appearing,
Sooner these than those in hearing.

"Therefore, *Pan,* if thou mayst be
Made to listen unto me,
Grant, I say (if seely man
May make treaty to god *Pan*),
That I, without thy denying,
May be still to thee relying.

"Only for my two loves' sake,*
In whose love I pleasure take,
Only two do me delight
With their ever-pleasing sight,
Of all men to thee retaining,
Grant me with those two remaining.

"So shall I to thee always,
With my reedes, sound mighty praise;
And first Lambe that shall befall,
Yearely decke thine Altar shall:
If it please thee be reflected,
And I from thee not rejected."

So I left him in that place,
Taking pitty on his case,
Learning this among the rest,
That the meane estate is best,
Better filled with contenting,
Voyde of wishing and repenting.

—From *The Poems of Sir Philip Sidney,* 260, 262–264

*Sir Ed. D. and M. F. G.

place of the court. "Disprayse of a Courtly life" was the title that Francis Davison understandably gave to the second of these "Pastoralls."

It was in the same terms that Greville wrote his letter to John Coke to seek his advice on his plans "for philips long promysed tombe"; and Greville allowed himself in his letter the same "loving freedom" that he had exercised in his life of Sidney "wth out ceremonie to breake thorow all pleas of right or Inequalyty . . . let us bothe stryve to be equall judges betwen our selves." Anyone at the time who might have picked up and read that letter would have recognized the gesture. Greville is here writing the "familiar letter"—the intimate letter of friendship—that had become the quintessential expression of friendship among educated men, a literary convention as readily recognizable as the pastoral landscape of Sidney's poem. The familiar letters most widely studied by modern scholars are those that circulated earlier in the sixteenth century among the humanist circle of the great Dutch scholar Erasmus, but the form of the familiar letter was copied and repeated throughout the following century.[7] One can see it set out in the letters that Antonio Pérez wrote, the renegade secretary of Philip II, while part of the circle around the earl of Essex when he visited England in the 1590s. Love between men is the theme of these letters. Typical of many more is the letter of Pérez in which a mere note arranging a meeting in the morning becomes an elaborate reflection on the nature of one man's desire for another.

Hodiè desideraui te convenire. Breuius dixissem, te desideraui. Nam qui amat, in orbem sui desiderii circumfertur. Verè in orbem, quia à corde, amoris centro, huc illuc fertur desiderium, & amatum tanquam orbem hâc illâc aggreditur. Non in visu, non in colloquutione, non denique in vnâ solùm actione, nec in vnius partis consequutione requiescit amor. Totum amatum circundet, & possideat necesse est. Vale, & multo manè me expecta.

[Today I desired to meet you. I should say that more briefly. I desired *you*, for he who loves is carried around in the orbit of his desire: truly in the orbit, for desire is carried hither and thither by the heart, the center of love, and approaches the beloved just as in orbit on this side and on that. Not in sight, not in speech—not just in one action alone, nor in the effect of one part—does love rest: it encompasses the beloved entirely, and it will inevitably possess him. Farewell, and very early in the morning expect me.][8]

Fulke Greville's letter to John Coke was cast in the same accustomed mode of the familiar letter, and the conventions in Philip Sidney's poem are as recognizable. The comparison of the true friend with the feigned was a staple of the prescriptive literature of friendship, the numerous guides to avoiding the pitfalls of friendship of which Francis Bacon's essays on friendship were once a part.[9] These guides are now read only by historians (if at all), and the same is the case with the familiar letter; but both were given an enduring expression in the Elizabethan literature of friendship, that engaging library of poems and plays of which Philip Sidney's "Pastoralls"—and Shakespeare's far more famous sonnets—were part and which are now firmly within the canon of English literature. It is perhaps for that reason that the change they seem to mark is so persuasive.

But is it *too* persuasive? It leaves some nagging questions unanswered, albeit at first sight apparently inconsequential ones. One of them is the question *why* Fulke Greville never built the memorial that he had planned for Philip Sidney and himself in St. Paul's Cathedral. It may seem niggardly, even small-minded, to ask that question about such a gesture; but it is curiously difficult to answer. Greville was immensely wealthy, and in 1615 he was the recently appointed chancellor of the exchequer at the court of James I, and this would have been by no means the first such memorial in the retrochoir of St. Paul's, yet the memorial was not built, and it is very difficult to say why. Another such quizzical detail concerns those letters of Antonio Pérez: not the letters in themselves, as their genre is not difficult to grasp, but why there were so *many* of them. By his own estimation Pérez must have been able to produce at least one new Latin epistle every day—some days several—at a time when he was engaged in the difficult task of establishing a place for himself as one of the secretaries of the earl of Essex, men whose role was to act as the earl's go-between with the world, to gather intelligence and to see to his affairs.[10] Yet these are very often not practical business notes dealing with administration and political affairs but self-conscious literary productions composed in an elaborate mannerist style, whose subject overwhelmingly is the delight (and sorrows) of friendship. If the number of such letters is striking, the circumstances of their survival are even more so; for a good many of them have survived (and are now in Lambeth Palace Library) because of the copies made as they passed through his hands by Anthony Bacon, one of the hardworking secretaries of the earl of Essex, as he went about his daily tasks. Taken at face value, Bacon's copies of these letters are as inexplicable as the effort devoted to their composition by a man on the make like Pérez in the hard-nosed world of Elizabethan England. The insistent implication is that, in some way that is not immediately obvious, they figured in that very practical world of power and place into which Pérez was seeking to insert himself.

That implication suggests a further possibility. Is that rationale, whatever it was, also the reason why the familiar letters of the time have survived not by chance as isolated manuscripts but in collections of such familiar letters carefully gathered together by their recipients or their authors? When one looks at the close details of these letters, that pragmatic world is not as absent from them as it might at first seem. The preface to Fulke Greville's readiness "wth out ceremonie to breake thorow all pleas of right or Inequalyty" is this opening to his letter.

Mr Cooke howsoever some misprisions of unkindnes stand hetherto undecyded betwen us. In respect that when no competent Judge is chosen, ther can no defynytyve sentence be given. yet the opportunyty of this Justly discharged servant going neer you, & the occasion it selfe, easily encourage me, wth out ceremonie to breake thorow all pleas of right or Inequalyty, and in

the Language of old acquantence bothe to salute & Impart freely wth you,
know therfor, that this Latin Epistle enclosed, is written by a man cald over
by me to reede this Intended lecture of story.

Greville is taking Coke's advice about a scholar he has invited to England to
give a history ("story") lecture or lectures (Greville would later endow the
first history chair at Cambridge). He deals with the man's possible scholarly
abilities and then turns confidentially to seek Coke's advice about the appropriateness of his plans for Sidney's tomb. But a detail that Coke might
well have been expected to pick up is a phrase in the description that Greville gives him of this scholar that one might at first pass over: "by nation he
is a northerne briton." A "northerne briton" was a Scotsman, but the term
"briton" was one that was enthusiastically countenanced by King James I,
who on his accession to the English throne had sought to persuade his two
nations, Scotland and England now ruled by the same king, that they should
also be really and effectively one "Britain." History in seventeenth-century
England was not merely an academic study: as contemporaries were well
aware, it had ready political associations, in the contested claims of crown
and parliament as in those of popery and the reformed religion. Is Greville
delicately—and indirectly—suggesting that his lecturer will be politically
acceptable? Coke's reply was that "this mans contrie hath advantage both
to suppress exception, and to countenance a new creditor wth the voge and
authoritie of the tyme."[11] The emphasis is surely on the word "this": *this*
man's country overrules the exception that might be taken to a foreigner.
Are both of them talking with a studied indirection about the politics of
the court?

      And what of that odd remark "yet the opportunyty of this Justly dis-
charged servant going neer you"? Why does Greville need to commend the
bearer of the letter? That Coke had it in his hand was evidence enough that
the bearer had done his work, as well as if the letter had been brought by
the common carter. The curious comment draws into the picture the bearer
of the letter, who is otherwise now invisible to us. The explanation is perhaps to be found by a parallel in a postscript Greville adds to the letter following his signature. As one can see from the correction in the manuscript,
the postscript he initially attached was this: "Yf ever we meete agayn, you
shall faythefully know what was in my power to have done for you, & have
accepted for my own advancement, yf you ether had come up, uppon my
earnest letter." But his concern to add the postscript has distracted him, and
he stops in the flow of writing and corrects the term he has used to "invy-
tation long agoe by your father" and then continues "or the last modest one

made by my letter to and for your selfe." That first invitation had not been delivered in a *letter* but by a message, and the invitation Greville made had apparently carried weight in a world of affairs—"what was in my power to have done for you"—weighty enough to have led to Coke's resistance. That past resistance, which stands "hetherto undecyded betwen us," forms the opening of Greville's letter but then becomes (to our eyes now at least) invisible in this letter of gentle friendship, until this earnest postscript. Did the business similarly come, one wonders, in a message carried by the bearer he commends and with it the world of power and politics that the letter alludes to only indirectly?

If Fulke Greville's letter is an indirect trace of a world of affairs, could the same also be the case with Philip Sidney's "Pastorall" depiction of their friendship? The pagan setting necessarily invites an oblique reading. It beckons the reader to look beyond its surface meaning and from the mutual love of shepherds in a pagan countryside to male friendship in the court of a monarch of the reformed religion, from which such friendship is separated not by geography but by rhetoric. The identity of the three friends in this poem is an open secret, which Francis Davison in editing the poem is at pains to demonstrate he shares. Greville's letter and Sidney's poem alike are exercises in intimacy, but it is an intimacy that then potentially has its spectators; and they are not alone in that. The same is true of Antonio Pérez's passionate Latin letters, which he (as well as Anthony Bacon) carefully copied before parting with them and which Pérez published in Paris in 1603 as *Ant. Perezii ad Comitem Essexivm, singularem Angliae Magnatem, & at Alios Epistolarvm Centuria vna.* The letter I quoted earlier is taken from that edition. The title of Pérez's collection—which draws such attention to the power and standing of the recipients of the letters it contains—indicates how much its potential audience was set in such a world of power and politics. Publication in sixteenth- and seventeenth-century England was not merely synonymous with printing; the circulation of manuscripts was still common and unlike printing corresponded to (and defined) a reading audience. The multiple surviving manuscripts of Greville's life of Philip Sidney are a consequence of a defined (and defining) circulation of that kind.[12] Sidney's "Pastoralls" would have circulated in manuscript, as would Pérez's letters; and the ultimate publication of Pérez's letters in print was the wider extension of the currency they had always possessed. That publication had a potential dynamic of its own in a world of affairs is the ironic implication of James Howell's *Epistolae Ho Elianae: Familiar Letters Domestic & Forren Partly Historical. Political. Phylosophical. by James Howel Esqr. one of the Clerks of his Ma*ties *most Ho*ble *Privy Counsel* of 1645: the letters they contain written to his friend Daniel Caldwall

ostensibly when they were young men—quintessential familiar letters all—
were largely (if not wholly) concocted long after the event, when James
Howell was put to it to earn his living while incarcerated in the Fleet prison.

A sustained look at the details of these documents does not support the
judgment that they are detached from a world of affairs, despite the contempt
for friendship of that kind in Sidney's "Pastorall." Its presence is indirect,
even studiously indirect; but in some material sense they evidently figured
within it. Yet the collections of familiar letters in sixteenth- and seventeenth-
century England were not mere artifice, or perhaps one should say that they
were not artifice alone. In the familiar letters that Michael Hickes, the patronage secretary of Lord Burghley, exchanged with his friend John Stubbe,
one sees the elegant sentiments of sixteenth-century friendship being exchanged between them, that "nec mihi nec tibi" is "the Law of Ffreindship"
and "that true note of a true friend that is to reprove to admonishe, to ex-
hort, to pray for." Adages like this could have been taken straight out of the
popular guides to the pitfalls of friendship that are echoed in Sidney's poem.
But these letters document also an intense personal friendship that began
when Hickes and Stubbe were students together in Cambridge, and in its
time included both passion and jealousy. In 1570 we see Hickes writing
Stubbe an emotional and jealous letter complaining of his friendship with
a friend of their Lincoln's Inn days. Which of the two, he asks angrily, do
you love the best? And one can see from a teasing letter Stubbe sent him in
1575 that he was still prickly about the friendship several years later. The
"Law of Ffreindship" that Stubbe quotes is in the course of his reassur-
ances, and the adage on a true friend immediately follows Hickes's anguish
over Stubbe's loss of his right hand: "these few lynes, in this ragged pece of
paper, and wrytten with the lefte hand," he wrote, declared his love for him.
There are also in these letters evident expressions of affection in quieter
times and a glimpse in a late letter of John Stubbe of that youth, as he put
it, that they spent together.[13]

One can see the same combination of convention and affection in the
letters of James Thickness and John Evelyn[14] and of Tobie Matthew and
Francis Bacon.[15] Bacon first helped Matthew in his advancement and then
in the scandal that followed his conversion to Catholicism. Matthew did
the same for Bacon in his disgrace and acted both as a critic and translator
of his writings. There is a striking isolated illustration of the same combination in a letter written to Casiodoro de Reina, the minister for several
years of the Spanish reformed congregation in London, by his friend and
collaborator Antonio del Corro after a long and anxious separation. If it
had not been for his wife, he writes, he would have hastened to him long

ago, the very day "vide y conosci quan impossible me era biuir sin v. m." [I saw and realized how impossible it was for me to live without you]. He then goes on to explain that in desperation he had set off impetuously to find Reina, without even knowing where to set out for, when "almost miraculously" he received Reina's letter. He then turns from this emotional introduction to the business in hand: the arrangements he is making for the printing of Reina's translation of the Bible into Spanish.[16] Within friendships like this such language is not mere artifice. But it did not belong to such friendships alone: it figured also within a wider world; Michael Hickes and John Stubbe when they began to write their familiar letters were young men practicing between themselves the grand gestures that they thought preferment might one day bring them in that world.

Friendship in the World

Without grasping what that encompassing context was—and how these conventions might figure within it—one has simply not begun to grasp what was signified by documents like these. Even less can we begin to understand what a gesture like the memorial that Fulke Greville had planned might mean in that very public space of St. Paul's Cathedral. The intimacy between two men like Greville and Philip Sidney appears to have figured paradoxically also in a public context, and if one looks beyond the close detail of these gestures to the outline of their lives, it soon becomes apparent why that was. What one does not see, though, is evidence for the notion that these gestures of friendship marked a profound dislocation with the past: the transformation of friendship into an essentially private relationship, necessarily set apart from the commerce and practice of the world. From the moment of his birth, Sidney caught and held the gaze of the world. That very name "Philip" given to him at his christening signified the hopes and fears he would arouse. His godfather Philip II of Spain—from whom he took his name—became the husband of the queen of England, Mary, in the same year that his godparents lifted Sidney from the font. The bond of *compaternitas* that act created between his family and that of Mary Tudor signaled the ambitions of his family that came to focus on him as its only surviving male heir. At his death Sidney was the heir of two of the greatest magnates in the land, his uncles Ambrose Dudley, the earl of Warwick, and Robert Dudley, the great earl of Leicester; and for a time it had seemed possible to some that a Dudley heir might inherit the throne of England if Elizabeth were to die childless. With King Philip II on the throne of Spain, his godson might rule England. Time was to show how fantastic

these hopes were, but they were none the less dazzling; and Sidney's formidable family had played a part in the smaller fortunes of his friend Greville
from the friendship's inception. It was probably Sir Henry Sidney, Philip
Sidney's father, who sponsored Greville's first appearance at court; and it
was also Sir Henry Sidney who by his recommendation made the lucrative
opening for Greville within the administration of the Welsh Council.[17]

If Philip Sidney became Greville's friend at court, men like Greville provided for him the beginnings of what would have become his own household and secretariat had he lived. The same was true of the third of the three
figures in Sidney's "Pastorall": Edward Dyer. Dyer had been part of the
household of the earl of Leicester, to which Sidney was the heir, since Sidney had been a child; and Dyer provided Sidney with a pair of eyes and ears
within the Leicester household and a friend to act there for him. One sees
him in 1583, for example, vigorously supporting the attempts Sidney was
making to become the captain of the Isle of Wight.[18] Friendship like this
created a understanding that would bring its return. In his essay "Of Followers and Friends" Francis Bacon enumerated three kinds of favor that
followers and friends might look for: one was "protection from wrong," another was the "recommendation" of the kind Sidney's father provided for
Greville in the Welsh Council, but the third and the one Francis Bacon puts
first is "countenance": the *appearance* of friendship in the public eye that was
itself a kind of currency that could be turned to advantage, when others
sought to make use of it for themselves.[19] The familiar letter was part of the
coin of that currency. To seek in their expressions of disinterested affection
an authenticity in a postromantic sense is to miss their nature as material tokens of friendship that advertised the countenance of a friend and were designed to be preserved and circulated. It is then intelligible why Antonio
Pérez should have devoted so much effort to their production (and circulation) and why a hard-headed secretary of the earl of Essex like Anthony Bacon copied Pérez's familiar letters as they came through his hands. The earl
of Essex's countenance was a currency that could be devalued by counter-
feits or inflation, and Anthony Bacon was keeping a prudent eye on what
Pérez was about.

Familiar letters have survived because of the use that was made of them,
and it is arguably their survival that now tells us most about the role they
once played. Philip Sidney's "Two Pastoralls" were a gift of the like kind
from his own hand. As he well knew, they would have provided Fulke Greville and Edward Dyer as they circulated with the countenance that it was
his duty to give his followers and friends. Such a gift from Philip Sidney
could have been turned to profit as readily as the position that Sir Henry

Sidney had secured for Greville in the Welsh Council. The account of Philip Sidney that Greville was able to write was also, in a sense, such a gift. *The Life of the Renowned Sir Philip Sidney* (as it came to be known) is the title it carried when it appeared in print in 1652, a title designed to attract for it a buying public. The manuscripts of the work bear no such title: rather the one title found there is that of the manuscript of Trinity College, Cambridge: *A Dedication to Sir Philip Sidney.*[20] As that title indicates, its literary form was a dedicatory opening to a literary manuscript that guaranteed its propriety through the "countenance" of an influential patron. Greville's *Dedication* was written after Sidney died; but the countenance that Sidney already had given Greville, in gestures like the "Two Pastoralls," guaranteed the uninterrupted propriety of such a dedication.

Letters like those of Antonio Pérez—or a poem of particular friendship by the great Philip Sidney—are not transparent windows through which we can now observe the past. They are the remaining traces left by the practices of friendship, of commendation and countenance that once employed them: material remains in the most literal sense, as much so as the artifacts that might be dug up by an archaeologist. If in terms like these we then return to that letter Fulke Greville sent John Coke in the autumn of 1615, the perspective subtly alters, and eventually it provides an explanation for the puzzling failure of Greville to fulfill the plan it described for Sidney's long-promised tomb. That puzzle encapsulates in miniature how much the historian can (or should) build on the gestures of friendship in the sixteenth and seventeenth century. The casual reader, picking up this letter where it remained among the papers of the marquess of Lothian in Melbourne Hall in Derbyshire, would scarcely have grasped that Coke was corresponding with a man who had recently become one of the most powerful men in England. The prospects of Fulke Greville at the court of Elizabeth I did not survive the change of reign, when in 1603 James VI of Scotland became Queen Elizabeth's successor as James I of England. Crucially, Greville lacked the support at court of Robert Cecil (the son of the great secretary of Queen Elizabeth), who had carried much of his father's influence at the court of Elizabeth into that of King James. Left without the patron he needed, Greville retired to his native Warwickshire and to his still considerable wealth. Robert Cecil's death in 1612 gave Greville the chance he needed; and in October 1614, by skillfully cultivating both the support of the king's favorite Robert Carr, the earl of Somerset, and that of the Howard faction, he was appointed to the great office of chancellor of the exchequer. *This* was the man who in the following year was writing to John Coke. Although the plain face of this gentle letter disguises that fact, the endorsement on the letter written later by Coke's son emphatically does not: "1615, Sept 4 Mr Chancelor of the Exchequer from London."

In 1615 Philip Sidney had been dead for nearly thirty years; although Fulke Greville had far from forgotten him, Greville was now a man over sixty, and his friendship with Sidney was a memory of his youth, not of his old age. It is John Coke, not Sidney, who takes the center stage in this project. The letter carefully avoids drawing any attention to the position Greville now commands—and to a contemporary reading this letter that fact above all would have been the most striking thing about it. Greville is careful not to press Coke on that past resistance that stands "hetherto undecyded betwen us," which one only glimpses between the lines; he presses him only on matters of scholarship and of poetry: on the qualifications of the candidate for the history lectures that he has in mind to endow and on his concerns about the verses for "philips long promysed tombe." The verses are earnestly enclosed "fyer hotte" for Coke's opinion: "now gentle Mr Cooke be pleased to Judge, add, change, or diminishe, for all this may yet be done, wthout any change, but of thoughts, for wth loving freedom I shalbe your debtor." He signs himself with the word that has hovered over the letter: "your infirme loving frend."

To this he adds his urgent postscript: "Yf ever we meete agayn, you shall faythefully know what was in my power to have done for you." But this is not how a familiar letter should conclude; and the intimacy returns with a further postscript and the love of "letters" in a different sense.

> [F]arewel agayn good Jhon, & let us bothe stryve to be equall judges betwen our selves.
>
> Frend Jhon thes verses for the Table ar hastely don & as you may see finished whyle he was coping I feare lengthe and some other things in them but yf you allow the way I can easily contract & alter the rest by leysure.

Greville is respecting the convention that any strife between them could only be the honest exchanges between friends with a shared love of literature: no more than between the shepherds of Philip Sidney's "Pastorall," "Striving with my Mates in Song."

For a man like Coke, this was as elegant a gift from Greville as the one Sidney in his "Pastorall" had given Greville, and was a gift that Coke had earned. Coke was in effect Greville's "secretary" as Greville and Edward Dyer had been for Sidney twenty years before. In 1590 Greville had appointed Coke as his estate agent, and from that point Coke was the recipient of Greville's generous support, a support he returned when Greville lost his influence at court. After 1603, Coke continued to look after Greville's accounts and to supply him with information.[21] Was this letter part of his reward now that Greville had come into his kingdom? By the autumn of 1615 Greville was in a position to give Coke the countenance that he had not been able to give him for the previous ten long years; and could he have given it in a more eloquent form, than in a letter of intimate friendship between them about no less a project than the tomb of the great and long-revered Sir Philip Sidney?

This letter did not survive by chance. It survived because Coke carefully preserved it after his reply with the elegant Latin letter of commendation that apparently arrived with it, composed as a token of his skill by the foreign scholar that Greville had "cald over": "& you for honors sake made object of it." No contemporary could have imagined that he would have done otherwise. The letter of intimate friendship (and on such a subject) that he had received from the now great chancellor of the exchequer was a gift worth jewels. To all who might see it, it showed that John Coke was his man: "secretly transacte your opinion in englishe wth me as I do wth you." Greville's word "secretly" was well chosen, as he knew. The "secretary" was a man who could keep a *secret,* and Greville's letter sets out, for those who might be shown it, that same trope of secrecy offered and received, which Sidney had once given Greville in his "Pastoralls" and to which their editor Francis Davison had so carefully drawn attention. The letter conveyed to anyone who might be shown it the open secret of the position of a secretary, a role that has since changed greatly not only in gender but also in status. It conveyed the countenance in a world of power and affairs that Greville owed Coke, and with it Greville turns to include Coke in his project for the tomb of the great Sir Philip Sidney: "& secretly transacte your opinion in englishe wth me as I do wth you. I send you herewth the inscriptions fyer hotte for philips long promysed tombe." Greville could not have given Coke a more dazzling calling card than a letter such as this.

But let us now take the argument a step farther. Did the letter not also potentially fulfill the same service for Greville as it did for Coke? Greville would have expected Coke to have been ready to circulate a familiar letter from a figure such as Greville was in 1615, much as Anthony Bacon would have expected the same of Antonio Pérez on receiving such a letter from the earl of Essex; but in seeking Coke's advice on Sidney's tomb, he was not only admitting Coke into the circumference of their friendship: he was also reminding a watching world that Greville had been the friend of the great Sir Philip Sidney. Sidney's death had not removed the magic of his name: it had rather grown with it. Greville's dedication to him of his literary works had already claimed the posthumous countenance of his memory, and the circulation of his letter to Coke now did the same.

Seen in this light, there is no mystery to be explained in Greville's apparent neglect in not building the magnificent joint memorial to himself and Sidney in St. Paul's Cathedral that his letter projects. The advertisement of that project provided by his letter to John Coke was not necessarily a means to that end but an end in itself. Was this then a cynical manipulation of the memory of a man he had long ceased to love, if indeed he had ever been more than his patron and friend at court? The difficulty with that judgment is that it is undermined by a gesture Greville was to make when he prepared for his own death. Greville's tomb lies in the tiny chapter house of St. Mary's Church in his native Warwick, above his remains in the crypt below. The setting of the tomb seems to discourage spectators. The chapter house lies off a dark room at the north end of the nave, and the monument fills the chapter house, leaving little space for visitors. The light is provided only by the constricted windows set high in the wall, which leave the marble sarcophagus in a gloom that makes the inscription on the stone difficult to read—or rather would do were it not for the floodlights that the modern churchwardens have felt impelled to introduce to attract tourists. The setting retains a forlorn and neglected air, and when I visited it, the devout ladies who care for the church told me that it has a way of attracting to itself the unwanted objects temporarily discarded elsewhere. The monument has a stark grandeur, due in part to the black and honey-colored marble but principally to its reticence. It carries none of the heraldic arms and inscriptions recording family and marriage that one would expect on such a tomb. Their place is taken by a single inscription in Roman capitals that records the three relationships, in solemn ascending order, by which Greville chose to be remembered: "Fvlke Grevill," it reads, "Servant to Qveene Elizabeth," "Conceller to King Iames," "and Frend to Sir Philip Sidney."

Greville's tomb elevates his friendship with Sidney to the central relationship of his life in a gesture that contrasts starkly with the public splendor of his project for St. Paul's Cathedral. The line below "Trophaevm Peccati" (death is the "trophy of sin") completes the terse inscription, and the gravity of the monument is underlined by the nearby presence of the magnificent fifteenth-century Beauchamp chapel. As Jean Wilson has pointed out, Philip Sidney's uncles Ambrose Dudley, the earl of Warwick, and Robert Dudley, the earl of Leicester, had intended to turn the Beauchamp chapel into a Dudley family mausoleum; and the gaudy Tudor tombs are placed there as close as they could have been to the tomb of the great Richard Beauchamp, the fifteenth-century earl of Warwick.[22] These monuments contain in ample measure the gilded ornamentation and armorial decoration of the memorial Greville had projected for himself and Sidney in St. Paul's Cathedral, but which he set aside in the somber and obscure monument in the dim chapter house of St. Mary's Warwick.

Greville's final gesture is his own commentary on the project in his letter to Coke. His letter laid his claim to a tomb with Sidney such as those the Dudleys placed in the Beauchamp chapel, and he knew that Coke would ensure that all the world—or all the world that mattered—would be made aware of his claim to the countenance of Sidney's memory. It was an exercise in rhetoric that did not need to be translated into stone and gilding. But it was not a cynical pretense. To judge it so is to ignore the conviction of his contemporaries, that the gestures of friendship rightly and necessarily figured in a public sphere. In Greville's letter to Coke, Sidney continued to act for Greville beyond death as a friend should; and in his quiet final gesture, Greville acknowledged and returned that friendship. The one was a statement for his own time and place; the other, if I may put it this way, was for us.

Friendship as Danger

The collections of familiar letters that survived in the great houses of England were as rhetorical as the poetry and drama of the English Renaissance, but this rhetoric was not set apart from a world of affairs: it was rather a way of negotiating its dangers. The principal difference between the friendship of the modern world and the friendship of traditional society is that, in the traditional societies that this book describes, friendship was *dangerous*, and it was so because friendship signified in a public sphere. That was as true of England in the sixteenth century as it had been of the fourteenth. That persistence of meaning soon becomes apparent merely through listening for the word "friend." Lending money was a "kynd of freindshipp," Michael Hickes told John Stubbe (but one he thought Stubbe too ready to demonstrate).[23] The "voices of yourselves, your tenants and such other friends as you can procure": that was how Sir William Wentworth, an influential northern landowner, was asked to give his support in an election to James I's first parliament by the lord president of the Council of the North, Baron Sheffield.[24] "Yf the man be as he now semeth, hit were petty [a pity] to loose him," wrote the harassed earl of Leicester to Elizabeth's great secretary Francis Walsingham from the expeditionary force in the Low Countries, "for he is in dede mervelously frended."[25] The earl of Leicester had employed the same term earlier in the year—and in the same way—when he wrote to his agents recruiting for the expeditionary force, charging them to recruit soldiers for the expedition from among his "good friends and servaunts."[26] These terms describe a terrain familiar to political historians but seen here from a different vantage point. The William Wentworth to whom Baron Sheffield was writing was the father of the great Sir Thomas Wentworth, who was to play such a part in the politics of seventeenth-century England after he succeeded to his father's position in Yorkshire, and the networks of local influence that one glimpses in expressions like this are the social fabric that sustained that grand narrative of seventeenth-century history that political historians have so long mulled over.

This network did not operate only at the apex of society. In the spring of 1640, John Wilson, the parish priest of Arlington (near Lewes in Sussex), noted in his parish register that Robert Williams, one of his parishioners, had married Mary Godly, not in the parish church of Arlington but at that in Dunnington near Chichester: as he put it, "because his freinds were against the match." His parishioner Robert Williams would have kept company with other farmers and laborers like himself: the kind of group one sees in the depositions of the local justices of the peace, perhaps with the addition of the local tailor or a servant, drinking (and quarreling) together. It was not the opposition of companions such as this that would have made Williams escape to Dunnington to be married. It was rather the opposition of those who might think they had a material interest in the marriage he made, including his family: they evidently had other plans for him. That is what that expression "friends" means here, as it does in the church courts (where the term was frequently employed in marriage cases). The opposition of his "friends" in this sense was not sufficient to stop Williams from returning to Arlington after the marriage, and ten months later his daughter was born there and called Mary as her mother was, and within the year John Wilson had buried the little creature; but the opposition to Robert Williams's match would evidently have been enough to have disrupted the wedding had he attempted to wed Mary Godly at the door of the parish church in Arlington.[27] The term employed by his parish priest in describing this opposition is the same term as that used by the earl of Leicester when recruiting for the expedition to the Low Countries or that used by the lord president of the Council of the North when whipping up support for the elections to James I's first parliament. In this expression in the Arlington parish register one sees the same network of local influence, but from below rather than from above.

The "friend" in this sense was someone whose interests were tied to your own. Even if this tie were irksome—such as that between a debtor and a creditor—it was sufficient to make you use influence on their behalf, or expect them to use theirs for you, to obtain a payment perhaps, or to settle a dispute. That evocative collective term "our friends" (or its chilling counterpart "friendless") represented your hold on a potentially hostile world. Such bonds were precarious and carried with them a possibly unwelcome—even resented—burden that made them dangerous. "Vnder this name of Friendship, which name comonly to our vnderstandings, is the messenger of Peace, is included much daunger": that is William Cornwallis in his essay "Of Friendship and Factions." "To co[n]clude," as he puts it, "speaking of this, every way appeares danger." As the historian David Wootton has pointed out, the attraction of the guides to friendship like that of William Cornwallis was the practical advice they offered on how to have what one might call safe friendship: as in, do not be in a hurry to make a friend; make friends only of those who seem to shun friendship; or test a friendship before relying on it. When Erasmus asserted "Amicitia aequalitas"—or "Friendship stands in true equality" as Richard Edwards put it in his play *Damon and Pithias*—he was echoing Cicero, but the sharp point is explained by Cornwallis: "It is daungerous if we enjoy a friend much our superiour to doo him offices not easily requited, such impossibilities make him desperate, and desirous to cancell that obligation with Some Action, that you shall not afterwards be able to complaine of his Ingratitude."[28]

Cornwallis's "Of Friendship and Factions" appeared in 1600 at a time when he was seeking, as Antonio Pérez had done before him, to make a way for himself as an influential secretary in the household of an Elizabethan nobleman and in the circle around the earl of Essex. As with Pérez, his writings were designed elegantly to draw attention to himself. He did not find the post he sought (as few did), but becoming a secretary in the household of the earl of Essex would not have diminished for him the uncertainty of friendship. Secrets are an equivocal possession, which can be resented.

> That part of Friendship which cammaunds secrets I would not have delivered too soone, this is the preciousest thing you can give him, for thereby you make your selfe his prisoner, vntill his Advise or assistance requres it, and he should not have them, for it may be his honestie would keepe them, but his tongue cannot: feare or corruptio[n] doth much with men, especially when the discouery endaungers not his owne body.[29]

When Philip Sidney suspected that his father's secretary, Edmund Molyneux, was opening the letters he sent to his father, this is the letter he sent him.[30]

Mr Molyneux: Few words are best. My letters to my father have come to
the eyes of some; neither can I condemn any but you for it. If it be so, you
have played the very knave with me, and so I will make you know if I have
good proof of it. But that for so much as is past. For that is to come, I assure you before God that if ever I know you do so much as read any letter I
write to my father, without his commandment, or my consent, I will thrust
my dagger into you. And trust to it, for I speak it in earnest. In the mean
time, farewell. From Court this last of May 1578.

By me
Philip
Sidney

This was the man to whose fortunes Fulke Greville was tying himself; and
they were profoundly equivocal. Elizabeth I never trusted Philip Sidney or
the designs of his family and friends in which he had played an instrumental role from the moment of his birth. That very name "Philip," given for
his godfather Philip II of Spain—and her enemy—would have been a
prickly reminder not to trust him too far. A shared failure to find preferment at the court was the common ground of his friendship with Fulke
Greville, a dangerous basis for any friendship, and especially so when Greville maintained a precarious balance with the opposing factions at the
court of Elizabeth. What would have happened if one had succeeded where
the other did not? Sidney was not a man to be tried too far. His early death
never put that question to the test, but one can see such a question mark
suspended over their friendship.

Friendships like this hung on a thread, and that stance of an entirely altruistic friendship—exemplified in Sidney's "Pastoralls"—was designed
to negotiate the dangers of such friendship. The countenance of friendship
was directed outward to the world at large, but this rhetoric was directed
inward to the friends themselves. Honor in traditional society was a precarious commodity, and this careful stance was designed to negotiate it: a
convention expected to be respected when a favor was offered or sought. Its
familiarity within the circle of the earl of Essex—so much so as to make it
almost an automatic reaction—could be illustrated from almost any of the
letters of Antonio Pérez, but the point is perhaps best made by a letter written home by Perez's secretary in 1595, a man called Godfrey Aleyn, in an account Aleyn gives his father of a conversation he had one day with his master. Aleyn's letter contains none of the literary artifice of his master's letters.
These are letters of the kind that sons with little money have always sent

their fathers. Yet in writing to his father he demonstrates a sharp awareness of the conventions to be followed when a favor was offered or sought.

> My Mr called me vnto him th'other daye and amongst many promises he willed me to tell him what thinge I wold moste desyer he shold doe for me. I aunswered for him that I onely desyered him to love me. He againe asked me (as not being satisfied with that aunswere), and I aunswered him againe the same. He then assured me that he loved me as his owne sonne and wold doe as much for me as for his owne sonne, and willed me earnestly to tell him of anything wherin his lres might pleasure me, and he protested to me that he wold both wright to the Queen and to my Lord in my behalf and that soe earnestly that I shold not be denyed my sute, saying further that my Lord promised to doe me any pleasure soe I did please him with my service. Therfore I praye you learne oute some sute that I might in tyme sett him in hand, and of the obteining of it. I doe not once doubte whatsoeuer it be, allthough it be worth a thowsand pounds by the yeare.

Aleyn was following the expected convention in his repeated response: "I onely desyered him to love me"; and that this was a convention is evident from the calculation with which he then sets about adding up how much he is likely to make through his master's influence. This letter survives apparently because it was seized when he and his father were arrested and Godfrey Aleyn charged with petty treason for copying and passing on his master's letters addressed to the earl of Essex. The stance of a disinterested affection that Aleyn carefully adopted when his master spoke to him was the convention required of him on such an occasion.[31]

His master introduced to the earl of Essex two rich merchants, Jerónimo López and Laurence des Bouverie, with the same calculation and protestations of affection,[32] and one of his epistles addressed to Thomas Smith, a secretary of the earl of Essex, expresses the same conventional assertion as the young Aleyn had made to him. Its occasion is merely a note asking to see Thomas Smith, but Pérez opens the letter by declaring that Smith will suspect him—as a mendicant stranger—of an ulterior motive. The word Pérez uses for stranger is "peregrinus," and the letter spins itself into a rhetorical elaboration of what the word signifies, an erudite exercise designed to illustrate the same claim that Aleyn so carefully maintained: that all he desires is to be loved; the letter ends with an appeal as witness to the truth of what it says to the friendship of Thomas Smith with Henry Savile, who was another of Essex's scholarly secretaries, and with an elegant comparison of their friendship to one of the colleges of the universities. If he is a stranger, he says, he is only a stranger to *love*.

> Sabellum tuum saluere iubeo millies, & amplius, & quia tuus amicus est, & quia aueo eius amicitiam. O par beatum, & vtinam per me impar! Heus vos recipite peregrinum in collegium vestre amicitie, peregriunum in amando. Beatior numerus impar. Valete ambo.

> [I command you to greet your Sabellus for me a thousand times and more, both because he is your friend and because I long for his friendship. O fortunate pair, and would that for me you were not. Come now, admit a poor stranger into the college of your friendship, a stranger to love. An uneven number is more fortunate. Farewell to you both.]³³

This is Aleyn's denial dressed in the elegant clothes of Renaissance humanism, the same as in Philip Sidney's "Pastorall" or as in a multitude of poems and plays written in the English Renaissance.

When Fulke Greville wrote his letter to John Coke, he too was negotiating such a dangerous moment in their friendship, probably the most dangerous in a friendship that lasted a lifetime. "Mr Cooke howsoever some misprisions of unkindnes stand hetherto undecyded between us." In these opening words, Greville lays the danger on the table; and then it disappears from view, until that urgent emphatic postscript before the "familiar" tone returns and closes the letter. What it alludes to is that, when Greville had lost his position at the court, Coke had not always done his bidding, but now Greville was in a position to press it: and both of them knew it. That knowledge was dangerous to them both. Greville could now do Coke much harm, but an obedient but resentful man makes a dangerous friend. The request had apparently not been great. In 1610 Greville had asked Coke to come to him in London, and Coke had refused. Greville had pressed the request again with offers of an annual allowance, a house for Coke's family, and "other benefits."³⁴ Greville turns back to those rejected gifts and Coke's continued resistance in his postscript: "Yf ever we meete agayn, you shall faythefully know what was in my power to have done for you, & have accepted for my own advancement." Is the word "faythefully" a pull on the string?³⁵ Does the phrase "my own advancement" make the point a little too clear? Is the menacingly conditional construction a threat? In the circumstances Coke might have been forgiven for thinking them so. But these are only the smallest of details, visible if at all only to those privy to the past. To anyone else's eye, the countenance of the letter is everything an envied secretary could have asked for:

dazzlingly so. No man in Jacobean England could be diminished by accepting such a gift, and—if Coke would take the gift proffered—it enabled Greville and Coke to reestablish their friendship in the very altered circumstances that now prevailed: between the exile who was pressing a request in 1610 and the powerful figure who was the author of this letter in the autumn of 1615. Greville's letter tactfully ends only with the disagreement that might subsist between two friends with a shared love of literature, but it repeats and potentially cancels the dangerous uncertainty of that phrase "Yf ever we meete agayn." He fears the length of his verses "and some other things in them." But he could easily contract the verses and alter the rest "if you allow the way."

Coke knew well what the letter meant. "Right honorable I am glad if it may pleaseth you." So he first began with conventional politeness but swiftly corrected himself: there was to be no uncertainty in this reply. "Right honorable I am glad when it pleaseth you to accept my dutie and thanckfulnes in anie service." With that word "anie" all is said, and Coke turns with the freedom of friendship to his frank advice on matters of scholarship and letters and on the projected tomb of the great but long dead Philip Sidney. They are back in the pastoral landscape, and the moment of danger has been negotiated. The careful convention we see here was not their invention, and that was why they could employ it. It allowed one party to accept the equivocal obligation that accompanied a gift without losing face; and it allowed the other, by indicating that he knew the language in which that gift should be offered, to show that he knew the limits beyond which it would not be pressed.[36]

Is this then to claim that this language of friendship was precisely the *opposite* of what it appears to be? Certainly this language is no more a transparent window than the familiar letter, but neither is it a distorting mirror in which all we can see is the very fear and power that it denies. Does that judgment correspond to the trust Fulke Greville rightly placed in John Coke to bury his remains? It was Coke whom Greville appointed as his executor and who arranged for the burial of his body in the church of St. Mary's Warwick, below the monument that marked his youthful love for Philip Sidney.[37] Take also the sonnet of William Shakespeare that I placed at the head of this chapter, probably the most famous statement in all literature of that lifting of the spirit that comes when the lover thinks of the beloved.

> When in disgrace with Fortune and mens eyes,
> I all alone beweepe my out-cast state,
> And trouble deafe heaven with my bootlesse cries,
> And looke upon my selfe and curse my fate.
> Wishing me like to one more rich in hope,

Featur'd like him, like him with friends possest,
Desiring this mans art, and that mans skope,
With what I most injoy contented least,
Yet in these thoughts my selfe almost despising,
Haplye I thinke on thee, and then my state,
(Like to the Larke at breake of daye arising)
From sullen earth sings himns at Heavens gate,
For thy sweet love remembred such welth brings,
That then I skorne to change my state with Kings.

As the literary critic John Barrell has pointed out, this sonnet can also be read—word by word and line by line—as the complaint of an impecunious poet of the time seeking a financial subvention from his patron. Its context is a sonnet sequence that begins with the humanist poet offering his earnest advice to the aristocratic young man in his care, to whom the sonnets are first addressed, much as Edward Dyer or Fulke Greville might have properly have offered theirs in verse to Philip Sidney; but the sequence soon turns from education into love and a passionate absorption that turns into a black jealousy when aroused by the woman who steps into the erotic triangle. The sonnet has long been read as a supreme declaration of such a transforming love, but it lays itself open to another interpretation. Are those "friends" that the poet lacks the same kind of "friends" as those with which Sir William Wentworth or the earl of Leicester was possessed (or the humble Robert Williams more equivocally)? If they are, then the "love" that "remembred such welth brings" is the same "love" that Godfrey Aleyn protested was all that he desired of his master, although he was able to calculate it with precision in terms of hard cash. The complaint of the impecunious poet, as John Barrell has pointed out, was a commonplace of the English Renaissance. Here is Thomas Nashe's memory of Sir Philip Sidney:

> Gentle Sir Phillip Sidney, thou knewst what belongd to a Scholler, thou knewst what paines, what toyle, what trauel, conduct to perfection: wel couldst thou giue euery Vertue his enouragement, every Art his due, euery writer his desert: cause none more vertuous, witty, or learned than thy selfe. But thou art dead in thy graue, and hast left too few successors of thy glory, too few to cherish the Sons of the Muses, or water those budding hopes with their plenty, which thy bounty erst planted.[38]

If this complaint is the same as in Shakespeare's twenty-ninth sonnet, then the poet's "disgrace with Fortune and mens eyes" is his poverty; his "out-cast state" his financial state; to be "rich in hope" the prospect of gain; the "skope" he envies is not the literary scope of others but that which wealth brings them and their "art" the skill they have in obtaining it—the "art of Love" that in Philip Sidney's poem makes for success in a worldly court. But this is not to claim that Shakespeare's declarations are as hollow as those of Antonio Pérez, any more than it is to claim that the letters of Michael Hickes and John Stubbe are an elaborate sham: nor is it to claim that the response to Shakespeare's sonnet for the last four hundred years has been a vast misunderstanding. The point is rather (and simply) the one John Barrell makes, that the language Shakespeare is using had (as he puts it) the power to appropriate for its own purposes the most expansive and the most hyperbolic expressions of authenticity and that the pathos of the poem derives from the narrator's *simultaneous* desire and inability to escape from that fact.[39] Shakespeare's twenty-ninth sonnet is not only the statement of a universal human experience. It is rooted in its own time and place, to which it points with precision.

The language of love between men that one sees in the English Renaissance is simply that: a language and a convention. It could be heartfelt, as it could be hollow; but wherever it lay on a spectrum between the two, such language between men always and necessarily signified in the public context of power and place that to modern eyes it seems to belie. There lay its force and the enabling power it could possess. It is deceptively easy to describe friendship between men in sixteenth- and seventeenth-century England. The accounts they themselves gave of the workings of friendship persuasively invite an interpretation in recognizably modern terms of an essentially private and altruistic relation (and one among educated men grounded in a common love of literature). This chapter does not argue that that stance was a cynical pretense. Manifestly it often was not, but I have argued that its rhetoric played an enabling role amid the practices of friendship in traditional society, of which the tokens of friendship that historians hold in their hands are the tangible remaining traces. The rhetoric of an entirely altruistic affection negotiated the dangers that pressed close on friendship when it signified in a precarious public sphere. It provided a language in which a man's acquiescence could be required and given without requiring him to lose face or his honor.

Friendship and History

A rhetorical mechanism of this kind did not mark any radical discontinuity with the past. The extensive archaeology of the familiar letter illustrates that perspective. The familiar letter was not the invention of the new humanism of the sixteenth century, which shaped the education of men such as Philip Sidney and Fulke Greville or Edward Dyer and John Coke. Men such as these shared a common distaste for the learning of the medieval schoolmen, and one would get no inkling from their writings that in the familiar letter they were employing a device for negotiating the equivocal demands of friendship that had been the hallmark of churchmen since the eleventh century. In the twelfth century, John of Salisbury secured political and financial support for himself and his friends by letters of friendship that tactfully avoid an explicit reference to the business in hand. Those of Peter of Celle and of Anselm in the eleventh century as abbot of Bec would have done the same, carried by messengers hurrying to and fro between Bec and Canterbury; and the same was true of the letters of the eleventh-century Pope Gregory VII to King William I of England. Gregory VII's letters are frequently apparently composed of his prayers for the welfare of his correspondents and his earnest requests that they should pray for him, but as I. S. Robinson has pointed out, the principal instrument he employed to enforce his reforms was the political influence he could exert through his friendship network and which he directed by these letters. His letters to William rejoiced in the friendship in which a common love of St. Peter had for so long joined them but at the same time tacitly articulated the political vulnerability that drew the papacy and the Anglo-Norman kingdom together. The pressing business that accompanied letters like those of John of Salisbury, Anselm, or Gregory VII was carried by the messenger or was reserved for other documents. There is a vivid illustration of this in a gentle letter of monastic friendship that Stephen Langton sent Thurstan, the abbot of Sherborne in Dorset, in 1131 (or at a date close thereto). As Chrysogonus Waddell has pointed out, the immediate context for Langton's letter was the tensions produced by the arrival in England of the radical Cistercian reforms emanating from Langton's abbey of Cîteaux. Elsewhere such tensions had erupted into confrontation and violence in traditional Benedictine communities like that at Sherborne. Langton's engagingly respectful letter was designed to defuse those tensions, and it has survived because the newly arrived Cistercian radicals at Rievaulx, who appear to have been the bearers of this letter, were well aware of its fraught context and took care to keep a copy.[40]

A device such as the familiar letter presupposes a literate culture. The popular stock of stories about friendship were rather the stuff of performances in a tavern or at noisy church ales. They were perhaps ballads recited by a traveling performer on a bench at a fair or to the crowds that one might have seen eating and drinking in the hall of a great house in the English countryside. The place friendship continued to occupy in these stories is a measure of the extent to which they continued to articulate the hopes and fears that English men and women held about friendship. The ballad of *Adam Bell*, one of the ballads of sworn brotherhood, appeared as a printed quarto volume around 1550, a form that corresponded to the manuscripts that would have been read by burgesses and their families a century earlier. The cheap chapbook version of *Adam Bell* that appeared in 1668 would have been peddled by traveling chapmen at a price accessible to much of the rural population.[41] Printed documents like these reflect indirectly this largely oral culture, but there is a revealing glimpse of its continued vitality (and the place of the stories of sworn friendship within it) in an aside that George Puttenham makes in his *Arte of English Poesie*, which appeared in 1589. Its context is a passage in which he is discussing rhyme and his view that the "ouer busie and too speedy returne of one maner of tune" is to be avoided. He makes though an exception in passing, and his aside gives an intriguing glimpse of this robust oral culture at a date close to the end of the sixteenth century.

> [V]nlesse it be in small & popular Musickes song by these Cantabanqui vpon benches and barrels heads where they haue none other audience then boys or countrey fellowes that passe by them in the streete, or else by blind harpers or such like tauerne minstrels that giue a fit of mirth for a groat, & their matters being for the most part stories of old time, as the tale of Sir Topas, the reportes of Beuis of Southampton, Guy of Warwicke, Adam Bell, and Clymme of the Clough & such other old Romances or historicall rimes, made puroposely for recreation of the comon people at sse diners & brideales, and in the tauernes & alehouses and such other places of base resort.[42]

It was also at this point, in the later sixteenth century, that the ballad of *Bewick and Graham* was composed, at least in the form we now have it, one of the most haunting and enduring of all the ballads of sworn brotherhood.[43] *Bewick and Graham*'s provenance in the later sixteenth century is powerfully telling of the persistence of traditional notions about friendship. So is the familiar letter written by a twelfth-century churchman. The same is true also of the humanist "secretary." The role of the secretary was no more the creation of the humanists of the sixteenth century than was the familiar letter—the intimate friend who acted for a great man and was his go-between with the world—although the writings of the humanists themselves give no inkling of this. The *secretarius* of a great man was a medieval figure, and it was precisely this term that was employed in the fourteenth century by the *Annales Paulini* to characterize the role of Edward II's sworn brother Piers Gaveston: "Petrum vero de Gavastone fecit," it notes, "secretarium et camerarium regni summum" [Indeed he made Piers Gaveston the highest secretary and chamberlain of the realm].[44]

Of course there were evident differences. The fourteenth century was more likely to employ imagery derived from the Scriptures than from the classics and its Latin to be modeled on Jerome than on Cicero or Tacitus, and no humanist of the sixteenth century would have described the deaths of Sir John Clanvowe and his sworn brother Sir William Neville in the terms used by the *Westminster Chronicle*, despite the Ciceronian trope of the friend as a second self. Neville's readiness to die with his friend is rather reminiscent of the vow of Amys and Amylion to be faithful unto death— "trouth plight while thei leved in londe"—and of the two sworn brothers in the *Knightes Tale*, sworn "til that the deeth departe shal us tweyne." Guy and his sworn brother Tirry in the romance of *Guy of Warwick* make the same vow as Amys and Amylion—"Wyll we nowe trowthe plyght / And be felows day and nyght / And, whyll þat we be leuande, / Nodur fayle odur in no lande?"—and Neville's grief is expressed in the same terms as that of Tirry's refusal to eat or drink when his sworn brother leaves him.[45]

The common tomb of William Neville and John Clanvowe—with which the last chapter opened—seems itself almost like a passage out of a medieval romance. In the Latin version of the story of Amys and Amylion, composed by a churchman before the fourteenth century, the two sworn friends die fighting for Charlemagne and are buried in separate tombs. In the course of the night their bodies move together and are found in the morning lying side by side. The gesture made by the friends of Clanvowe and Neville in burying them together was very probably colored by medieval romance of this kind, as it appears to have colored the account in the *Westminster Chronicle* of their death.[46]

These were the clothes in which friendship was dressed, and the outline of the world it inhabited is still recognizable two centuries later on. Philip Sidney and Fulke Greville were allies at court as Neville and Clanvowe had been two centuries earlier; and although Elizabeth I was shrewd enough not to give them the positions of trust that Richard II had given Neville and Clanvowe, she employed them together in diplomatic missions abroad as Richard II had employed Neville and Clanvowe. The imagery of a kinship akin to marriage on the joint memorial that Greville had projected for them—which appeared so strikingly reminiscent of the tomb monument of Neville and Clanvowe—was no sport and was to be given enduring form in the chapter house of St. Mary's Warwick. A network of family and friends remained as necessary for advancing oneself in the sixteenth century as it had been in the fourteenth century. Ironically, perhaps the clearest illustration of that truism is the phenomenal progress of the humanist-educated "secretaries" themselves, for it was their skills in obtaining patronage that advanced them rather than the skills in philology and classical learning that they thought prudent to place at the forefront.

The history of friendship uncovers for the historian a level of English society that is not easy to see, a bedrock of social relations less susceptible to religious and political change than the documents produced by those upheavals might suggest. The coming of a reformed religion under a monarch with a powerfully strengthened arm gave rise to tensions that would break out in violence (and repression), but the shape of English society was not swept away. At this level of society, the changes that one sees manifest themselves only slowly, and over long periods of time, often adjusting and adapting to changing circumstances rather than announcing a radical break with the past.

Religion in England was not surrendered easily into the hands of zealots, and friendship remained closely associated with Christianity among traditional-minded Christians on both sides of the Reformation divide. The dead remained the touchstone of the degree to which friendship and Christianity were linked in the minds of English men and women. The Reformation in England challenged friendship's customary forms. The prayers of the saints for those on earth—and those of the living for the holy souls in purgatory—had expressed the friendship that subsisted across death. Although Fulke Greville's project for Philip Sidney's tomb would have replaced the shrine of St. Erkenwald with a monument that marked the body of the champion of the reformed religion (which is how Greville had presented Sidney), the unquestioned appropriateness of their joint monument there illustrates how closely friendship continued to be associated with the sites of Christianity.

The monuments to the dead in the churches of the reformed religion in England continued to express the friendship that linked the living with the dead and provided a model for the friendship that ought to subsist between the living. The tombs of friends buried together like William Neville and John Clanvowe no longer implicitly (or explicitly) sought the prayers of those who might pass by, which might release them from the joyful sufferings of purgatory, and the common sight of masses for the dead ceased with the Reformation, but traditional Christians no more abandoned a belief in the friendship between the living and the dead than they did a belief in the friendship among the living. Greville's final gesture to Sidney in St. Mary's Warwick expresses that conviction between two convinced adherents of the reformed faith. It acknowledged the posthumous countenance of a friend to which Greville had laid claim in his project for St. Paul's Cathedral, and this obscure final gesture reflects the still self-evident assumption that the obligations of friendship were not canceled by death. The inscription that Greville had composed for the memorial in St. Paul's survives only in fragments embodied in John Coke's reply, but a line still rings out: "The sympathies of pure sparcks whch . . . remaineth betwenn the spirits of the living and the dead." That sentiment would have been fully intelligible in the Christianity of England two centuries earlier, among all its adherents whether or not they had been supporters of the early reformers among the Lollard preachers, as Neville and Clanvowe had been.[47]

Similarly, the eucharistic practice of sealing friendship came under pressure amid the religious changes of the sixteenth century. Among the zealots of Reformation and Counter Reformation alike, the Eucharist became a symbol of religious conformity; and such a pragmatic use of the Eucharist must have become increasingly difficult to maintain, when it did not depend on a distinctive office or the rubrics of canonists. But in this respect the Reformation merely took changes already under way a stage farther. As Miri Rubin has pointed out, the fifteenth century already shows a tendency to withdraw and reappropriate the Eucharist, and the appearance in English parish churches from the later fourteenth century of more opaque screens between nave and choir was a symbolic expression of that instinct.[48]

But in one crucial respect the new humanist learning did bring to the gestures of friendship something quite new: a manipulation of the sense of history itself. History was always central to the humanist program, and Greville's endowment of the first history chair at Cambridge was a part of that program. It was the humanist scholars of the sixteenth century who constructed the notion of a "feudal" Middle Ages, and they did so with one eye to the contemporary political implications that notion might have for their patrons. These wider implications, both then and since, have given the concept a life well beyond its actual usefulness to historians as a conceptual tool, given the number and often contradictory definitions of the term. The implication for England was that, if the kingdom had once been a feudal estate, held by tenure ultimately of the Crown, the claims of Parliament in the seventeenth century were not of the immemorial nature its proponents claimed for it.[49] The argument was to be reversed by the Victorian constitutional historians in the nineteenth century and reversed again by their Marxist critics. Whether England had been a feudal society—more than superficially and for a short period—was the football in that game. But in the argument's later career, the "feudal" Middle Ages were to lose the rhetoric with which humanist scholarship had originally endowed them. For the humanists, the outlines of "feudal" law were recovered by the purity of their edited texts, freed by them from an opaque overlay of medieval glosses; and the notion of feudalism they constructed easily lent itself also to the caricature of the violent and disruptive squirearchy of the past, from which the humanist-educated secretaries of the sixteenth century were anxious to distinguish themselves. That caricature effaced the figure of the learned and courtly knight, like Sir John Clanvowe: the author of the beguiling *Boke of Cupide* (and of a theological treatise) and the friend (with Sir William Neville) of Chaucer.[50] The rhetorical force of this contrast strengthened that rhetoric of an altruistic friendship between men that had always eased the precarious uncertainties of friendship and honor in traditional society: it tactfully detached the exercise of friendship between men from the past and placed it in the study, in the "closet" of two scholarly friends, among their books.

At points one can observe that process taking place. One such is a moment in the public quarrel between Gabriel Harvey and Thomas Nashe in the 1590s, which began when Harvey's brother, the Reverend Richard Harvey, published a collection of sermons with a prefatory epistle attacking Thomas Nashe for publishing a provocative preface to Robert Greene's *Menaphon*, without the proper "countenance" of a literary patron that (he intimates) he himself has secured. As Lorna Hutson has pointed out, the attack directly touched the connections being made by the authorities in the troubled 1590s between literary publication without a patron and political subversion, a connection that made explicit the notion of surveillance that had always been latent in literary patronage.[51] Nashe's response was in his *Pierce Penilesse: His Svpplication to the Divell*. In the course of his rebuttal, Gabriel Harvey was to make an attack on Nashe and an invitation to him that Nashe was to find very difficult to avoid.

He calls Nashe Robert Greene's sworn brother: "his sworne brother, M. Pierce Pennilesse . . . his inwardest companion." The implication was that Nashe had come to Greene's side merely because he was in collusion with him, and it articulated precisely those fears of conspiracy that had underlaid the force of Richard Harvey's original attack. It was a difficult charge for Nashe: as a man educated in the humanist learning, quite as much as Gabriel Harvey, he was reluctant to defend the friendship created by sworn brotherhood in its own traditional terms; and in his *Strange Newes* of 1593 he attempted to brush the matter off with the nonchalant claim that "neither was I Greenes companion any more than for a carowse or two."

Gabriel Harvey sensed that he had drawn blood and later that year (in his
Pierces Supererogation) returned to the charge. It was Thomas Nashe, he argued,
who was in need of a friend to rescue him from his ignorance and folly, "such
a deuoted freend, and inseparable companion, as Aeneas was to Achates,
Pylades to Orestes, Diomedes to Vlysses, Achilles to Patroclus, and Hercules
to Theseus"; and doubtless then—as Harvey adds the poison—he would
have been utterly undone, for such a friend would have shown him his folly.
Then he adds this invitation. "Compare old, and new histories, of farr, &
neere countries: and you shall finde, the late manner of Sworne Brothers, to
be no new fashion, but an auncient guise, and heroicall order."[52]

The *late* manner of sworn brothers? The expression "late manner" here
means *recent* manner, or as Harvey puts it, a "new fashion." In that expression Harvey has swept away half a thousand years of history, that and more.
He thereupon takes up his own invitation and (at length) turns to true and
proper friendship in precisely those terms of an altruistic affection that were
the staple of the treatises on friendship in the sixteenth and seventeenth century: "Life is sweet, but not without sweete societie: & an inward affectionate frend, (as it were an other The same, or a second Selfe,) the very life of
life, and the sweet-harte of the hart." He illustrates his argument from the
classical texts at hand on the shelves and in the cupboards of the humanist-
educated men of the sixteenth century. One could not of course have expected a humanist like Gabriel Harvey to tell again the stories of Amys and
Amylion or of Adam Bell and Clym of the Clough, but that carefully effac-
ing phrase—"the late manner of Sworne Brothers"—effaces the history also
of men like William Neville and John Clanvowe or Nicholas Molyneux
and John Winter or that glimpse one catches in Richard Strangways's notebook of the familiar sight in fifteenth-century England of the sworn brothers of more than a century before. In its place is an engaging historical illusion, constructed out of the classical rhetoric of the new humanist learning,
to which Harvey lays claim. His point is not to criticize the help of a friend:
the point is that Greene has had the wrong kind of friend.

In large measure this was all shadow boxing. Although there was some
personal animus between Thomas Nashe and Gabriel Harvey, the need to
reply to an offense in print was fundamentally for both of them an excuse
to draw attention to themselves, a means of advertising their abilities to become a secretary in the household of an Elizabethan nobleman; in the dedicatory epistle to *Pierces Supererogation* Harvey firmly implies that such a post
is already properly within his grasp. But a claim to patronage was an equivocal claim in the eyes of those who might mistrust the power it would

give—not least over their patron. Gabriel Harvey's tactful effacement of history was as rhetorical a response to those fears as the careful indirection of the familiar letter. It demonstrated that he knew the limits on a secretary's role, by demonstrating that he also knew the proper language in which such an office should be sought.[53]

William Cornwallis made the same gesture in his essay "Of Loue." "I laugh, and wonder, at the straunge occasions that men take now a dayes to say they love," he writes, and the love he is writing of is the love between friends: "if their new-fangled inuentions can finde out any occasion, they are sworn brothers."[54] "Inuentions" is here being used in the now obsolete sense of "fashions," as in Gabriel Harvey's "new fashion," but Cornwallis's sharp point lies in that phrase "now a dayes." The contrast he implies is with the classics and the altruistic friendship of its literary models, which compose his essay and to which he too lays claim. In publishing his essays, like Harvey, he is advertising his suitability for preferment; and like Harvey he knew the rules of the game. The rules of that game are set out in the frontispiece that accompanied the 1632 edition of his essays.[55] The illustration shows two men, evidently friends, sitting together in the same study. The one (on the left) is reading from a volume, but his pen lies ready to hand by the paper on which he is making his extracts. The other, equally intent, has picked up his pen and is writing. On the desk of the second there is no book to be seen, for he is evidently writing a letter: the sheet spread across the table is covered already with writing, as he adds what appears to be a postscript or an annotation before folding the letter into a parcel and sealing it with wax. The arches they sit below suggest a classical rather than a Gothic building, and the open arcade suggests Renaissance Italy rather than rainy Stuart England. The two men stand as icons for the two instruments that the humanism of the English Renaissance employed in negotiating the uncertainties of friendship between men in traditional society. One was as old as that society: the familiar letter that the figure on the right is evidently writing. The other was their own distinctive creation, but it worked to the same end. No one in the early seventeenth-century could have imagined that a figure in such a setting was reading a romance or a ballad. He would be reading the classics, and the extracts he is taking from them include the truisms of friendship between men that equip him for the role in which his companion is engaged. These classics are the newly purified editions of the humanist learning freed from medieval glosses, in which he and his friend have been educated: the purity of the texts held in the hands of the one corresponds to the purity of the friendship being employed by the other.

The Hard Facts of Friendship

The stance of an intimate and altruistic friendship is everywhere evident in the writings of the men educated in the new humanist learning of the sixteenth century. Does this appearance mark the beginnings of a modern understanding of friendship, as an essentially private tie that does not (or rather perhaps should not) obtrude on a world of affairs and politics? That is the question that has been posed by this chapter. It is a persuasive argument: too persuasive perhaps, because such a sweeping conclusion, I have argued, skirts the enabling rhetoric that stance afforded in traditional society. The humanist scholars created a new embellishment of that rhetoric, but one that was to persist far beyond its time and place: a manipulation of the sense of history itself. The appearance that friendship between men was shaped afresh in sixteenth-century England by the ideals of a newly rediscovered classical world is a tactful illusion, not a sudden break with the past: a new response to the long-familiar uncertainties of friendships between men that carried obligations that were frequently irksome and always dangerous. For a man's honor could be at stake in the manner in which the obligations of friendship were made and called upon. The stance of a generous altruism, of an inward affectionate friend, was a tactful rhetoric that helped to negotiate those dangers, a language in which the hard facts of friendship could be spoken.

It is no easy task to understand those facts from the viewpoint of the individuals in the past for whom they were an everyday reality. As these first two chapters have been designed to demonstrate, there is no shortcut around that problem. It does not give way before a historian's judgment, however robust, on what constitutes the real facts of the matter and what can be dismissed as mere rhetoric. Nor will it be found in positing a dramatic break with the past conveniently placed between one historical era and the next. These solutions are imposed from outside and unravel among the bewildering diversity of the evidence and its stubborn refusal to allow itself to be neatly partitioned into categories of fact and mere rhetoric. There is, though, a potential inlet to that elusive inner viewpoint, in the evident connection that traditional society in England persisted in making between its own understanding of friendship and the rites, the places, and (perhaps to a lesser extent) the persons of its religion, whether or not these connections were set out in the writings of the canonists and jurists of the time now conveniently presented in modern editions that sit on the shelves of university libraries. Their apparent absence from those readily accessible volumes makes it easy to dismiss them, but, as these last two chapters have been intended also to demonstrate, the outline of what they were still remains in the practices of friendship that they animated and in the surviving traces of those practices still to be seen, traces often in the most material sense. The tomb monument of William Neville and John Clanvowe is one such trace, of the place that friendship was perceived properly to occupy in the liturgies and rites of traditional Christians. That projected for Fulke Greville and Philip Sidney is a trace of the practices of countenance and commendation that corresponded to that proper place and that determinedly continued to do so even when the forces of reform and counterreform asserted themselves at the altar. One can place by these a third such tomb, which is a trace of something different.

It is the tomb of two men who lived in the same England as William Neville and his friend John Clanvowe, who very probably knew of them, and who like them were buried in the same grave, as a husband and wife might have been. But these men were not figures who might have been taken out of the pages of a medieval romance, like Sir William Neville and Sir John Clanvowe: two knights who had died together on the military pilgrimage to liberate the holy city of Jerusalem from Moslem rule. They were rather priests and scholars; and for nearly three centuries the monument that marked their tomb lay in the midst of the choir of Merton College, Oxford. Its design, to which I now turn, is a vivid reminder of such friendships; but it points also to the pressing ethical question that was perceived to lie at their heart. If the historian of friendship is ready to put aside the unavailing attempt to impose an order on the diversity of evidence about friendship in traditional society, and rather listens to what that diversity is saying, it tells its own story; and the story is among the oldest that humankind has ever told, sitting around the hearth. It is the story of what it means to have a family.

CHAPTER 3

Families and Friends

Near the cross where Jesus hung stood his mother, with her sister, Mary wife of Clopas, and Mary of Magdala. Jesus saw his mother, with the disciple whom he loved standing beside her. He said to her, "Mother, there is your son"; and to the disciple, "There is your mother"; and from that moment the disciple took her into his home.

The tomb of John Bloxham and John Whytton may easily be passed by unnoticed. The monumental brass that was placed above their tomb when they were buried together in the chapel of Merton College, Oxford, now lies in a neglected corner of the lofty chamber—intended as the crossing of a nave that was never built—that visitors now pass through on their way to the choir beyond the screen. That setting would have been little more inviting in the fifteenth century, when the north transept where their monumental brass now lies served as a busy and noisy parish church, entered by a door that opened onto the bustling street outside: but it was not here that the monument lay when at the end of the fourteenth century the remains of John Whytton were laid in the tomb of his friend John Bloxham. To see its intended setting one must walk from the north transept down into the body of the church and climb up the steps that lead into the choir. (See fig. 3.)

There must have been few across the centuries who have entered the choir of Merton College for the first time without, for a moment, catching their breath. The antechamber gives way to a chapel filled with light through the medieval stained-glass windows that line its walls: it was here, at the very middle of the chapel and at the steps to the altar, that the memorial brass to John Bloxham and John Whytton once lay, sparkling in the light. It was a setting where human and celestial figures might seem to stand side by side. A fourteenth-century fellow of the college kneels in the stained-glass windows by a saint, and the prophets and apostles painted on the choir stalls seemed to stand with the fellows of the college as witnesses of the drama unfolding at the altar. Bloxham and Whytton themselves appear on their memorial brass like two saints, depicted there as if raised up on a column for all beneath them to see, under canopies that echo those of the saints in the stained-glass windows about them. But these are clearly men of bone and blood. Both have the tonsure of a cleric, and Bloxham—on the more honorable side, the dexter, to the viewer's left—is dressed as a bachelor of divinity. Their features are finely etched as if drawn from life as they stand side by side, with their hands joined in prayer and their eyes fixed on a distant point that still meets the gaze of the onlooker across the six centuries that divide them from us.

John Whytton and John Bloxham met when Whytton arrived as a young scholar at Merton College near the year 1364. Bloxham was probably already by then a youthful fellow of the college and was later to become its warden. As the scroll beneath the figures on their monument recounts, on Bloxham's death, at the end of a friendship of more than twenty years, Whytton prepared this tomb in which they would both lie together in death and provided for the great memorial brass marking their friendship that lay above it. In such a setting one can sense the self-confidence of that gesture, yet to the modern eye its meaning becomes more opaque as one probes the apparently confusing imagery of the monument. In one respect, the imagery on the monument seems to employ the same marital analogy as the impalement of arms on the tomb of William Neville and John Clanvowe, the tomb of the two knights with which this book began. Bloxham and Whytton lived in the same England as those two knights and would have known of them; and the tombs employ the same marital analogy: the one in the marital "impalement" of arms; the other in the familiar iconography employed in the fourteenth century for the common tomb of a husband and wife, where the two figures are depicted together side by side in their joint tomb, their hands joined in prayer, and looking straight at the viewer. The arrangement is almost too common to require illustration: a familiar sight in many medieval English parish churches. One can see it, for example, in the memorial brass illustrated here from the same period from the tomb of William Grevel and his wife Marion in the parish church of Chipping Campden in Gloucestershire (see fig. 4).

But if the conventional arrangement of this brass in Merton College suggests a marital analogy, the iconography at the foot of the monument seems to employ an analogy of a different and contrasted kind. At the base of the column on which their figures stand is depicted a lamb with a Latin cross and banner and beneath it a scroll carrying the names of the two men,

Figure 4
The monumental brass from the tomb of William and Marion Grevel,
St. James, Chipping Campden.

"Johannes Bloxham : Johannes Whytton." The function of the scroll is not
to identify them. Given the size of the brass and its setting (which is more
than 120 inches long), when one is standing above the two figures one cannot see the design at the base of the monument, and vice versa. The task of
identifying them is done in the conventional manner by the scroll immediately below their images, which gives their names and explains who they
were. The second scroll rather draws attention to their *names* themselves,
John—"Johannes"—and its threefold coincidence: threefold because the

lamb with the cross and banner is the icon of St. *John* the Baptist. The engraver further emphasized the point by the careful spelling out, letter by letter, of "Johannes" on the scroll without the abbreviation that would have
been more normal (and as indeed is employed in the scroll immediately beneath their figures). In modern culture kinship is identified with our sur-
names, not our first names; but in the fourteenth century it was common to
take one's first name from a godparent, so that one's names indicated as it
were two ancestries: a physical ancestry in the last name and a "spiritual"
ancestry in the first. What this design appears to be doing is identifying St.
John the Baptist not as the patron of these two men, their *patronus*, but as
their *patrinus:* as their spiritual godfather and thus each other as spiritual
brothers, in not a marital but a fraternal analogy. Were John Bloxham and
John Whytton then sworn brothers as William Neville and John Clanvowe
seem to have been? It seems probable that they were and that that is what
the design implies—or rather it is what the design at the foot of the monument implies, for this explanation leaves the visible resemblance of their
tomb to that of a husband and wife curiously *un*explained.[1]

    That confusion (to the modern eye at least) in the kinship imagery em-
ployed seems only the more intractable when one compares the promises of
a betrothal recognized in canon law with those used for sworn brotherhood,
preserved in the glimpses one catches of them in the romances and ballads
of sworn brotherhood: the two appear substantially the same. "I plight thee
my troth"—a familiar formula for a betrothal—sits beside the "Togeder
were trouth plight" of *Amys and Amylion* and the "We beþ wed-breþren and
trewþe-ipliʒt" of Floris and Blancheflour, as well as the "Treuþe bitven hem
is pliʒt" of *Guy of Warwick* (and the "trewðe fest," i.e., troth plight of Isaac
and Abimelech in *The Story of Genesis and Exodus*).

    The same point is nicely made for the term used for sworn brotherhood
in the ballad *Bewick and Graham*, "a man that's faith and troth to me," by an
exchange recorded in a case heard in the courts at York at around the time
when *Bewick and Graham* (at least in the form we now have it) was composed.
As the documents in York for this marital case note, when Isabel Clark said
to William Hosier, "William here I give you my hand and faith of my body
to marry you," her kinsman and witness stepped in quickly: "That binds no
matrimony," he said and told her she must give "her faith and troth," which
she then did.[2] A "wed" in Middle English was a pledge or a covenant, and
the vows both of sworn brotherhood and of a betrothal alike—as binding
promises—were "weddings": the reason that the fourteenth-century poem
Athelston can employ the same term "weddyd" to refer interchangeably (and
with equal force) to a both a "sworn" brother and to a married wife.[3] The

otherwise puzzling logic that I set out in my first chapter, employed by both Richard Strangways and Giraldus de Barri, is that the formula for a betrothal and that for "wedded" brotherhood were in large measure the same: Richard Strangways when he attributes an impalement of arms to two men because they were, as he puts it, "sworn brothryn"; Giraldus de Barri when he ascribes to sworn brotherhood the binding force of a betrothal—together with the solemnity of the spiritual kinship, the *compaternitas* or godbrotherhood created by a baptism, that the tomb monument of John Bloxham and John Whytton also evokes.

Nor is kinship distinguished in these terms from friendship. Giraldus de Barri characterizes the motive for the ritual he describes as "friendship" ("ad majorem *amicitiae* confirmationem"). In the romance of *Floris and Blancheflour* the "frend in Babiloyne" to whom the traveler is directed is introduced by that phrase "We beþ wed-breþen and trewþe-ipliȝt,"[4] and in the romance of *Guy of Warwick* the same ritual kiss that makes Guy and Tirry "treuþe-pliȝt & sworn breþer" is also able to make two men "frendes."[5] While one manuscript of the *Anglo-Saxon Chronicle* characterizes Edmund Ironside's compact with Cnut as one of "wed" brotherhood, another variously describes it as a compact of friendship;[6] and the fourteenth-century cleric who composed the *Vita Edwardi Secundi* described a sworn brother, a "frater adoptivus," as an "amicus" [friend].[7] What a fourteenth-century chronicler characterizes as a "fraternitatis fedus" [a covenant of brotherhood], the author of the Latin *Amys and Amylion* described as a "fedus amicicie" [covenant of friendship].[8] In the sixteenth century William Painter described the two sworn brothers in "the fifty-ninth nouell" of his *Palace of Pleasure* as "two Gentlemen, which from the tyme of their youth lived in such great and perfecte *amitie*,"[9] and in Robert Greene's play *Frier Bacon and frier Bongay* (from the sixteenth century also) the two young scholars introduce themselves simply as "we are … sworne brothers, as our fathers liues as friendes."[10]

In expressions like this, different kinds of kinship terminology overlap and shade into each other and are not clearly distinguished from friendship. To select one element as the substance—or to discount others as mere rhetoric—would be to fail to do justice to the plain insistence of these expressions, however confusing or conceptually difficult they may now appear to us, half a thousand years later. The aim of this chapter is to be attentive to those terms: to attempt to recover the inner logic of this language, from within as it were and in its own concerns. My starting point is an attempt to unravel that persistent association of friendship with the sites of Christianity, illustrated so dramatically in the setting of the tomb monument of John Bloxham and John Whytton. It eventually proves an inlet (I shall argue)

both to the terms in which friendship was represented and to the ethical uncertainty that lay at the heart of that response.

Friendship and Traditional Religion

Recent years have seen a major reassessment among historians of the sworn
friendship of traditional society, but these writings show a curious myopia toward the distinctively religious issues it raises. The seminal work was Pierre
Chaplais's *Piers Gaveston: Edward II's Adoptive Brother*, which drew attention to
the neglected studies of sworn friendship undertaken by antiquarians since
the seventeenth century, but in Chaplais's book the ecclesiastical setting for
ritual brotherhood is dealt with summarily and by a cursory hypothesis.

> In pagan societies, the adoption ceremony sometimes included a ritual in
> which each of the two prospective brothers opened a vein and gave his part-
> ner some of his blood to drink, or a mixture of the two bloods was drunk
> by both; thus they could truly say that they were "brothers of one blood."
> The same ritual is known to have been occasionally observed by Christians,
> although it seems to have been more usual for them to take part in a com-
> munion service in which the two partners shared the same host.[11]

Chaplais's book influenced a subsequent symposium on ritual brotherhood in the scholarly journal *Traditio* that contained a study by the American historian Claudia Rapp of the *adelphopoiesis*, the traditional Greek rite for
"making brothers" or "sisters." Rapp's paper had a firm grasp on the place
the *adelphopoiesis* occupied in Byzantine culture but had no discussion of the
detail of the liturgy beyond the bare fact of its use, and is as brusque as
Pierre Chaplais.

> In secular society . . . the practice of ritual brotherhood was taken for granted
> and supported by the church, which sanctioned it through a ritual . . . By the
> twelfth century, the church authorities began to view with a critical eye the
> *adelphopoiesis* relations that involved laymen and declared that they were cat-
> egorically forbidden by the church . . . But these ecclesiastical authorities
> still refrained from threatening any form of punishment. And the inclusion
> of the office in the *euchologia* shows that, despite their disapproval, the ritual
> continued to be practiced even into post-Byzantine times.[12]

It is striking how curiously featureless these passages are. *Why* did Latin
Christians regard the Eucharist as significant, in the context of ritual broth-

erhood? Why does the *adelphopoiesis* take the particular form one sees in the liturgical collections—this form rather than any other? The arbitrariness in Chaplais's hypothesis, almost the casualness, of the transition from one ritual practice to another tacitly shares the scant ecclesiology in the passage from Rapp that identifies the "church" not with Chaplais's "Christians" but with the "ecclesiastical authorities." Although neither Rapp nor Chaplais is explicit on the point, both are adopting here a view that takes it as axiomatic that "popular" religion will necessarily lack the definition that canon lawyers and systematic theologians give to official religion, a view that renders popular religion as something necessarily featureless and—ultimately—unintelligible, the assumption Peter Brown has accurately characterized as a "two-tiered" view of religion.[13]

The eloquent setting of the tomb of John Bloxham and John Whytton unsettles that distinction, and it was no isolated or eccentric gesture. In 1499 William Jekkes, a priest during the fifteenth century in the church of Salle in Norfolk, provided in his will for the burial of his body within the church of Salle close to that of his friend and fellow priest Simon Bulleyne: like Bloxham and Whytton, they had been friends together within the same community, sufficiently close as to wish to lie in death together.[14] More than a century later, that same gesture is still recognizable when John Browne, one of the fellows of Gonville and Caius College in Stuart Cambridge, provided for his burial in the antechapel of the college in 1619 near the tomb of his friend Thomas Orrell: his lost friend, "amici sui desideratissimi," in the phrase in the annals. Browne and Orrell had met in their youth when they were students at the college, and later became fellows there together. Orrell died in his twenties, but the memory of their youthful friendship was evidently still alive to Browne when he made his will more than fifteen years later.[15] The annals of the college quote the epitaph that Browne composed for the (now lost) tomb of Orrell: "amicitiâ candidus," that he had been in every sense a good friend. It is also at this point that the tombs of two women buried side by side in a similar way come into view. One such is the early seventeenth-century tomb of Ann Chitting and Mary Barber in the church of St. James in Bury, in Suffolk, which Ann's son Henry Chitting mentions in his papers.[16] Is the appearance of female friends buried together something new in the seventeenth century? Or is it simply that they become more visible at this point, as the evidence becomes more abundant and the light brighter? Whatever one makes of that question, the implication is not that the gesture was losing its force. Whether the gesture is that of the friends of John Bloxham and John Whytton who buried them together in the chapel of Merton College—or that of the friends William Neville and

John Clanvowe in the church of the Dominican friars in distant Constantinople—it is still visibly the same as that in the burial of William Jekkes and Simon Bulleyne in a parish church in Norfolk at the close of the fifteenth century and that of Thomas Orrell and John Browne in the chapel of Gonville and Caius in Stuart England more than a century later.

Its persistence only makes it potentially the more telling. What then was signified, to the world outside, when two friends were buried together in a church, within the same grave? The familiarity of the tombs and memorials to the dead in the parish churches of England is why that question seems at first to require so little explanation; but the question remains, and it rightly requires an answer. In one respect the explanation lies in an expression of reverence for the bodies of the dead, but that explanation alone misses the symmetry between this gesture, at the end of a friendship that it marks so publicly, and the eucharistic practice that (in the fourteenth century at least) could have marked its beginning *in the same setting:* the practice that was the subject of my first chapter. When one turns to descriptions of that practice by contemporaries, what one finds is the insistence on the *place:* "they come together in some holy place with the man with whom they are eager to be united." Those are the words of Giraldus in the twelfth century, and the same concern recurs in the document recording the brotherhood in arms of two English esquires in the army of Henry V, also discussed at that point in the first chapter: its closing insistence that the covenant was made in the church of St. Martin at Harfleur. Why, if terms of the agreement were the substance of the matter, does it insist on this point? *Why* does it record that the setting was that of a church? And why the church of *St. Martin?* Why did it matter?

The answer that Giraldus de Barri gives was that it was a "holy place." But then what made it holy? In the most tangible of terms, the repeated answer one sees is that it was the presence of Christ and the saints. For Juvénal des Ursins the oaths of ritual brothers were oaths "sworn on the precious body of Jesus Christ," in hearing the mass together in the presence of "the Body of Our Lord" on the altar. In 1307 Edward II and his sworn brother Gaveston were said to make their oaths together "upon God's body" and upon the other relics there, like two sworn brothers out of the romances, as Amys and Amylion swore their brotherhood "where were relics of the saints." Giraldus combines the Eucharist and the saints in the same tangible terms. His "holy place," as he puts it, is that "before the altar and in the presence of relics of the saints." In these expressions it is the tangible presence of the Body of Christ and the presence of the relics of the saints that seal the oaths, not merely the place itself: they are what make the setting holy. Is their presence why it was also fitting that the bodies of two sworn brothers should in the end lie in the same place? So, it would seem, judged the churchman who wrote the Latin version of *Amys and Amylion*, for in his account the bodies of the two sworn brothers become themselves like the relics of saints, miraculously preserved together by the altar in the church built for them, as if awaiting other men who will come after them to swear their own brotherhood there.[17]

As the sixteenth century in England rolled across the beliefs of even traditional-minded Christians, that sense of the tangible presence of the saints was to falter; but the Eucharist did not, and its association with the creation of friendship remained. The Holy Communion in the Lord's Supper remained the setting in which those present, in the mysterious and lovely words of the reformed English liturgy, became "partakers of his most blessed body and blood";[18] in some respects, the changes introduced by a reformed religion rather sharpened the sense of its presence within mundane society than undermined it. As the historian passes from the friendship of the fifteenth century, the path one follows narrows, but the persistent association of friendship with the Holy Communion in the Lord's Supper remains a visible track. It continues to point to those beliefs about friendship that traditional-minded Christians on both sides of the Reformation divide persisted stubbornly in holding. Time has taken its toll of the evidence. Any memorial that William Jekkes may have left is now lost, as is the memorial brass to Ann Chitting. We now know of the burial of John Browne beside his friend Thomas Orrell only from the college annals of Gonville and Caius. But the chapel of their college in Cambridge has preserved another such monument from the same time, and it casts a penetrating light on traditional friendship as it emerged into the seventeenth century across the upheavals of the religious and political changes of the preceding century.

When the master of Gonville and Caius, the greatly loved Dr. John Gostlin, dictated his will on 19 October 1626, he knew that his death (which was to come two days later) was close. His thoughts turned, as they often had during his life, to his friend Dr. Thomas Legge, who had died nearly twenty years before in the summer of 1607. Thomas Legge and John Gostlin appear to have met when Gostlin arrived as a youthful scholar at Gonville and Caius on a cold November day in 1582, when Legge was already a fellow and master of the college. This was a time in which the religious tensions in England were plain for all to see, tensions that had already pressed hard on the life of the college and would also shape the friendship of these two men. The document prepared at Dr. Gostlin's dictation that October in 1626 has long since disappeared, but we know of its terms from the copy that his friend and younger disciple William Moore (the university librarian and the benefactor of the college library) later made in the annals of Gonville and Caius that he was commissioned to complete. The description of their friendship that Moore added in the annals (and that of John Browne and Thomas Orrell) gives an incisive guide as to how such friendships could be understood by their contemporaries, comments to which I shall return; but in the chapel of the college Gostlin left his own record of his friendship with Legge. His will provided for his burial by the body of Legge, but a monument in the chapel already appears to have graphically marked that wish and remains there to this day.[19]

On the south wall of the chapel is Gostlin's monument, apparently placed there in 1619 (see fig. 5). It depicts Legge kneeling with his hands joined together in prayer under a canopy supported by two pillars, in scarlet robe and hood. The inscriptions record his doctorate of laws, his mastership of the college, and his death in 1607 at the age of 72. The design is properly conventional and is modeled on that of the eminent Dr. Stephen Perse, whose monument is on the north wall of the chapel; but to this design Gostlin added a striking element. Below the figure of Legge, a heart in flames is depicted held aloft by two hands, with the inscription below.

IVNXIT AMOR VIVOS SIC IVNGAT TERRA SEPVLTOS

GOSTLINI RELIQVVM . COR TIBI LEGGVS HABES

[Love joined them living. So may the earth join them in their burial.
O Legge, Gostlin's heart you have still with you.]

The setting in the chapel appears to be the work of John Gostlin. On Legge's death it was determined by the fellows that a memorial should be made, but their evident intention was to have placed the memorial in the new building funded by his legacy. But as Christopher Brooke (the modern historian of Gonville and Caius) has surmised,[20] Gostlin appears to have arranged for the memorial to be placed in the chapel; and as he did so he added, as part of that gesture, his lasting memorial to his friendship with Legge. It was a strikingly personal gesture—its design as far as I know is unique—but it was also public and redolent of that persistent association that continued to be made in England between friendship and the Eucharist; for in the early part of the seventeenth century it was in this setting, sitting in the Elizabethan manner in their pews in the chapel, that the fellows and scholars of the college would have received the communion together at the Lord's Supper. That continuing association is movingly explicit in the

Figure 5
The memorial of Thomas Legge in the chapel of Gonville and Caius College,
Cambridge. The inscription "Iunxit amor vivos . . ." lies on the slanted face
below the two hands holding the Sacred Heart.

account of Gostlin's death left by Thomas Wake, a fellow of the college
who remained with him in his last days.

As he approached death, Dr. Gostlin asked to receive communion with
the fellows of the college and talked to them there about the nature of
friendship. But first, he asked them to forgive him.

[H]aving given him absolution, according to the form set down in our Book
of Common Prayer, he sayd he was desirous to receive the Communion, w^{ch}
the next day was administred unto him by my self, 7 of the senior fellows

being Communicants with him; & albeit very feeble, yet with help being brought down, unto his lower chamber, in ye presence of us all, before his receiving ye Sacrament: He began thus. It pleased God yesterday to send his Angell unto me, for so I term his Priest upon Earth, unto whome I made a generall confession of my sins, after wh^{ch} he gave me absolution, whereupon I received much spirituall comfort, & some ease also of my Body. And now again I do confess unto you all, that I have been a great sinner, & I do desire you all to forgiue me, for I hold Tully's Rule, nemini injuriam facere, to have been good, had he not made this addition, nisi lacessitus. And therefore St Austin sayd, that he spoyled the best Rule by this additament, for that wh^{ch} our Savior sayd, was spoken of old; love your Friends, & hate your enemies, was but fermentum Pharisaeorum, the malice of human corruption. Having spoken this, I administered the Sacrament. Then having received the Communion, calling us again unto him he spoke thus. When I am dead & gone, obserue strictly the prescript Form of the Liturgy: For let y^m say what they will, that invert & alter it by pieces, It is true obedience & service to God, to observe what the Church hath commanded. Let me entreat you, to loue one another, to bear with one another's infirmities, & not to retain malice in your hearts. Frequent ejaculations in his sickness. Pater misericordiarum miserere mei. Abyssus miseriae invocat abyssum misericordiae. Jesus, Jeusu, sis mihi Jesus. Cupio dissolvi et esse cum Christo. The time of his sickness I constantly read prayers unto him, twice a day at least, & reading ye penitential Psalms, himself answer'd, my self reading one verse, & he another. Delivered upon occasion, speaking of the College, that he always held a mastership, & Governor's place in a College, to be a place of honor & credit, & not of profit.[21]

The Eucharist of traditional Christianity was designed to restore defective human relations in the world about it, and that work was the work of kinship and of friendship. That conviction—so self-evident to our ancestors as hardly needing to be enunciated—has up to this point underlaid this book, since the ritual kiss depicted on the tomb monument of William Neville and John Clanvowe with which it began, the same *osculum pacis* that the priest in the old mass had taken from the Body of Christ on the altar and that had then passed among those present: each receiving it from his neighbor and passing it on in return. Its scriptural basis lay in the discourse at Jesus' last supper with his disciples in the fourth Gospel, in his parting gift to them of his peace and friendship (John 14:27, 15:15). Its practical working out was that of the imperative implied by the version of Luke 2:14 given in the Latin Bible, the hymn sung by the angels when announcing the nativity of Christ: "Gloria in altissimis Deo, et in terra pax hominibus bonae voluntatis" [Glory be to God on high, and on earth peace *to men of good will*]. Its condition was that addition, that to receive that gift we must also give it, bear with one another's infirmities, and not bear malice in our hearts. It is that traditional conviction that John Gostlin was enunciating in the account of his death. The general communions of Easter or Whitsunday required reconciliation between those making their communions together, for them to affirm and reaffirm the proper bonds of friendship that held society together. It was an opportunity to step down, without losing face, from quarrels of which their participants (or their neighbors) had grown weary. Communion among the laity became infrequent in the thirteenth century (not at the Reformation) as it became reserved for the periodic general communions of social tradition. A pair or a group of friends could still make their communions together, but the model of the general communions invested the act with those powerfully social and constraining implications. The plainness and more mundane quality of the reformed communion rather asserted that significance than abolished it.

The socially unitive role of Christianity in the world about it was to come under severe pressure, on both sides of the Reformation divide, during the religious upheavals of the sixteenth century. When reform and counterreform set Christians one against the other, it could seem a diversion from the struggle—or worse—and puritans and papists alike set out to diminish its troubling presence. The Tudor reformers struck the kiss of peace from the reformed Prayer Book of England and sought to deny any recognition in canon law that baptism could create the "godbrotherhood" of *compaternitas*, concerns shared also by the Council of Trent and a resurgent Catholicism. Within only a generation of the Tudor reformers, the king's Irish subjects were to find newly minted Catholic bishops arriving fresh from Rome with prejudices that the Tudor reformers would have recognized and the same motives: forbidding the kiss of peace in private masses, restricting it elsewhere to a clerical elite, and firmly placing in the way of the social use of baptism the obstacles that the Council of Trent had devised, as the synod of Drogheda in 1614 put it, whether "amicitiae ineundae aut alia ex causa" [for the sake of forming a friendship or for any other cause].[22]

For some this seemed like the religion of the lukewarm, but for others it was its very point, why Christianity mattered and how it had earned its keep. For these the value of religion's claims was that it helped men and women to live in peace and friendship with religion, not set men at each other's throats. The convictions that such traditional-minded Christians persisted stubbornly in holding were not easily abandoned, a story that the historian John Bossy has told on a broad canvas across England and France, Germany and Italy; but in the lives of John Gostlin and Thomas Legge we can see that stubborn persistence set out in a miniature that tells in its own way a wider story. Gostlin and Legge appear to have held such views, and their friendship was as much a part of traditional Christianity as that of John Bloxham and John Whytton, commemorated in the choir of Merton College two centuries before, whom they so much resembled. Its course is perhaps a measure of how resilient such traditional views would prove to be.

In 1582 when Gostlin arrived in Gonville and Caius, the obstacles such views faced were all too evident. Under the mastership of Legge, Gonville and Caius seemed ready to nurture papists and puritans alike in a heady brew. Figure after figure that was to emerge as a Jesuit or Catholic priest in the years that followed passed through Gonville and Caius during Legge's mastership. The most famous of these was arguably Richard Holtby, who was to become the superior of the Jesuits in England after the execution of Henry Garnett in 1606 and who for more than thirty years avoided the spies and pursuers who hunted him around the country; another was the Catholic martyr John Fingley. But under the mastership of Legge many of the fellows were of a radically different persuasion, men such as the zealous reformer John Paman. The storm was inevitable and broke in the same year that John Gostlin arrived at the college. It took the form of a violent denunciation addressed to Lord Burghley, the chancellor of the university, from a majority of the fellows, who complained in their petition that Legge's regime had made the college a popish seminary.[23] The letter was outrageous and extravagant, but it was a potentially deadly business. Lord Burghley was not only the chancellor of the university. He was also the great secretary of Elizabeth I, at a time when a captured Catholic priest could expect to be tortured and executed in the public gaze as a warning, not for the punishment of heresy but for treason against a queen who had been deposed by the pope of Rome. Only a few years later in 1586 John Fingley was to suffer such a grim martyrdom for his priesthood.

Legge was no papist, and he was to sit out the storm of 1582, still the master of the college (it was the remonstrants rather than he who would eventually take their leave); but as the modern historian of the college has put it, "it may be that the excitements of 1582 taught him caution, though it seems clear that they did not cure him of his tolerance."[24] When Legge died in 1607, John Gostlin was to be drawn directly into the reviving storm. After Legge's death the fellows immediately elected Gostlin as his successor, with a rapidity that suggested the awareness of the opposition their election would prompt. If so, they were right to anticipate it. The events of 1582 had blown over, but they had not been forgotten, and the university authorities summarily and firmly set aside the election and put the biblical scholar William Branthwaite in Gostlin's place, someone whom they evidently judged they could trust to hold the college in better order, in contrast to Gostlin, who evidently held tolerant views all too like those Legge had held.

Gostlin retired to Devon, where the college had connections and where he practiced as a doctor of medicine in the years that followed. But if in 1607 the authorities in the university had not forgotten the potentially disastrous events of 1582, the fellows of the college were no more inclined to forget John Gostlin. When William Branthwaite died in the winter of 1619, the fellows persisted stubbornly in electing Gostlin again to the mastership—despite the suspicions of his tolerant views that were still abroad at the royal court in London. "Before the breath was out of Branthwaite's body," as John Venn, the great nineteenth-century historian of the college, put it,[25] a letter had arrived from King James (or at least in his name) with a warning in this regard; but this time the fellows acted with more circumspection, and the election was allowed to stand by drawing on the aid of powerful friends at court.

Thus at the beginning of the new year in 1619, the fellows of Gonville and Caius had at last the man they desired to be their master as the successor to Legge, the man who, as he lay dying seven years later, asked them to receive the communion with him and to talk to them about Christian friendship, which required them to bear with the infirmities of others and not bear malice in their hearts. The college had bowed to the new forces of reforming zeal (or of the counterreform that were their Catholic equivalent), but these had not entered its spirit, where an older conviction prevailed. The monument that Gostlin—and the other fellows with him—placed in the chapel in that triumphant year of 1619 marked that persistence. It represented Gostlin's love for Legge in powerfully personal terms and still does. But it also marked the traditional place that friendship stubbornly continued to occupy within English Christianity, which it exemplified, as it was designed to do.

In the century before, men like Gostlin and Legge could have regarded communion together as affirming their friendship. Did they still see their communions together in the chapel of Gonville and Caius as doing so? The comments of their contemporaries support that view, describing the sworn brotherhood that had been a familiar sight in the fifteenth century not as a distant memory but as a contemporary phenomenon; Gabriel Harvey and William Cornwallis did so in the passages I quoted at the end of the last chapter. Contemporary descriptions like these correspond to the continuing vitality of the ballads and stories of sworn brotherhood. These were still being performed in taverns and fairs, and they were still being created. Somewhere in the Borders, as Gostlin arrived at Gonville and Caius in

1582, the ballad *Bewick and Graham* was being composed and sung for the first time, perhaps the most enduring of all the ballads of sworn brotherhood. The two young scholars in Robert Greene's sixteenth-century play *Frier Bacon and frier Bongay*—who introduce themselves as "sworne brothers, as our fathers liues as friendes"—represent a familiar pair in the sixteenth-century universities, although the play is ostensibly set in the thirteenth century: two young men arriving together at one of the universities from the same county, already linked there as they are by ties of family and local patronage, one the son of a tenant who held his land by copyhold from the father of the other.[26]

The most telling comment in this regard is by a contemporary who knew John Gostlin intimately, William Moore, the continuator of the college annals, who used a revealing phrase when he came to the monument to Legge and Gostlin's inscription, which he quoted. "They had lived," he said, "conjunctissime": "qui cum eo conjunctissime vixerat."[27] The term implies a formal and binding union, one created alike by friendship or by kinship—a "conjunx" is for example a husband or wife—a term like the "wedded" of Middle English, which could be used comfortably both for a "wedded" or sworn brother and for a "wedded" wife. He had evidently chosen the term with care and employed it again when he mentioned John Browne's wish to be buried by the body of the friend of his youth, Thomas Orrell: "quasi in fatis esset, vt qui in vita essent coniunctissimi etiam post fata ossa permiscerent et Cineres" [as if in their deaths the bones and ashes of those who in life were *coniunctissimi* should also be united after their deaths].[28] If there is a term that characterizes those whom humankind has thought it appropriate to bury together, it is that word "conjunctissimi," whether husbands and wives, parents and children, sisters and brothers. One might propose the translation "family" were it not that in the society of which I am writing it comprehended also friends.

The term links these men directly to the sworn brothers of the fifteenth century. "Quos Deus sicut unamini concordia et dilectione in vita coniunxit, ita et in morte eos separari noluit" [God did not wish to divide in death those whom in life he had joined (*coniunxit*) as one in unity and love].[29] These are the words with which the culminating miracle of the medieval Latin *Amys and Amylion* begins: the miracle of the two sworn brothers whose bodies move together to lie in death side by side. Are they not also the terms of John Gostlin's inscription: "Iunxit amor vivos sic iungat terra sepultos" [Love joined them living. So may the earth join them in their burial]? Had William Moore and Gostlin read or heard a version of the story of Amys and Amylion that corresponded to the form of the Latin story, with its

Christian conclusion? They might have done so, although it may have been among the diversions of student life akin to the spurs and the horses, the singing that so offended the godly party at Gonville and Caius, and (it has to be said) the drunken fighting of Cambridge student life. The ballads they heard in the tavern—and joined in their refrains—might well have included the story of Amys and Amylion or more homely variants such as the ballads of Adam Bell and Clym of the Clough or Christy Graham and his bully Bewick. *Amys and Amylion* was most certainly not set in the curriculum of a humanist education, but the university curriculum (on its own at least) is a poor guide to student life in sixteenth-century Cambridge. The humanist scholars of the sixteenth century used the language of the new learning, but they also knew the language of the friendship of the past because they still lived in its world and breathed its air, and William Moore carefully collected manuscripts of the romances.[30]

In the traditional society that the zealots of reform eyed with suspicion, Christian charity could never be detached from the actual bonds of friendship that permeated the social world about it. Without them it was an abstraction that was unlikely to touch the lives of men and women. Gostlin's monument to his friendship with Legge in the chapel of Gonville and Caius celebrated one of those bonds, but it stood for them all; and the Eucharist that reaffirmed their friendship was the common union that knit all friendship together. The confidence of that gesture is as tangible as that in the monument of John Bloxham and John Whytton, at the center of Merton College chapel, and for the same reason. Both lay at the heart of the traditional view of Christianity's work they affirmed, in a compass no bigger than the brass above the tomb of two friends or a heart in flames below a monument in a college chapel in Cambridge.

One might well wonder, in such a setting, how representative was John Gostlin's gesture. Did the enclosing walls of a Cambridge college protect it from a changing world taking shape outside? In effect, does a Cambridge college demonstrate the persistence of friendship's place within traditional religion precisely because it was disappearing elsewhere? The question is a pertinent one, but one ought to hesitate before following its lead. That wider world could intervene swiftly in the affairs of a Cambridge or an Oxford college, as it did in Gonville and Caius on the death of Legge and on that of his successor. Nor was an Oxford or a Cambridge college a world apart; in economic terms it functioned in ways markedly similar to any of the great houses of England: its tenants and its properties were visibly similar. The orthodoxy and compliance of an Oxford or Cambridge college was as much a cause of concern to the authorities as that of the household of any noble family. Traditional views of friendship may be visible in a seventeenth-century college less because of its distinctiveness than because of the readiness of subsequent generations there to preserve the monuments and records of the past. That judgment of the question becomes the stronger, if we turn from Gonville and Caius where Gostlin was now safely ensconced as master to the center of power in the kingdom, at the court of King James I: power that seemed increasingly in the closing years of James's reign to be brokered by one individual: George Villiers, the great duke of Buckingham and the intimate friend of King James I. If the friendships of a Cambridge college were indeed not something set apart from a wider world of power and place but mirrored it, one might expect to see their outline evident here also: that and friendship's continued place within the religion of English men and women.

It is that question I now propose to explore. A way into it is a letter that King James sent the duke of Buckingham, set out below, undated but written at some point toward the close of his life, a letter that—inexplicably to modern eyes—appears to speak of a "marriage" between them, a term that recalls the tomb monument of John Bloxham and John Whytton. The letter is among the Tanner manuscripts in the Bodleian Library and consists of a single folded sheet. The recipient is not explicitly named, but the letter's close resemblance to James's letters to the duke of Buckingham leave no doubt that he is the person to whom this ardent note was sent.[31]

> My onlie sweete & deare chylde, notwithstanding of youre desyring me not to wrytte yesterdaye, yett hadde I written in the euening, if at my comming in out of the parke suche á drowzienes hadd not comed upon me, as I was forced to sitte & sleep in my chaire halfe an howre & yett I can not contente myselfe, withowt sending you this p^{rst} praying god that I maye haue a ioyefull & confortable meeting with you, & that we maye mak at this christenmasse a new mariage, euer to be kept hearafter, for, god so loue me, as I desyre onlie to liue in this worlde, for youre saike, & that I hadde rather liue banished in anie pairt of the earth with you, then liue á sorrowefull widdowes lyfe without you, & so god blesse you my sweete chylde & wyfe & grawnte that ye may euer be á conforte to youre deere daide & husbande.
>
>   James R.

To the reader now turning over the volume that contains this letter, among the manuscripts of Duke Humfrey's Library at the Bodleian, it is not now at all clear what James envisaged in his hope that he and Buckingham would "mak at this christenmasse a new mariage, euer to be kept hearafter"; nor in what sense could James regard himself as Buckingham's "husbande" or he as his "wyfe." There is a clue to the first of these at least, in a surviving letter that Buckingham sent James around this time. At the end of this letter, Buckingham turns again to the words he had spoken to James when he had last parted from him: words that he does not repeat—Buckingham's urgency conveys how much they would have remained in James's mind—but words that evidently turned on the fidelity of Buckingham's loyalty to James, fidelity that had apparently been called radically in doubt: "to conclude," he writes "lett this paper aserure you that the last words I spoke to you are so trew that I will not onelie giue my word sware upon the holie euangile but take the blessed sacrement upon them."[32]

The "blessed sacrement" is that in the Holy Communion, and Buckingham's passionate avowal takes the same form as that of James in his letter, for in the reformed church of James's reign the Christmas that James anticipated was one of the three days when its members received the sacrament of Holy Communion in the Lord's Supper. The canons of 1604 required the Lord's Supper to be celebrated three times a year. In George Herbert's *Countrey Parson* they are explicitly those of "Easter, Christmasse, Whitsuntide."[33] What James is looking forward to is what Buckingham offers to him in this letter: they will seal their friendship and its fidelity by receiving the Holy Communion in the general communion at Christmas together, before the eyes of all. In his letter James uses "marriage" to mean the act of a "wedding": the solemn exchange of promises (the "wed") that could create kinship among those it encompassed.[34] The term is of the same provenance as the "wedded" or "sworn" brothers that had been a familiar part of English society from at least the fifteenth century (and very probably for long before that). The terms James employs repeat the covenant of two such "wedded" brothers. "They will liue and dye together": that was how William Cornwallis described the oath of two sworn brothers in 1600, but two centuries earlier the terms one sees are the same despite Chaucer's irony, "I shal never fro thee go, but be thine own sworn brother."[35] In the seventeenth century the setting is no longer the old mass, and the tangible presence of the saints in their relics no longer plays a part; but James's letter moves with the same logic, from the fidelity between them that will be sealed at this coming Christmas in the communion in the Lord's Supper to the vow that God will then hold in his keeping, for the words "for, god so loue me" are those of an oath whose terms are the same: "for, god so loue me, as I desyre onlie to liue in this worlde, for youre saike."

If Roger Lockyer, the great modern historian of the duke of Buckingham, is right in dating these two letters to 1624, then James's letter not only anticipated the final crisis of James's reign, it was directly instrumental in it.[36] For the historians of the nineteenth century the friendship of traditional English society was a diversion (or worse) from the constitutional developments they were seeking to trace: whether the putative "bastard feudalism" they perceived as obstructing the onward march of the royal administration, or the royal "favorites" such as the duke of Buckingham and Piers Gaveston, the earl of Cornwall, before him, who supposedly corrupted it. It was a view that was to have an abiding influence among British historians across the twentieth century and obscured the extent to which the formal and objective character that friendship could possess in traditional society enabled men like Gaveston or Buckingham to act as the king's instrument. The publication in 1981 of Roger Lockyer's *Buckingham: The Life and Political Career of George Villiers, First Duke of Buckingham* was to break definitively with that judgment by treating Buckingham as a serious politician. In Lockyer's view a figure like the duke of Buckingham represented the dynamic element in absolute monarchy, its capacity to innovate, and one that drew conservative reaction to itself and away from the king. A few years later, J. S. Hamilton was to reassess Piers Gaveston in similar terms and similarly assail the view that Gaveston had been a figure without political or constitutional significance.

In 1623 the duke of Buckingham reached out beyond that role and attempted to grasp from an apparently ill and failing monarch a role akin to that the count-duke of Olivares occupied in the Spain of Philip IV or that Cardinal Richelieu exercised over Louis XIII, summed up in Lockyer's terse characterization as a role that "does not depend upon the ruler's affections ... the key to this particular relationship is the dependence not of the favourite but of the monarch."[37] In October 1623 the duke of Buckingham had returned with new determination from the ill-conceived attempt to find a bride for James's son, Charles, at the Spanish court. The instrument that articulated his determination for a dominating role was to impel England under his leadership into the war that was spreading from the Palatinate and that was to engulf Europe for a generation: precisely the prospect against which James had pitted himself. Under the pressure of Buckingham and Charles, added to that of his advisers and a bellicose public opinion, James gave way and in December 1623 consented to calling a Parliament that would provide the finances and impetus for such a war. The stage seemed set for a dramatic reversal in England's foreign policy—and government.

At the Parliament that met in February 1624, James seemed to have abandoned the reins of government, and it was not he but the duke of Buckingham who addressed the Parliament in the great hall at the palace of Whitehall, where they were accustomed to wait on the king. As the historian of the

Stuarts put it, "If Buckingham had said, 'I am the King,' he could not have expressed himself more plainly."[38] At this critical juncture the Spanish ambassadors played their hand and succeeded, against all Buckingham's provisions, in reaching the king directly with a message, which warned James that Buckingham was planning to immure him in one of his country houses and to rule de facto in his place. James listened, and he acted. As Roger Lockyer puts it, "The Spanish charges against Buckingham were so skilfully woven around a core of truth that James could not simply dismiss them as unfounded."[39] He declared his disbelief in the accusations but ordered his privy councilors to affirm solemnly on oath that they had not been involved in any plot against him. He decided to put formal interrogatories to them, probing what truth if any lay in the accusations. James's action provided him, as had been intended, with the instrument he needed definitively to reassert his authority. At this crisis, Buckingham's health broke down gravely and dramatically, as it could do under stress, and he retired to New Hall, his country house in Essex, to recover. It was later there that Roger Lockyer places his letter to James, offering to take the sacrament on those urgent last words he had spoken to James. As his bid failed and he withdrew to his sickbed, the watchful eyes that inhabited the court would have followed him closely, going perhaps to his fall, perhaps even to his death.[40]

James's response was compounded of two intertwined elements. One was the memory of that young man who had captivated him and had always been able to make him laugh and warm his heart and whom he had never ceased to love. James's passionate response to Buckingham's illness, immediate and unreserved, was a real measure of that love. But the other element that shaped James's response was the pressing conviction of his world about the nature of friendship. I know of no occasion from the eleventh to the seventeenth century when it was ever claimed that the infidelity of one friend could release the other from the covenant he had made with him: for good or ill, they were bound together. These two elements came together easily in James's response: the duke of Buckingham was not to fall from power or from James's love. It is not difficult to judge what James said in response to those urgent parting words of Buckingham; but he did something also: he wrote a letter.

As summer turned into winter—the winter that was to be James's last—James's letter that we have in the Tanner manuscripts appears to have been the earnest of his response. Is there a trace of the potential instrumentality of this letter in its repeated insistence on the palpable reality of the letter itself? For this curiously is a letter about letter writing. Its opening is Buckingham's insistence that James should *not* write; and James's "present" is the letter itself, that James despite Buckingham's earnest entreaties would not rest without placing in his hands. That insistence corresponds to the curious device by which it then translates the *oral* form of an oath before witnesses into a written document, which the bearer brought to the hands of the duke of Buckingham. The intimate tone of this letter can distract us today from the countenance such a familiar letter was capable of providing in a wider world of politics and affairs, an instrumentality evident from that point in 1623 when such letters began to flow from James to Buckingham in Spain. Their intimate tone does not prepare one for the careful count James kept of the letters he sent Buckingham during that time: the diplomatic quagmire Buckingham and Charles were stepping over, however, does. They would have provided Buckingham with James's undeniable countenance and corresponded to the honor of the dukedom that flew with them also to Buckingham in Spain.

The rhetoric of intimacy had its own persuasive power in a wider world, and the traces of that world can still be discerned in this letter. Some of the details are very small; others are written in a bold hand. One such detail is the absence of the broken wax seal and the familiar recognizable direction to "the Lord Duque of Buckingham" on the outer membrane. If the letter traveled alone, why are they missing here?[41] Another is the now invisible bearer, for a letter from the king of England was carried by no common carter. At times in his letters to Buckingham James would draw attention to their bearer. On such occasions was James commending the message that the bearer was carrying? Another such trace is the survival of this apparently intimate letter. For if this letter were intended only for the eyes of the duke of Buckingham, as on its surface it appears to be, why was it preserved and why was it handed on? But the most striking trace of that wider world in which this letter potentially figured is paradoxically the one that seems directly to evade it. This is a letter written in James's own recognizable hand. Noblemen in seventeenth-century England did not need to write their own letters, least of all the king of England; for such an office they employed a "secretary" who would act as their scribe and often read out to his patron the scrawled and abbreviated "secretary" hand of the time; in one of his letters to Buckingham, James describes the marquess of Hamilton hovering at his shoulder, offering to act as his secretary and to read out Buckingham's letter for him (and by implication for those also who might also be present).[42] The author's own handwriting authenticated a letter as nothing else could, and made of the letter a gift and a token of intimacy that had a currency of its own. "I haue forgotten to write my legable hand in this letter forgive me": when Buckingham wrote that improbable postscript, in one of his letters to James, he was ensuring that all those who might hear these words being read out were being left in no doubt about the intimacy he shared with the king of England.[43]

In the closing months of 1624 those eyes that had followed the duke of Buckingham as he left the court were watching still, and were waiting perhaps to pick over his fall; if Roger Lockyer's dating of these letters to 1624 is right, then James's letter was potentially a sign for those watchers as much as for the duke of Buckingham himself. In their communion together at Christmas James planned to give the duke of Buckingham that public mark of their bond that those same watching eyes would see and have their cue to draw back, but it was not to be. When the Christmas of 1624 came, James was too ill to leave his room and attend chapel, and he died only three months later.[44] The frail and ill man who wrote that letter may well have known that he might not be able to give Buckingham that solemn mark of friendship as he had planned. But did he now need to? This letter in his own hand anticipated and made that gesture for him, for all who might see it. In this letter the act was not only as good as done, it was done; and that is perhaps why after finishing it James struck out one of its closing words, probably the last words he ever sent the duke of Buckingham. He had first concluded the letter "youre deere daide & maister," but he paused and struck out the word "maister." In its place he wrote "husbande." The covenant of friendship that James had planned to give the duke of Buckingham in the sacrament at Christmas 1624 provides a context for judging the beliefs of a man like John Gostlin, for whom the Eucharist was the evident instrument of friendship: for James's intended gesture lay in no hidden corner but was rather one between the greatest magnate in the land and the supreme governor of the reformed English church.

A curious detail remains unexplained by this. James had not written that he would make a marriage with Buckingham at this coming Christmas. What he had written was that he would make a *new* marriage. What then was that first "marriage"? For the answer we are directed by the letters between Buckingham and James, which take us back vividly into the force of a world of ritual kinship. If Buckingham's letters to James are the guide, that first "marriage" between them had been made at Wallingford House, Buckingham's London house (now where the Admiralty buildings stand overlooking St. James's Park), near the royal palace of Whitehall on the morning of 30 March 1622: when James had stood as godparent at the baptism of Buckingham's first child.[45] That act created a kinship between James and Buckingham that made them each other's "gossip," that godbrotherhood of *compaternitas* that in mundane terms was the principal creation of a baptism, rather than any subsequent responsibility for the religious care of the child. The importance of the kinship it created between them is made explicit in virtually every letter between James and Buckingham, who habitually opened his letters by addressing James as his "gossip." The king's role in the baptism was immediately public knowledge, sufficiently so for John Chamberlain to write the same day with the news. He added the confident assertion that the child, who was a girl, would be called Jacobina, a feminine form of James, although she was actually to be named Mary after her godmother, the countess of Buckingham, Mary Villiers. When James had heard of the next pregnancy of Buckingham's wife, the lady Katherine, he had written to Buckingham: "I hoape it is a goode sygne, that I shal shortlie be a gosseppe ouer againe, for I muste be thy perpetuall gosseppe."[46] The dukedom that was conferred on Buckingham in Spain had affirmed in public and insistent terms the force of that kinship to James, for Buckingham was the first duke in England in nearly a century not to have royal blood in his body.[47] It had been through baptism not blood that Buckingham had been incorporated into James's family, and in 1624 it was James's design that the friendship that kinship in baptism had created would be publicly reaffirmed in the Eucharist, for all the world to see: and let it draw back. James understood Buckingham probably better than any man in the world and what had been in Buckingham's mind and heart; but like John Gostlin, he also knew how a good Christian should die, bearing with the infirmities of others and not bearing malice in his heart.

This argument of course leaves still unexplained *why* James should have identified himself as Buckingham's husband and Buckingham as his wife. My argument has been that the expression "marriage" in James's letter referred to a marriage as the "wedding," the covenant to a marriage that in the traditional society this book describes was properly made between the "friends" of the two parties, between their parents and families and indeed between all those who might have an interest in the projected marriage: it was they who made the match. But such a covenant could also be made in the "spiritual" brotherhood among the parents and godparents of a child, the *compatres* and *commatres* created at its baptism, the "gossips" of vernacular English. In 1622 James and Buckingham became such spiritual "gossips" to each other, and the repeated place of that term in their letters underscores the scale of its importance for them: it was that kinship, I have argued, that James intended publicly to reassert by their communions together in 1624. But such a covenant and kinship could also be made between two "wedded" brothers, directly by the oath itself and without the symbolic instrumentality of in the one case the bride or in the other the child: it is because of that affinity that the terms of James's oath corresponded so closely to that of two "sworn" brothers. The common element in each—whether the "wedding" of a marriage, the ritual brotherhood created through the promises of baptism, or that created by the oaths of two "wedded" brothers—is that the kinship they created was made not by blood but by promise.

The terms of James's oath are then those of a *brother*, not a husband, and that enlargement of the language of kinship in the terms "husband" and "wife" is something to be seen over and again in the terms in which James and Buckingham characterized their friendship in their letters, in which different kinds of kinship terminology overlap and mix together in an apparently bewildering profusion. Their friendship is both the kinship created by ritual and that created by blood; not only "gossip," "husband," and "wife" but also the "boy" that a father might call his child or the "dad" that then as now was the term a child used to address its father. Their friendship is present not only in that resonant word "friend" but also in the term "servant," which in this society was a relation of friendship as the word "boy" could also connote a servant (of any age). Some of the terms they employ are precise and accurate, such as the "gossip" both employ or the "scholar" that fitted disarmingly James's early attempts to educate the youthful Buckingham. Others are jokes, like Buckingham's teasing "slave" and "dog" or James's earnest pun on "steward": like a good steward or Stuart, he would care for Buckingham's interests. The strings of words in which James would arrange these terms seem designed only to emphasize their confusion: "youre deere daide & husbande" or "thy deare dade & christen gosseppe" swell and grow into proliferating and exuberant processions, "youre deare dade, gosseppe, & stewarde" or "my sweete deare chylde, skoller & freende."[48]

Yet this is no eccentricity of James and Buckingham, although the elaborate prose of the early seventeenth century gave it ample scope. It displays, with the exuberance of the seventeenth-century baroque, the same conflation to be seen in the tomb monument of John Bloxham and John Whytton with which this chapter opened, in which two sworn brothers seem to stand together on their tomb like a husband and wife. More mundanely, that same overlapping terminology is to be found across the traditional society of England: in the "conjunctissimi" glimpsed in the annals of a Cambridge college; among the depositions of a court in York set by a ballad of the common people; with a churchman composing a fourteenth-century chronicle as well as in a play written by a man educated in the shining new humanist learning of the sixteenth century: that apparent confusion to the modern eye was the conundrum with which this chapter opened. The letters between James I and the duke of Buckingham make unavoidable, at last, the same conclusion, however difficult it may seem: for the officious historian to pick through these terms—selecting some and discarding others—would be a dusty pedantry that fails to grasp what this evidence is saying directly and with such confidence: the confusion lies not in these terms from the past but with us.

Friendship and the Family

That the "family" can be defined in several different ways—in terms of blood relations for example, but also as a common household, or in terms of marriage—has tended to be a technical point of interest only to sociologists and anthropologists, as in modern society these different definitions coincide closely, where the family living together in the same household is conventionally the group of parents and their children linked by blood or marriage.[49] In the past these potentially differing definitions often did not coincide so nearly, and one major cause of this mismatch was the several forms of what one might call voluntary kinship, kinship created not by blood but by ritual or a promise. Modern society recognizes only one such "voluntary" kinship, in marriage. In the past others have subsisted alongside it. One was the kinship established by baptism, kinship relations of the kind I have sought to trace in this chapter. Another was that created by a betrothal, the agreement to a marriage that might precede the marriage itself by several years but which created binding relations that stood with those created by marriage and baptism. A third was the kinship created by a vow of sworn brotherhood.

Their cumulative effect was that an individual lived in a potential plurality of families, in the strict sense of the term. He or she could be part of one such family in terms of blood relations and simultaneously incorporated into another in terms of the ritual kinship created by betrothal or marriage, by baptism, or by a "sworn" brotherhood. My argument here has not been to identify each of the individuals I have recounted as necessarily having been made ritual kin within these customary forms, although they may have been and some certainly were. It is rather that the outline of their friendships—a friendship that signified as kinship—unlocks the larger whole of which their friendships were perceived to be a part. Kinship did not obliterate the boundaries of families. "Spiritual" kinship remained distinct from that created by birth or marriage, and sworn brotherhood did not extend to others beyond those who made the promise that created it. Their cumulative effect was rather to embed the family within a wider and encompassing network of the friendship that kinship was perceived to create. That network has been peculiarly difficult to see from the vantage point of a modern historian. Its presence was created by those very mismatches that had the ability to overlap and in doing so be drawn outward, mismatches that modern society lacks: where all definitions of the family are perceived to delineate the same group and no kinship is perceived to be, in the strict sense of the word, artificial and the product of human agency. For the later historian to attempt with determined pedantry to undo the connections made in the traces of kinship that the past has left is to miss the point that that apparent confusion, in which different kinds of kinship terminology overlapped and shaded into each other, corresponded with precision to the actual social context in which they figured.

In the traditional society this book describes, the friendship that kinship could create was in itself only one part of a larger whole that presses on the confines of this book. At one level of society, it was replicated in the wider influence of the great households of the English countryside, which the colleges at Oxford and Cambridge so closely resembled. At another, in the bonds created by fraternities and trade guilds. At yet another in the houses of call in which tramping artisans in the same trade lodged together in the town in which they were working, under their own governance rather than that of their masters. It could reappear in the practices of fostering and adoption, which might create links extending throughout the lives of the individuals touched by them, and in the movement of adolescents between families to act as servants in other households, often of a higher social standing, with their own family receiving children from elsewhere: and in doing so linking household with household. Within this wider frame, a multiplicity in the forms of kinship readily overlapped and created that web of obligations and friendship that held the society of England together.

Within it was placed the family in our contemporary (and more limited) sense of a group of parents and their children. If one analogy to the relation between kinship and the wider friendship it could create is that of an interlocking network—the image I have used—a more graphic one is perhaps that of a set of Chinese boxes, lying one inside the other: to grasp the place the family held in traditional society and the friendship in which it was embedded, one has to find the keys that unlock these differing definitions and open them, one by one. Such a course draws the historian's eye away from the friendship that might subsist between two men or two women, even if one was the king of England and the other the great duke of Buckingham, to the place their friendship might play within the world their families inhabited—from friends to families—as it does when one probes (as chapter 2 did) the friendship of two men like Philip Sidney and Fulke Greville.

Sidney's pastoral depiction of his friendship with Greville and Edward Dyer was as much a gift that figured in that world as the letters from Sidney's father, letters in a different sense, that secured Greville's position in the Welsh Council and could serve to smooth the way for his first appearance at the court. In return, Greville and Dyer provided for Sidney the beginnings of the household he would have needed had he lived and succeeded his uncles, the earls of Warwick and of Leicester.

Two centuries before, the friendship of two knights, William Neville and John Clanvowe, inescapably was embedded in the needs of their families, although it eludes the categories that modern society might bring to it. To grasp a friendship like theirs in its own terms, one needs to follow the rhetorical clue given by the imagery of kinship on their tomb. Its context took shape when Neville and Clanvowe first appear closely associated, soon after January 1373, when Clanvowe entered the service of Edward III on the death of Humphrey Bohun, the earl of Hereford; and the close association of Neville and Clanvowe at the royal court was to touch the wider fortunes of their families. The Clanvowe family were members of the Herefordshire gentry; while still a minor John Clanvowe had already inherited his father's lands in the county. William Neville was a younger son of one of the greatest families in England, the Nevilles of Raby in County Durham, a family that with the Percys virtually ruled the northern counties, from their positions as wardens of the marches and as agents of the king. William's career at the royal court was to provide a continuing link between the monarchy and the authority in the north of his elder brother, John Neville, the lord of Raby. The Nevilles' interests lay almost entirely in the northern counties and to that extent at least lacked a wider national base. The effect of William Neville's close association with John Clanvowe was significantly to widen the family's base at the royal court.

In 1385 one has a close view of this at work when we see Clanvowe being included with Neville in the potentially delicate matter of the commission led by William Neville's brother Alexander Neville, the archbishop of York, to inspect the readiness of the castles, forts, and men in the Scottish marches—a commission that included the readiness of the men under John Neville as lord of Raby.[50] By 1385 John Clanvowe had become a substantial figure at the court and in the administration. Both he and William Neville had become royal chamber knights together in 1381 and were instrumental in the development by Richard II of the machinery of household government, to a degree unparalleled since the reign of Edward II, and were placed by him in key positions of trust, in the one case in the north and in the other in Wales and the Welsh marches. The commission in 1385 was given detailed instructions and was clearly intended to judge the readiness of the Scottish marches critically and for themselves. It was a sensitive business, but Clanvowe's sworn brotherhood with William Neville ensured that, when John Neville welcomed him to Raby, he was welcoming no potentially uncertain stranger, alongside his brothers William and Archbishop Alexander.

Philip Sidney and Fulke Greville not only pursued their friendship together in recognizably the same terms as did William Neville and John Clanvowe: allies at the royal court, employed by the sovereign in the risks of diplomacy abroad, and commemorated together in the same tomb with an imagery corresponding directly to the kinship in which their friendship figured. These connections were in substantial measure employed at the service of the same family. Fulke Greville's mother was Anne Neville, the daughter of Ralph Neville, the fourth earl of Westmorland and the successor at Raby Castle of his ancestor, the elder brother of William Neville, John Neville, the lord of Raby before him; and when Fulke Greville took the title of Lord Brooke of Beauchamp's Court, he was celebrating in that name his descent from the Willoughby family through his grandmother (and Willoughby heiress) Elizabeth Willoughby, a family that had been linked to the Nevilles and the Beauchamps (the family of the earls of Warwick) by a succession of marriages stretching back over the previous two centuries. Philip Sidney and Fulke Greville—from the moment of their births—had figured within the plans of their families, as had William Neville and John Clanvowe, whom they so much resemble: the kinship that their friendships created was not only theirs but that of their families.

A visit as important as that of William Neville and John Clanvowe to Raby in 1385—a visible link between the royal administration and the authority of John Neville as lord of Raby—would have been accompanied in the splendor of the great hall at Raby (and in the nearby Neville family church of St. Mary Staindrop) by public ritual at its grandest. It is in that setting that Neville and Clanvowe would have exchanged the formal gesture of the kiss of peace, which they are depicted exchanging on their tomb memorial—a gesture that would have signified eloquently at such a moment in a wider context than the growing friendship between these two men alone. Had one read the heraldry of their tomb monument in this wider light, it would have spoken eloquently how little their friendship was their own alone and how much that of their families and kin. The two heraldic helmets on their tomb, arranged as if in a stylized depiction of the kiss of peace, are unusual (if not unique) only in that there are *two* shields in the design below. When in the fourteenth century the heraldic arms of two families were united by the marriage of an heiress, the two resulting helms could be arranged in this same way, to mark the union of the two families: face to face as here, as if in a stylized depiction of the kiss of peace.[51] The two helms would then have surmounted only one shield. But how many shields are there here? The marital "impalement" of arms renders the two shields the same: as if, as the *Westminster Chronicle* puts it of these two sworn friends, the one were the other. In these two sworn friends, as in the marriage of an heiress, the heraldic arrangement marks the union not only of two individuals but of two families; the very existence of the tomb is a measure of how much that was the case. Two men like Neville and Clanvowe with apparently Lollard beliefs—those of the early reformers—would conventionally not have approved of funeral pomp or elaborate tombs, for which the Lollard preachers had little liking. But it was not they who made this tomb in which they were laid. The tomb was the work of their friends, and as a number of historians have pointed out, until the eighteenth century in England "friends" remained a category that comprehended rather than excluded kin.[52] That we have this tomb monument at all is a graphic measure of how much the friendship of these two men was the property of such "friends."

The reformers in England, perhaps with limited success, removed the kiss of peace from its place in the Eucharist: the kinship and friendship it marked seemed to them a distraction from the zeal for the Lord's religion that the times demanded. But the same formal embrace—in the same public context of a family's hold within its community—appears again in the inscription on the tombs of Ann Chitting and her friend Mary Barber in the church of St. James in Bury that I mentioned earlier in this chapter. The monument itself has been lost, but the inscription survives among the papers of Ann Chitting's son, the Suffolk antiquary Henry Chitting. As Henry Chitting's papers elegantly underline, the friendship that it commemorated between these two women articulated a link between households like that of the sworn brotherhood of William Neville and John Clanvowe. These papers are Henry Chitting's topographical collections of Suffolk churches made by him in the second decade of the seventeenth century, intended (as their modern editor Diarmaid MacCulloch points out) for the Suffolk gentry among whom Chitting's manuscripts circulated and whose connections they celebrated. Mary Barber was the niece of Francis Boldero, the powerful servant and official of the lord keeper Sir Nicholas Bacon, the Chitting family's patron. It is this connection that the monument expresses—as Henry Chitting carefully indicates in his note—in the arms of Mary Barber that "impale" the arms of her husband with those of her own family, the Bolderos. The description of her friendship with Ann Chitting that follows in the inscription—and the embrace that ritually encapsulates it—is then placed in that context. Diarmaid MacCulloch transcribes the note that Henry Chitting made of the monument thus (in which "ut ante" means "as before" and indicates that Mary Barber's "scucheon" "impales" the arms of Roger Barber, that the note describes, with those of the Bolderos, and there lies the point).

Here lyeth the body of Roger Barber Esq'r the husband of Mary Barber who was of the age of 62 yeares he died the 6 of June A. D'ni 1606.

Under it is a scucheon of his coat and crest and mantle, vidilicet argent 2 chevrons inter 3 flurdeluces gules, his crest is a bull head argent out of a crowne gules

next to him lyes

Mary his wife who lived maried together 28 yeares had 12 children she died 6 Septemb: 1600, and further upon Barber ut ante impales Boldero, per pale or and azure a saltier counterchanged.

by her lyes

An Chittinge widow of Thomas Chitting of Ickworth gen. with theis verses in brasse.

Here lyes interd the dead body of Ann,
late wife of Thomas Chitting gentlema'
of Ickworth by whom she had children three
Henry, John, Mary, she liv'd vertuously
Her sowle did travell on the Epiphanye
like the wisemen her saviour to see
and though her body lyes here buried
her better part survives and is not dead

Henry her sonn her body here did place
next to her freind whose soules in heave' imbrace
They lived and loved like two most vertuous wights
Whose bodyes death wold sever he unites
Decessit 6 Januarij A. D'ni
1606 aetatis suae 59.[53]

The Uses of Friendship

This chapter opened with the questions posed by the tomb monument of John Bloxham and John Whytton, in the chapel of Merton College; questions that were only to be underlined as it followed the history of such friendships, into the seventeenth century. One of these insistent question marks was the opacity of the terms employed in the design of their tomb, in which different forms of kinship seem to overlap and shade into each other. The argument of this chapter has been that that perceived "confusion" (to the modern eye) serves as a distant mirror to a defining conviction of modern society: that all definitions of the family delineate the same conjugal group. In the traditional society that Bloxham and Whytton inhabited, that "confusion" corresponded with precision to the actual social context in which such friendships figured: a society in which diverse forms of voluntary kinship could overlap and create that web of obligations that was its frame.

Such friendships were placed in a view of religion's role that had deep and abiding roots: that has also been the argument of this chapter. The bonds of friendship extended beyond any exclusively religious domain, but they could be created by the rituals of baptism and betrothal at the church door and reaffirmed by communion at the altar within, at the steps to which in Merton College chapel the tomb of Bloxham and Whytton once lay. Here lies the reason why the religious beliefs (and practices) of this society provide a path back to its friendship. In this light religion's proper role was to aid society to live in peace and friendship. It was that conviction that imparted the confidence one still can sense in the monument to the friendship of Bloxham and Whytton at the heart of the chapel of Merton College. It was that conviction also that would be reasserted in the monument that John Gostlin placed in the chapel of Gonville and Caius in that triumphant conclusion of 1619.

Such monuments are not, of course, windows on the past. They are representations of an ideal, of figures as ethereal as the heroes of the romances that they so much resemble. Like Amis and Amylion made saints by their friendship, the figures of Bloxham and Whytton stand as if placed among the saints that crowd the windows around them. But to recognize that these figures are ideals is not to say that they are not real. The obligations of friendship, as my last chapter sought to show, could be irksome and resented and the moment and manner of their calling dangerous; the ideals of friendship helped to negotiate those dangers: they allowed the obligations of friendship to be called not in the language of main force or through the pressure of a community but in the terms of such ideals, ideals that did not call in question a man's honor or require him to lose face.

One can perhaps sharpen the point: the diverse forms of voluntary kinship created the obligations of friendship in distinctive ways, and there lay their strength, the point I propose now to pursue. Of these diverse forms, the one that might impinge least on a family's future expectations was the sworn brotherhood of two men like William Neville and John Clanvowe, and for that reason they were likely to have been allowed a degree of freedom in their choice that would have been impossible for the kinship created by baptism or betrothal. Sworn brotherhood did not create potential impediments to marriage among their kin, as both baptism and a betrothal did; nor did it require the transfer of property or raise expectations of inheritance. The property William Neville lacked as a younger son was obtained by his marriage to an heiress before 1366 (John Clanvowe may not have married), and assistance from the family of one's sworn brother depended more on goodwill than on a settled obligation (the reverse was also the case).[54] Although John Neville as the lord of Raby would have greeted Clanvowe in 1385 with all the gestures of friendship, he evidently felt no need to include Clanvowe in his will.[55] Simon Bulleyne shared a grave with his friend William Jekkes, as Neville did with Clanvowe, but when he died at the end of the fifteenth century, he left his friend his personal effects rather than his substantial property, his writing desk and his chest (as Philip Sidney was to leave his books to Fulke Greville and Edward Dyer).[56] Sworn brothers rather pledged their oath, to stand by each other in well and woe: an oath potentially awesome in its scope, but foremost a commitment of person to person, not of property. Such a bond was well suited to two landless adventurers like Nicholas Molyneux and John Winter, but it was characteristically more widely a young man's business. Piers Gaveston and the future King Edward II met as young men at the court of Edward I and became sworn brothers there. John Bloxham and John Whytton were still young men when they first met, at Merton College in 1364. In the romances sworn brotherhood is no less a young man's affair: Amis and Amilyon (and Bewick and Grahame) are specifically said still to be youths when they became sworn brothers.[57] In the seventeenth century, John Browne and Thomas Orrell still appear in this mold, as did Philip Sidney and Fulke Greville before them.

Unlike sworn brotherhood, the kinship created by baptism carried direct implications for a family's future strategy akin to those of a betrothal. Godparenthood at least could create expectations of inheritance, and the impediments to marriage applied to "spiritual" kinship as well as that created by marriage. Impediments to marriage also had their uses: a "forgotten" impediment was a convenient means of obtaining what was in effect a divorce. These were implications that the sixteenth-century reformers sought to curtail, but Elizabeth I's brusque rejection of the proposal in parliament of the Reformatio Legum Ecclesiasticarum cut short in England the changes taking place elsewhere in Europe. The godbrotherhood of her successor

James I and his "Christian gossip" George Villiers was a product neither of the world of politics that they inhabited nor of the seventeenth century. The England of the fifteenth century that one sees in the work of Philippa Maddern and Alison Hanham convey that point: in the one case among the gentry of fifteenth-century Norfolk and in the other among the wool merchants of London. Maddern's account catches in persuasive detail how the *compaternitas* of godbrotherhood could be used to create friendship between Norfolk neighbors, such as Simeon Fyncham and Laurence Trussbut, who stood as godfather to Simeon's son Laurence (and gave him his name), as Simeon Fyncham similarly stood as godparent to his neighbor's son Simeon Rykkys and gave him his name also. Hanham depicts the same ties at work among the merchants of London, where two wool merchants like Richard Cely and William Maryon could secure their friendship by William's standing as godparent to Richard Cely's son. The spiritual kinship between the two families was renewed in the next generation: William Maryon stood as godparent to one of the daughters of the younger Richard Cely, and his brother George Cely became godfather in return, as it were, to one of the sons of William Maryon's sister. The matriarch Agnes Cely—the mother of George and of his brother Richard—further secured the link between the two families by standing as godmother at the baptism of the daughter of William Maryon's nephew and by giving the child her name, Agnes. Two families such as this, linked by ties of spiritual kinship back and forth across the generations, were "perpetual gossips" to each other in King James's phrase, as James himself had sought to bind his family with that of George Villiers.[58]

At the accession of Elizabeth, parish registers frequently ceased to record the names of godparents. Others continued to do so into the eighteenth century, either generally or sporadically; and the importance that the associated naming practices could continue to hold is evident in the numerous extracts that Charles Cox made in his careful antiquarian book on the parish registers of England. The sporadic entries are perhaps the most telling, emphasized as they often are within the register by especially large entries.[59] The kinship of two godbrothers or two sworn brothers could be as indisputable as that formed by marriage; but kinship of this kind shared a crucial distinction to that of a betrothal or a marriage in its ability to forge links across social divisions where marriage would have been unthinkable. The kinship of two godbrothers (or two sworn brothers) did not *extend* the family, as a betrothal or a marriage did: it rather befriended it, from within and without. This did not diminish a godbrother's presence. William Maryon was a substantial part of his godbrother's household, as Piers Gaveston had been part of that of his sworn brother Edward. "[M]y master and my mistress, my master Richard Cely and William Maryon and all our household be in good heal[th]" was how the Cely household was reported to George Cely, and Maryon took a part in all the family's affairs, including its resentments. The stern advice he administered to the easy-going George was ill received, by a young man more fond of spending money on horses with the hot-blooded gentlemen soldiers of Calais than of attending to business. But Maryon's substantial place within the domestic circle of the Cely family did not stand in the way of his being also godfather to their factor at Calais, a dependent and humble "cousin" of the Celys whose position was crucial for their interests. Spiritual kinship between "gossips" had similarly secured the link with the family's factor in the days of the older Richard Cely, when their factor Thomas Kesten had been the godbrother of both George Cely and his brother Robert: "Reverent and worshipful sir and my special friend and gossip" was how Kesten, now fallen on hard times, was able to write to George in 1479. In fifteenth-century Norfolk, one of Simeon Fyncham's neighbors, Edmund Norman of Filby, was able to become godbrother to his much more prestigious neighbor Robert Clere of Stokesby by standing as godparent to Clere's child. Rosemary O'Day has illustrated how Walter Bagot, a member of Parliament and justice of the peace, could be godbrother to his friends and clients in sixteenth-century Staffordshire. In sixteenth-century London, one can see from the register of All Hallows-in-the-Wall how spiritual kinship could continue to be used to forge links between individuals associated with the workaday world of the queen's household.[60] An entry in the register of Albrighton, near Wolverhampton, in 1638 records a baronet and his kinsman standing as godparents to the son of a "sawier," whose trade was to saw wood in a saw pit, "to doe good unto a poore man," as the register puts it.[61]

The limits of ritual brotherhood enabled it to play a directly practical role in a family's affairs. Young George Cely probably learned his trade from his "gossip" Thomas Kesten, judging by the pamphlet Alison Hanham identified containing a record of sales written by them together.[62] In the century before, the sworn brotherhood of Piers Gaveston and Edward appears to have provided, in the eyes of Edward's father, the formidable Edward I, a proper context for Edward's training as a knight, unaffected by the social disparity between them. As J. S. Hamilton has pointed out, it appears to have been Edward I who introduced Gaveston into his son's household after being impressed by Gaveston's service in Flanders in 1297, a view that is borne out by his appearance in Edward I's household retinue by 1297–1298. Judging by the only contemporary chronicle to give an explanation for

Gaveston's transfer to the household of the young prince, Edward I appears to have intended Gaveston (who was apparently the oldest member of the prince's household) as a model for him.[63] In the same way that sworn brotherhood appears in actuality and in the romances as a young man's business, it also appears in both in terms similar to the education of the young prince Edward. Christy Graham in the ballad of Bewick and Graham—whose story I retold in the first chapter—is the heir of a great house in the sixteenth-century border country near Scotland, trained in the house of Sir Robert Bewick, the neighbor and friend of his father, Lord Graham. His teacher in Sir Robert's house was his sworn brother, his "bully," Sir Robert's son; and when Christy Graham comes to fight with him at his father's command, his "bully" Bewick greets him in just such terms.

> O no! not so, O bully Grahame!
> That eer such a word should spoken be!
> I was thy master, thou was my scholar:
> So well as I have learnëd thee.[64]

When, in seventeenth-century England, James I was to characterize his "christen gosseppe" George Villiers in the same terms, as his "scholar," he was employing the same familiar traditional view of the role.

Marriage and betrothal; godparenthood, godbrothers and godsisters; and sworn brotherhood—among these three the last was the most circumscribed, but it was that limitation that could make it a reliable element within a family strategy where these others might fail. It crucially elided those expectations of inheritance that could leave families bitterly divided. As J. R. Lander has pointed out, the Nevilles would have become an overwhelming force in English politics if they had acted together, which they did not.[65] The more limited kinship of sworn brotherhood potentially elided such quarrels. This is presumably the reason why Edward II arranged for the marriage of Piers Gaveston, who was already his sworn brother, to his niece Margaret de Clare. Three centuries later it is still the reason why the joint tomb projected by Fulke Greville for himself and Philip Sidney in St. Paul's Cathedral connotes a much closer union with Sidney than the relation he already occupied as his "cousin."

The most fundamental threat to a family's strategy was not though the quarrels that might erupt over property and inheritance, however bitter: it was rather death, which could always without warning cut away the ground from any family strategy. The arrival of the black death in England during the childhood of William Neville and John Clanvowe underlined that hard fact. The provision of a sworn brother was one possible response, which could if necessary stand in the gap; and this is a thread that runs through its history. One can see it at work in the care Edward II took of Gaveston's family after Gaveston's death: endowing his widow Margaret with lands and income and providing for her daughter Joan to be raised at the convent at Amesbury and for her dowry and betrothal (although the care he took came to nothing when the girl died at age thirteen).[66] In the fifteenth century Nicholas Molyneux and John Winter made careful provision of the same kind when they prepared the written agreement of their ritual brotherhood, providing that if either were to die the survivor was to "nourish" his brother's children and to pay for their schooling, and funds for their maintenance were provided in the agreement. If both were to die without children, their assets were to be sold to provide for masses to be said, for their souls and for those of their parents.[67] In testamentary terms, the role of the sworn brother was not that of beneficiary but *executor:* the role formally entrusted to Nicholas Molyneux by John Winter's will, as John Gostlin was executor for the will of Thomas Legge and as Fulke Greville had charge of Philip Sidney's papers (and helped to carry the pall at his funeral). In sixteenth-century Staffordshire, the Walter Bagot mentioned above acted swiftly when the son of one of his clients and godbrothers was left fatherless, sending his godson Walter Edge with two of his sons to study together at Oxford, with Edge probably acting also as their personal servant. In these terms Edward II had acted for his sworn brother Piers Gaveston, providing for his burial and the care of his tomb and for the maintenance of his family.[68] The strength of the bond is apparent in John Winter's rightly placed confidence that he could trust the man he had cheated nevertheless to be the executor of his will. To take the assets such men bequeathed each other as the measure is to miss the point. The potential strength of their role lay in their very freedom from that expectation of inheritance.

One should look rather to the things they entrusted to their care. Most eloquently this was their bodies: Fulke Greville's plans for Philip Sidney's tomb in old St. Paul's laid claim to that charge, as did John Gostlin's care for the remains of Thomas Legge, and John Browne's for those of Thomas Orrell, as Edward II had cared for the remains of his sworn brother three centuries before. The final line of the inscription on their tomb below the figures of John Bloxham and John Whytton record Whytton's care of that charge. Equally intimate are the possessions they left each other: Simon Bulleyne's writing desk and Philip Sidney's books—and a manuscript of his *Arcadia*. But in a wider commonwealth, beyond their intimacy and the

memories of their youth, what figured first and most tellingly was that they
left each other their families.

Amice Cristi Johannes

The ethics of friendship began to turn on the family connection. They are
not easy to hear in the records readily available to historians, the records left
by officials of church and state (and preserved by their successors). A canon
lawyer might be less concerned with the wider friendship that a betrothal
could create than with ensuring whether the consent of the bride (and bride-
groom) had been given, if they were of an age to give it. A liturgist might be
more concerned to stress the religious education of a child than the friendship
its baptism secured between its parents and its godparents. A sheriff or a justice of the peace would be even less concerned with such questions so long
as the king's peace was not endangered. There are moments, though, when
one can hear their voice. One such moment is John Gostlin's final discourse
on friendship when he received the Eucharist with the fellows of Gonville
and Caius as he lay dying. In the seventeenth century his voice comes late in
the day, but in the forenoon of the fifteenth century there is another such
moment. It is a religious lyric, addressed to St. John as Christ's friend—
Amice Cristi—and like many of the religious lyrics of its time, its engaging
directness disguises how much it is the product of theology and ethics.

> Prey for vs the Prynce of Pees,
> Amice Cristi Johannes.
>
> To the now, Cristes dere derlyng,
> That were a maydyn* bothe eld and yyng,
> Myn herte is set to the to syng,
> Amice Christi Johannes.
>
> For thou were so clene a may,[†]
> The preuytes[‡] of heuene forsothe thou say
> Qwan[§] on Crystys brest thov lay,
> Amice Christi Johannes.
>
> Qwan Cryst beforn Pylat was browth,
> Thov clene maydyn, forsok him nouth;
> To deye wyth hym was al thy thowth,
> Amice Christi Johannes.

Crystys moder was the betake,
A maydyn to ben a maydenys make;^{||}
Thov be oure helpe we be not forsake,
Amice Christi Johannes.[69]

    [*]virgin   [†]virgin   [‡]secrets   [§]when   ^{||}companion

No one could imagine that the friendship of Christ and St. John depicted here reflected any friendship one might find in fifteenth-century England: a lyric such as this reflects the same elevated ideal as that depicted on the tomb monument of John Bloxham and John Whytton. But fifteenth-century England was a society where a man needed all the friends he could find, and one might be a saint such as this. The fourteenth-century fellow of Merton depicted in the windows of its chapel, kneeling by the saints depicted there, is presumably making a prayer for help such as this.

Was the language proper for a prayer to such a friend also a way of talking about the kind of friendship that ought to subsist on earth as well as in heaven?[70] It is that possibility I propose to explore here, and its justification lies in that religious lyrics such as this were designed not only for admiration but to be used. Their practical context was preaching and is evident in their presence in the manuscript notebooks of the preaching friars. The ingenuous "Christmas carol" is a creation of the sixteenth century, not the fifteenth, and took shape precisely as the religious lyric lost the homiletic use that had previously shaped it. Precisely how this lyric was used one cannot be sure; and although it is not inconceivable that the lyric might have been sung in such a setting, more probably one should rather imagine the preacher quoting a lyric like this, verse by verse, as the sermon progressed, dwelling on the vivid scenes it depicts and using the verses to drive home his points in a dramatic and memorable form. The evident popularity of this lyric is suggested by its presence in more manuscripts (as a carol) than any other (as well as in more musical settings than any other polyphonic carol). A second justification for the question I have posed is its genre, as one of a number of such lyrics on St. John as Christ's friend; this genre evidently drew to itself the persuasive ideals of friendship that a preacher in fifteenth-century England might draw on as he sought to sway his audience, ethics that extended far beyond the narrow concerns of a liturgist or canon lawyer.

The St. John addressed is the figure traditionally identified as the author of the fourth Gospel in the Bible, and the disciple "quem diligebat Iesus" [whom Jesus loved] mentioned there as well as the author of the apocalyptic book that closes the Bible. The scheme of the lyric is a distinctively Johannine

one. Of the three scenes depicted in the lyric, the first and the last are unique
to the fourth Gospel: the first, the beloved disciple lying in the bosom of
Christ; the second, Christ's trial before Pilate; and the third, the scene at the
foot of the cross when the dying Christ entrusts the care of his mother to
his friend John (the passage that is the epigraph for this chapter). The identification of Christ as the "Prince of Peace," with which the lyric opens, is
similarly Johannine and is derived from Christ's discourse in the fourth
Gospel at the beginning of the passion narrative, his parting gift of his peace
to his disciples, in which for the first time he calls them his "friends."[71]

> Pacem relinquo vobis, pacem meam do vobis: non quomodo mundus dat,
> ego do vobis ... Iam non dicam vos servos: quia servus nescit quid faciat
> dominus eius. Vos autem dixi amicos: quia omnia quaecumque audivi a Pa-
> tre meo, nota feci vobis.

> [Peace I bequeath to you, my own peace I give you, a peace the world can-
> not give, this is my gift to you ... I shall not call you servants any more, be-
> cause a servant does not know his master's business; I call you friends, be-
> cause I have made known to you everything I have learned from my Father.]

Two lyrics addressed to St. John are found uniquely in a manuscript apparently associated with Beverley Minster in Yorkshire, a manuscript that
also contains the Latin processional hymn in honor of St. John, "Psallimus
Cantantes." In the same way that "Psallimus Cantantes" would have been
used in the mass or the festal office in honor of St. John, one can well envisage this lyric to St. John being similarly used in the minster as an adjunct
to preaching, perhaps in the course of the Sunday afternoon sermons during Lent, when the church would have been crowded with laypeople in
preparation for Easter, an audience for whom the vernacular (with a smat-
tering of Latin) would have been appropriate, an audience (as it was described by the medieval philologist D. M. Grisdale in a similar context) "of
trades-people and the country folk and perhaps also a few of the upper
classes together with a sprinkling, how great or small it is impossible to say,
of ecclesiastics secular or regular."[72]

There is probably a trace of the homiletic context in the movement in the
lyric between the plural of the prayer that forms the refrain—"Prey for *vs*
the Prynce of Pees"—and the single voice of the preacher in "Myn herte is
set to the to syng," or as another version of the lyric puts it more directly:
"I shall you tell of Crystes derling." But the most fundamental trace of its

homiletic context is its indirection, in its reference to settings that it assumes its audience will already know or will have explained to them by a preacher, "Qwan on Crystys brest thov lay" or "Qwan Cryst beforn Pylat was browth" and so on. Such a preacher in fifteenth-century England, quite possibly a friar, would seek to bring his message home to his audience in terms they could recognize; and the lyric adds details to the gospel story that deftly translated the scene into the world of his time. The version I have given here is that derived from the manuscript in Trinity College, Cambridge, written (it would appear) in the first half of the fifteenth century: at a time shortly after the deaths of the sworn brothers who have figured in this book, men such as William Neville and John Clanvowe or John Bloxham and John Whytton; at the same point when Nicholas Molyneux and John Winter were making their oaths to each other in the church of St. Martin at Harfleur and when one catches a glimpse in Richard Strangways's notebook of the familiar sight of the sworn brothers of fifteenth-century England.

These details added to the gospel account translate the friendship of Christ and St. John into the terms of their friendship. One of these is the lyric's assertion that "To deye wyth hym was al thy thowth," for this is not in the gospel account.[73] What we are hearing here are the promises of the sworn brothers that we have heard over and again earlier in this book: in the *Knightes Tale*, that they will never fail each other "for to dyen in the peyne, til that the deeth departe shal us tweyne," in *Amys and Amylion* to hold together "while thei leved." It is the fatal promise of Christy Graham to his sworn brother: "I swear I'll be the first that die" that one still hears in King James's oath to George Villiers that "for, god so loue me, as I desyre onlie to liue in this worlde, for youre saike" and in William Cornwallis's report of the oath of two sworn brothers that "they will liue and dye together." In this lyric John has been transformed into Christ's sworn brother, in the same manner that the thirteenth-century poem of *Genesis and Exodus* presented Isaac as the sworn brother of Abimelech and Abram as the "breðre sworen" of Mamre, Eschol, and Aner in his retelling of the Old Testament narrative (for readers who, as its introduction puts it, knew no book learning).[74]

The translation was evidently a familiar one, which a preacher could use to press home John's closeness to Christ.

As he in his passion to his dere moder
Toke the for her keper, her son, and his brother,
Pray that owr hartes may most of all other
Jhesum semper amare.

Those verses are from another of this genre of lyrics to John as Christ's friend,[75] and its presentation of John as Christ's sworn *brother* is also made explicit—in a homiletic context—in the manuscript of a sermon apparently preached in a monastic cathedral church in the north of England (reminiscent of Beverley) between 1389 and 1404, judging by its reference to Pope Boniface IX. The sermon dwells on the dialogue between Christ and Mary at the foot of the cross, in which John in the same way becomes Christ's sworn brother.

> "Now Modir'," a seiþ, "gode Modir', be noþinge desamaied nor' disesid for
> Me, vor' I go streith to þe vadir' of heuene'. nor' be nat aferit who schal cum-
> fort þe & do þe solas hir' whan Ich am ago'. vor I schal leue her' wiþ þe Ion,
> Myn owne der' broþere, þat schal rule þe & loke to þe as to his owne modir'."[76]

A second such detail—which translates the lyric into the familiar world of late medieval England—is the line in which the lyric affirms that "[t]he preuytes of heuene forsothe thou say / Qwan on Crystys brest thov lay." This too is not in the gospel account. "Preuytes" are secrets, and the line makes John the "secretarius" of Christ in the court of heaven, as Piers Gaveston was made "secretarium et camerarium regni summum" [the highest secretary and chamberlain of the realm] in the court on earth of his sworn brother Edward II: the role discussed in the last chapter that was to become the "secretary" of the sixteenth century, educated in the new humanist learning and privy to his patron's secrets. In the familiar notion of the fifteenth century, the secrets John learned there, when he lay in the bosom of Christ, were the secrets to be revealed in the apocalypse with which the Bible closes.

A third is that phrase "the Prynce of Pees" with which the lyric opens, emphasized by another version in which John himself may be being presented as "the Prynce of Pece" and his fidelity to Christ conflated with Christ's own death, which the mass commemorates.[77] A lay audience in the fifteenth century was more likely to identify this with the "peace," the "pax," that they exchanged in the mass than in the terms of the text of the fourth Gospel: the familiar gesture that in the mass preceded communion (or stood in its place) when the priest took the peace of God as it were from the altar and it passed among those present, each receiving it from his neighbor and passing it on in return; the ritual act I described in the first chapter of this book that is arguably the gesture depicted on the tombstone of William Neville and John Clanvowe. The association with the mass is made explicit in the lyric to John as Christ's friend that opens with the "cena Domini" [the Lord's Supper] that then and for centuries after was a familiar vernacular term for the Eucharist. The fourth Gospel does not contain the account, given in the other Gospels, of the institution of the Eucharist at the Lord's Supper. This detail the author of the lyric added to the account that the fourth Gospel does give of John lying in the bosom of Christ.

> To Almyghty God pray for pees,
> Amice Christi Johannes.

> O glorius Johan Euangelyste,
> Best belouyd with Jhesu Cryst,
> In cena Domini vpon hys bryst
> Eius vidisti archana.*[78]

*You saw his secrets.

It is this familiar ritual among friends and neighbors in the fifteenth century that the "peace" of this lyric would most readily have suggested for a lay audience. It imparts to John's friendship with Christ a homely value that corresponded to the work of the Eucharist in traditional Christianity—the same moral tradition that was expressed in John Gostlin's last supper with his confreres in Gonville and Caius: the peace that was the positive bond of friendship, not peace as the opposite of war or as the effect of victory.

When traditional Christianity comprehended sworn brotherhood within the mass, it was responding to that understanding of the Eucharist. The tomb monument of William Neville and John Clanvowe expresses that understanding in graphic terms by placing the "wedded" brotherhood implied by their "impaled" arms beside the kiss of peace that it also depicts, the one as the counterpart to the other. Peace is also the leading term in the heady trio with which the monk chronicler of Worcester Abbey characterized a vow of ritual brotherhood, "pace, amicitia, fraternitate, et pacto et sacramentis confirmata" [peace, friendship, and brotherhood made fast by bond and oaths].[79] Henry of Huntingdon simply says "osculum pacis invicem datum est" [they exchanged the kiss of peace].[80] The "sub religionis et pacis obtentu" [appearance of piety and peace] that Giraldus de Barri firmly places at the beginning of the account that I quoted in the first chapter would have been immediately comprehensible to his audience in these terms. The scriptural basis for such a response to sworn brotherhood lay in the accounts in 1 and 2 Samuel of David's ritual brotherhood with Jonathan before the Lord (from which the epigraph for chapter 1 is taken),[81] and the familiar text of the Latin Vulgate version appears to have influenced several of the accounts

of sworn brotherhood written by ecclesiastics: the same term *foedus* employed
in 1 Samuel is used both by William of Malmesbury in this connection and
by the cleric who composed the account of Edward II's sworn brotherhood
with Pier Gaveston in the Cottonian manuscripts; the sealing of David and
Jonathan's ritual brotherhood by the symbolic gift of personal objects is
echoed in the *Worcester Chronicle* and the kiss of peace between David and
Jonathan of 1 Samuel is echoed in Henry of Huntingdon's terms.[82]

But the climax of the poem is not the fidelity of John, as if it stood alone.
Its movement is in the same direction as in the friendships that this chapter
has been following: from friendship to family. In this, perhaps more than in
anything else, it translates the friendship of Christ and John into the ethics
of fifteenth-century England, to their place in a world of moral responsibility beyond mutual support, however faithful. The end of the lyric, in
ethics as well as in narrative, is the scene at the foot of the cross in which
Christ entrusts his mother to John's care: the paradoxical depiction of the
divine Christ, in the mystery of the incarnation, entrusting the care of his
mother—the Virgin Mary and the mother of God—to the man who, after the manner of the flesh, was his own sworn brother.

Friendship's Doubts

There is—at this point in the argument—a "but" to be added. If the ethics
of friendship pointed to a wider moral responsibility beyond mere fidelity
and mutual support, can one not detect in that wider ground a reservation
about friendship itself? Let me give an example, from the passage in William
Cornwallis's essay "Of Loue" on the motives that might prompt sworn
brotherhood. Two men might become sworn brothers, he warns, simply because both are poor—or both are rich.

> I laugh, and wonder, at the straunge occasions that men take now a dayes to
> say they love: If they meete with a fellowe at a Feaste, or in a Potte, If their
> Delightes bee anye thing a kinne, or theyr Faces anye thing alike; If their
> Countries be one, or their landes neare adioyning; if they be both rich, or
> both poore, or indeed if their new-fangled inuentions can finde out any oc-
> casion, they are sworn brothers, they will liue and dye together: but they
> scarce sleep in this mind, the one comes to make vse of the other, and that
> spoyles all; he entered this league not to impaire, but to profit himselfe.[83]

Might two men have become sworn brothers simply because they were both
poor, as Cornwallis claims? There is a surprising edge to the details in Corn-

wallis's hostile account, when compared to the sworn brothers of my first chapter. The two officials in Chaucer's *Freres Tale* swear brotherhood as spontaneously as in Cornwallis's characterization (or as the future king Edward II and Piers Gaveston are said to have done) and the peasant farmers in Chaucer's *Pardoners Tale* swear brotherhood in a tavern. As Cornwallis implies, sworn brotherhood was indeed used to reinforce bonds of local friendship between men who were neighbors, and his description that "they will liue and dye together" is an accurate account of the form that the vow of two sworn brothers recognizably took. If his characterization (however hostile) was accurate in these details, might he not also have been accurate in claiming that two men could become sworn brothers simply because they were poor?

The claim would have had an edge, and a man like Cornwallis knew how to manipulate the fears of the privileged world he was seeking to enter when he published his essays in 1600; close to their surface lay fears of sedition. But what might—at one level—appear as sedition might seem like something else to those outside. The ballad of Adam Bell and Clym of the Clough is such a tale of two yeoman farmers who swear brotherhood simply because they are poor: no gentlemen, but men who had worked their land with their own hands and having fallen foul of the law become outlaws. Their bloody violence, when they break into Carlisle to rescue William of Cloudesly, might well have sent a shiver through the audience in the hall of a great house on a winter's evening.

> They called the porter to a councell,
> And wronge hys necke in two,
> And kest hym in a depe dongeon,
> And toke the keys him fro.

But judging by the patchwork of verses in the ballad, the same storyteller might have given his tale a different color in another setting and for another audience. The censorship that could be exercised over print hardly applied to a performer in a tavern or at a fair: and such a detail as the porter's neck wrung in two might easily have been replaced there with the sadistic justice of the peace:

> "Thou speakest proudely," sayd the iustyce;
> "I shall hange the with my hande":
> Full well that herde his bretheren two,
> There styll as they dyd stande.

One wonders what the response might then have been to the boldness of Adam Bell and Clym of the Clough?

> They loused theyr arowes bothe at ones,
> Of no man had they drede;
> The one hyt the iustyce, the other the sheryf,
> That bothe theyr sydes gan blede.[84]

Whether the response was a (not entirely disagreeable) fright or a roar of approval from a less than sober audience at a fair might well have turned on the occasion and the time, the implications of the tune that the performer chose, and the antics and gestures he or she applied—this was the craft of such storytellers and how they earned their keep.

But if two men might become sworn brothers simply because they were both poor, what of that other claim: that they might become sworn brothers simply because they were both rich? The rich needed friends as much as the poor. How innocuous was a league of that kind likely to be? Among the humanist-educated men of the sixteenth century like William Cornwallis, one readily sees the fears of collusion that sworn brotherhood aroused: men like this were anxious to distinguish themselves from the equivocal mechanisms of friendship, by which men had traditionally advanced themselves—and all the more so because of the degree to which they themselves employed them. When Gabriel Harvey accused Thomas Nashe of coming to Robert Greene's defense because he was his sworn brother, he was wielding with precision the reservations his contemporaries held about sworn brotherhood, sufficient to draw blood.

Are these reservations something new in the sixteenth century? Or are they only then more apparent? In the tomb monuments of William Neville and John Clanvowe or John Bloxham and John Whytton there seems to be no trace of them, but they were I think there; and the telltale clue to their presence is that very eucharistic practice that accommodated such sworn friendship, which this chapter has followed from the eleventh century to the seventeenth. No doubt the chronicler Juvénal des Ursins was voicing a widely held view when he described the sworn brotherhood of the dukes of Orléans and Burgundy in the fifteenth century as "an oath sworn on the precious body of Jesus Christ," but is that not to gloss in a broad expression the insistent detail that their vows to each other were not made within the mass? The "lords of Orléans and of Burgundy heard the mass together and received the Body of Our Lord; *and before doing this* they swore true love and brotherhood together."[85] The same detail reappears in the twelfth-century account given by Giraldus de Barri: "*Finally* with a celebration of the mass and the prayers of priests, they are joined indissolubly as if by a betrothal."[86] In the evidence provided by Juvénal des Ursins and Giraldus de Barri alike, the mass is not the setting for the vows of sworn brotherhood but rather follows; and in the careful proprieties of Giraldus's satire, the separation in time is accompanied by a corresponding separation in space, between door and altar. "Postmodum ecclesiam intrantes" [Then going into the church]: Giraldus's telltale phrase indicates what would have been self-evident to his audience. They correspond to the familiar rubric "ante ostium Ecclesiae" [before the door of the church] in the betrothal liturgies. A betrothal was made at the church door. It was there that the rites of baptism began. It was there also, at the church door, that the vows of sworn brotherhood were exchanged, the two sworn brothers then receiving Holy Communion together in the mass within that followed. The spacious porches of many English parish churches are a trace of rituals at the church door like this.[87] The reforms of the sixteenth century preserved that careful line. King James's letter to the duke of Buckingham (and the duke's to him) look forward to a reaffirmation of the league between them in the Eucharist, but it had not been made there; and John Gostlin's gesture in the chapel of Gonville and Caius recalled a bond reaffirmed but not necessarily created in the Eucharist. To read this eucharistic practice as an unreserved endorsement of the vows of ritual brotherhood is crucially to miss the careful boundary at the same time being drawn by the shape of such a liturgy: the communion was not the setting for the vows of sworn brotherhood, it was a response to them, an amplification of their significance, a public embodiment of them in a wide world of ethical obligation.

It is not difficult to see the reason for that reserve. The dangers of friendship, the subject of the last chapter, were ethical as well as pragmatic. Friendship required fidelity, but what if that fidelity required one to act *un*-ethically? How then was friendship to be distinguished from mere collusion and cynical self-advancement? That was the rub, and there was no simple nostrum that could avoid it, although the indirection of the language of friendship provided a circumspect path about it. The problem lay in the ends to which friendship might be put. When in the romance of Amys and Amylion the two sworn brothers make their vows to each other, they vow not to fail each other: not only in "wele" and "wo" but also not in "wrong and ryght," and the formula equivocally does not restrict the vow only to the wrongs *suffered*.[88] A potential for wrong as well as a potential for right: there lay the ethical problem.

But was there not also a more fundamental dilemma, beyond the particular motives that might prompt the sworn friendship of two men? I have argued in this chapter that the friendship created by a vow of sworn brotherhood— or that created by the godbrotherhood of baptism or by a betrothal—were part of the wider fabric of obligation and friendship that constituted England's traditional society. The unreserved vows of sworn brothers were set within the constraints of this wider and potentially compromising world. How probable or likely then were they? Amis and Amylion could be certain of being made saints by their friendship only within the pages of a romance.

The eucharistic practice that I have followed in this chapter was, I would suggest, a response to that dilemma and one that points the historian to the ethical problem at its heart. The nature of this response is easier to grasp if one views it from the wider perspective provided by the two halves of Europe, the Greek and Byzantine East and the Latin and Roman West, which from the eleventh century began to encounter each other again. Sworn brotherhood was as much a property of the Greek half of Europe as its Latin counterpart, and the crusaders had no difficulty in recognizing the Greek *adelphopoiesis* (the Slav *pobratimstvo*) as the equivalent of the sworn brotherhood of the Latin West:[89] it employed the same language of brotherhood; the ritual kiss arguably played the same prominent part in its ritual;[90] and in the troubled history of its canon law one can see in explicit terms the same reservations with which Catholic Europe regarded its western counterpart. Ritual brotherhood, warned a twelfth-century Greek ecclesiastic, could lead to "many sins,"[91] and Byzantine canon law has variously attempted to restrict the rite or to preclude its use altogether, although apparently with limited success, judging by its continuing inclusion in the liturgical collections. The *adelphopoiesis* was to remain as current in the sixteenth and seventeenth centuries as its equivalent in the West.

From at least the fourteenth century, the Franciscan friars in Dalmatia were employing a rite for creating sworn brothers among Latin Catholics— an *Ordo ad fratres faciendum*—that corresponded to the *pobratimstvo* familiar among their neighbors that incorporated at least one of its prayers, in a Latin translation. The rite printed here is taken from a fourteenth-century manuscript in the library of the Catholic parish church of St. John in Trogir, in modern Croatia, on the Adriatic coast.[92] According to a note at the end, the manuscript was completed in 1394. It includes masses for various Franciscan saints and appears to have been compiled by Catholic Franciscan friars when they arrived around 1370 in the area, where they were subsequently to exercise a considerable role. The opening of the missal, "Incipit ordo missalis canonicorum secundum consuetudinem romane curie," identifies it as the Roman Missal, at least apparently as far as these Franciscan friars were concerned.

Its modern editor, the Dominican scholar O. Antonin Zaninović, appended documents from the historical archives in Dubrovnik in the second half of the fifteenth century, describing the use of the rite (and the kiss of peace in this context) by two Dubrovnik musicians earlier in the century, close to the time when Nicholas Molyneux and John Winter swore their brotherhood in the church at Harfleur in France. He also adds the recollections of the rite among elderly people to whom he spoke. "*Pobrastimstvo* created kinship with the whole household so that no one from that house could marry anyone from the house of the other *pobratim*."

Was this the rite that was used in the Latin West? This may have been the case. The Trogir manuscript appears to have drawn on a number of manuscript sources, its author adapting and combining them. The last of the four prayers in the rite follows closely a prayer in the *pobratimstvo* and appears to be a translation from the Slavonic,[93] but I have been unable to find the same close parallels for the first three prayers. A Latin rite like the *Ordo ad fratres faciendum* may well prove to have been used more widely than in Dalmatia alone, but one needs to be cautious in making that judgment, and not only because the impediment to marriage described by Zaninović suggests a status in canon law (at least to that respondent) that evidently was not present in the West. The principal reason for doubt lies in what at first sight might seem only a technical point, which I will come to in a moment; but the most evident difference is something immediately tangible. The presence of this office in the Trogir manuscript (as in the Greek and Slavonic manuscripts) is a material trace of the presiding role played by the priest, as he read from the manuscript or held it in his hands: explicitly recognizing the brotherhood or sisterhood of the rite in his function as a priest, and in doing so taking the center of the stage. In the East the character of the rite was evidently given by the official who performed it, but in the Latin West it was given rather by the setting in which it took place, that "holy place," as I argued at the onset of this chapter, of which Giraldus wrote in such resonant terms. In the Latin West a priest was required to say the mass; but the practice appears in these terms more a customary use of the Eucharist directed to social ends, among men and women who no doubt regarded themselves as good Christians, but not a matter for canon law or needing a specific liturgical office. At the heart of the practice in the Latin West was not the office or indeed the role of the priest but the *setting*. It is on that point that I want to pause.

The characteristic setting for the creation of ritual brotherhood in the Latin West was not a distinctive liturgy at the altar. Its setting in the descriptions that one reads seems to be the porch and church door where the vows of sworn brotherhood could be exchanged. Nor was the church door the only place where they could be made. In Chaucer's *Pardoners Tale* the setting for the vows of the tale's sworn brothers is a tavern. The *Pardoners Tale* is set in Flanders, as the sworn brotherhood of the *Shipmannes Tale* is set in France. In the *Freres Tale* (which is set in England) the vows are made in the countryside. Chaucer might have intended to suggest an impropriety here, but I think this was not necessarily the case. One has to remember that betrothals promising a marriage could also be made without any impropriety in both of these settings and in England continued to be, well into the seventeenth century.[94]

The distinction is not that between a secular form in the Latin West and an ecclesiastical form among the Greeks and Slavs. A judgment like this would employ precisely the scant ecclesiology that I criticized earlier in this chapter, identifying the church only with its officials. A setting outside a church building could be seen as making the vows *more* Christian, part of the moral economy of religion rather than a narrowly sacerdotal matter. But the implication—that the vows were regarded as complete without the mass that followed—is underlined by the vows of sworn brotherhood depicted in the *Freres Tale* and the *Pardoners Tale.* The vows in these two tales are clearly complete without priestly blessing, and they suggest that this would have been the case also with vows of sworn brotherhood made at the church door, whether or not followed by communion within the church. The point is rather that the church door was a setting that signified in *both* a religious and a secular context: the first in being physically part of the church building, the second in being an open space that ensured that the vows were publicly known (an evident fact then emphasized by the procession around the church that Giraldus de Barri mentions), sufficiently public that the community could stand as witnesses (or perhaps objectors) to them. This was also the significance of the term "publice" [in public] used in the Lanercrost chronicle of Edward II and Piers Gaveston, "et vocavit ipsum publice fratrem suum": that he had called him his brother in public and before witnesses.[95]

In this, Latin Christianity was making a careful, theological connection across the dangers of mutual appropriation that were present when the communion sealed the oath of two sworn brothers in the eyes of those around them. That dilemma was felt both among Greek Christians and Latin Christians, but the differing liturgical responses were shaped within two distinctive theological worlds. The general communion of social tradition required reconciliation between those making their communions together and was an opportunity to step down from quarrels, without losing face, of which participants or their neighbors had grown weary: an enabling rhetoric that allowed one to step down not under duress but under the higher demands of the sacrament. Its impact was to make communion for the laity rare and correspondingly awesome. Two individuals could still make their communions together, but when they did, the general communions invested that act with the same powerfully constraining social implications. So much was common property to Greek and Latin Christianity alike: the differing responses to sworn brotherhood lie in what might at first seem a technical detail, but it is, I would suggest, something much more. In the *adelphopoiesis* and the *pobratimstvo* the bread and wine are not consecrated by the priest: the elements are rather brought to the liturgy *already* consecrated. The *Ordo ad fratres faciendum* evidently adopted the same device. That the Trogir manuscript assumed that the elements would be preconsecrated as in the *pobratimstvo* is strongly suggested by its provision of a communion antiphon but not an offertory antiphon—a part of the mass directly attached to the consecration—and suggests that strictly the rite is indeed as the manuscript describes it, an "ordo," not a "missa"—a "rite," not the mass itself.

In Catholic and Orthodox theology alike, when the bread and wine in the mass are taken, blessed, and broken by the priest, they are *changed* into the body and blood of Christ. In that sense the *adelphopoiesis* and its Slavonic equivalent are not strictly eucharistic at all. Their shape is rather a distinctively Greek liturgy of praise. Characteristically the prayers of the *adelphopoiesis* (and the *pobratimstvo*) open with the praise of God as creator, as king, and as savior and place the blessing of the participants that follows in that context.

Lord God almighty who created man in his own image and likeness and gave him eternal life . . .
Lord our God, who has granted our petitions for our salvation . . .
Lord our God, you are the perfecter of love and teacher of the world and saviour of all.[96]

The prayers of the *Ordo ad fratres faciendum* show the traces of the same liturgical form. Such a blessing—strictly a blessing of God—places such rites with those for the cutting of a boy's hair or beard, for a betrothal, the prayers for rain, first fruits, or the blessing of seed corn that are also found in the manuscripts that contain the *adelphopoiesis* or its Slavonic equivalent: things that have a natural integrity and potential of their own, to which the believer responds in praise of their creator.[97]

A Catholic Rite for Making Brothers
This rite is taken from a fourteenth-century manuscript in the library of the
Catholic parish church of St. John in Trogir, in modern Croatia, on the
Adriatic coast.

Ordo ad fratres faciendum

Introitus.
Suscepimus, Deus, misericordiam tuam in medio templi tui secundum
nomen tuum, Deus, ita et laus tua in fines terrae iustitia plena est dextera tua.

Ps.
Magnus Dominus et laudabilis nimis in civitate Dei nostri in monte sancto
eius. Gloria Patri et Sicut erat.

Kyrie eleison, Christe eleison, Kyrie eleison.
Pater noster . . . Et ne nos inducas in tentationem.
R Sed libera nos a malo.
Salvos fac servos tuos. Deus meus, sperantes in te. Mitte eis, Domine, aux-
ilium de sancto. Et de Sion teure eos. teure eos.

Domine, exaudi orationem meam. Et clamor meus ad te veniat.

Dominus vobiscum. Et cum spiritu tuo.

Oratio:
Intercedente pro nobis et vobis beata et gloriosa semperque unigeniti Dei
genitrice Maria et beato Petro apostolorum principe cui tradidit Dominus
potestatem in coelis et in terra ligandi atque solvendi et peccata populi
dimittendi, ipse vos absolvat ab omnibus vestris peccatis praeteritis, praesentibus et futuris et liberet vos ab omni malo. Per . . .

Oratio:
Deus, qui sanctis apostolis tuis praeceptum dedisti, ut sancta divinitate se
invicem fratres vocarent, et Petrum et Paulum, Jacobum et Johanem fratres
constituisti bene✝dic hos famulos tuos ill. et ill. qui se tuo nomine fratres con-
stituunt, ut amodo deinceps per te hic et in futuro valeant coronari. Per . . .

A rite for making brothers.

Introit.
We have received your mercy, O God, in the midst of your temple. O God, even as your name, so does your praise extend to the ends of the earth. Your right hand is full of righteousness (Ps. 47:10–11)

Psalm.
Great is the Lord and highly to be praised in the city of our God upon his holy hill. (Ps. 47, with doxology following "Glory be to the Father").

Lord have mercy, Christ have mercy, Lord have mercy.
The Lord's Prayer—"Our Father."
My God, save your servants. That put their trust in you (based on Ps. 85:2). O Lord, send them help from the sanctuary. And watch over them out of Sion (based on Ps. 19:3).

O Lord, hear my prayer. And let my cry come unto you (Ps. 101:2).

The Lord be with you. And with your spirit.

Prayer:
Through the intercession of the blessed and glorious Mary Mother of the eternally begotten Son of God, for us and for you, and of the blessed Peter prince of the apostles, to whom the Lord gave power in heaven and on earth to bind and loose and to absolve the sins of his people, may he release you from all your sins, past, present and to come and deliver you from every evil. Through . . .

Prayer:
O God, who commanded your holy apostles that by holy divinity they should call each other brothers and united Peter and Paul, James and John as brothers, ble✝ss these your servants [name] and [name] who in your name unite themselves as brothers, so that now and henceforth they may be worthy to be crowned by you here and in the age to come. Through . . .

Oratio:

Omnipotens Deus noster, qui es ante saecula et permanes in saecula saeculorum, qui dignatus es visitare humanum genus per uterum Dei Genitricis
et virginis Mariae, emitte sanctum angelum tuum super hos famulos tuos ill.
et ill. ut se diligant, sicut dilexerunt se sancti apostoli tui Petrus et Paulus, et
Andreas et Jacobus, et Johanes et Thomas, Jacobus, Philippus, Matthaeus,
Simon, Thadeus, Matthias et sancti martyres tui Sergius et Bachus, Cosmas
et Damianus, non dilectione carnali, sed fide et dilectione Spiritus Sancti, ut
in ipsa dilectione permaneant omnibus diebus vitae suae. Per . . .

Epistola:
Gaudete, perfecti estote: Require in benedictione navis novae.

Tractus:
Ecce quam bonum et quam iucundum habitare fratres in unum. Sicut unguen-
tum in capite eius quod descendit in barbam, barbam Aaron.

Evangelium:
Ambulans Dominus Jesus iuxta mare Galileae . . . Require in festo sancti
Andreae apostoli.

Communio:
Ecce quam bonum et quam iucundum habitare fratres in unum.

Oratio:
Dominator, Domine Deus noster, qui fecisti hominem ad ymaginem et
similitudinem tuam, qui iusisti sanctis apostolis tuis Philippo et Bartholo-
maeo fratres fieri, non colligatos carnalis consuetudine, sed fide et Spiritu
Sancto et quomodo sanctos martires Sergius et Bachum fratres dignatus es
vocare, ita bene✝dic hos famulos tuos ill. et ill., non colligatos carnali consuetudine, sed fide et Spiritu Sancto, da inter eos esse amorem sine odio et
sine scandalo omnibus diebus vitae suae, per intercessionem sanctae Dei
Genetrice et Virginis Mariae et beati ill. omniumque sanctorum, quia te de-
cet omnis honor et gloria, et adorare Patrem et Filium et Spiritum Sanctum
nunc et semper et per infinita saecula saeculorum. Amen.

Prayer:

O Lord our God Almighty, who was and is and is to come, who did not disdain to be born of humankind in the womb of the Virgin Mary Mother of God, send your holy angel upon these your servants [name] and [name] that they may love each other, as your holy apostles Peter and Paul loved each other, and Andrew and James, and John and Thomas, James, Philip, Matthew, Simon, Thaddeus, Matthias and your holy martyrs Sergius and Bacchus, Cosmas and Damian, not through the bonds of birth, but through faith and by the love of the Holy Spirit, and that they may abide in the same love all the days of their life. Through . . .

The Epistle—from Paul's Epistle to the Philippians, chapter 4.

Tract.

"Behold, how good and joyful it is for brethren to dwell together. It is like the ointment upon the head that ran down unto Aaron's beard" (Ps. 132:1–2).

The Gospel—from the Gospel of Matthew, chapter 4.

Communion.

Behold, how good and joyful it is for brethren to dwell together (Ps. 132:1).

Prayer:

O Lord, our God Almighty who created man in your own image and likeness, and who willed your holy apostles Philip and Bartholomew to be made brothers, not bound by the bonds of birth, but through faith and by the Holy Spirit, and in like manner granted the holy martyrs Sergius and Bacchus to be called brothers, so ble✝ss these your servants [name] and [name], not united by the bonds of birth but through faith and the Holy Spirit, grant them love without enmity and without stumbling all the days of their life, through the intercession of the holy Virgin Mary, Mother of God, [name], and all the saints, for yours is the praise, the glory and the worship of the Father and the Son and the Holy Spirit, now and forever, world without end. Amen.

This same distinction has also been detected by historical liturgists in the differing rites for marriage in Greek and Latin Christianity, a Latin rite that came to be shaped from the eleventh century by the exchange of promises followed by communion and a Greek liturgy preserving an older liturgical tradition that locates the liturgical action in a prayer of praise. In the one case this has been described as the support and clothing of a promise, whereas in the other it is the celebration and receiving of a gift.[98] The fully eucharistic response to sworn brotherhood in the Latin West was rather in the eleventh century something fundamentally new, an expression of that wider desire to place the Eucharist at the center of social life that swept across Latin Europe in the eleventh century and that took as one of its many forms the desire to employ the Eucharist in binding a covenant or an oath.[99]

As much as its Greek equivalent, the eucharistic practice of the Latin West takes the historian back to the ethical dilemma within sworn brotherhood; but its basis there was a distinctively Augustinian understanding of grace, of the kind that shaped Christianity in the West. Both cultures recognized the good in the vows of sworn brothers only as something still incomplete and yet to be realized, as a potential only: but while the one (in the Latin West) characteristically viewed the potential good as it were from below, in a world of defective human relations, the other sees it as it were from above, from the viewpoint of the integrity of creation. In the one case, the response was a ritual shaped by the Eucharist, as a source of sustaining grace in an imperfect world. In the other, the shape of the liturgy was a prayer of praise for its creator. This second was a much older liturgical tradition, but it had carried and still carried the problem that praise must be spoken. A distinctive office emerged in Greek and Slav Christianity for the creation of ritual brotherhood and sisterhood, and with it a troubled canon law that repeatedly sought to legislate explicitly for its ambiguities and repeatedly failed to do so. Significantly the Latin rite employed in Dalmatia was dogged by the same troubled canon law as its Slav counterpart, and corresponding concerns about its status in canon law may prove to be a trace of its use elsewhere.[100] In the Latin West more widely, that troubled history appears to have been eluded by enfolding sworn brotherhood tacitly within the existing forms of the Eucharist.

Did it do so at the cost of an accommodating ambiguity? Greek Christianity responded with circumspection, only recognizing the potential good in the vows of sworn brothers and sisters. Latin Christianity conceded a great deal more. But a judgment that this was solely tacking with the wind fails to grasp the nature of this response, as it would have been experienced from within. Why, to put the point sharply, did individuals in this culture *wish* to

seal the bond by communion at the altar at all? The repeated answer this culture gives—however foreign it may seem to us now—is that there these were
oaths "upon God's body" and upon the relics of the saints: there the bodies
of the saints lay, in their relics preserved by the altar, and there the communicants became partakers of Christ's own body and blood. As traditional
society was touched by the currents of religious reform, the relics came to
eclipse the communion; but it is the communion that most directly unlocks
for the later historian what this answer meant, precisely because the vener-
ation of relics can seem to modern eyes so grotesque. The disproportion between these dry remains and the devotion directed to them seems to make
nonsense of the act, but there lay the point. For the devotion to make sense,
it was absolutely necessary to perceive these relics in substance as something
other than they appeared to be.

What was that? "Heaven" has always been a vague and undefined belief
in traditional Orthodox Christianity, lacking any clearly explicit place in the
creed. What the creeds look toward is the resurrection of the dead: "Et
exspecto resurrectionem mortuorum" [And I look for the resurrection of the
dead].[101] If the saints will share in that general resurrection, their dry and des-
iccated remains are, in a real and substantial sense, not the end; their destiny
is to be embodied again—and they will then stand as witnesses: that is the
point. If the vows of sworn brothers are made beside the relics of the saints,
then those saints hold those vows in their keeping and on the day of the resurrection will stand as witnesses to the fidelity—or the infidelity—of the
oath takers. And if those vows are sealed in the Eucharist? Then Christ himself becomes witness to them. Oaths are the instruments of an oral culture and
are bound by the testimony of witnesses, but witnesses could be found not
only among one's neighbors or friends, they could also be sought among figures that were celestial and divine; and within the terms of that imaginative
world, such a prospect was awesome and compelling beyond all words. The
saints and Christ himself would stand as witnesses to the fidelity of the oath.

Is this not what the tomb monument of William Neville and John Clanvowe was designed to convey? One ought perhaps to have guessed this from
the onset, for over and again this culture's response to the equivocal unity
of two sworn brothers was in terms of the oath itself: in the expressions it
employed to characterize them, as "sworn" or "wedded" brothers, fratres
"iurati," "conjurati," "foederati," "confederati," "adjurati"; in the language
of "league," of "fedus" and "foedera" that their descriptions employ; in the
stories about sworn friendship that turn on the testing of that oath; and in
the compelling imagery on their tombs. What the design of these tombs depict is their *vow,* here on the tomb of these two knights in the kiss of peace

that affirmed it and in the "wedded" imagery that corresponded to it. Is it not then intelligible why the bodies of two such sworn brothers should have been placed by the altar to await the resurrection there? There they lay by the relics of the saints and the body of Christ, the witnesses who at the resurrection would rise with them and affirm the fidelity of that oath. The bodies of William Neville and John Clanvowe are likely long since to have turned to dust or been scattered, but their tomb asserts that their vow has not, that it touched something that would never die. It asserts that at the resurrection Christ himself will stand by them and witness to their fidelity.

This was indeed to tack with the wind. By allowing the vows of sworn brothers to be confirmed by the Eucharist, Latin Christianity gave them a potentially binding force far more constraining within the terms of their imaginative world than the witness of any priest, but this was not a mere appropriation of religion to secular ends. Steadfastly this persisted in looking toward two ends. For the Eucharist to be celebrated for sworn brothers, for their friends and their families implied—for the gesture to have meaning—that in some sense it was *not* being celebrated for their enemies (or even that it was being celebrated against them). But the Eucharist affirmed that Christ died for all, and the change wrought in the bread and wine by their consecration transformed these elements into a universal sacramental sign that knew no boundaries: it was that sign that was then offered and received in communion.[102] It was the genius of Latin Christianity to have recognized that the Eucharist needed no protection, that it was its own protection: the very celestial and divine figures who stood as witnesses to the oath of two sworn brothers would also stand as witnesses to that acceptance of that universal sign.

To draw my conclusions together, this chapter has argued that the bound friendship of traditional culture was dogged by suspicions of collusion and self-advancement, of which its ideals seem to show no trace. The actual practices of friendship tell a different and fuller story, whether these are the practices of countenance and commendation explored in the last chapter or the eucharistic practice followed in this. To rediscover these practices, one needs to look at the material evidence left by their presence not as transparent windows on the past but as the tools once employed, artifacts in the most material sense that still bear the traces of the practices that produced them. Indeed, in this light the ideals of friendship themselves appear as such instruments, precisely because of their capacity tactfully to efface and negotiate the dangers of friendship.

These dangers were not only pragmatic. They were also ethical, a product of the equivocal place friendship occupied, caught within the network of obligation and kinship that cemented the traditional society of England. This wider place gave to friendship the formal and objective character with which this book began. It gave it also its equivocal capacity, to help men and women to live in peace and friendship among themselves, across their divisions, but also its capacity to intensify those very divisions. The ethics of friendship were a response to the potential for a peaceful life. Its tactfully enabling gestures were a way of negotiating the dangers of divisiveness.

A short question remains, a simple but perhaps a troubling one; and it may well have struck the reader at several points as unasked. It concerns that kiss arguably depicted on the tomb monument of William Neville and John Clanvowe, a gesture that has marked each stage of my argument. The question was put by the reader in church history in the University of Cambridge, Dr. Eamon Duffy, during a discussion with the historian of ritual, Professor John Bossy, in a BBC radio program in 1999, which discussed the tomb monument of these two fourteenth-century knights. Its immediate context was a discussion of the various forms taken by the ritual kiss, the kiss of peace. This simple question is, Did not lovers also kiss?

JOHN BOSSY: Kissing, at least according to St Paul, is a general demonstration of Christian charity: you greet one another with a "holy kiss," which means it is a spiritual kiss rather than a carnal kiss; you perform the kiss of peace either as it were statutorily at mass at the time of communion, or in preparation for communion, or as an alternative to communion.

EAMON DUFFY: If Neville and Clanvowe kiss, what sort of a kiss is being exchanged?

JOHN BOSSY: I would think it would be a kiss of peace and that the object of it would be to create some special relation of brotherhood between them, but it would be a holy kiss in my opinion. Certainly St Augustine says there are three sorts of kisses: there is the holy kiss; there is the kiss of betrayal, the Judas kiss; and there is the impure kiss; and you have to be careful that you do not get one when you want the other one.

EAMON DUFFY: Lovers kissed too in the Middle Ages. Do you think medieval people felt an ambivalence that the same gesture might have such different meanings?

JOHN BOSSY: Yes, I was talking about non-sexual kissing, holy kissing as I would say before: as soon as you get into non-holy kissing, then you are in a dark area, where nobody knows quite what is going on.[103]

One could sharpen the question. The perception that a kiss is being depicted on this monument depends on the reversal of one of the shields below, so that the two shields tilt toward each other. Shields in heraldry, if presented *à couché* (i.e., as tilted) are inclined to the dexter, the viewer's left; here the shield on the left has been reversed and tilts to the sinister, the viewer's right. The two shields then appear aligned with the bodies below, as if they were turned toward each other in death, in their final bed and in a sense in their final embrace. But why should that design not be given a *sexual* rather than a ritual interpretation?

The opinion of a modern herald—for achievements of arms are still granted—is likely to be disconcertingly brief: one modern work sharply dismisses the arrangement of arms *à couché* with the brief and acid comment that it is "an excuse for bad taste."[104] The answer is of course that of St. Paul, that the kiss of friendship should be a "holy kiss," a chaste kiss. Perhaps the most compelling statement of this assertion across the traditional culture of England (certainly the most lovely) is Shakespeare's twentieth sonnet, expressed there in Shakespeare's explicit and earthy language. Despite the poet's passion for the young man, and despite the captivating and ambiguous beauty of a face "which steales mens eyes and womens soules amaseth," Nature (the poet acknowledges) has added "one thing to my purpose nothing": this is a love which at its end transcends "loues vse."

> A Womans face with natures owne hand painted,
> Haste thou the Master Mistris of my passion,
> A womans gentle hart but not acquainted
> With shifting change as is false womens fashion,
> An eye more bright than theirs, lesse false in rowling:
> Gilding the object where-vpon it gazeth,
> A man in hew all Hews in his controwling,
> Which steales mens eyes and womens soules amaseth,
> And for a woman wert thou first created,
> Till nature as she wrought thee fell a dotinge,
> And by addition me of thee defeated,
> By adding one thing to my purpose nothing.
> But since she prickt thee out for womens pleasure,
> Mine be thy loue and thy loues vse their treasure.[105]

But is Shakespeare's point so clear? I have given here the text as it first appeared in the quarto of 1609, without the modern editor's apostrophe that reads "loves" as a possessive. But what does that "but" in the penultimate line reverse—the desire of the opening lines or the "defeat" of the lines that follow? Voice the *s* in "vse" (as the verb) and read "loues" as a plural that is not a possessive, and see what then happens to the sexual ambiguity in that suggestion that the young man was "prickt ... out for womens pleasure." Part of the wit of the sonnet lies in recognizing it—potentially—as a reworking in just these earthy terms of Martial's obscene twenty-second epigram (in book II of the epigrams).[106] Yet the last lines of Martial's epigram are themselves a parody of the lines of Turnus to Aeneas at the end of the *Aeneid:* "utere sorte tua" (literally "use your chance"), or as Dryden was to put it, "Use what the Gods, and thy good Fortune give"; or as C. Day Lewis more directly, "Yours was the luck. Make the most of it"—the transcendent sentiment that lies at the other side of the ambiguity in Shakespeare's dazzling tour de force. Shakespeare's sonnet can be read *both* as asserting the chastity of friendship in the most transcendent of terms *and* as rejecting it in the most bawdy and explicit of terms.

Have we not been here before? Shakespeare's twenty-ninth sonnet, to the same young man, can be read (as I argued in chapter 2) both as an expression of that lifting of the spirit that comes when the friend thinks of the beloved *and*, in brutal contrast, as the request of an impecunious poet for a financial subvention from his patron. John Barrell's view was that the poem presses on the limits of language itself: that in its final lines it "tries but fails to move within the orbit of another discourse, or even to find a language which would not be discursive at all, which would escape the limitations which the discursive nature of language imposes on all our utterances."[107] But is there not also another and perhaps simpler view? Were Shakespeare's verbal pyrotechnics designed neither to produce a declaration of love nor a purse of gold—but laughter, at the sheer audacity of the feat? That question raises a disconcerting possibility. Has something much simpler been missed in the analysis I have followed so painfully, to this point: in its earnest discussion of kinship, its language of natural families and of "extended families," of friendship formed by gift giving and friendship formed by ritual. Have its conclusions, perhaps, been like those of an earnest anthropologist scrutinizing the peoples of an island lapped by the sea in Polynesia, without grasping that he was, very gently, being teased? Whatever one makes of it, there is unmistakably the sound of laughter to be heard, and toward that sound I now propose to walk.

CHAPTER 4

The Body of the Friend

On the night before he suffered, he took bread into his holy and venerable hands, and lifting up his eyes to thee and giving thanks, he blessed it, broke it, and gave it to his disciples, saying: "Take, all of you, and eat of this: for this is my body."

Seventeenth-century Cambridge is still visible as one walks along the streets and paths of Cambridge today; the view of Trinity College from the bridge over the river in the early days of October has changed little in the last three centuries, in a pattern composed as much by the youthful students strolling by the river and the autumn leaves drifting on the water as in the lofty profile of Trinity College library. Two young men among those walking by the river in seventeenth-century Cambridge were John Finch and Thomas Baines, who met as students at nearby Christ's College during the troubled civil war years of the 1640s and formed there a friendship that was to endure across their lives. Their remains still lie buried, side by side, in the chapel of Christ's College, Cambridge. The walk from Trinity Bridge brings one to Christ's College across the busy market street, but to find its austere (but beautiful) sixteenth-century chapel one must pass through the protecting college gatehouse and cross the enclosed court that opens up before one. By the communion table in the chapel is the monument that marks their burial there together, and as one enters the chapel it draws any visitor's eye (see fig. 6).[1]

Sir Thomas Baines died in September 1681 in Constantinople, where Sir John Finch had been the ambassador of Charles II; his remains were brought by his friend to England, where Finch was himself to die the following year. The monument signed by the sculptor Joseph Catterns marks their burial together in the vault nearby and is a graphic expression of the nature of their friendship. The two halves of the monument are each surmounted by a

Figure 6
The monument of Sir John Finch and Sir Thomas Baines in the chapel of
Christ's College, Cambridge.

portrait of one of the friends; and the monument is linked by the image of
a knotted cloth, set between the two tables of the inscription, that corresponds to the single flaming funerary urn set above, in a visual pun on the
marriage or love knot. That same terminology of a marriage had already
been employed by Finch in the inscription he left to the memory of Baines
in Constantinople. In it he had described their friendship as an "Animorum
Connubium": a marriage of souls.[2]

Two centuries before, that image would have traced for the historian the
evident outline of the sworn "brothers" of fifteenth-century England, whose
"wedded" brotherhood lent itself easily to such marital imagery. Were the
contemporaries of Finch and Baines, at the end of the seventeenth century,

able to interpret their friendship in the same terms? Brotherhood in arms was still a familiar relation in France in the later seventeenth century, judging by a letter of Madam de Sévigné in 1674, and the French term used by the English merchants in Constantinople to characterize Sir Thomas Baines, the "chevalier," may be a trace of this historical background.[3] What is certain, however, is that the terms Finch used here were no eccentricity at the end of the seventeenth century. The expression "conjunctissimus meus" ("Nunc de Integerrimo et Conjunctissimo Meo Bainesio") that he employed in the inscription he left in Constantinople is the same term that William Moore had used earlier in the seventeenth century to explain the wish of John Gostlin and Thomas Legge (and of John Browne and Thomas Orrell) to be buried together in the nearby chapel of Gonville and Caius; and at this point, at the end of the seventeenth century, there is an explicit intellectual context for the terms of this monument. In describing their friendship as a "marriage of souls," Finch used the same term employed by Jeremy Taylor, the Caroline divine (and later bishop) in his *Discourse of Friendship*, a work that was reprinted some seven times between 1657, when it first appeared, and 1684, when the monument in Christ's College was completed. The closing lines of the inscription on the Christ's College monument also look back to Taylor's work.

> Ut Studia, Fortunas, Consilia, immo Animas vivi qui
> miscuerant
> Iidem suos defuncti sacros tandem miscerent cineres.

> [So that they who while living had mingled their interests, fortunes, counsels, nay rather souls, might in the same manner, in death, at last mingle their sacred ashes.][4]

Both inscriptions draw on the same passage in Jeremy Taylor's *Discourse*, in which he describes friendships as "marriages of the soul, and of fortunes and interests, and counsels." The context for this remark was Taylor's sharp awareness of what was implied by the view that the good of marriage lay in the friendship it communicated without which society itself would not subsist: such friendship is, as he put it, is "all the bands that this world hath": a view that would have been as readily intelligible in the fifteenth century as it evidently still was to a conservative Anglican like Taylor. The implication he draws is this.

> Add to this, that other friendships are part of this, they are marriages too, less indeed than the other, because they cannot, must not be all that en-

dearment which the other is; yet that being the principal, is the measure of the rest, and all are to be honoured by like dignities, and measured by the same rules, and conducted by their portion of the same laws: but as friendships are marriages of the soul, and of fortunes and interests, and counsels; so they are brotherhoods too; and I often think of the excellencies of friendships in the words of David, who certainly was the best friend in the world, Ecce quam bonum et quam jucundum fratres habitare in unum: it is good and it is pleasant that brethren should also live like friends.[5]

These are brotherhoods, he goes on to argue, like those of David and Jonathan, brotherhoods made social and confederate, as he puts it, by something more than nature. "It was my brother Jonathan," said David; such brothers contracting such friendships are "the beauties of society, and the pleasures of life, and the festivity of minds" (Ps. 133:1). Jeremy Taylor's terms are those in which this monument is designed, and it conveys, at the end of the seventeenth century in England, that formal and objective character that friendship could evidently still possess, so curiously unfamiliar to the modern eye, that was the subject of my first chapter.

Its setting by the communion table also marks the traditional place of such friendship in religion's role that I explored in chapter 3, and the significance of that setting is subtly emphasized by the design of the surrounding woodwork and the inscriptions above the communion table. The woodwork (added between 1702 and 1703) frames the monument with brackets and a canopylike pediment and extends across to the setting of the communion table (where the scrolls on the monument are repeated in the scrolls in the woodwork that flank the cartouche above). The inscriptions reemphasize the connection. That on the cartouche, "SVRSVM CORDA" [lift up your hearts], looks back to the opening image of the monument's inscription, that these were two of the most devoted friends "quibus Cor erat unum" [who had but one heart]: as the inscription that until recently lay below, "VNVM CORPVS ET VNVS SIPRITVS" [there is one body and one spirit], looked back to the closing lines of the inscription that I quoted above.[6] If the inscriptions above the communion table draw the eye back to the bodies of two friends awaiting the resurrection together there, they also draw the eye down to that other body, the Church, which is the Body of Christ in the epistles of St. Paul, celebrating the Lord's Supper at the communion table below. At the end of the seventeenth century the Lord's Supper in Christ's College would have been celebrated in Latin, in a translation of the prayer book authorized by Charles II. The words "sursum corda" were the opening words of the prayer in the Lord's Supper recounting the institution of the Eucharist: as the inscription below, "unum corpus et unus spritus," are taken from the lesson in the prayer book for the seventeenth Sunday after Trinity, from Paul's Epistle to the Ephesians. Paul urges his readers to keep the unity of the Spirit "in vinculo pacis" [in the bond of peace], for there is, as he puts it, but "one body and one spirit": that same association of peace as well in the human breast as in the soul that had been marked by the kiss of peace in the old mass.[7] If the friendship of this monument is a spiritual friendship, the signs in which that friendship is represented here are correspondingly those of an intimate and *physical* closeness, as tangible as the bread and wine consumed in the Lord's Supper: above all in the tangible presence of the bodies of these two friends lying together in death, but also in the single funerary urn that surmounts the monument; in the embraces of his friend as Baines lay dying, which the monument also reverently records; and in the final kiss of peace with which his friend received his last breath, recorded on the inscription left by Finch in Constantinople, "Dum inter Amplexus et Gemitus, ultimum Ipsius Spiritum Exciperem" [when between embraces and sighs I received his last breath].

Were such embraces only appropriate for the moment of death? This was not the view of Jeremy Taylor. He puts it in an engagingly homely image.

> Give him gifts and upbraid him not, and refuse not his kindnesses, and be sure never to despise the smallness or the impropriety of them. Confirmatur amor beneficio accepto; "a gift," saith Solomon, "fasteneth friendship"; for as an eye that dwells long upon a star must be refreshed with lesser beauties and strengthened with greens and looking-glasses, lest the sight become amazed with too great a splendour; so must the love of friends sometimes be refreshed with material and low caresses; lest by striving to be too divine it become less humane: it must be allowed its share of both.[8]

But is Taylor's point so clear? Why does he use that odd description of an embrace as a *gift*? This monument seems a private, almost secluded gesture, protected as much by the Latin of its inscription as by the gateway of Christ's College: neither would have been easily accessible to the populace outside; but as one deciphers the Latin of its inscription, that impression receives a jolt. It leaves one unprepared for how much of the inscription's terms concern not the friendship between these two men but the worldly connections of Sir John Finch: the cousin of the earl of Winchilsea, and the brother of the earl of Nottingham, a figure who appears prominently in the inscription in his own right. The inscription elides the more humble background of Sir Thomas Baines, who was later remembered as having been

Finch's "sizar," or personal servant, when they were students at Cambridge, a common role for a bright but impecunious student in seventeenth-century Cambridge (as the antiquary John Ward recounted the matter):

> They have a tradition at Christ's college, that while Mr. Finch was a student there, taking too great liberties, his sizar, Thomas Baynes, very tenderly admonished him of his misconduct; which at first he resented, but upon reflection complied with his advice, and ever after made him his constant and bosom freind.[9]

Baines was later to act for Finch as his secretary and the go-between with the world that protected a man like Finch. The great connections and place occupied by Finch form a patina of references that run across the face of the inscription, in which his gifts again insistently reappear.

> Comitis Nottingamiensis Frater, Non magis Iuris quam Iustitiae consulti, Regiae Majestati a consiliis secretioribus summiq Angliae Cancellarii ... Principi, Patriae, atq Ecclesiae Anglicanae charissimi ... A serenissimo Rege Angliae per Decennium Legatus ... in usus pios Quater mille libras Anglicanas huic Christi Collegio donavit Ad duos socios totidemq scholares in Collegio alendos Et ad augendum libris quinquagenis reditum. Magistri annum ... huc delatus ab illustrissimo Domino D. FINCHIO HENEAGII Comitis Nottingamiensis filio Primogenito.

> [Brother of the earl of Nottingham, a man not more versed in jurisprudence than in justice, a member of the king's majesty's Privy Council and lord chancellor of England ... most dear to his prince, his country and to the Church of England ... the other sent as ambassador for a decade from the most Serene King of England ... gave to Christ's College, for pious purposes, four thousand English pounds to support two fellows and the same number of scholars in the college and to augment the master's annual stipend by fifty pounds ... brought here by the illustrious Lord Daniel Finch the eldest son of Heneage Finch, earl of Nottingham.]

These references correspond to the references the inscription also makes to the college *itself*, in this context.

> [S]ub amantissimi Tutoris HENRICI MORI auspicijs hoc ipso in Collegio initae ... ad sacellum hoc ... huic Christi Collegio ... in Collegion ... hic ...

[Begun in this same college under the auspices of their most loving tutor Henry More . . . to this chapel . . . to Christ's College . . . in the College . . . here . . .]

The effect is to place the latter firmly within the former: to advertise to any who might be able to read its terms the place that Christ's College properly occupied in such a world of power and place.

The abrupt path from the bodies of two men, lying so intimately together, to the power and wealth about them may seem to the modern eye brash and disconcerting, perhaps even vulgar; but they evidently did not seem so to their friends who commissioned this monument. I propose in this chapter to follow the nature of the path that beckons to the historian in this inscription, from the intimacy of families and friends that this book has traced up to this point, to that greater world beyond them in which they figured; and I shall argue paradoxically that the instrument that leads from the one to the other is precisely the giving of such gifts.[10]

Embrace

The royal court of Charles II was part of the engine of that world. In 1650, as the now inseparable Finch and Baines set about the visit to Italy that followed their years at Cambridge, an account of the royal court appeared that casts an unusually clear light on the social world in which their tomb monument would eventually be set. The court it described was not that of Charles II but that of his grandfather James I; but the account below, published thirty-five years after the event, assumes that the gesture it describes would still be readily intelligible to its readers. Its setting is the hunting lodge that James I maintained at Royston among the woods and fields of Hertfordshire, and the gesture it describes proves to have a ready meaning far beyond the conventions of the court. The description appears in the memoirs of Sir Anthony Weldon, who at the time of the incident recounted was an office holder in James I's court. The earl referred to is Robert Carr, James's friend and now the earl of Somerset, who is saying his farewells to James before returning to London and to the commission of inquiry that was to lead to his ruin. The date is the autumn of 1615.

> The Earl of Somerset never parted from him with more seeming affection than at this time, when he knew Somerset should never see him more; and had you seen that seeming affection (as the author himself did) you would

rather have believed he was in his rising than setting. The Earl when he kissed his hand, the King hung about his neck slabbering his cheeks, saying "For God's sake when shall I see thee again? On my soul, I shall neither eat nor sleep until you come again." The Earl told him on Monday (this being on the Friday) "For God's sake let me." Said the King "shall I? Shall I?" then lolled about his neck, then "For God's sake give thy Lady this kiss for me" in the same manner at the stair's head, at the middle of the stairs, and at the stair's foot. The Earl was not in his coach when the King used these very words (in the hearing of 4 servants, of whom one was Somerset's great creature and of the bedchamber, who reported it instantly to the author of this history) "I shall never see his face more."[11]

Weldon's charge is that these gestures were a formality and a sham, that James had no intention of fulfilling what they indicated. For the social historian that is curiously helpful, for it detaches the gestures being described from what we might or might not make of James's relationship with Robert Carr and leaves them floating free as public signs with an understood meaning. What then was that meaning?

In one respect at least the picture Weldon gives needs a hefty discount. The publication of his memoirs in 1650 immediately followed the fall of the Stuart monarchy, and at this point the restoration of Charles II in 1660 could scarcely have been predicted with any confidence. This is also the account of a man with a grudge. By the time Weldon prepared the manuscript from which this account was probably drawn by its editor, he was no longer the courtier we see here. He had lost his post and was a bitter man. We therefore need to make some allowance for his malice. To slabber Robert Carr's cheeks was certainly to kiss him and to hang about his neck was to embrace him, but the colorful language in which these are described is Weldon's own. The clue several centuries later on as to how to read this gesture lies in that reference to the staircase at Royston, where James chose to embrace Carr. This was no casual choice. It was there, at the midpoint of the stairs, that James chose in 1623 to welcome back his son Charles and the duke of Buckingham (who was to be Carr's successor in the king's favor) from the Spanish journey, unseduced by popery or Spanish princesses, and when the church bells rang for them across the length of a mightily relieved Protestant England. On that occasion James had descended the stairs to their midpoint to meet them, a piece of carefully symbolic domestic geography. In Weldon's description James has accompanied Carr not only to that point but all the way to the foot of the stairs and at each point—at the head of the stairs, at the midpoint, and at their foot—he embraced Carr before the eyes of all the court.

The embrace he gave Carr was a gesture not only expected of a king or of King James. Indeed it was so readily intelligible a gesture precisely because it was so familiar.

> But I doubt not so soon as his name shall come into the knowledge of men and his worthiness be sounded in the trump of fame, but that he shall be not only kissed but also beloved of all, embraced of the most, and wondered at of the best.

That was the editor of the *Shepheardes Calender* in 1579, introducing its hopeful author.[12] The author was Edmund Spenser, and according to John Aubrey's anecdote this was indeed how Sir Philip Sidney was to acknowledge him (and to make amends for his initial neglect).

> Among others Mr. Edmund Spencer made his addresse to him, and brought his Faery Queen. Sir Philip was busy at his study, and his servant delivered Mr. Spencer's booke to his master, who layd it by, thinking it might be such kind of stuffe as he was frequently troubled with. Mr. Spencer stayd so long that his patience was wearied, and he went his way discontented, and never intended to come again. When Sir Philip perused it, he was so exceedingly delighted with it, that he was extremely sorry he was gonne, and where to send for him he knew not. After much enquiry he learned his lodgeing, and sent for him, mightily caressed [him], and ordered his servant to give him . . . pounds in gold.

"From this time there was a great friendship between them, to his dying day," adds John Aubrey, but the story has survived not only because Aubrey recorded it but also because those embraces were evidently a sufficiently *public* gesture for Aubrey to have heard of them:[13] at the beginning of Davenant's play *The Cruel Brother* of 1627 one of the characters points to just such public embraces as evidence of a certain Lucio's influence with the duke;[14] and it is in such terms that Thomas Howard recorded Robert Carr's rise to power at the court of James I.

> The Prince leaneth on his arm, pinches his cheek, smooths his ruffled garment . . . We are almost worn out in our endeavours to keep pace with this fellow in his duty and labour to gain favour, but all in vain; where it endeth I cannot guess, but honours are talked of speedily for him.[15]

The gesture was as old as the friendship between men that this book has described: three centuries before it was in these terms that the fourteenth-century chronicle of the monastery of St. Albans had described Edward II's reception of Piers Gaveston on his return from France in 1308—and the growing resentment of Edward's other magnates.

Inter quos Petrum occurrentem, datis osculis et ingeminatis amplexibus, familiaritate venerabatur singulari. Quae familiaritas specialis, a magnatibus praeconcepta, invidiae fomitem ministravit.

[He adored Piers with a singular familiarity when he saw him among them, giving him kisses and repeated embraces; which special familiarity, already known to the magnates, furnished fuel to their jealousy.][16]

When James sought to reconcile Carr to the rising George Villiers (the duke of Buckingham to be) by encouraging Carr to recognize Villiers as his friend, it was this gesture he asked Carr to give Villiers, as Anthony Weldon recounts it in his memoirs. The speaker is the king's servant Sir Humphrey May.

"My Lord, Sir George Villiers will come to you to offer his service and desire to be your creature; and therefore refuse him not, embrace him, and your Lordship shall still stand a great man, though not the sole favourite." My Lord seemed averse. Sir Humphrey then told him in plain terms that he was sent by the King to advise it, and that Villiers would come to him to cast himself into his protection, to take his rise under the shadow of his wings. Sir Humphrey May was not parted from my Lord half an hour, but in comes Sir George Villiers and used these very words "My Lord, I desire to be your servant and your creature and shall desire to take my Court preferment under your favour and your Lordship, and your Lordship shall find me as faithful a servant unto you as ever did serve you."[17]

The displaced Carr did not embrace Villiers, however, but offered to break his neck (a reply, Weldon added, that savored more of spirit than wisdom). Had the gesture been given as James had asked, it would have been the public sign of a man under Carr's protection, his faithful servant and friend, his "creature" as Villiers put it. For Weldon, the cynical nature of James's hypocrisy was that James had given Carr this gesture before the eyes of all the Court on the very eve of Carr's fall. As Weldon put it, one would have rather thought that he was in his rising than in his setting.

This publicly displayed intimacy is what Francis Bacon, writing at the time in his essay "Of Followers and Friends," called "countenance," the appearance of a friend's evident favor; and the influence it advertised was a gift that could readily be turned to advantage.[18] This is what Henry Howard later advised the then greatly powerful Robert Carr:

> There is no better way to pare their nails . . . than by some withdrawing of your favourable countenance, which I do assure you is a groundyard to their boldness and a discharge of many watchful ears and eyes.[19]

Such kisses and embraces were for such "watchful ears and eyes" as these. The material gifts that turned the wheels of seventeenth-century society are still readily apparent, the gift of offices especially and the flow of fees and sweeteners they could bring. Less apparent are the symbolic gifts that could be as readily exploited. Arguably the most eloquent of these was the physical intimacy we see here, from which a wider intimacy could be read: the gift, one might perhaps call it, of the body. Both Carr and James potentially benefited through a gesture like the one Weldon described that day at Royston. Carr benefited from being powerfully reinforced as James's friend. James benefited through the tacit obligation it placed Carr under. But while the benefit for Carr was immediate in the countenance it gave him, for James the benefit was deferred to when he might call on it. The gesture he had given Carr was for James a form of symbolic capital—part of what contemporaries characterized as "honour"—and it was the deferral of its return that created a continuing relationship between them. This gift—in this case false coin according to Weldon—was what James give Carr that day.

Table

The public embrace was only one of the bodily signs of friendship. Another was eating together, and this was the point of James's claim that he would not eat without the departing Carr. It was the table that perhaps most of all transformed the stranger into the friend. The common table was part of the symbolic geography of all the great houses of seventeenth-century England, centers of influence far beyond their roles as homes for the English aristocracy; and James's lodge at Royston shared in this symbolism. The buildings themselves were often constructions of the sixteenth century or later, but well into the seventeenth century their domestic symbolism was still visibly of a kind with the great houses of the medieval aristocracy; and in the courtesy books of the Middle Ages the "service" of a lord was firstly service at the table, in cutting the food, filling the cup, and so on. These were tasks that were carried out for a lord by his gentry supporters acting as his personal servants, and they conferred the same countenance as the public embrace of the kind we see here.

They did so because the wider role of the great house required it to contain different levels of society as part of one household, whether or not always physically present, and the symbolism of the body and the bodily functions such as the common table readily represented its nature.[20] By the seventeenth century one can see this visual symbolism most clearly in the communal eating and drinking in the colleges and halls of the universities. The fellows and fellow commoners (the more wealthy students) would eat at the high table in the great hall. The scholars would sit apart, and the numerous poorer students (often working their way as servants in the colleges) would sit farther apart or be waiting on the tables. The visible effect would not have been greatly different than that produced by the crowds of tenants and visitors eating or drinking in the hall of a great house. The great halls in the seventeenth-century universities reflected an older architectural pattern that had largely been abandoned in the great houses by the later fourteenth century, but the move of the high table that had taken place in the great houses from the dais in the great hall to the great chamber above only further emphasized the procession of the dishes first to the high table and then back down, for what was left to be eaten by those further down the social scale.

The friendship represented by the eating and drinking in the great hall illustrates a part of the workings of seventeenth-century friendship that is not apparent when a gesture such as the friend's embrace is seen in isolation. The formal nature of such friendship was not a mutuality of interest but a mutuality of ethics. The point is implicit in that term "beneficium" that Jeremy Taylor used in the passage from his *Discourse of Friendship* that I quoted above: "confirmatur amor beneficio accepto" [a gift—i.e., a "beneficium"—fasteneth friendship]. The term is that in Seneca's *De Beneficiis,* which became a more readily familiar part of humanist learning with the editions of Seneca's works published by Justus Lipsius in the 1570s but more popularly, in England, with the translations of Arthur Golding in 1578 (and Thomas Lodge in 1614). As Linda Levy Peck has characterized the term, "Within this Senecan tradition, duty and rights, the meat of feudal and Kantian relationships, did not exhaust the ties between people. Instead, 'benefites [were] . . . a thing that most of al other knitteth men togither in fellowship.'" The "benefit" was not extorted: rather a man's honor required it to be given with an open hand; it could profit the giver, but not if it meant to profit him alone. "Such benefits, given freely, in moderation, and received gratefully, circulated throughout society, and constituted 'the chief bond of human society.'"²¹ Such a "benefit" did not reside in the material value of the gift, however great, and the countenance given by the friend's embrace was potentially such a gift. It was one that could impose an obligation on the recipient, but that was not necessarily an obligation to the giver. It could be met, or rather passed on, to a third party and so reaffirm the solidarity of a group. The progress and return of the food in the great hall reflected an obligation of that kind, identifying those taking part as common insiders at precisely the points where the symbolic system emphasized social divisions. Those at the high table ate first and so on down the social chain; but the dish was the same, and your restraint was the gift that passed on.

Gestures of this kind did more than indicate bonds of friendship, as a signpost might indicate a town: they created them. This perhaps most of all requires an act of imagination on our parts. It is a way of thinking that is now largely alien, in which representation is constitutive and not merely mimetic; but there is perhaps an inlet to it in that recurring association with the friendship created in the Eucharist. Could this not have been understood in the same terms in which the friendship of the great house was reproduced, by the sharing of the food from the high table in the great hall? In each the elements were taken first to the high table, or to the altar, and distributed as its gifts. Similarly, could not the *osculum pacis*, the kiss of peace that preceded the communion (or stood in its place), correspondingly be seen as another form of the familiar bestowal of the embrace? In both contexts it carried with it friendship's obligations and was not given lightly.

To interpret these analogies as an appropriation of the Eucharist to secular ends would not only be an anachronism; it would elide the fact that the *same* symbols of communion signified in both contexts. A defining characteristic of such a traditional view of religion's role was that—in distinction to what sought to supplant it on both sides of the Reformation divide—it straddled such a division, and here lay much of the reason for its tenacity. Its supplanting would have entailed divorcing religion from the symbolic systems outside it. There were those, both in Milan and in Geneva, who were ready to make that sacrifice. But how feasible was it that it could ever have been achieved—or rather at what price? The analogy is also illuminating in reverse—and here lies that inlet I suggested. Although even traditional-minded Christians might increasingly disagree on how this was the case, the Eucharist was and remained the experience of a transformative rite that changed the significance of the bread and wine brought to it: through a mechanism of the same kind the table changed the stranger into the friend.

Bed

What then of that other claim that James made, that he would not sleep until Robert Carr returned? If eating and drinking created friendship, so too did sleeping together. This is the significance of the comment in Anthony Weldon's account that Carr's "great creature" was "of the bedchamber," and the symbolism it drew on was as old as that of the common table. Here is John Paston writing home hopefully to his mother in 1479: "I think that Sir George Brown, Sir James Radcliffe, and other of mine acquaintance which wait most upon the King and lie nightly in his chamber will put to their good wills."[22] The implication is still the same as in this gratified note from early in the seventeenth century: "His Majesty understanding of our coming presently sent for us into his bed-chamber and did use us very graciously,"[23] and the gesture was alive near the century's end when in 1678 John Evelyn proudly recorded in his diary "I had a private audience of his Majesty in his bed-chamber."[24]

The intelligibility of the gesture was not restricted to the royal bedchamber. Into the seventeenth century the inhabitants of England slept in beds or pallets set up at night, and (as one can see from their size) such makeshift beds were usually shared, in houses where rooms led casually one into the other: arrangements that made who shared a bed with whom into an evident fact. It was also a potentially meaningful one, for beds are not only places where people sleep: they are also places where people talk, and the epithet "bedfellow" readily suggested the influential intimacy of a friend. At the same point that John Paston was writing home to his mother from the court, Richard Cely in Calais was receiving news from home in the same terms. "Also, sir, ye shall understand that my Lord of St John's bedfellow was here with my mistress your mother now late, within these three days, and he said that my Lord sent him hither for to wit whether that ye were i-comen home or none."[25] John Chamberlain glossed the epithet "bedfellow" as indicating who was "the chief man" about William Cecil, Lord Roos;[26] and it is in that sense that the countess of Oxford used the word when she complained about the influence a certain John Hunt was exercising over her son, the earl of Oxford: "Hunt hath impudently presumed to be his bedfellow and otherwise used him most unrespectively."[27] Ann Bacon uses "bed-companion" in the same sense in a letter to Anthony Bacon in 1594: "your brother ... keepeth that bloody Pérez, as I told him then, yea as a coach-companion and bed-companion."[28] The glamour it could exercise is played out to comic effect in George Chapman's Jacobean play *The Gentleman Usher*, when the gullible gentleman usher is seduced into acting as pander by the embrace and shared bed of a young nobleman, who then broaches the delicate subject in the intimacy of their lying together.[29] As the audience would have been well aware, it was not only a woman's seduction that could be discussed in the intimacy of a shared bed. The most striking illustration I know of this is an entry that Bishop William Laud made in his diary in August 1625: "That night in a dream the Duke of Buckingham seemed to me to ascend into my bed, where he carried himself with much love towards me, after such rest wherein weary men are wont exceedingly to rejoice; and likewise many seemed to me to enter the chamber who did see this."[30] Laud's dream is of his potential patron and friend at the court of Charles I, the great duke of Buckingham; but the point of the dream is its conclusion, that the powerful mark of favor he was dreaming of was public. It is in this sense also that we should read the now famous remark of the (then future) duke of Buckingham when he looked back with gratitude in a letter to James I, to that night when first "the bed's head could not be found between the master and his dog."[31]

Historians of the royal court have persuasively demonstrated how the gentlemen of the royal bedchamber were deliberately employed as a tool of government, but what was being employed in this was not the sacred nature of monarchy. The stratagem the court employed was so effective because it was so common and readily intelligible.[32] In the universities the sleeping arrangements were as carefully orchestrated as the eating and drinking in the great halls. It was common for a tutor to share his room with a student who acted as his personal servant. Where the student might act as the tutor's patron, however, the dependence was reversed, so much so that a tutor in sixteenth-century Oxford discovered that he was in danger of having surrendered his rights over a valuable young man by allowing him to share the cubicle of another tutor.[33] Perhaps the most striking illustration to us now of bodily symbolism of this kind is that which arose out of the emptying of the chamber pot, a ubiquitous fact in premodern housing of all kinds. For someone to dispose of someone else's bodily wastes could carry the same indication of intimacy as sleeping or eating together, to which it was of course an adjunct. The groom of the stool at James's court at Royston was Sir Thomas Erskine, and he was able to write with some pride on the precise details of the state of the king's stool. His pride was not misplaced, for his role fixed his position by the king. He was also entitled to sleep on a pallet at the foot of the king's bed and to be alone with the king in the coach.[34] His role was in its effect the same one that Lady Ann Bacon had complained of Antonio Pérez occupying in the household of Francis Bacon "as a coach-companion and bed-companion," and was but the same role writ large of a poor student in a Cambridge college in emptying his tutor's chamber pot.

The mundane significance of physical intimacy stood behind its eloquent part in the romances of friendship, and it continued to do so as much in its daily use as in a poem or a play or a piece of imaginative literature. When in the Latin *Amys and Amylion* the angel Raphael is sent by God to one of the two sworn friends during the night—"Amice, dormis?" [*Amicus*, are you sleeping?]—he thinks that it is his friend speaking, who is his bedfellow while his wife is away: "Minime dormio, socie karissime" [I cannot sleep, my beloved comrade], he replies.[35] It is the appealing image in Tirry's dream of his sworn brother in the romance of *Guy of Warwick.*

Also me thoght, that syr Gye
Was here be me, full sekerlye*
And my hed in hys armes lay

*surely

Earlier in the poem it had been no dream: "Tho lay terry down to grounde, / And slepid in Gyes armes a stounde."[36] Such comments give a vantage point from which to judge the elegant garments in which masculine friendship was often dressed in Elizabethan and Jacobean England. Typical of the carefully beautiful manner in which it was usually presented is the picture of Euphues's friendship with his friend Philautus in John Lyly's Elizabethan novel *Euphues,* which employs the same gestures of embrace, table (board), and bed:

> But after many embracings and protestations one to another they walked to dinner, where they wanted neither meat, neither music, neither any other pastime; and having banqueted, to digest their sweet confections they danced all that afternoon. They used not only one board but one bed, one book (if so be it they thought not one too many). Their friendship augmented every day, insomuch that the one could not refrain the company of the other one minute. All things went in common between them, which all men accounted commendable.[37]

This is idealized, of course, and there are literary echoes here, especially of Cicero's essay on friendship *De Amicitia* and of the numerous ornate treatises on love that popularized Ciceronian and Neoplatonic ideas on friendship; the same could be said of the familiar letters between friends of chapter 2: but when one looks at the details of this account, one sees something surprisingly more mundane. Its material is made up virtually entirely of the conventions I have been writing of: the embraces and the protestations of friendship, the common table and the shared bed. Its idealization consisted rather in what it missed out: its tactful omission of those bonds of mutual concern of which the familiar everyday signs were such conventions. The engaging artifice is part of a tough reality, and the realistic comment to set by it is that of Francis Bacon at the end of his essay on followers and friends when he says that such friendship as there is in this world is in truth between those "whose fortunes" as he puts it "may comprehend the one the other."[38]

Seen in this frame, the tombs of friends buried together come into focus; not only that of John Finch and Thomas Baines, but those I have described stretching back to the fourteenth century and beyond. To the modern eye such tombs reflect on death and transcendence, and so they did to our ancestors, but to them they were also (and more simply) that final bed in which such friends might at last lie together.

Body and Society

It is not greatly difficult to reconstruct this symbolic system from the pieces one sees. They cohere too easily. But identifying the place this symbolism occupied within seventeenth-century society more widely is a great deal more precarious. The evidence I have used has largely been derived from the life of the great households. But is it simply that the light is strongest here? The evidence available to any historian of premodern England is overwhelmingly that left by the elite. That is true even of evidence in administrative records that appear to provide accurate information about the common people, such as court records. The information recorded (and the information excluded) was the choice of those who controlled those records, and we see the outline of their concerns in the evidence remaining. No sources automatically relieve the historian from the extremely difficult judgment on how to generalize from the evidence that remains. It is that question I propose to turn to in the context of this symbolic system.

One reason for being open to the possibility that this symbolism was not uniquely a function of the great houses is that the great houses were far from being populated only by the gentry. I have already mentioned the tenants and visitors that would have been part of the crowd in the hall. Nor was the way of life in the great house altogether different from that of the farmer living and eating in the same house with the farm's laborers. Similarly the colleges, whose halls replicated those of the medieval great houses, were by no means wholly places of education for the wealthy. They contained others studying alongside them, who might be maintained there by a bishop or a local corporation. More likely, however, such students maintained themselves by working as servants to the colleges or to the wealthier students. Would not the signs I have described be intelligible to them in other contexts also?

Arguably the most abrupt difference between the great houses and society more widely is the point I have so far avoided: the great houses were overwhelmingly a world of men. At first sight, this fact more than any other seems to make it impossible to generalize from them to society at large. It is the guide we are looking for, however, or rather it leads us to it if we follow its trail. James's lodge at Royston was almost entirely composed of men, members of the Court and servants alike. That was true of all the great houses of the time. The names of the members of the household of the earl of Derby in 1587, for example, contain only two female servants in comparison to the overwhelming roll call of male names—the Johns and Henrys and Edwards and Richards and so on, in the hall, the chamber, the kitchens, the offices, the stable, the pantry, and the cellar.[39] The Northumberland household earlier in the century[40] and the Warwick household a century before that[41] show a similar overwhelming majority of men. The same was true of the colleges at the universities, which admitted only male students and employed only male servants, insofar as the work was not carried out by the poorer students themselves.[42] It is difficult to imagine a wider view of this gift of the body that I have described that did not take account of the apparent fact—in this evidence at least—that the body being given was male.

The explanation is not that the great houses and the colleges were masculine enclaves cut off from contact with women. They had extensive links with the many women who were traders supplying its needs, or who were its tenants, or who worked on the land or with the animals belonging to the house. The point is rather that these women did not live and work within it. When a great house needed work that women normally did—such as washing clothes or looking after cattle—this work was carried out by women outside the house whenever it could be, by the river or a well or in the fields. In this respect the women associated with the great house were in a position not fundamentally different from that of the women who supplied the house's needs as traders rather than as servants. They ate, they drank, and they slept outside the great house. When they were unmarried (as many would have been, given the stage of life service represented), they would have lived together with other single women in a tenement or in a group of cottages. Such groups of women are a visible feature of sixteenth- and seventeenth-century England and were often organized around the shared work.[43] The maleness of the great house is the corresponding phenomenon to these groups of women living and working together; one can see the same phenomenon with unmarried itinerant male journeymen living with other men in the same trade in the town.[44] Nor was it the case that work in large measure determined where only the unmarried inhabitants of seventeenth-century England ate, drank, and slept. It was true for most people, as little domestic housing of the time allowed for food to be cooked safely or for washing, either the body or clothes. Hence the ubiquitous bakers and laundresses of this society, and the stalls and street vendors where cooked food could be bought. When survival was as pressed as it was for most of the inhabitants of this society, eating, drinking, and sleeping tended to be carried out as close as possible to where someone worked, whether or not they had a marital home. Sundays and holidays apart, it was the place of work that often determined where these activities needed to be carried out; and these pressures would have applied to a married servant as much as to an unmarried one.

In this way the constraints of work shaped the greater extent to which in this society, in comparison to our own, the daily cycle of working, eating and drinking, the bodily functions, and sleeping was carried on outside the marital home. Service in the great houses was men's work, and that fact in large measure determined for its inhabitants where this daily cycle was carried out. But service in the great house was characterized in this way when the service was carried out by gentlemen as well as by menial servants, as such work was not labor alone. When social life was shaped as widely by work as this, "work" was not only an economic activity. It was also a means by which social relationships could be established and given meaning.[45]

The symbolism of the body of the friend was such a means. From this vantage point, the symbolic gift of the friend's body does not appear as a gift between men only, nor was it a gift that carried a meaning only in the context of a great house. The guide to its place in seventeenth-century society is the nature of the sign itself rather than the immediate context in which we now see it several centuries on. But it is no accident that the meaning of this symbolic system is now clearest to us in such a context of power and place. The gift of the body was a sign of power and security in the friend, and wherever power was diffused—into whatever levels it seeped— so too was potentially diffused the gift of the friend's body. The word "love" in this society could comprehend as easily the public relation of friends as the more private meaning we give the word today, but wherever on that wide spectrum the gift of a friend's body might lie, it gestured toward a place of comforting safety in an insecure world.

Letter

At first view the humanism of the sixteenth century appeared to have put aside such bodily gestures with disdain, but one need only lift a corner of its rhetoric to see how much it still drew on them and their continuing vitality. That awareness of the past is graphically illustrated in the famous paired portraits by Quentin Metsys that Erasmus and his fellow humanist scholar Peter Gilles sent to Thomas More in the autumn of 1517; portraits that, as Lisa Jardine has argued, were self-consciously designed to have an iconic status: depicting Erasmus as international teacher and "man of letters." In the paired pictures the two friends no longer appear set among the figures of the saints as John Bloxham and John Whytton had been presented at the end of the fourteenth century. They appear seated together among Erasmus's books in his study in Louvain. Gilles looks across the table to Erasmus, who looks up from the work he is composing—his *Paraphrase of St. Paul's Epistle to the Romans*—to the book to which Gilles is gesturing, which Thomas More is evidently expected to recognize as his *Utopia* and which Gilles had seen through the press for him at the end of the previous year. The book projects beyond the frame of the picture, and the gesture draws the unseen observer, More himself, into the intimacy of these two friends seated in Erasmus's study.[46]

As Lisa Jardine points out, at the center of this picture rests a book. Erasmus explains that gesture in the familiar letter to Peter Gilles that had served as the dedication of his *Parabolae sive Similia.*

Vulgare quidem et crassum istud amicorum genus, Petre amicorum candidissime, quorum vt omnis vitae, ita necessitudinis quoque ratio in corporibus sita est, si quando procul seiunctos agere contigerit, anulos, pugiunculos, pileolos, atque alia id genus symbola crebro solent inuicem missitare; videlicet ne vel consuetudinis intermissione languescat beneuolentia, vel longa temporum ac locorum intercapedine prorsus emoriatur. Nos vero, quibus animorum coniunctione societateque studiorum, omnis amicitiae ratio constat, cur non potius animi xeniolis et literatis symbolis identidem alter alterum salutemus?

[Friends of the commonplace and homespun sort, my open-hearted Peter, have their idea of relationship, like their whole lives, attached to material things; and if ever they have to face a separation, they favor a frequent exchange of rings, knives, caps, and other tokens of the kind, for fear that their affection may cool when intercourse is interrupted or actually die away through the interposition of long tracts of time and space. But you and I, whose idea of friendship rests wholly in a meeting of minds and the enjoyment of studies in common, might well greet one another from time to time with presents for the mind and keepsakes of a literary description.][47]

The term Erasmus uses here for "material things" is "in corporibus," a word that could also imply *bodily* things, and the examples he gives—rings, knives, caps—are objects that can be worn on the body: when given as gifts they are its trace and stood in its place. Erasmus's point is that this is a friendship sealed by the exchange of *literary* gifts, a meeting not of bodies but of minds.

Thomas More made the point explicit in the verses included in his letter to Peter Gilles on receiving the picture. In one of these verses he speaks in his own voice, but first the picture itself speaks.

TABELLA LOQVITUR
Quanti olim fuerant Pollux et Castor amici,
    Erasmum tantos Egidiumque fero.
Morus ab his dolet esse loco, coniunctus amore
    Tam propre quam quisquam vix queat esse sibi.
Sic desyderio est consultum absentis, vt horum
    Reddat amans animum littera, corpus ego.

[The Painting Speaks
I represent Erasmus and Giles as as close friends as once were Castor and Pollux. More, bound to them by as great a love as any man could entertain for his own self, grieves at his physical separation from them. So the measure they took, in response to the yearnings of the absent friend, was that loving letters should make their souls present to him, and I their bodies.][48]

The translation is that offered by Lisa Jardine in her seminal work on Erasmus,[49] and (as both Jardine and the historian of intellectual history David Wootton have argued, albeit in somewhat different terms) the "amans littera" (Jardine's "loving letters") are such literary gifts as Erasmus's "presents for the mind and keepsakes of a literary description"—gifts such as More's *Utopia*.[50]

They are to my mind right. Yet the design of the portrait also employs precisely the *bodily* tokens that Erasmus disdained, and More's letter I would suggest deftly acknowledges that fact and in doing so negotiates the difficult terrain that lay between them. With his right hand Peter Gilles gestures toward the book, but in his left hand he holds a letter, evidently (to anyone close enough to read the address written on the outside) a familiar letter of friendship.

V[iro] Il[lus]trissimo Petro
Egidio Amico charissimo
Anverpiae

[To the Illustrious Peter
Gilles, beloved friend
at Antwerp][51]

The address serves of course to identify Peter Gilles, as the books on the shelves in the portraits identify this as the study of their author Erasmus; but the letter also identifies its sender. The handwriting as Thomas More points out in his letter is recognizably More's own, as that in the work Erasmus is shown as writing is Erasmus's distinctive hand: as much (if not more) a token of the body than the rings, knives, and caps that Erasmus so disparaged. "[R]emitte rogo ad me," More writes, "duplicabit miraculum apposita cum tabella. Sin aut perierit aut vobis vsui erit, ego experiar mee manus imitatorem ipse rursus imitari" [Do please let me have the letter back: it will double the effect if it is kept handy alongside the picture. If it has been lost, or if you have a use for it, I will see whether I in my turn can imitate the man who imitates my hand so well].[52]

Why does Thomas More need the return of the letter, when he could reproduce the effect of his own hand merely by picking up his pen? This is of course—if I may point out the obvious—a joke, as that curious word "littera" is a pun, employing a term that can also mean "handwriting." "Littera" in the senses in which it may be used here—as an instance of writing, or as a class of literary works, or as literary activities more generally—is more usually put in the plural than in the singular employed here.[53] The unusual form here allowed the pun: as "keepsakes of a literary description" a "littera" was a spiritual token, but as More evidently well knew, as "handwriting" it was a *bodily* token.

The joke and the pun alike have the same insouciant effect: to draw attention to the traces in the painting of More's own hand. In modern society handwriting signifies so little that the historian is apt to pass over the significance of the familiar letter being written in the sender's own hand, a significance that springs into view when one sees it being employed by a nobleman, who would have had a "secretary" not only to write his letters for him but for whom that was a trust, even a privilege. For the sender to write the letter in his own hand passed that privileged intimacy to the recipient. It was for this reason that at the crisis of 1624 James I wrote his letter to the duke of Buckingham (discussed in chapter 3) in his recognizable italic hand, despite the pain of the arthritis in his hands—nothing could have added more weight to the formidable token it represented for the duke of Buckingham than that mark of James's countenance. Fulke Greville's letter—addressed "[t]o my verie loving freend Mr Jhonn Cooke"[54]—(discussed in chapter 2)—employed the same device when it marked his peace offering to John Coke in the changed circumstances of 1615. The elegant Latin commendation that came with it—written by the scholar in his schoolroom italic script—was in substance a joke, a foil to the real mark of intimacy that Greville offered to Coke in this letter seeking his advice on the tomb of Sir Philip Sidney, written in his scrawled, ugly, and utterly distinctive hand.

The familiar letter as a token of the friend's body was no more a creation of humanism than the familiar letter itself. In the eleventh century the daughter of the anti-king Rudolf of Swabia had similarly sought a letter from Pope Gregory VII written in his own hand;[55] but the more irregular handwriting of the sixteenth century was to give the device an apt vehicle. Unlike the formal scripts that the new print culture replaced, it readily conveyed the individual trace of the author's hand, and the opportunity it provided served the needs of the new humanist scholars finely. It allowed them at once both to employ the bodily tokens by which men had always marked their friendships and at the same time rhetorically distinguished their friendships from those of the past, in a self-conscious humanist transformation of the gift of the friend's body into the gift of persuasive "letters."

More and Erasmus were enabled by such a rhetorical gesture in 1517 to negotiate the potentially dangerous sands that stood between them. Peter Gilles's gesture in the portrait draws the viewer's eye to the letter he is holding in his other hand, but on his hand there is a ring, and that ring draws the eye to the ring on the hand of Erasmus, its reflection as it were in the other panel. More would have recognized that ring as his gift to Erasmus—although probably he alone would have done so. The identification arises from a note that Erasmus made of his money and rings in April 1534, which has survived among Erasmus's papers. Several of the rings are carefully recorded by him as gifts and include four having been given to him by More: three with sapphires and one with a cameo bearing the engraved figure of a woman looking over her shoulder. This last appears to be the ring Erasmus is wearing. As Gilles holds the letter so that the viewer can see the handwriting in which its address is written, Erasmus also turns his hand as he writes to display the cameo on his ring; and as More would have recognized his own hand in the one, he would also have recognized his gift to Erasmus of that ring in the other, together with what such a gift implied.[56] By 1517 Desiderius Erasmus was in the eyes of many the greatest scholar alive in Europe, and men like Peter Gilles or Thomas More were his students and followers: but in more brutally material terms this was by no means necessarily the case. In a letter in 1516 to the French humanist Guillaume Budé (who unlike Erasmus was married), Erasmus had complained albeit with exaggeration of "vnicam vxorem mean oppono tɲn katapaton penian, quam nec adhuc humeris excutere possum, adeo ton misounta philei" [my one sole wife, that accursed Penury, whom I still cannot shake off my shoulders, such is her love for him that hates her].[57]

By contrast, in 1517 Thomas More was already a commanding figure in the administration of the law and the courts and in the merchant community of the City of London. He had direct access to a wider world and had all the signs of a brilliant public life before him: a man who might provide Erasmus with that access to patronage that Erasmus sought. The tokens of friendship in Metsys's panels made a claim to that friendship, but how was it to be given without making Erasmus More's man in the eyes of the world? That was the rub.

In this portrait More saw that claim, but the claim was visible only to him: the book to which Gilles gestures was evidently untitled, and to an observer who did not know the context, it might appear to be one of the works of Erasmus. The handwriting on the letter Gilles holds in his hand would be equally opaque, the same observer might assume it to be a letter from Erasmus, and few, if any, beyond More would recognize the ring as his gift. In the copy that Erasmus may have retained in Louvain, that invitation is hidden, for in that version the paper Gilles holds has been rolled up and the handwriting that it bears cannot be seen. The picture sent to More was an invitation but a guarded one. It invited him to provide Erasmus with the countenance he sought but, in the manner in which he did so, to indicate that he knew the limits beyond which it would not be pressed.

More fully understood what was being asked of him. Copies of his letter acknowledging the gift—and acknowledging the hand as his own— would early have circulated in manuscript. The manuscript version we have is the copy Erasmus himself had made, and the letter was soon to appear in print in Johann Froben's *Auctarium selectarum aliquot epistolarum* of 1518 and again in his *Epistolae D. Erasmi Roterodami ad diuersos* in 1521, with an editorial note that draws attention to the identification of More's hand.[58] But More's response was also offered to Erasmus in what he did not say as much as in what he did, for the gift of the ring—a gift of that "commonplace and homespun sort"—remained only between Erasmus and More. That tactful excision played its part in the enabling rhetorical gesture. It left Quentin Metsys's picture as an image of a friendship that subsisted wholly in a shared love of learning that stood (but only in rhetoric) in the place of the bodily tokens of the past. A gift such as More's *Utopia* would leave its recipient no less the independent scholar.

Laughter

In Thomas More's letter one can hear again that laughter that seemed to unsettle the conclusions of chapter 3. This is the shared laughter of men paying each other the compliment that they know what is appearance and what is not, but several centuries later on can the historian be so confident? Does that laughter suggest that the ethics of friendship may not be altogether what they seem to us now? It is that difficult question I propose now to explore.

One hears again this same laughter in a letter written to Robert Carr in the year in which he became the earl of Somerset. Like that of Thomas More, this letter contains a joke about a letter and its hand; but it also draws out what was only implicit there. If the familiar letter could be a token of the body of the friend, could it not then also be a token of its erotics? Its author was that immensely intelligent man Henry Howard, the first earl of Northampton, and the context for his letter lay in his designs to ensure his continuance in power after the death in 1612 of his friend and supporter at court Robert Cecil, the earl of Salisbury: the loss of that friendship required a new alliance, and Howard saw it in the brilliant figure of Robert Carr, whose friendship with the king seemed in 1613 to be carrying all before it. The seal of that alliance was to be the marriage of Carr with Howard's grandniece Frances Howard, the countess of Essex. When Howard wrote his letter in 1613, he was replying to a letter that Carr had evidently written to him in his own hand, to which Carr had elegantly drawn attention by the contrivance—now perhaps a recognizable one—of an apology for his handwriting. Howard's letter begins by picking up that gesture.

> Swete Lord
> Thinke not that I can finde paine in that which giue me greatest pleasur which is any thinge which procedes out of your pen and flowes from your mind . . . that am nowe as well acquainted with your hand as with my owne, and though it wear but that which a man takes in crackinge a swete nutte to

tast the kirnell or but lyke the payne which my Lady fraunces shall feele
when the swete streame followes.[59]

The image extends the erotic relationship to include Howard, and it is entirely appropriate that it should, for it united also two men. Howard's erotic
metaphor here is a familiar device. After George Villiers had succeeded to
Carr's place in the king's eyes, he was to use a similar erotic image in con-
cluding one of his letters to the king. He hopes, he writes, to make a speedy
end to the business and "in thereby getting libertie to make the speedier hast
to lay my selfe at your feete, for neuer none longed more to be in the armes
of his mistris."[60]

This was the language not only of James's court. In the preceding reign,
Antonio Pérez had written a letter to the earl of Essex in which he likened
himself to the mistress of the newly arrived secretary that Essex had sent
him, the brilliant Robert Naunton. "Nauntonun tuum amicum ad me mit-
tis, vt apud me siet, et me celet, et ambiat, tanquam amicam" [Naunton,
your friend, you send me that he may be near me and conceal and protect
me like a mistress]. Pérez's image is of course a joke—"sed, quid tu irrides
amicam senem, et Castitatem meam?" [but why do you laugh at an old mistress and my virtue?]—but the later historian may have the uneasy feeling
that these are jokes to which he or she is not fully a party. In such familiar
letters something is being said and not being said at the same time.[61]

It is a humor that could be rough and cruel, as in the message James I included for Henry Howard in a letter to Robert Cecil. The letter is heavily
laden with earthy humor, and in James's rough way it was intended to be
affectionate. This was despite the reminder to Howard of his father's execution by Henry VIII. James's message for Howard was a response to his
jocular annoyance at seeing James's sons prospering so well. James's reply
was his intention of producing more such sons to annoy Howard: "but be
he sure I will immediately upon my return have his head for this labour and
in as great haste as King Henry my noble predecessor got his father's, who
could not go ad centrum terre without it, but in one point I am greedier
than he was, for whereas the head alone served him, I will have body and all
together."[62] It could be teasing, as in the prospect John Stubbe offered his
college friend Michael Hickes concerning a certain John Drury, of whose
friendship Hickes had been jealous. (Which of us both, he had written, do
you love best?) "This term," Stubbe cheerfully volunteered, "he is like
enough to be your bedfellow."[63] Or it could be charmingly salacious, as in
the affectionate wish James Thickness included in a letter to the young John
Evelyn, who was in Rome and had written to his friend about the things he

had seen: "The scholar's wife," Thickness wrote in reply, "wished herself a book: and I a statue, to be the object of that fair mind, those dear eyes, those curious hands, which enliven antiquity as well in a friend as in a ruin."[64]

For all its insouciance, Thickness's letter was a formal familiar letter of friendship (although with a young man's good humor it turns at its end to a venison pasty and "the drinking of yᵣ health"). When Thickness and Evelyn exchanged their letters, they were practicing between themselves the eloquent gestures they hoped preferment would bring them, as indeed were John Stubbe and Michael Hickes; and nearby among the manuscripts in the British Library there is a passage in a letter from the duke of Buckingham to James I that seems to recall something very similar in the bed of the king of England. Much of the charm of George Villiers lay in his ability to make King James laugh: write to me merrily, he had said;[65] and his letters were often composed of an earthy (and scatological) humor that suited James's affection for him. Is this passage in that spirit? What it recalls appears remarkably like those curious hands in the letter of the youthful James Thickness.

> [T]here is this difference betwixt that noble hand and hart, one may surfitt by the one, but not by the other, and soner by yours then his one, therefore giue me leaue to stope with mine, that hand which hath bine but tow redie to execute the motions and affections of that kind obligeing hart to me.[66]

What are we to make of it? One explanation has been to see expressions like these as the evidence of a covert homosexuality, but the problem with such an argument is that it eventually gives way under its own weight. Those who have read such comments in this light at the court of James I appear not to have grasped that a similar humor also characterized the courts of James's predecessors Queen Elizabeth and Henry VIII, and those who have read the apparent homoeroticism in the writings of the unorthodox Christopher Marlowe have done so without grasping that the same suggestive imagery reappears also in the poetry of John Donne or the devoutly religious Richard Crashaw.[67]

The explanation of a covert homosexuality also fits ill with what such figures had to say about the sin of Sodom. The evidence does not suggest any softness toward sodomy on their part, although the "sodomy" of seventeenth-century England differed from the modern notion of "homosexuality" in a number of fundamental ways, not least in being vaguer. The passionate conventions of the familiar letter did not suggest the sodomitical. The minister of the Spanish reformed church in London, Casiodoro de Reina, received such a familiar letter from his friend and collaborator Antonio del Corro, after a long and anxious separation. In it Corro writes that, if it had not been for his wife, he would have hastened to Reina long ago, the very day as he puts it that "vide y conosci quan impossible me era biuir sin v.m." [I saw and realized how impossible it was for me to live without you]; and like the sworn brother in the Latin romance of *Amys and Amylion*, Corro describes how he had set out in desperation and impetuously to look for Reina without even knowing where to search, when "casi milagrosamente" [almost miraculously] Reina's letter arrived. Yet when Antonio del Corro preached in London on the sin of the sodomites in St. Paul's letter to the Romans, he elaborated the horror of the sin with all the exuberance of a popular preacher.[68]

The familiar letters between Tobie Matthew and Francis Bacon show the same combination of affection and usefulness one sees elsewhere.[69] Bacon helped him in his career and in the scandal that followed his conversion to Catholicism. Matthew did the same for Bacon in his disgrace and acted both as a critic and translator of his writings. Yet for Matthew sodomy was also one of "those crimes which are against nature ... ever to be detested and punished."[70] Nor did Antonio Pérez apparently see a sodomitical implication to his joke. After his flight from Spain, the Inquisition had charged him with being a sodomite (as well as a heretic and a traitor), and it would have been quite out of character for him to have added fuel to the charge. He was careful to avoid the claim that he was a heretic by the permission he obtained when he visited England to practice Catholicism. Why would he then have taken a different attitude to the charge that he was a sodomite? When he included this letter in the collection of letters he subsequently published in Paris, there was in his mind no suggestion that it might be a dangerous inlet to the Inquisition's charge of sodomy. When he had completed the letter, folded it, and sealed it, he added below the outer direction to earl of Essex the parting words "En su mano": that it had been written in his own hand, the recognizable gesture of the familiar letter written in the friend's own hand. The body on which Pérez's joke turned was not that of the sodomite but the body of the *friend*, for which the familiar letter stood.[71] In this respect King James did not differ, who in his *Basilikon Dôron* described sodomy as one of those crimes that a king was "bounde in Conscience neuer to forgiue."[72]

The shared bed and the embraces of masculine friendship suggested the sodomitical no more than the conventions of the familiar letter. Although Jeremy Taylor's *Discourse of Friendship* evidently influenced the moving terms of the monument of John Finch and Thomas Baines, his *Unum Necessarium* still characterized those guilty of sodomy as abominable, and the embraces and protestations of Euphues and Philautus (and the bed) they shared sit beside John Lyly's description of the sodomite as "a most dangerous and infectious beast."[73] The point is nicely made for the later historian by Archbishop Laud's deadly opponent the parliamentarian William Prynne, who when he edited his diary explicitly attempted to read into it the abominable sin of Sodom; but when he came to Laud's dream of sleeping with the duke of Buckingham, he merely transcribed it: its meaning was evidently too obvious to do otherwise.[74]

Are these jokes about sexuality at all? If they are, one would be hard put to explain them in such terms. But does one need to? Arguably what is common to all of these jokes is not sexuality but manliness. In James Thickness's letter do those curious hands find something more tangibly physical—and indicatively male? Is not Henry Howard's joke to Robert Carr a compliment to his ready manliness of the same kind? The context for James's joke at the expense of Henry Howard is similarly a boisterous and earthy letter from James among his male companions in the country, his "corporation, that is, of fooles, horses, & doggis." Before James's joke comes his message to Robert Cecil's niece with "a tribute of kisses" that "muste be kept counsall" from the queen and is followed by his greetings to Thomas Howard (the earl of Suffolk) that was to have been to "honest Suffoke" but which James changed into "honest bigge Suffoke" by adding "bigge" above the line, with the injunction that "& the greatter an honest thing be, it is the better." With that broad joke he turns to his "enuyouse enemie" Henry Howard and his expressions of envy at seeing James's sons prosper so well. "I hoape with goddis grace within few yeares to multiplie his greifes by sum moe sutche prikkes in his eyes," and with that the hapless Howard becomes the victim of the same humor. What the wandering hands of the young John Evelyn found in his friend, judging by such a context, was his manhood.

The argument of chapter 3, which the laughter of such documents seemed at first to unsettle, was that the wider ethics of friendship turned on the perceived ability of friendship to secure the boundaries of family and kin: that it created links of kinship across social barriers otherwise unbridgeable; that it evaded the quarrels over inheritance that could divide families; and crucially that it could stand in the place of a friend left empty by death, in the care of his children and family. These were the responsibilities James assumed when he received the children of George Villiers from their baptism. But if that ethical framework lay in the reproduction (and survival) of family and kin, where then lay the impropriety of such humor? If the one was about the male phallus, then unarguably so was the other. Laughter does not always come from mockery; it can be a sign rather of its opposite: that something can be a source of humor precisely because it is secure. This is the humor of men who might father children, whose friendships celebrated that fact and would if need be see that task through to its end. A man's honor depended on that. It depended also on the recognition that his motives for his friendship were open-hearted, that willingness to give with an open hand without calculation or self-interest. The one fixed the place of friendship within the natural order, the other equally firmly within the moral order; and both alike were acknowledged in conventions and boundaries that the historian must recover to do justice to the past—or indeed to be a historian at all.[75]

In modern society most people are likely to be more familiar with the bodies of the opposite sex than with their own. This is rather the humor of men for whom the male body, its sight, touch, and smell, was an everyday reality and (if the argument of this chapter is right) a reassuring instrument by which a man's place in society might be claimed and protected. Certainly this was not the humor of the nice and fastidious Puritan (or indeed of the Counter Reformation moralist), but the men who celebrated their manliness in jokes such as these did not, I think, feel the need to obtain the permission of a clergyman. What we are hearing here are *jokes*. Antonio Pérez's joke rested on a real distinction between the joke itself and the actuality. It turned the world upside down. In it, it is the master who becomes the conventionally weaker part and the servant the powerful: it is Pérez and not the secretary who becomes the mistress. That was why the joke was only a joke and not to be taken seriously. The same was true of George Villiers's depiction of King James as his mistress: as all the world knew, he was emphatically his master.

Jokes like this are not evidence of what men did between the sheets of a bed; they are rather evidence of what they *said* between the pages of a letter, and it is there that this humor had its context. The two letters from Buckingham to James from which I have quoted were set apart from a world of affairs only in rhetoric. Each is evidently in Buckingham's distinctive handwriting and consists of a sheet folded so that part of the sheet would have formed the outer cover for the letters—where one would have looked for the remains of the broken wax seal. The absence of a seal suggests that these letters were designed to be accompanied (within an encompassing sheet) by *other* letters or papers—which are invisible to us now—that might carry the business and could be destroyed. The postscript—"I haue inclosed tow or three letters of the Condi of Oliuares to Gundemar where by you will iudg of his kind carefullness of your sone"—confirms that surmise. Buckingham appears to have written the first of the two letters from which I have quoted at some point early in March 1623, shortly after his arrival in Spain with

James's son Charles to conduct the dangerous and difficult negotiations for Charles's marriage to the infanta Maria, the daughter of Philip III of Spain. Buckingham's absence from England risked leaving his position by the king dangerously vacant and those who resented his influence with the freer hand. Is this what was in Buckingham's mind in writing this letter?[76]

> Dere dad and gosope
> The cheefest aduertisment of all, wee omitted in oure other letter which was to lett you know how wee like, your daughter, his wife, and my ladie mistris, without flatterie I thinke there is not a sweeter creature in the world babie charles him selfe is so tuchd at the hart, that he confesses all he euer yett saw, is nothinge to her, and swares if that he want her there shall be blose, I shall louse no time in hasteing there coniuntion, in which I shall ples him her you, and my selfe most of all in thereby getting libertie to make the speedier hast to lay my selfe at your feete for neuer none longed more to be in the armes of his mistris, so craueing your blessing
> I end.

> I haue inclosed tow or three letters
> of the Condi of Oliuares to Gundemar   Your humble slaue
> where by you will iudg of his kind   and doge,
> carefullness of your sone   steenie

The point of course is that repeated "we" in the opening of the letter. George Villiers is writing a joint letter with the heir to the throne of England that places him on as near as equal a level as he could dare assume, and he is doing so in a letter that others are likely to see or to hear being read aloud to the king. It is a reminder to a watching court of who he still is, and that is the point of that closing joke. The nature of a caricature—and this joke is such—is that it is not mimetic: the laughter lies in the one point that *is* mimetic, and here that point of contact is the physical intimacy on which the joke of James as his mistress turns: the public embrace, the common table, and the shared bed that this chapter has followed. The point is evident in that other analogy that the letter makes. Its writer is also his humble slave and "dog," and a dog will lie happily by its master's bed, like a gentleman of the bedchamber at the Jacobean court; but what a dog appreciates most of all are those nights when a fond master allows him to share his bed, as George Villiers remembered that night when first "the bed's head could not be found between the master and his dog." The joke reminds a watching court that Villiers is still the bedfellow of King James I.

The humor in a second letter of George Villiers to King James came also at such a dangerous moment, although that might not be immediately evident to us now. The letter was written shortly after the patent reached Buckingham in Spain creating him a duke, the first without royal blood for near on a hundred years. There could be no question of not accepting the gift, and the countenance it gave him at the Spanish court was directed to the negotiations there, which were proving increasingly difficult. Like James's gesture in standing as godfather to his daughter, it indicated that he was James's own kin. But a gift so immense as a dukedom for a man like George Villiers was potentially compromising. A code of friendship should not come into conflict with a code of manly honor. In the eyes of the world it might make him James's man. The problem that faced Buckingham in this letter was how he could accept while guarding his honor.[77]

The answer Buckingham finds lies in James's hand, with which the letter begins: "Dere dad and gossope, It can not but haue bine an infenite truble to haue written so longe a letter and so sone espetiallie at this painefull time of your armes." The opening of the letter left no one in doubt that the letter he had received offering him his dukedom had been written in James's own hand, but the image Buckingham then chooses cautiously opens to view the quandary he is in, by its analogy of himself as Adam (and Adam's first disobedience) and James as his Maker. "I confess trewlie I ame not a gott sorie for the paynes you haue taken, this might argue I loue my selfe better then my maker, but my disobedience in this with my humble obedience in all my future actions shall wittnes the contrarie," and with this the letter turns back again to James's hand, "I can bouldlie say, it is not in the power of your large bountifull hand and hart euer hereafter eyther to encreace my dutie and loue to you, or to ouer ualue my selfe as you doe by thinkeing it fitt I should be sett so fare beyond my fellows." But then comes his reservation, in the terms we have already seen. He first appears to have continued, "I can not now name these tow things but I must expres her," but that word "now" evidently evoked a memory. He crosses out these words and continues: "there is this difference betwixt that noble hand and hart, one may surfitt by the one, but not by the other, and soner by yours then his one, therefore giue me leave to stope with mine, that hand which hath bine but tow redie to execute the motions and affections of that kind obligeing hart to me."

Did James laugh? After this opening, as the letter extends to a detailed page of argument, he sets out the reasons for refusing this gift, reasons that all would know were largely formal: the dangerous precedent it would set for James's son; the lack of distinction in Spain between the children of a duke and those of a king; and the disproportion of his estate. The first two are merely the occasion for an expression of loyalty to Charles. The last had been amply overcome, not only by James's generosity, which Buckingham acknowledges, but also by that fortune that his position by the king enabled him to obtain; and all the world knew it: that was his problem. The solution, for which his opening had prepared, lay in James's letter and the traces James's letter bore of his own hand, to which he now returns.

[T]his I say is still a good argument for me to refuse, but you haue not bine contented to rest here when I thought you had done more than enugh and as much as you could, but hath found out a way which to my harts satisfaction [is] fare beyond all, for with this letter you haue furniched and inriched my cabinet with so pretious a wittness of your ualuation of me as in future times it can not be sayde that I rise as most courtiers doe, throug importunitie, for which caracter of me and incomparabe fauor from you, I will sine with as contented nay as proude a hart
Your poure steenie
as ducke of buckingham

The valuation James had made of him—as his bedfellow and in his letter—was as a *man* and a friend. If that had been the point of the joke (if such it is), then the handwritten letter that Buckingham received was a persuasive token of that estimation. If the letter indeed contained the double entendre it seems to do, the laughter of King James at his saucy letter at such a moment would have settled that fact beyond any possible doubt for those watching eyes and listening ears. George Villiers, the duke of Buckingham, was no Henry Howard; but he had a shrewd understanding of how the world in which he lived worked.

Desire

The desire for the gift of the friend's body, as I have called it, does not correspond easily to anything in our culture several centuries on, but one can recapture the magnetism it could then exert through one of the stories in William Painter's *Palace of Pleasure*. For the modern reader this needs some teasing out, as the immense popularity of this collection of stories lay in the purchase they exercised on the fantasies of their sixteenth-century readership. The story opens with a symbolism that may by now be familiar. "Besides the country of Perche, there were two gentlemen, which from the time of their youth lived in such great and perfect amity, as there was between them but one heart, one bed, one house, one table, and one purse." The one

bed, one house, and one table is something already met, as the physical intimacy that was the friend's gift. The story's first readers would also have
been alert to that final addition, the one purse, to which the narrator returns.

> Long time continued this perfect friendship: between whom there was but
> one will and one word, no difference in either of them. Insomuch as they
> not only seemed to be two brethren, but also they appeared in all sem-
> blances to be but one man. One of them chanced to marry. Notwithstand-
> ing they gave not over their friendship, but persevered in their usual amity
> as they were wont to do. And when they happened to be strained to straight
> lodging, the married gentleman would not stick to suffer his friend to lie
> with him and his wife. But yet you ought for friendship sake to consider that
> the married man lay in the mids. Their goods were common between them,
> and the marriage did yield no cause to hinder their assured amity.

In time that amity was poisoned, by the married friend conceiving a suspicion of his wife's fidelity with his friend. The curious twist to the modern reader is that the story does not present the problem as one of jealousy
or sexual desire but in the *secrecy* that led the one friend to keep his suspicions from the other.

> I know well enough that jealousy is a passion so intolerable as love itself.
> And when you shall conceive that opinion of jealousy, yea and it were of my-
> self, I should do you no wrong, for yourself were not able to keep it. But of
> one thing which is in your power, I have good matter whereof to complain,
> and that is because you will conceal from me, your malady, sith there was
> no passion or opinion which you conceived, that before this time you kept
> secret from me. Likewise for my own part if I were amorous of your wife,
> you ought not to impute it as a fault unto me, because it is a fire which I bear
> not in my hands, to use at my pleasure. But if I kept it to myself from you,
> and endeavour to make your wife know it by demonstration of my love, I
> might then be accounted that untrustiest friend that ever lived.[78]

The moral of the tale, as Painter goes on to recount it, is that what de-
stroys their friendship is not jealousy over a woman but secrecy between
friends. Within the setting of the story is the role of the Elizabethan "secretary": the coveted route to advancement in the household of an Elizabethan noblemen for the army of poor but able graduates that the sixteenth-
century universities produced in such numbers. The origin of their title was
that they could keep a "secret" and act as their patron's go-betweens with

the world. It is that role that is being decked out here in the trappings of
this fable about secrecy and that animated the story for its sixteenth-century
readership. The setting of the story as that of two intimate friends unveiled
rather than concealed its placement in sixteenth-century society for its original readers, for the one heart the two friends shared is that stance of a disinterested affection one sees in the formal "familiar" sixteenth-century letter of friendship, often passionately expressed in ways reminiscent of James's
protestations to Robert Carr.

The story's open secret is that of a sixteenth-century secretaryship, and
from this setting comes the symbolism of the body of the friend with which
the story opens and the intimacy on which it then turns. The one house and
the one table are the coveted position in the household of a patron, the one
bed is the intimacy they gave access to, and the one purse is the reward these
could bring. The readers of Painter's book were most unlikely to have had
such a coveted post: they were rather the kind of men that dreamed of having one, and that dream was the fantasy this story played on: its moral was
that they should be trusted, and its fantasy was that one day they might be.
This fantasy was encouraged because the author tantalizingly presents himself in the familiar letter to the earl of Warwick that opens the volume as in
actuality himself possessing just such a relationship. The excitement the
story was designed to arouse—almost pornographic in its virtual setting—
is directed not toward the body of the friend's wife, the tale of adultery that
we might now be inclined to see as the narrative structure, but toward the
body of the male friend himself.

The Silence between the Lines

The body of the friend has been the missing piece within the argument of
this book, an instrument that brought into being friendship's obligations.
Friendship was not given lightly. Given solemnly and before witnesses, its
gestures gave to the obligations of friendship the objective character that
made them indistinguishable from those of kinship. Less evident to later
historians are the resentment and dangers those obligations carried with
them, dangers that were ethical as well as pragmatic. How could friendship
be distinguished from mere collusion or from a cynical self-advancement?
One response to that ethical uncertainty was the eucharistic rite that I have
followed from the eleventh to the seventeenth century as a guide through a
terrain that at times seemed bewildering. A pragmatic response to its dangers was the indirection (and laughter) of the language of friendship, a

means of testing the ground before that dangerous moment when the obligations of friendship were created or called upon.

Yet it is likely now to have become apparent to the reader that the tangible presence of the body of the friend has also made unavoidable a problem that has several times surfaced and been put aside. Why are its terms so silent about women? The problem first appeared in connection with that eucharistic rite whose path I have followed, as the traces of its use (in England at least) are between men. Yet female children were baptized as well as male children, and women as well as men received Holy Communion. The historian needs to be wary of making an argument from silence. It may be more *visible* between men, but that it was restricted to them is another matter. But the problem surfaced again with the public embraces, the common tables, and the shared beds of this chapter, which seem to signify largely if not entirely in a world of men. Tables and beds were shared as much by women as men.[79] One now sees these gestures of physical intimacy most clearly among the men of the great households, but these were not masculine enclaves cut off from women. The guide to the place of such gestures, I have argued, was the nature of the signs themselves rather than necessarily the context in which we now see them most clearly several centuries later. But how often can one make that argument?

The problem returns and is not to be gainsaid in the bodily humor of friendship, for the body that comes into view there is unambiguously (and indicatively) male. That perhaps more than any other reason has justified the pages devoted to its insistently phallic humor. It suggests that the problem is more than one of merely finding the evidence, that the silence itself may be part of the evidence. There is a possible test of that question. Women are not as visible as men in the historical record because they often lacked the property and influence of which such records are often the trace, but an argument like that will not apply to their place in the *stories* of the past, and the stories of sworn friendship have been one of the threads in this book. Do women figure there? The answer is emphatically yes, not as friends, but as the enemies of friendship.

Friendship is not symmetrical between men and women in these stories. In the romance *Athelston* the wrongs suffered by the sworn brothers are reversed, while those suffered by a wife are not.[80] In the versions of *Amys and Amylion*, when one of the friends is stricken with leprosy, the response of his wife is to drive him out or to try to kill him. His friend takes him in and cares for him. In Chaucer's *Knightes Tale* the two sworn brothers are divided not by friendship but through a woman (as they are in William Painter's story).

Yet if one cannot walk past the silence in these stories about the friendship of women, even less can one account for the nightmare quality that silence assumes. A part of the story of *Amys and Amylion* has so far not found a place in my argument: the explanation of why it is that the two sworn brothers lie together in death not with their wives but with each other. The answer in part is this. When the angel Raphael is sent by God to Amicus lying with his friend in their bed—"Amice, dormis?" [*Amicus*, are you sleeping?]—the message he bears is how his leprosy may be cured. The blood of Amelius's children, the angel tells him, will effect the cure. Amelius must sacrifice them to save his friend: so he does, and what lies between him and his fidelity is his wife. The moment for the test of that fidelity comes when she is at church: Amelius severs the heads of his children, collects the blood, and in that blood as if in a second baptism his friend is saved. God confirms the rightness of his fidelity, the children are restored to life by divine intervention, and—on the day that Amicus is healed—his wife is slain by the devils who have entered her. *That* is the reason that Amicus lies in death not beside his wife but beside his friend.[81]

Is there anything in what I have written that can explain that story? If there is, I cannot see it. Stories like this are not, of course, transparent windows on the past; they are stories about its dreams and its fears, but the lack of symmetry in them is telling. It is the same problem, writ large, as the more mundane problem of the absence of women from that historical evidence on which my account has been based. This is not a mere silence. This society does not, evidently will not, explain this lack of symmetry but rather asserts it. The historian must either accept such fears as irrational—and ultimately therefore inexplicable—or accept the role (at the last) of a reluctant protagonist and press the past for an account that goes beyond what it is ready to give. There is an evident shadow across the world of friendship that I have described that the past itself is unwilling to explain, and if the work is to be taken through to its end, the task is to follow that shadow to the figure from which it is being cast, to look it in the face, and to give it its name.

CHAPTER 5

Friends and Enemies

While he was still speaking a crowd appeared with the man called Judas, one of the Twelve, at their head. He came up to Jesus to kiss him; but Jesus said, "Judas, would you betray the Son of Man with a kiss?"

As one walks down Rome's Via di Montoro toward the Via Giulia, one seems to pass suddenly from the Rome of the Middle Ages into the High Renaissance. The narrow and dark alleys of the fifteenth century open onto the Via di Monserrato, a street of baroque churches and fine palaces that at its end culminates in the piazza before the Palazzo Farnese. That abrupt transition would have been marked for any visitor to Rome at the end of the sixteenth century by the cries and hammering of the workmen restoring this quarter of the city, as a newly resurgent Catholicism was transforming the streets and buildings as well as the religious fervor of Rome. This was the triumphalist Rome of the Counter Reformation, and when Felice Peretti became its bishop as the energetic reformer Pope Sixtus V, little seemed to stand in the way of its triumph beyond a handful of quarreling rebels in the Low Countries and the heretic queen of England.

One such visitor in the spring of 1586 was an Englishman named Robert Morton; and the Venerable English College in the Via di Monserrato, where Morton stayed during his visit to Rome, remains today a living link with that time. At the end of the sixteenth century, the hospice for English pilgrims to Rome had been transformed into a seminary for zealous young Englishmen training there for the priesthood, men who would take the oath to return on the dangerous mission to win back England for the Catholic faith. After his visit, Morton left a monument in the church of the English college, which can still be seen there today and remains a graphic witness to the idealism and the defiance that the friendship of traditional society could ignite (see fig. 7).[1]

D O M

R D NICHOLAO MORTONO PRO ANGELO

SACRAE THEOLOGIAE DOCTORI CLARO QVI

AMICIS CHARS CAETERISQ BONIS OIB PRO

FIDE CATHOLICA IN PATRIA AMISSIS AO

EXILII SVI XXV AETATIS VERO LXVI ROMAE

MORTVVS E A D MDLXXXVII D XXVII M IA

SEPELIRIQ VOLVIT EODEM TVMVLO CVM R

D SETONO CVM QVO EADE RELIGIOIS

CAVSA EX ANGLIA AVFVGIT ROMAQ SIMVL

VENIT

ROBERTVS MORTONVS NEPOS AMATISSIMO

PATRVO POSVIT

[To the Reverend Nicholas Morton
priest, Englishman and a celebrated doctor of sacred theology,
who having lost his dearest friends and all his other goods
in his native country for the sake of the Catholic Faith
died at Rome in the 25th year of his exile and the 66th of his age
in the year of Our Lord 1587, on the 27th day of the month of January.
It was his wish to be buried in the same tomb with the Reverend John Seton
with whom he fled from England for the same cause, that of religion,
and who came to Rome at the same time.
Robert Morton, his nephew, erected this tablet to a most loving uncle.]

Like John Bloxham and John Whytton before them, Nicholas Morton and John Seton had been priests and scholars, fellows of Cambridge colleges: Morton of Trinity College and Seton of St. John's College (and the author of one of the most popular native logic textbooks to be used in sixteenth-century England), but each also played an active role in England's attempted return to Catholicism under Queen Mary. When in 1558 Mary died childless, to be succeeded as queen by Elizabeth, that attempt lay in ruins, and Morton and Seton went together to Rome as exiles. By 1587 Seton had been dead for twenty years, and this testimony to Morton's enduring wish to be buried with his friend is a telling measure not only of the strength of their friendship but also of the ideals it articulated. In this inscription Morton's wish to be buried with his friend corresponds defiantly to the loss of

Figure 7
The memorial plaque of Father Nicholas Morton and Father John Seton at
the Venerable English College, Rome.

worldly place and possessions, and its setting in the English college speaks
eloquently of what that choice was understood by their contemporaries to
signify. Below the inscription are the skull and the bones of their remains,
but above, these are transformed by the design in which an angel with its
wings outspread in flight ascends to the cross that surmounts the monument, and the cartouche (bearing heraldic arms) is supported by palm leaves
symbolizing victory over death and the grave. The cross here is bare, without the figure of the crucified Christ. The cross rather drew the eye across
the chapel to the high altar and to the dramatic painting by Durante Alberti
placed above it. In Alberti's painting God the Father is depicted enthroned
with the Holy Spirit holding the body of the crucified Christ; and part of
the globe of the earth is visible below, where the outline of England can be
seen. The cross from which Christ has been lifted (the same cross as on this
monument) hangs in space between the two, and from his wounds Christ's

blood falls across the universe. As it falls onto England below, it bursts into flame. "IGNEM VENI MITTERE IN TERRÂ" is the motto held aloft by an angel like that on the monument. "I have come to bring fire onto the earth."

Robert Morton's monument was designed to correspond to that defiant motto. In December 1586 Robert Morton returned to the English college and stayed there with Nicholas Morton for eleven days: his farewell to his uncle, who was to die a few weeks later, but also a discussion that was to shape Robert Morton's own life and the memory he was to leave behind him. His own decision to enter the seminary and in April 1587 to take the oath to risk his life as a priest in England coincided with his placing this monument in the chapel of the college. The *Liber Ruber* still held in the college, recording those who took the oath, contains the entry for Robert Morton in April 1587 with the defiant addition placed prominently by Morton at the end "propria manu scripsit," that it had been written in his own hand. Later that year he became a priest and, as he had vowed, returned to England and the mission. When the following year the news reached the college that Morton had suffered martyrdom for his priesthood in Lincoln's Inn Fields, it was by this monument, in the church of the English college, that the defiant students gathered to sing the *Te Deum Laudamus* before the painting of the crucified Christ: "We praise thee, O God, we acknowledge thee to be the Lord. All the earth doth worship thee . . . The noble army of Martyrs, praise thee."[2] To come to this monument aware of the uncertainties that dogged the ethics of friendship in traditional society is to be aware of how much the friendship it articulated represented a defiant answer to those doubts for the zealous young men who read its terms. Nicholas Morton and John Seton had given up everything—this is what it is saying—not for each other but rather together for something greater that touched the stars.

It comes correspondingly as a shock to grasp how their contemporaries in England who did not share their Catholic faith might have interpreted a friendship of two men in such a context: in a popish college of young men administered by the Jesuits, as the English college was, Ignatius of Loyola's Society of Jesus. However extraordinary it may seem to us now, the assumption such contemporaries appear to have carried is that two such men would have been defiant and outspoken sodomites. Ephraim Pagitt's greatly popular *Heresiography* ("a description of the Hereticks and Sectaries of these latter times," as he put it) was to contend not only that the Jesuits tolerated the sin of the sodomites but that they openly defended it.

These are the most pernicious and dangerous sort of all others. These are not ignorant Sots like the Anabaptists, and others, but educated and brought up in all manner of humane learning, and so more able to doe mischiefe. These take upon them to justifie all the Errours and abominations of Antichrist; yea, their Idolatries, and Sodomiticall uncleannesse they will defend and maintaine.[3]

The association of popery with sodomy is a familiar device amid the anti-Catholic propaganda of the Reformation, but the problem with making sense of it is that it is not explained there: it is rather asserted and its characteristic logic is simply circular. This is how the reformed Cambridge theologian William Perkins explained it, in terms of the inevitable influence of papal Rome itself.

[T]he Church of Rome is that Sodom wherein the two prophets were slain (Revelation 11:8). It is there so called because it matcheth Sodom in her sins in that it teacheth the sins of Sodom in making laws to inhibit lawful marriage in sundry sorts of men, to tolerate fornication and such filthiness. Yea, not only by the scriptures but in many other sundry, ancient, and some of their own records it is manifest that Rome is a Sodom.[4]

An argument such as this seems not only to defy sense but also the absence of any evidence that the historian can now see. One cannot judge whether Ephraim Pagitt and William Perkins (or others like them) actually believed these claims: one can only say that they made them. But *why* did they make them? Why in effect did they expect them to be believed?

Claims like this occupy for a historian the uncomfortable ground constituted by fantasy, and it is tempting swiftly to dispose of the problem by a robust judgment on the historian's part that moves to more readily intelligible ground. The passages below are taken from two historians who have responded in such a ready manner, but the terms in which they do so illustrate sharply how quickly the historian can then come to an uncomfortable dead end. Certainly both appear to find evidence for their judgment. The first is from a recent study that attributes the prejudice against homosexuality in the England of James I not to questions of religion but to underlying anxieties about gender and a fear of effeminacy. The second is from a major English historian who could be taken to have identified the psychological origins of that fear.

Sodomy was always understood in gendered terms . . . Always somewhere lurking in the background of prejudice against sex between males there was a revulsion against—or rather a fear of—effeminacy . . . In the late sixteenth

and early seventeenth centuries, the fear that effeminacy led to sodomy and
became a sign of sodomy was spelled out in anti-theatrical tracts which argued that when boys dressed in women's clothing on the stage, it threatened
to make the actors themselves more feminine; it even threatened to effemi-
nize male observers in the audience . . . the connection between effeminacy
and sodomy is as plain as day in the anti-theatrical tracts of Philip Stubbes,
John Rainolds and William Prynne.[5]

What seems undeniable is that there was an acutely felt anxiety in Tudor and
early Stuart England about how women could best be governed and controlled . . . The popular literature of the time is full of tales of frustrated adolescent heroines . . . So it would not have surprised Shakespeare's playgoers
to find Desdemona pleading before the Venetian senate to be allowed to accompany Othello to Cyprus in order that her marriage could be consum-
mated . . . Women's desire, once awoken, was seen as unquenchable . . . The
dilemmas felt by men about women were based not so much on simple mi-
sogyny as upon anxiety and fears about women's assertiveness and independence in speech and action, fears which often came back to their sexuality.[6]

The fears of women (and consequently of effeminacy) that Anthony Fletcher
conveys in the second quotation provide in Michael Young's terms an intelligible explanation for expressions of hostility to homosexuality. Yet a
troubling aspect of these two accounts is their consequent inability to explain
why men should have felt these fears. Neither study presents any evidence that
women in the sixteenth and seventeenth centuries were more assertive or sexually voracious, or why they should have been perceived to be so. The unspoken assumption in both of these passages is that, because the prejudice in
these fears was irrational, it is therefore ultimately inexplicable. Its character
(from the viewpoint of the historian) is simply that it would give way eventually to more rational conceptions of gender in modern terms, to which
the study by Fletcher then turns. That gap in the argument corresponds to
the accompanying assumption that the sources these descriptions employ
are plain windows onto such fears (expressed in that image of transparency
that Young employs), that these comments are historical evidence of what
their authors feared rather than strictly only of what they *said* they feared.
Were the two the same? I propose in this chapter to explore the possibility
that they were not, that these expressions of fear may be the traces of strategies that were not necessarily designed to identify the ends they served—
and that *that* is why the fears they voice appear so curiously inexplicable.

An inlet to that possibility is given by the curiously unacknowledged symmetry between two images that exercised a compelling grip on the imagination of traditional society in England, if the many references left to them are a reliable guide. One is the image of the masculine friend that has been the subject of this book. The other is the figure called the sodomite. The reaction these two images prompted was wildly different; the one was universally admired, the other execrated and feared: yet in their uncompromising symmetry they paralleled each other in an uncanny way. Why this was and what it tells us of traditional society in England is what I have set out to explore in this chapter. It begins then among the shadows, on the edge of social life, in dreams and fantasies. But I shall argue that if we follow their outline we will emerge eventually into the daylight, in the very center of this culture. But we will go by a road, which I hope to lay open in this chapter, which this culture itself was unwilling to acknowledge was there.

An Unnatural Intimacy

The "sodomite" of the sixteenth century differed from the modern "homosexual" in a number of fundamental ways. One was that it escaped the notion of a distinct homosexual minority, although sodomy was nonetheless regarded with a readily expressed horror. In principle it was a crime that anyone was capable of, like murder or blasphemy. This is the New England minister Thomas Shepard in his *Sincere Convert* of 1641.

> [T]hy heart is a foul sink of all atheism, sodomy, blasphemy, murder, whoredom, adultery, witchcraft, buggery; so that, if thou hast any good thing in thee, it is but as a drop of rosewater in a bowl of poison; where fallen it is all corrupted. It is true thou feelest not all these things stirring in thee at one time . . . but they are in thee like a nest of snakes in an old hedge. Although they break not out into thy life, they lie lurking in thy heart.

"Sodomy" and Shepard's "buggery" were overlapping (and equally vague) terms: the first was the scholarly word, the second the vulgar, which Shepard is here using for emphasis. It was, according to John Rainolds, not only a "monstrous sin against nature" but also one to which "men's natural corruption and viciousness is prone." It was sometimes attributed to drunkenness, and a sixteenth-century minister accused of sodomy said when first confronted that what he had done he had done in his sleep. The logic is the same as that of Shepard. It was not part of the individual's nature: it was part of all human nature and could surface when the mind was dulled or sleeping, much as someone might commit murder in a drunken fit or in a dream.[7]

But the notion of sodomy differed from our contemporary idea of homosexuality in a number of other ways also. It covered more hazily a whole range of sexual acts, of which sexual acts between people of the same sex were only a part. It was closer to an idea like debauchery. Another difference is suggested by the phrase John Rainolds uses: for all its vagueness, it was thought of as an essentially masculine sin, a distinctively "masculine bestiality."[8] But it differed also in that it was not only a sexual crime. It was also a political and a religious crime, and it is on this point that I propose to dwell here. One can see this sharply outlined in the accusations made in Elizabeth's reign against the rebellious nobleman Edward de Vere by his erstwhile fellow conspirators. The picture they draw is of a man who was not only a sodomite but also an enemy of society: a traitor and a man given to lawless violence against his enemies. He was also, they tell us, a habitual liar, an atheist, and a blasphemer. The charge of sodomy was not merely added to the list. It symbolized it. If this man was a rebel against nature, was it surprising that he was also a rebel against society and the truth (or the Truth) that supported it? Sodomy, the jurist Edward Coke wrote, was "crimen laesae majestatis, a sin horrible committed against the king: and this is either against the king celestial or terrestrial." It was in this way that the ubiquitous association of sodomy with treason and heresy was put together and why one encounters it so commonly in the polemics of Reformation Europe.[9] Ephraim Pagitt's claims of the Jesuits' defense of sodomy is preceded and given its base by a more political charge. "The Jesuites also teach it to be not only lawfull, but also meritorious to lay hands upon the Lords Anoynted, and to murther Hereticke Kings after the Pope hath declared them to bee such."[10]

After 1570 this was no light claim. In 1570 the austere Pope Pius V—the very embodiment of the Counter Reformation—had publicly declared Elizabeth of England to be a heretic and excommunicate. As the buildings and streets of Rome were being rebuilt in 1586, other workmen in ports along the coast of Spain and Portugal would soon be fitting an armada designed to bring to England the fearsome and bloodied troops of the formidable Alessandro Farnese, the duke of Parma, and to restore the Catholic faith by brute force of arms. The Robert Morton with whom this chapter opened was martyred on 28 August 1588, as the reaction in England to the arrival of the Armada reached its climax. In my third chapter, on families and friends, I discussed that equivocal capacity the ideals of friendship could possess to articulate what might seem—from one viewpoint—fidelity but from another sedition. The terms of the monument Robert Morton left in the Venerable English College in Rome can be seen indirectly to articulate the wider issues of authority at stake in the college itself in 1579 when the students successfully rebelled against its government. One of the choices put forward by the students to be rector at that time was Robert Morton's uncle, Nicholas Morton, commemorated in this monument with his friend John Seton. What was at issue in the events of 1579 was, as John Bossy has explained them, an irreconcilable difference of opinion about the purpose of the foundation: a house of studies to enable the exiles to secure employment abroad while they awaited the inevitable return of England to Rome or a missionary activism. The latter—the view that was to triumph in the college and that was expressed by the missionary oath—emphatically did not entail rebellion against the sovereign, but it created a tension between the ideals of missionary activism and those that had characterized the church in England under Mary, which presupposed obedience to the sovereign: a tension that was exemplified in Nicholas Morton's visit to England as the northern rebellion of 1569 took shape. The description by the later rector of the college, Robert Persons, of the zealous students in 1579 would not have been lost on his contemporaries. They made, as he put it, "their consciences the ground of all their proceedings," and

many did imagine to see a certayne company of Lawrences, Sebastians and the like intractable fellowes, who brought Emperours and princes to desperation to deal with them, for that they could neyther with giving or taking away, neyther with faire wordes nor with foule bring them to condesend to any one little poynt that they misliked. Many also strangers made this consequent; if these fellowes stand thus immovable before such Princes in Rome, what will they do in England before the Heretiques?[11]

For the earnest young men in the English college in Rome, the fire in Durante Alberti's painting by the monument Morton left in its church was the fire of their faith—not that of invasion. The painting dates from 1583, and at the time of Robert Morton's visit was a dramatic recent addition to the church; its motto "Ignem veni mittere in terrâ" is a quotation from the Gospel according to Luke (12:49), where it refers to Jesus' coming passion in Jerusalem. Earlier in the Gospel Jesus rebukes two of the apostles for seeking to bring fire down on the Samaritan village that would not receive him, "quia facies eius erat euntis in Ierusalem" [because his face was set toward Jerusalem] (Luke 9:51–56). The body of the crucified Christ depicted in the painting was that made present on the altar below, and the setting of Nicholas Morton's monument was no less eucharistic and irenic than that of John Finch and Thomas Baines would be by the communion table in

Christ's College a century later. But to many English men and women the fire consuming England in Durante Alberti's painting might well have presaged, in their eyes, a different conflagration. The part shaped the whole, and the Jesuit's "plotting of Treasons," of which Ephraim Pagitt had no doubt, was for such men and women imbued with the propaganda of the Reformation evidence enough that they would defend and maintain both treason and sodomy alike.

The intimacy of the masculine friend, the subject of chapter 4, was an image far removed from this, an image of intimacy between men in stark contrast to the "uncivil" image of the sodomite, although in some respects they occupied a similar terrain. Each required a physical closeness, and the gestures of the one—in the embrace and the shared bed—were indeed sometimes also those of the other; but the conventions of friendship were set a world away from the wild sin of Sodom by the placid orderliness of the relationships they expressed. The anarchic crime of which Edward Coke wrote was evidently a different thing. In 1629 the preacher John Harris expanded on the destruction of Sodom before the House of Commons in the fast sermon for that year and puts the point nicely. "Indeed, peccatum nefandum, that sin not fit to be named, the high hand of God hath kept out of our Countrey, and euer may it remaine a stranger."[12] The sodomite was not the friend: he was the stranger.

The distinction between the two was then apparently sharp and clearly marked: the one was expressed in orderly "civil" relations, the other in subversive; and this simple distinction explains a good deal of what we see. But it does not explain quite all. On occasion one can also come across a document that appears—against all expectations—to be putting the two together and reading a sodomitical meaning by such a monstrous image into just those conventions of friendship which elsewhere seemed protected from that interpretation. Rare though they are, these documents are not to be dismissed as mere curiosities, and I propose to look at two such documents closely, for they suggest that this distinction was neither as sharp nor as clearly marked as the contemporaries of John Harris or Edward Coke would have us believe. They cast an unexpectedly bright light on that hidden road I mentioned: the unacknowledged connection between the unmentionable vice of Sodom and the friendship that all accounted commendable.

One of these documents is a denunciation made in 1601 by a paid informer named William Reynolds, whose subject was a certain Piers Edmonds, a soldier who had been in Ireland with the earl of Southampton before Southampton joined Essex's ill-fated rebellion of that year. Edmonds, he implies, was likely to have been a rebel as his master had been; and into this implication Reynolds weaves a story of an unnatural intimacy between the two men that told its own tale.[13]

> I do marvel also what became of Piers Edmonds, called Captain Piers or Captain Edmonds, the Earl of Essex man, born in Strand near me, one which has had many rewards and preferments by the Earl Essex. His villainy I have often complained of. He dwells in London. He was corporal general of the horse in Ireland under the Earl of Southampton. He ate and drank at his table and lay in his tent. The Earl of Southampton gave him a horse which Edmonds refused a hundred marks for him. The Earl Southampton would coll [embrace] and hug him in his arms and play wantonly with him. This Piers began to fawn and flatter me in Ireland, offering me great courtesy, telling me what pay, graces and gifts the earls bestowed upon him, thereby seeming to move and animate me to desire and look for the like favour. But I could never love and affect them to make them my friends, especially Essex, whose mind I ever mistrusted.

Behind this account is the familiar stereotype that the man guilty of "unnatural filthiness" would be also very likely a traitor. But the evidence Reynolds points to so menacingly—the table they shared, the common tent in which they slept, and the embraces Reynolds saw—were all the conventional signs of friendship that I described in chapter 4; and that the characters in this drama understood them in this way is strongly suggested by the openness of Edmonds's boasting and the public nature of these embraces, for they must indeed have been public if someone like Reynolds could have been a witness to them.

A document such as this poses an interesting question about what its author is doing, but first the other such document I mentioned. This works in a similar way but is far more famous. The relationship of Edward and Gaveston in Christopher Marlowe's sixteenth-century play *Edward II* is of a piece with all that I have said of friendship in this book and is the spectacular center of the play, in that it is Edward's love for Gaveston and Gaveston's rise to power that prompt the rebellion of Edward's resentful nobles and his ensuing tragedy and death. Modern critics of the play have recognized that its conventions are those of sixteenth-century, not fourteenth-century, England. But those who have written of the apparently openly "homosexual" nature of the play have not grasped its irony or that the intense emotion, the passionate language, and the embraces we see between these two men have ready parallels in Elizabethan England in the daily conventions of friendship without being signs of a sodomitical relationship. When we look for signs of overt sexuality, what we see are rather Edward as a father and his determination to marry Gaveston to his niece. The latter is no incidental detail, nor is it an accident that she is referred to quite simply as the king's niece, as her role is to unite Gaveston and Edward as well as to give Gaveston a wife. In the same way Henry Howard, the earl of Northampton, in the daylight world of Jacobean England would seek to bind himself to the powerful Robert Carr by Carr's marriage to his grandniece Frances Howard.[14]

The gestures of friendship in this play are those this book has followed and open with those two quintessential expressions of the friendship between men in sixteenth-century England: the familiar letter and the public embrace.

[*Enter* Gaveston *reading on a letter that was brought him from the king.*]

My father is deceast, come Gaveston,
And share the kingdom with thy dearest friend.
Ah words that make me surfet with delight:
What greater blisse can hap to *Gaveston*,
Then live and be the favorit of a king?
Sweete prince I come, these these thy amorous lines,
Might have enforst me to have swum from France,
And like Leander gaspt upon the sande,
So thou wouldst smile and take me in thy armes.

Gaveston's sexual image—for Leander swam the Hellespont to be with Hero—is a product of the same sexual imagery that, as Marlowe's play was being published and read for the first time, Antonio Pérez was employing in his letters to the industrious (and influential) secretary of the earl of Essex, Anthony Bacon, busy making a secure place for himself in the household of the earl. So is Edward's:

Welcome to *Tinmouth*, welcome to thy friend,
Thy absence made me droope, and pine away,
For as the lovers of faire *Danae*,
When she was lockt up in a brasen tower,
Desirde her more, and waxt outragious,
So did it sure with me: and now thy sight
Is sweeter farre, then was thy parting hence
Bitter and irkesome to my sobbing heart.

The passionate language is the stuff of the romances of male friendship, of Guy and Tirry or of Amys and Amylion, but its sexual image might as well have been Pérez writing to one of the secretaries of the earl of Essex. The link is that confident masculinity that I described in the last chapter, expressed alike in sexual potency as in the bonds that bound men: "amant enim clientes sicut vxores maritos viros viriles," wrote Pérez in one of his letters to the earl of Essex [clients love masculine men, as wives their husbands].[15]

To interpret Edward's friendship with Gaveston in the play as homosexual is not only to employ an anachronism, it is also to miss the extent to which it employs the familiar conventions that negotiated the uncertainties of the risky world of masculine friendship in sixteenth-century England, a rhetoric that this book has followed. Gaveston's protestation of his love for Edward—"It shall suffice me to enjoy your love"—is in the same carefully conventional form as that of the calculating secretary of Antonio Pérez making his report to his father: "I aunswered for him that I onely desyred him to love me." What the queen's watchful eyes see in the play—"He claps his cheekes, and hanges about his neck, / Smiles in his face, and whispers in his eares"—is the same as that the jaundiced Anthony Weldon reported—"The Earl when he kissed his hand, the King hung about his neck slabbering his cheeks"—or the watching eyes of Thomas Howard saw when anatomizing the rise to power of Robert Carr: "The Prince leaneth on his arm, pinches his cheek, smooths his ruffled garment . . . We are almost worn out in our endeavours to keep pace with this fellow in his duty and labour to gain favour." The opening of the play is its epitome. Its pressing depiction of the friendship between Edward and Gaveston can be read with precision and more historical sense as the urgent measures that any new ruler in sixteenth-century England needed to take on acquiring the throne of England. Edward—like Mary in 1553 or Elizabeth in 1559—is taking the necessary steps to acquire a body of "friends" to secure his position, as we see Gaveston doing in his turn and as his opponent Mortimer later says he will do: "Mine enemies will I plague, my friends advance."[16]

Yet there are in the relationship of Edward and Gaveston dark suggestions of sodomy. It is there in the sexual ambiguity of the opening. When the naked and lovely boy in Gaveston's entertainment for Edward holds a bush "to hide those parts which men delight to see," is it the body of the boy that is being hidden or of the goddess he is playing? It is there in the later comparison of Gaveston to the classical Ganymede, the beautiful youth caught up by Zeus to be his cupbearer. Giles Fletcher could compare Christ's ascension without embarrassment to the fate of Ganymede, but "ganymede" was also used more crudely as a synonym for a catamite.[17] It is there also in Gaveston's foreign birth and Italianate ways, both of which were associated in Elizabethan England with sodomy.[18] It is there most clearly but most disturbingly in the hideous sodomitical murder of Edward at the end of the play. Yet this one clear statement of Edward's sodomitical sin is put in the hands of a man called Lightborne, whose name is but an Anglicized echo of Lucifer, the father of all lies. Marlowe describes in this play what could be a sodomitical relationship, but he places it wholly within the incompatible conventions of Elizabethan friendship, in a tension that he never allows to be resolved. The image we see is simultaneously both that of friendship and its caricature.[19]

Such unlikely texts as these of William Reynolds's denunciation and Marlowe's play prompt the same question. They appear to be bringing together images that were usually kept quite detached from each other. Why, we might well ask, did their authors think they would be believed? The answer casts a light on the society in which these documents were put together quite as much as it does on the documents themselves. The answer in short is this. As a contemporary would have seen far more readily than we do, some of the conventions of friendship are missing in these accounts, and the missing ones are precisely those that ensured that the intimacy of these conventions would be read in an acceptable frame of reference. They were not only missing in these accounts: by the end of the sixteenth century especially, they were also often missing in society at large. It is this that these documents point up. One missing assumption was that both masters and their close servingmen would be "gentle," men (as a work published in 1598, entitled *A Health to the Gentlemanly Profession of Seruingmen*, puts it) "made of their own metal, even a loaf of their own dough, which being done ... the gentleman received even a gentleman into his service."[20] It is this missing propriety that William Reynolds indirectly alludes to when he describes Piers Edmonds as a man born in the Strand "near me" or as another description of Edmonds puts it more bluntly, "a man of base birth"; and the nobles' frequently repeated complaints of Gaveston's "base" birth in *Edward II* make the same point.

A second assumption that is missing is that the bond between a master and such an intimate companion was personal, not mercenary. It this missing assumption that William Reynolds alludes to in the damning commentary he quietly adds to Piers Edmonds's boasting, beginning with that simple but all important participle, "seeming to move and animate me to desire and look for the like favour." His motives were as base as his origins: that is what Reynolds indirectly is telling his reader. Gaveston's motives are as suspect as Reynolds would have us believe Edmonds's were. The opening scene in the play makes that all too clear, as does the image Marlowe later has Gaveston unconsciously lapse into. It begins with the same—eminently proper—sentiment that Antonio Pérez's servant professed. It ends brutally different.

> It shall suffice me to enjoy your love,
> Which whiles I have I think myself as great
> As Caesar riding in the Roman streets
> With captive kings at his triumphant car.[21]

The absence of these two reassuring conventions left what remained open to a darker interpretation. What then was one seeing? If someone had acquired a place in society to which he was not entitled by nature and could then perhaps even lord it over those who were naturally his betters, the specter likely to be conjured up in the minds of an Elizabethan was not the orderly relationship of friendship between men but rather the profoundly disturbing image of the sodomite, that enemy not only of nature but of the order of society and the proper kinds and divisions within it. Perhaps, it darkly suggested, it was the signs of *this* that one was seeing? It is this fear that Reynolds and Marlowe played on with such skill.

Such documents warn one against making a mistake one might otherwise easily fall into; they clarify that what one is seeing in such a structure of ideas as I have described in this book is not a collective and automatic mentality, of any kind. It is rather a kind of code: the difference between the two lay in that a code was something individuals were still free to manipulate. They may not have done it very often, but the possibility of consciously manipulating the signs of this code, for their own benefit, was always there: and it is not an accident that the two clearest examples I have seen were created by authors whose task was to shape and manipulate meaning: to tell tales. But this was not merely sleight of hand, and it is this that makes these documents so revealing. These two authors were able to present such credible pictures precisely because the conventions that were so crucially absent in these accounts were also in practice often absent in daily life. It was because contemporaries were often *not* following the ideals of service that Elizabethans wrote their tracts expounding them, as the tracts themselves make clear. A master looking for a useful servant might well prefer the industrious servant who was poor but able and anxious to better himself to the better born one, and the protestations of disinterested friendship and service one reads so frequently were often hollow. These proprieties are the conventional niceties that all too often were no more than pretense.

"You may boldly write for his favour in this matter," a lawyer in Elizabethan London wrote. "You paid well for it."[22]

Such cynicism was probably always likely to have been justified, but something wider is at work here also. A broad hint of this is given in *A Health to the Gentlemanly Profession of Servingmen*. The decay in the conventions of service, its author tells us, was something that he could still remember. The Lisle letters support that judgment; in them we see the conventions of personal service still very much alive in the 1530s. Why then the change? According to the anonymous author of this work, the change was brought about by the decline in the openhanded "housekeeping" of the great house. It was also due, he tells us, to the replacement of gentlemen retainers by servants drawn from outside the gentry, a change that was referred to also by Walter Darell in his conduct book for servingmen, published in 1572. The gentleman servingman was being replaced with "the rich farmer's son," as Walter Darell puts it, a man who will "drudge in their business."[23]

Behind these complaints lies the sixteenth-century decline in the hordes of retainers in the great houses of an earlier England and the conventions of personal service associated with them, a change these tracts closely document. Such great households were by no means extinct in Elizabeth's reign. Lord Burghley was still able to say that it was his disease to have too many servants although there was little he could do about it, and early in the following century we still see Henry Howard, the earl of Northampton, taking into his household the sons of his gentry supporters.[24] But servingmen like these were increasingly an anachronism. The able and hardworking secretaries of the earl of Essex or of Lord Burghley were altogether more suited to their times. These were men trained in the new humanist learning and advanced through the universities and inns of court where they had studied and made their contacts, men such as Michael Hickes (who was the son of a mercer), the patronage secretary of Lord Burghley who figured earlier in this book in his letters of friendship to John Stubbe. As a social form the personal service of early Tudor England was in decay by the end of the sixteenth century, but as a cultural form it was not; here the language of "friendship," as a set of assumptions and expectations, was still very much alive. There was, though, a disparity between the two in precisely those elements that protected the intimacy that it involved from a charge of sodomy, and this provided a convenient inlet to charges of the kind that were laid at the prison door of the earl of Southampton and the hapless Piers Edmonds. To some degree that had probably always been the case, but by the end of the sixteenth century that disparity is evident. William Reynolds's account and the picture Christopher Marlowe gives in *Edward II* are in fact more accurate pictures of the ties of friendship in the late sixteenth century than the conventional ideal the Elizabethans were still apt to present, and it was this fact that made these descriptions so frighteningly effective.

A Deadly Alchemy

To take William Reynolds's allegations as evidence of a covert sexual relationship is to follow a phantom, cunningly made. But they put in a different light many of the charges of sodomy one sees. We cannot say whether there was a sexual relationship between Piers Edmonds and the earl of Southampton, and the malice of their accuser should make us cautious; but to leave the matter there is to miss the nature of such accusations. They did not need such a sexual relationship. They turned rather on a sharp-eyed recognition that the public signs of a male friendship—open to all the world to see—could be read in a different and sodomitical light than the one intended. But although we cannot say whether there was a sexual relationship between the earl of Southampton and the man who served under him in Ireland as corporal general of the horse, we can see within the accusation a familiar social outline. It is not alone in that. It is true also of a good many others: of Charles I's bishop John Atherton and Atherton's proctor, who were accused of sodomy in 1640 at the onset of the ruin of the Caroline church; of the sixteenth-century minister that I mentioned earlier, accused of sodomy with the servant who shared his bed, in a tale spread by his enemies in the émigré community to which he belonged; and of the earl of Castlehaven, who in 1631, in a prosecution full of anti-Catholic prejudice, was accused of sodomy with his servants. We will misunderstand these accusations if, beguiled by them, we uncritically assume the existence of the sexual relationship to which they appear to point, for the material from which they could be constructed was rather open and public to all. What such accusations have in common is rather the outline of a relationship that at other times might have been called friendship.[25]

The difference, according to the religious radical Henry Barrow, was no more than words. Barrow was no conventional reformed theologian like William Perkins but a radical who had no place in his view of society for magistrate or prince other than as the pliant instrument of the order he was seeking to establish, beliefs that led to his being hanged in 1593. The church he envisaged was a collection of separatist congregations set above the existing structures of society, in which he had then little investment; and the comprehensive church of the Elizabethan settlement appeared to him to be rotten to the core: "let their . . . open and secret lust (otherwise called love) most rife as in Sodom ... stand up to the faces of these priestes and prophets, being thus commonly and openly comitted in their church."[26] From outside the established order, Barrow was ready to make explicit a possibility that that order itself was reluctant to voice: the difference might lie only in what such "love" was to be called.

Christopher Marlowe appears to have stood radically outside established belief, and it was in such terms also that Marlowe rejected the basis of Christianity itself, if the claims shortly before his death of an informer called Richard Baines are to be believed. The "damnable Judgment of Religion, and scorn of Godes word" that Baines attributes to Marlowe in the manuscript that records his allegations contains this: "That St John the Evangelist was bedfellow to Christ and leaned alwaies in his bosome, that he vsed him as the sinners of Sodoma." The charge transmutes two of the three familiar signs of male friendship on which the last chapter turned: one the public embrace, the other the shared bed; it also contains the third, the common table, for every Christian knew that it was at his last supper with his disciples—at which Christ had instituted the Holy Eucharist—that St. John had leaned in his bosom. The seed of that transmutation lay in the same insidious detail that William Reynolds had woven into his denunciation of the base-born Piers Edmonds, a detail derived from the Scriptures themselves and included by Baines: that "all the apostles were fishermen and base fellowes"; and it worked to the same end, in leaving the intimacy that these familiar signs marked open to a troubling and sodomitical interpretation. By reading into them a fault line in Marlowe's own world, the insidious claim needed no more than the materials the Gospels themselves provided. The "scorn of Godes word" in such a charge lay in its implicit claim that the bond between Christ and the beloved disciple in John's Gospel lay only in the withholding—or the giving—of a word.[27]

Accusations like those of the informer William Reynolds are not evidence of what they charge; and the ease with which Reynolds was able to make his out of the most everyday materials should make us wary. We see in them rather the unwelcome difficulty his contemporaries had in drawing a line between those gestures of closeness among men that they desired so much and those that they feared. But to call someone a sodomite was to do more than invite public censure on what was thought of as a private vice. Its effect involved incomparably more than that. Let me give an illustration. In his autobiography Simonds D'Ewes gives a description of Francis Bacon, once lord chancellor to James I, in his disgrace, and it contains an accusation that the reader may well now find familiar.

For whereas presently upon his censure at this time his ambition was moderated, his pride humbled, and the means of his former injustice and corruption removed; yet would he not relinquish the practice of his most horrible and secret sin of sodomy, keeping still one Godrick a very effeminate faced youth to be his catamite and bedfellow, although he had discharged the most of his other household servants: which was the more to be admired [wondered at] because men generally after his fall began to discourse of that his unnatural crime which he had practised many years; deserting the bed of his lady, which he accounted as the italians and turks do, a poor and mean pleasure in respect of the other; and it was thought by some that he should have been tried at the bar of justice for it, and have satisfied the law most severe against that horrible villainy with the price of his blood; which caused some bold and forward man to write these verses following in a whole sheet of paper, and to cast it down in some part of York House in the Strand, where Viscount St Alban yet lay.

> Within this sty a hog* doth
> lie that must be hanged
> for sodomy.

But he never came to any public trial for this crime; nor did ever that I could hear forbear his old custom of making his servants his bedfellows so to avoid the scandal was raised of him, though he lived many years after this his fall in his lodgings in Gray's Inn in Holborn, in great want and penury.[28]

*Alluding both to his surname of Bacon and to that swinish abominable sin.

    Much of this plays over again the issues discussed in this chapter. There is the same social context for the charge of sodomy, here between a master and his servant. There is the same inconsistency between the description of his "secret" sin and the evident fact that many others (including the author) were aware of it. There is also the same insidious detail: his old custom was that he made his servants his bedfellows, and it worked to the same end. Simonds D'Ewes in fact lacks any direct evidence of the sodomy he is accusing Francis Bacon of; but in the impropriety of this detail—for this was a menial servant, no gentleman companion—lay the germ of a charge of sodomy and the suggestion that the shared bed of a master and his servant might mean something much darker. But this description is part of a larger description and only an incident in it. Its context in the manuscript is a broad indictment of the "injustice and corruption" D'Ewes mentions here, of the bribes that caused his downfall, and of the support given him in his corruption. But there was a problem in this. What distinguished this corruption from the normal workings of friendship? What distinguished, in effect, the bribes of the one from the flow of gifts and the ready use of influence of the other? Here this small description has its effect, for if successful it necessarily changed the frame of reference in which the whole was to be viewed. If this man was a sodomite, then was he not likely in all his doings to be the enemy of God's good order, in society as well in nature? That was the change it brought about. It could turn what seemed like gifts into bribes and what seemed like "countenance" into the support of infamy; it revealed what they really were. If successful it turned all to ruin, and it could work its alchemy by a manipulation of the signs of friendship, which it found so ready to hand.

Might one not have expected that transformation? The path this book has followed has wound about the rhetoric of friendship, and the reader who has remained with me this far has had more than once to return to that rhetoric with me, sometimes even to the same individuals and moments and bear with my doubts as to whether the historical evidence locked within it has been opened to view. At several points the basis for a robust judgment has seemed to emerge—each time a different answer—only then potentially to be undermined by those fault lines in the evidence that I have kept in sight, the troublingly unexplained details: its seeming contradictions, the sense of a joke that is not being shared or the presence of a nightmare that one cannot explain. Let me then rehearse my argument.

The rhetoric of friendship was not a mirror of the world in which it figured, self-consciously so: it is the surviving trace (sometimes in the most material form) of the practices that could negotiate those dangerous moments when the obligations of friendship were created or called upon. Those practices left friendship dependent on a rhetoric that could not be wholly assured, but could that lack of assurance not itself be picked up and used? Is it an accident that from the opening of this book the ideals of friendship have been most evident in accounts of the debasement of these ideals, accounts constructed to meet political ends? When Giraldus de Barri described the debasement of sworn brotherhood among the Irish, he did so to justify their conquest. When the author of *Athelston* constructed his romance around the corruption of sworn friendship, he was constructing a political allegory. The chroniclers of the fourteenth century had motives no less political in attributing the corruption of sworn brotherhood to the regime of Piers Gaveston. The logic of such claims drew on the realistic awareness that the ideals of friendship were not readily to be found even on the streets and in the houses of one's own town. Their seductive force lay in the luminous hope that a coming new order might make them so.

They made good propaganda, as much in the sixteenth century as in the fourteenth. In two incisive books Lorna Hutson and Alan Stewart have analyzed how the humanist scholars of the sixteenth century succeeded in diverting attention from their own equivocal position by manipulating the prejudices that governed the world of men in which they moved.[29] These rising new men owed their influential place as "secretaries" in the households of Tudor or Jacobean noblemen not to their blood but to their wits. They could manage a nobleman's estates, keep his accounts, evaluate the intelligence on which decisions rested, and act as his go-between in a world of affairs. These were men whom Walter Darell would have disparagingly characterized as the rich farmer's son who drudges in a nobleman's business. Such workaday posts were obtained not through the skills in philology and classical learning that they themselves placed in the foreground but by the familiar means of patronage and mechanisms of friendship between men, although the universities and the inns of court could provide a setting in which such contacts might be garnered. Darell was not alone in the resentment and suspicions the rise of such men prompted: their influence lay in their persuasive power, but for whose benefit was that persuasion being applied?

Such doubts had a new ground in the sixteenth century, but the prejudices that might distract from them did not. These continued to rest with those uneasy figures that evoked suspicions of just the kind that now could have been directed against the intimacy of the patron and his humanist-educated counselor. In distinguishing themselves from these old figures of suspicion, these new men sought (and in large measure succeeded) to divert attention from how much that intimacy potentially resembled them. One of these figures was the sodomite. When Shakespeare wrote his twentieth sonnet to the young nobleman to whom he was counselor and friend—the laughter of which seemed to unsettle the conclusions of an earlier chapter—he too was in such an equivocal position. Can one now perhaps appreciate how finely its laughter was judged? It exploited the instincts of the world of masculine friendship in which it figured in two complementary respects. The one was that culture's unwillingness to take seriously the ambiguous borderland between the "sodomite" and the shared beds and bonding of its male companionship, an unwillingness that figured in chapter 4. The other was its readiness to apprehend the "sodomite" rather in political and religious terms, as a traitor or a papist, that has figured in this chapter. The point was that, if the similarity of the humanist counselor to the "sodomite" was not to be taken seriously, then neither was his proximity to the subversion and conspiracy that the "sodomite" readily suggested. That gesture in Shakespeare's sonnet—which itself suggested an erotic interpretation to the intimacy of the humanist scholar and his patron (only to deny it)—was to be one of the trademarks of the humanist-educated men of the sixteenth and seventeenth centuries; and its presence in the poetry and drama of the English Renaissance that was their creation is now only its most visible legacy. The "erotic interpretation," as Alan Stewart puts it, was "a way of deflecting interest in a *political* interpretation, a separation of homoeroticism and politics, which later readers have been eager to embrace."[30] The ironic result several centuries later on is the honored place that that idyllic (but textual) homoeroticism far from mundane concerns has come to occupy in the canon of English literature.

If the figure of the "sodomite" was used to distract attention from the uncertainties in masculine friendship, the figure of the pliant woman could do the same, but in one respect there was a profound difference. When William Painter in his story in the *Palace of Pleasure* attributed the destruction of the "great and perfect amity" of two male friends to the presence of a woman, he was echoing an old prejudice that in the fourteenth century in Chaucer's *Knightes Tale* had divided its two ideal sworn brothers through the jealousy aroused by a woman. Chaucer's *Shipmannes Tale* sets out that fantasy. In the *Shipmannes Tale* a second set of sworn brothers—here a wealthy merchant and a lascivious and handsome monk—are both divided and restored in friendship through the lesser wit of a woman: in the merchant's wife who, at the start of the tale borrows money from the monk (who is abroad on the abbey's business) to buy finery and duly repays him with her favors. In the comic structure that ensues, the sworn oaths of marriage, sworn brotherhood, and religious life are each translated into money—and so become convertible—as the monk in his turn borrows money from the merchant: but when the merchant seeks repayment, the monk ingeniously replies that he has already repaid the money to his wife, which she cannot deny—but promises to repay her husband in bed. The fantasy the story articulates is that a man might successfully be *both* enemy and friend to another man, that he might both cheat him *and* be exonerated, and that the instrument to that end might lay in the lesser wit of a pliant woman. That fantasy was to retain its force amid the ambiguities that were negotiated in the sixteenth century.

The fictions that occupied the young men at the inns of court in the sixteenth century is Lorna Hutson's subject; and the logic of such stories, then as before, is that it if it is the nature of women to be open to seduction—

and therefore, the gentle logic follows on, not that of men—where then is the threat of persuasion in masculine friendship? In these fictions, as Hutson puts it, "women stand in, as victims, for the indirection or inadmissibility of rivalry between men."³¹

But it was not only in fiction that a woman could stand in as a victim for the rivalry between men. For much of the time the "sodomite" was a figure of fantasy readily recognized only in the stranger or the enemy.³² This was not so with women, who were always at hand and for whom the shared prejudices of men were no abstraction. The domination and "governance" of women provided—actually in household and in the streets—a ready basis on which men could co-operate and a thing on which they could truly unite. For a historian to represent the expressions of concern (however readily to be found) about how best women could be governed and controlled as a window onto men's fears of women is not only to misrepresent the past. It also unwittingly colludes with that strategy of displacement and victimization—to cover up the rivalry between men that it healed—and to do so not only in the past but in the present also.

An Impossible Space

The rhetoric of male friendship occupied an impossible space. For women it may have been different: that very place in the silence between the lines of the material from which this book has been constructed (as Valerie Traub has argued)³³ may have provided such a space. But it was only in Thomas More's land of *Utopia* that the adages of male friendship could be embodied. Fulke Greville's inscription on his tomb and its careful order—"servant to Qveene Elizabeth," "Concellor to King Iames," "and Frend to Sir Philip Sidney"—was a gesture of that impossible kind. Its triumphal distinction of friendship from service and from the role of a counselor was possible only in rhetoric: as he and all his world knew, the language of "friendship" was also part of the language of "service"; and as for the role of a counselor, "to take aduise of friends," as Francis Bacon had put it in his essay "Of Followers and Friends," "is euer honorable." In the subsequent editions, as Bacon's epigrammatic style twists around the hard realities of friendship, even its rhetoric begins to crumble. In the 1612 edition the addition of the word "some"—the "aduice of some few friends, is euer honourable"—shifts the weight from friendship as disinterested to a realistic judgment that it often was not. In the Latin edition the transformation is completed with the addition of the term "useful"—"to take advise of friends is really honorable and useful" ("... Honorabili sane et utile"). The disinterested character of friendship has been replaced by its *utility*.[34] It was a stony truth in Bacon's own life, as John Aubrey recounts it.[35]

> In his lordship's prosperity Sir Fulke Grevil, lord Brookes, was his great friend and acquaintance; but when he was in disgrace and want, he was so unworthy as to forbid his butler to let him have any more small beer, which he had often sent for, his stomach being nice, and the small beere of Grayes Inne not liking his pallet. This has donne his memorie more dishonour then Sir Philip Sydney's friendship engraven on his monument hath donne him honour.

In the stock of stories about friendship that were part of the property of the common people, one seems to hear the same story being told over and again, how the bound friendship of traditional society was undone by the kinship and obligation with which it was entwined. In the ballad *Bewick and Graham* the demands of friendship break against those of a son, when Christy Graham is faced with the dilemma of killing either his friend or his own father. In the ballad *Adam Bell* they break against those of a husband, when the idyll of the sworn brothers, outlaws together in the forest, is disrupted by the married man who has joined them, who must return to Carlisle to see his wife—with the sheriff and the justice lying in wait. In *Amys and Amylion* they are set hideously against the responsibilities of a father, when the fidelity to friend requires the sacrifice of children. These of course are not accounts of any social life that was actually lived: sworn brothers did not live in the greenwood, and it was only in the pages of a romance that a man might murder his children to save his friend. The pleasure they gave lay in their triumphant transformations. In *Amys and Amylion* the children are restored to life in the reversal of its conclusion. In *Bewick and Graham* the death of the two sworn friends restores the friendship of their fathers. When in the ballad *Adam Bell* the sworn brothers are pardoned and made men of the king's chamber, those ballad singers who knew their audience would have been rewarded with a rousing cheer—or laughter—and their pay.

A culture that could tell tales like these is not haunted by its fears. The uncertainty in masculine friendship was something its inhabitants were able to draw on and make use of. It protected a man's honor when the obligations of friendship were called upon, and it made for persuasive propaganda: the debasement of friendship was only too credible. It served at different points alike to justify to Catholic Europe the invasion of Ireland and the designs of an English queen who wished to be the supreme governor of her own church, but that convenient mechanism could not escape its own price. That same device could be and would be employed within, when the opportunity was offered or the occasion required. The outline of the "sodomite," the betrayer, or the foe were never very far from the flower-strewn world of masculine friendship, and they could never wholly be distinguished from it. A hard fact that those of power and influence preferred not to see but were willing, still, to make use of.

The rhetoric of friendship (and the precarious honor that it negotiated) rarely give direct access to its vulnerability, but there is one exceptional moment in this regard: a product of the subtle mind of Henry Howard, the earl of Northampton, and the extraordinary events of 1605 and the attempt—or supposed attempt—to destroy the king, his family, and the two houses of Parliament by gunpowder and explosion. I do not propose to enter here into the debates that have dogged these events: the extent to which there was indeed a plot or rather the extent to which it was a device of Robert Cecil, the earl of Salisbury and principal secretary to James I, to bolster his political objectives and influence with the king, for the point at which I want to pause is a moment in the speech of Henry Howard at the trial of Henry Garnett, the superior of the Jesuits in England and one of the accused. By this stage there could be no question of drawing back.

The problem concerned a technical detail in the formal indictment. It was this: the accused had agreed that they would, in its words,

> for the better concealing, as for the more effectual accomplishing of the sayd horrible Treasons . . . receiue seuerall corporall othes vpon the holy Euangelists, and the Sacrament of the Eucharist, That they the treasons aforesaid would traiterously conceale and keepe secret, and would not reueale them directly nor indirectly by words nor circumstances, nor euer would desist from the execution and finall accomplishment of the said Treasons, without the consent of some three of the foresaid false Traitors first in that behalfe traiterously had, And that thereupon aswell the said Thomas Winter, Guy Fawkes, Robert Keyes, and Thomas Bates, as the said Robert Catesby, Thomas Percy, John Wright, Christopher Wright, and Francis Tresham, did traiterously take the said seuerall corporall othes seuerally, and did receiue the Sacrament of the Eucharist aforesaid, by the hands of the sayd Henry Garnet, John Gerrard, Oswald Tesmond, and other Iesuites . . . to such intent and purpose as is aforesaid.[36]

Henry Howard held a traditional view of religion's role, both in the sense that he remained a Catholic and in that he still held the tenacious view that the proper work of religion was the creation of kinship and friendship and that at the heart of both lay the Eucharist. In binding their mutual fidelity in the Holy Communion, the conspirators would have been employing a device that for centuries had between friends "plighted faith and promise," as Howard put it in his judgment. But what then was that "intent and purpose," in the words of the indictment? The point was that God would have become the witness to an oath sealed in the Eucharist and hold it in his keeping: "as if God would be put in trust with the keeping" of the oath, as Howard put it. The problem Howard grasped was whether anyone could seriously believe that God would hold in his keeping an oath to commit murder? The "seale of the sacrament of Vnion was sette to this contract of blood, as if God would bee put in trust with the keeping of these prophane bands and obligations of conscience." That was the improbable claim within this indictment. But if such a claim was not credible, was the indictment itself credible? And if this part of the indictment unraveled, was there not a danger that the whole might begin to come to pieces?

Howard had seen the danger that this charge potentially posed for the indictment as a whole, and the answer he gave went to the heart of its defense: the intent was not to bind their fidelity, which God indeed would have held in his keeping, but their *infidelity*. "The purpose of these Gallants in binding faith and promise one to another by solemne oath . . . stood vpon the distrust that one reposed in anothers loue and moueless constancie." The point is unarguable. They swore their oath because they *distrusted* each other. But why does that judgment apply only to these conspirators? Why does it not apply to all those bound friends and sworn brothers who have peopled the pages of this book? If the friendship between such men was what it claimed to be, why did they need to bind it by oath? Why should God himself be a witness to it in the Eucharist (and the saints too in an earlier time)?

This book opened with the kiss of peace depicted on the tomb monument of William Neville and John Clanvowe that sealed their friendship, in the terms of the design on their tomb for time and eternity. But why was their love not enough? Could not the same question be asked of all those other bound friends like Neville and Clanvowe, across the centuries to the burial together of John Finch and Thomas Baines, united by the knot that symbolized their union? The implication of Henry Howard's incisive logic is this. The bound friendship of the past was predicated on suspicions of treachery and potential enmity, which the rhetoric of love and fidelity negotiated: the fear that the friend might prove, in the end, to be your enemy.

Were its rhetoric and its ideals then a lie? To say that the rhetoric of friendship occupied an impossible space—as I have—is not to say that it was a lie. Certainly, there are figures and moments throughout this book that correspond to Howard's logic; they stand out with a clear edge. One was the sworn brotherhood of Edmund Ironside and—his mortal adversary—Cnut in the eleventh century. Another that between Duke Louis of Orléans and Duke Jean of Burgundy—the man who would figure as his murderer—in the fifteenth century. Yet another was the reconciliation between King James I of England and the duke of Buckingham, which followed the events of 1624. These were cataclysmic events in the politics of their time. But such moments—however dark—do not overturn the evidence that stubbornly remains alongside them.

Does Howard's logic explain the grief that killed William Neville when his friend John Clanvowe died? Or Fulke Greville's obscure gesture in remembering Philip Sidney as his friend, in letters written on black marble that can hardly be read in the gloom of the chapter house of St. Mary's Warwick? Is it really credible that English men and women told stories about Amys and Amylion, Guy and Tirry, or Bewick and Graham or (long before) of Horn and Ayol or Octa and Ebissa and others like them and thought only and secretly of enmity? My readers can look for themselves at the tombs of the friends who lie together in death like the monument that John Gostlin left to his friendship with Thomas Legge and its burning heart, or the tomb John Whytton prepared for himself and John Bloxham to lie in: monuments that speak with more authority than I could ever muster. But my judgment is that it was not a lie: the evidence is patently too complex and too contradictory for that easy answer. To attempt to divide the formal friendships one sees in traditional society into neat categories would be an arbitrary task. When Nicholas Molyneux provided for the prayers for John Winter that might release him from the pains of purgatory, was he remembering the business partner who had exchanged the kiss of peace with him, or the love and brotherhood of his youth? When King James planned to seal his reconciliation with the duke of Buckingham in the Eucharist, was he reconciling himself with the magnate who would have seized the government of England from his hands in 1624, or the man he had always loved and still did?

Let me put this another way, one more concrete. Early in this book, in the working conclusion of my first chapter, I set out the explanations historians have put forward for the bound friendship of traditional society, sometimes in hostile disagreement with each other, whether violence, profit, or love. My criticism there applied to them alike: that these suggestions—if that is all we are to have—are an impoverished, a positivist view of history, that at root history is just plain facts, and that once a historian has concluded what they are about, he or she can then identify the reliable sources and dismiss others as mere rhetoric. The course I have pursued in the chapters that followed has been to reverse this: to take each of the sources of evidence from the past alike, precisely as rhetoric, and to look for the traces in them—often in the most material sense—of the practices that once produced them. Such a process is necessarily minute and painstaking, but eventually the social practices that left these traces emerge and can be reassembled from them—if there is world enough and time. What one then sees is a diverse set of practices that cannot be reduced to a single overarching motive but nonetheless employed the same rhetoric: practices of peacemaking, of countenance, of kinship. The same rhetoric that could ease the reconciliation of enemies could also enable the acceptance of a gift, or bind the affection of friends. It could enable adversaries to lay down a quarrel, without losing face. It could ease the passing of a gift, by its tactful indication that (as the language demonstrated in which a gift was offered) the giver also knew the limits beyond which the obligation it might create would not be pressed. And it could sustain by its binding force a true affection that might one day grow cold, through the infirmity of our natures.

The friendship of traditional society did indeed depend on an exchange of signs that could never wholly be assured, and its conventions and rituals sought to negotiate and transcend that ineluctable uncertainty: directly and in the concrete, eye to eye and face to face. Their rhetoric was Utopian; and however long one waits by the harbor, no ship will ever come to take us there. But that emphatically does not mean that the rhetoric was false. It was precisely in being Utopian that it protected an endangered honor, when the obligations of friendship were created or called upon, or when the heart grew cold. Traditional society had need of such Utopias, and knew well how to make use of them.

The story I have set out to tell in this book is drawing near its end; but one final question remains, to which I now turn. What happened to the world I have described?

CHAPTER 6

Friendship and Modernity

Ever when distress and sleep together
lay hold on the poor solitary,
he dreams that he is greeting and kissing his liege-lord,
and laying his hands and head on his knee—
just as he used to do when he enjoyed
the bounty of the throne in the days of old.
Then the friendless man awakes again
and sees before him the grey waves,
sees the sea-birds bathing and spreading their wings,
and rime falling, and snow mingled with hail.
    —"The Wanderer," tenth-century Anglo-Saxon poem

There head falls forward, fatigued at evening,
And dreams of home,
Waving from window, spread of welcome,
Kissing of wife under single sheet;
But waking sees
Bird-flocks nameless to him.
    —W. H. Auden, "The Wanderer," 1930

On the night of 17 October 1655 the sound of falling timbers and shattering stone pulled the fellows of Merton College from their rooms. The great roof above the south transept of the chapel had fallen in, shattering the monuments that lay below. Among the rubble a detail would stand out that marks a wider loss than the destruction of that night alone. One of the first to survey the damage was the antiquary Anthony Wood, hurrying across the way from his lodging in Merton Street, who "retriev'd the brass plates

... and transcrib'd and sav'd the inscriptions on them" (as he put it in his manuscripts). To a man like Wood, the destruction added painfully to the losses he had seen in the chapel of his old college; four years before he had witnessed the effacement of the "pictures of prophets, apostles, saints, &c. that had been painted on the back-side of the stalls in Merton coll. choire, in various and antique shapes, about the beginning of the raigne of King Henry 7 ... to the sorrow of curious men that were admirers of antient pictures." His efforts that day in 1655 preserved the inscription on a monument to two fellows of the college who had died early in the sixteenth century, and it is here that we might see a detail that seems to mark a passing world.[1]

The memorial brass that Anthony Wood preserved has been lost, but the matrix in the black marble slab that once held it remains in the south transept. One can still see the ghostly outline of two figures, standing together under a canopy flanked by pinnacles, as John Bloxham and John Whytton had been depicted on their great monumental brass in the nearby choir. Perhaps the most striking thing about the inscription that lay below the serene depiction of these two figures (as Anthony Wood recorded it) is its very taciturnity, its assumption that the reason *why* these two men are depicted together in death is so self-evident as to need no explanation.[2]

> Orate pro animbus Thome Harper, Bathonensis Diocesis, Sacre Theologie Professoris, et quondam hujus Collegii Custodis, et pro anima Radulphi Hamsterley Dunelmenis Diocesis, Socii istius Collegii et postea Collegii Universitatis Magistri, qui ambo fuerunt simul electi in istud Collegium.

> [Pray for the souls of Thomas Harper, of the Diocese of Bath, doctor of divinity, and at one time warden of this college, and for the soul of Ralph Hamsterley, of the Diocese of Durham, fellow of this college and later master of University College, who were both elected at the same time to this college.]

In 1490 the Ralph Hamsterley commemorated here had provided for the choir stalls, the loss of which Wood so bewailed; and before Hamsterley died in 1518, he provided for the memorial brass and the inscription that Wood later transcribed. By 1655, the brass had lain for a century and a half before the altar of St. Katherine in the south transept, where Hamsterley had provided for a chantry. The figure commemorated with him was the Thomas Harper who had been warden of Merton College from 1507 until his death the following year. Hamsterley and Harper had become fellows of the college together on the same day in 1476 and appear linked in its annals, evidently forming a friendship that still figured strongly in Hamsterley's mind as he approached death, sufficiently so for him to arrange, ten years after Harper's death, for this monument, which would depict them together and seek the prayers of the living for their souls.

Unlike John Bloxham and John Whytton, Hamsterley and Harper were not buried together. Harper died while away from the college at Bristol, where he was the vicar of St. Nicholas's church, and was buried there. Hamsterley apparently was buried in the church in Oddington, where he was rector (although this appears later to have been forgotten). The monument he left in the chancel of that church provides a startling contrast to the one in Merton, a contrast that marks graphically how he wished the future to remember him—and his friendship with Thomas Harper.

The serenity of the Merton monument is in stark contrast with that in Oddington church, which firmly and boldly bears no less an image than that of the body of Hamsterley wrapped in a shroud and being devoured by worms. "Vermib[us] hic donor et sic ostendere conor / Q[uo]d sicut hic ponor ponitur o[mn]is honor" is the inscription. It is engagingly translated by its historian as

I, here, to worms become a prey,
Try by this picture to say,
That as I lie here out of sight
So too must pass all earthly might.[3]

In contrast, his serene Merton monument depicted him with Thomas Harper, as Bloxham and Whytton had been presented, as if sanctified together by their friendship as Amys and Amylion had been. What the contrast between the two monuments graphically expresses is that it is their friendship—and what it touched—that would endure beyond the grave.

In the design of the Merton monument, the figures of the two men do not illustrate the inscription but complement it, two parts together making one whole. In this design the friendship that still links the living with the dead—expressed in the prayers that the inscription seeks—is united with the ideal friendship depicted in the image of the two men standing side by side beneath their canopy. In the monument as a whole, the friendship that subsists between the living and the dead and the friendship that properly subsists also between the living become models, the one for the other.

Yet this monument also bears the traces of the world that would supplant the world that Hamsterley and Harper inhabited. If you look closely at the lower half of the monument, you will see the remains of a later inscription, added at some point around the end of the seventeenth century or at the beginning of the eighteenth. The new inscription was evidently designed to rectify the loss of the inscription in 1655, but it did so in markedly different terms.

HIC JACET RADVLPHVS
HAMSTERLEY DVNEL
MENSIS QUONDAM
HVIVS COLLEGII SOCIVS
ET POSTEA COLL:
VNIVERSITAT MAGISTER
OBDORMIVIT IN
D'M'NO 4 NON.
AVG. 1518

[Here lies Ralph Hamsterley of the Diocese of Durham formerly fellow of this college and later master of University College. He fell asleep in the Lord on 2 August 1518.]

The prayers that linked the living and the dead are missing from this inscription and so is the friendship of Hamsterley and Harper. This excision marks a change that one can trace as one walks around the chapel of Merton College, and not only in the loss of those figures, which Anthony Wood recorded, that had stood with the fellows of the college as their friends and intercessors at the court of heaven. The windows in the transepts tell the same story as the "restoration" of the monument to Hamsterley and Harper: at some point between 1645 and 1650, the stained glass—which had contained scrolls seeking prayers for the donors—was taken out by the fellows. But within the terms of this book the most telling gesture lay in the choir and in the stripping (by 1673) of the great memorial brass to John Bloxham and John Whytton from the setting that it had occupied for three centuries at the center of the choir, to be casually laid aside in an empty space where room could be found for it in a corner of the antechoir.[4]

Friendship

These changes occurred more than a century after the Reformation in England, and the survival of the medieval stained glass in the choir is testimony that this was not the work of zealots. This was the work of the fellows themselves. Merton under Jonathan Goddard as warden (who was also the professor of physics at Gresham College) breathed the air of the new experimental philosophy. This was the Oxford where the lodgings of the warden of Wadham, John Wilkins, was the center of a group that prefigured the Royal Society. The new natural philosophy and chemistry of Robert Boyle, the mathematics of John Wallis, the astronomy of Seth Ward and Lawrence Rooke, and indeed the presence of Christopher Wren at All Souls and the restrained pragmatism of the physician Ralph Bathurst at Trinity College—these are all more representative of the Oxford of the 1650s than the religious zealots of a century before. It was this Oxford that would welcome the young John Locke as a student at Christ Church in 1652. In the eyes of the fellows of Merton College (if not those of an antiquary and a conservative like Anthony Wood), the changes exemplified in the chapel of Merton College were a rational reordering, specific and selective in its terms. What was evidently becoming antiquated, if not unintelligible, was the very forensic trail this book has been following: the place that friendship and kinship had occupied at the heart of religion's role, on earth as much as in heaven. It was something that evidently could now be assigned to a neglected corner of the antechoir or tacitly effaced from the inscription on a monument. There was a new spirit abroad.

The brass to John Bloxham and John Whytton was returned to the choir when the chapel was restored by William Butterfield and Gilbert Scott between 1842 and 1876, but the gesture did not endure; and when I visited the chapel in the summer of 1999, the brass had again been placed in the north transept, accommodating a modern liturgical reordering of the chapel corresponding to that of the seventeenth century.[5] The changes in Merton College chapel in the seventeenth century were a microcosm of the changes taking place across England at that time. In these changes the physical intimacy that not only symbolized but actually constituted friendship in the eyes of contemporaries lost its presence.

I earlier characterized those visible gestures at table or bed or in the public embrace as the gift of the friend's body. Most visibly, at this point the great houses of the English countryside ceased to provide the stage for such gestures of friendship across social divisions, a change that would be extended across the eighteenth century. The introduction of back stairs and of servants' dormitories located in basements removed the servants and numerous inhabitants of the great house from view. The open "prospect" of the eighteenth-century country house was an illusion produced by this seventeenth-century removal of servants from sight. The radical departure in this respect was Coleshill in Berkshire, designed around 1650 by Roger Pratt. Here the staircase was placed in the great hall, a momentous change in architectural terms that made the hall unsuitable for the rituals of communal eating that had

lain at the heart of the symbolic system of friendship. In Coleshill the servants and visitors to the house now ate in a separate hall next to the kitchen
in the basement. By the end of the seventeenth century this had become the
conventional arrangement and from the 1760s was extended by the introduction of bell systems, which allowed servants to be accommodated in a
separate wing. With these changes the crowds of male servants and other
visitors waiting on benches in the hall or sleeping close at hand or by a door,
once so ubiquitous, disappeared. Also in Coleshill's plan the rooms opened
off long central corridors running the whole length of the house, screening
the sharing of beds at night from view; and as the symbolism of the communal eating and drinking in the great hall was lost from sight, so too was
that of the "bedfellow": as great a change in historical terms.

The companions to these physical changes were corresponding changes
in the way of life in the great houses. They chart that bodily intimacy was
ceasing to be the intelligible sign it had been. Significantly, it was in the second half of the seventeenth century that gentlemen ceased to serve at the
table, the bed, or the stool (and with the introduction of backstairs the removal of the chamber pot ceased to be a public sight). It is at this point that
such service began to be regarded not as indicative of intimacy but as menial or degrading; and during the course of the eighteenth century, as the
lower servants disappeared from sight and from looking on, one ceased also
to see the crowds of tenants and visitors drinking in the great hall.[6]

Changes of the same kind are also apparent in the universities at this
point, which had long reflected the symbolic geography of the great houses.
During the course of the eighteenth century the practice fell away of the
poorer students' waiting at table or acting as personal servants, changes that
reflected the same change in attitude apparent in the disappearance of the
gentlemen servants in the great house. Students could still be required to
share rooms and beds when there was overcrowding, but as one can see from
their letters home, this was now thought to be onerous and a mere incon-
venience. There is no sign in these complaints of the meanings that had one
been attached to such intimacy.[7] The friendship of John Finch and Thomas
Baines commemorated in Christ's College, Cambridge (discussed in chapter 4) was touched by these changes. Finch and Baines were one with this
older world, a friendship later remembered as having been begun when
Baines was Finch's personal servant, or "sizar," at Cambridge; and before
Baines died, Finch drafted a dedication to him "as a Monument of Our
Friendship," as he put it.[8] Its form was the conventional familiar letter—
"this freedome Wee Indulge Each other" was the same "loving freedom"
that Fulke Greville had carefully advertised in the gift of his familiar letter to

John Coke earlier in this book—but it was, as all the world knew, rhetoric: the brother of the earl of Nottingham had indeed no need of the patronage formally implied by Baines's acceptance of a such dedication. It was rather Sir John Finch's gift to *him:* the rhetorical gesture of countenance owed to a man who had been his faithful secretary as well as his faithful friend. "No Wonder if our Thoughts became so familiar to Each other; that sometimes Wee forgott to whom they originally belong'd": the sentiment is Angell Day's in *The English Secretorie* at the end of the sixteenth century: for a master or a nobleman a faithful secretary is "the disposer of his verie thoughts."[9] The changing world these two men inhabited is perhaps best marked by the evident discomfort in the inscription on the monument in Christ's College as it circumvents the disparity in their families: "genus Verò si quaeris et necessitudines" [if you seek to know their lineage and families] is the question the monument asks but awkwardly answers only for the one.

That same changing world is evident in the opposition at the time to the monument to Granville Piper and Richard Wise in the church of St. Mary Magdalene in Launceston in Cornwall when it was erected in 1731. The monument in the north isle of the church closely resembles that to Finch and Baines in Christ's College, Cambridge. As there, the representations of the two friends are united by a single flaming funerary urn, which corresponds to the description of them below, which employs the same term "conjunctissimus" that Finch had used of Baines (and others before him).

> Vtque Vnanimes, et conjunctissimi in sua Vita fuerunt
> Ita post mortem jam non sunt divisi
> Fidissimum Amicorum Par.

> [And as in life they were one at heart and in kinship and friendship,
> so after death they were even then not divided
> most faithful pair of friends.]

Richard Wise would be remembered in Launceston as having been Granville Piper's manservant and later as his secretary, as Thomas Baines was remembered; but the controversy about the propriety of a monument to such a friendship that the monument prompted is something quite new in this book. Doubts had always attended the equivocal ethics of friendship, but the places in which one sees them were elsewhere: in the traditional stories about sworn friendship, in the suspicions of collusion that dogged it, and in the careful boundaries of the eucharistic practice that corresponded to it—never, as far as I am aware, in the setting of such monuments in an ecclesiastical context. The controversy that surrounded the erection of this monument in the 1730s was something new.[10]

It seems from the comments of visitors that England was diverging from a way of life that still continued for the time being across the Channel. The separation of servants that had become the norm in England was noted as surprising both by the German visitor Johann Wilhelm von Archenholz and by Pierre Grosley and François de La Rochefoucauld (and his tutor) when they visited England in the second half of the eighteenth century.[11] Surprised European visitors also noticed that Englishmen had replaced the embrace and the kiss with the handshake,[12] and it seems unlikely that the ritual kiss of peace discussed earlier in this book could have survived beyond this point. The Reformation and Counter Reformation alone were unlikely to have achieved this: the kiss of peace had never depended on a rubric, and to have removed it altogether from an ecclesiastical setting would have meant divorcing religion from the wider symbols of society and alliance, where the public kiss continued to retain its vitality. That of course was precisely the intention, but how realistic that was was another matter. When the gesture ceased to be intelligible in a secular context, it could hardly have survived in a religious context. When in 1749 an Englishman described the practice of two men kissing each other as a foreign and distasteful practice, he seems to have been unaware that it had ever been thought otherwise.[13]

As the formal gesture of a kiss was withdrawn from a public stage, so too was the rhetoric of a passionate attachment that had tactfully negotiated its dangerous uncertainties. The change is evident in a piece by the essayist Saint-Evremond, who spent much of the last forty years of his life in England until his death in 1703. The violent passion of friends like Orestes and Pylades, the essay argues, "are things we read, and see represented, which are not to be found in the commerce and practice of the world." Once it was precisely there that they had been employed.[14]

Civil Society

If the voice of this older world was Jeremy Taylor's claim that friendship is "all the bands that this world hath," then the most cogent voice of the confident new world replacing it was unquestionably the "civil society" of John Locke in his *Essay concerning the True Original, Extent, and End of Civil Government.* His chapter "Of Political or Civil Society" opens in these terms.

> God having made Man such a Creature, that, in his own Judgment, it was not good for him to be alone, put him under strong Obligations of Neces-

sity, Convenience, and Inclination to drive him into Society, as well fitted
him with Understanding and Language to continue and enjoy it . . . Where-
ever therefore any number of Men are so united into one Society, as to quit
every one his Executive Power of the Law of Nature, and to resign it to the
publick, there and there only is a Political, or Civil Society.[15]

"Society" here is not friendship, something *done*, active and immediate, in
the sense in which the old mass meant the term: "Nobis quoque pecatoribus
famulis tuis . . . partem aliquam et societatem donare digneris, cum tuis
sanctis Apostolis et Martyribus" [And to us sinners also, thy servants . . .
deign to grant some part and society with thy holy Apostles and Martyrs].
This was the sense in which the reformer John Stubbe (whom we met earlier in this book) employed the term, when he complained of the pope's
"absoluing our neyghbour kinges of any auncient leage or late oth of societie."[16] John Locke's "society" here is that notion of "society" as an abstraction familiar to us today. As the historian John Bossy argued in his in-
augural lecture at the University of York in 1981, "society" in John Locke's
formulation is crucially different, something that subsists as an objective en-
tity—a Great Something—over and beyond the individual, who is *in* it.[17]
In the terms of John Locke, the friendship of the world this book has described could figure only as anarchy.

No Man in Civil Society can be exempted from the Laws of it. For if any
Man may do, what he thinks fit . . . I ask, Whether he be not perfectly still
in the State of Nature, and so can be no part or Member of that Civil Society: unless any one will say, the State of Nature and Civil Society are one
and the same thing, which I have never yet found any one so great a Patron
of Anarchy as to affirm.[18]

The counterpart to John Locke's question would be the assertion of Immanuel Kant—and that of the eighteenth-century Enlightenment—that a
"rational" ethics requires the moral basis of friendship to reside in an undifferentiated benevolence "as if all were brothers submissive to a universal
father who wants the happiness of all."[19]

Kinship

It would be too simple a view to associate the eighteenth-century Enlightenment with this civil society, equating the Enlightenment view of friendship to civil society's suspicion about it. The traditional mechanisms of

friendship had their counterparts in the sixteenth or even the fifteenth century, and the aspirations of the eighteenth-century Enlightenment in ethics often led down to the Christian roots (as in the discussion between Dr. Johnson and the Quaker lady about friendship in the epigraph for this book). But if elective friendship was not part of the sinews of "civil" society—if indeed it could figure in its terms only as a patron of anarchy—what place was there for the wider ties of kinship? Before tackling that question, let me first review my argument in the early chapters of this book.

I argued that kinship and friendship turned on the same axis. In the society I described—"society" in the older sense, not that of John Locke—the good of kinship lay in the friendship (the "society") that it could create between individuals and between groups, who might otherwise be at enmity; and its rituals and rhetoric were designed to negotiate that precarious transition. The kinship that might have such an effect necessarily took a multiplicity of forms, created by promise as well as by blood, and by ritual and oath as well as by nature. It might spring from the love of parents and children, a brother or sister, or an uncle or aunt, nephew or niece—the love (in that once generic term) of a "cousin." But kinship might also be created directly, by human agency. Marriage was the most complete instrument of that agency: only marriage *extended* the family; but marriage was not the only form in which kinship could be created by ritual or promise. The "sworn brothers" and perhaps sisters of this book were another such, and they themselves are not a distinct and unique phenomenon. Their kinship overlapped both symbolically and actually with that created by a betrothal and with the "spiritual" kinship created by baptism. It once had had its counterpart in the confraternities and continued to have it in the houses of call of the tramping artisans. Its companions were the bonds created by adoption or by fostering, and the friendship that could be created between families by the practice of adolescents leaving their parents' home to act as servants in households higher in the social scale, often with their parents receiving children in similar circumstances from below: a gift across social divisions that curiously echoes the communal eating and drinking in the hall of a great house or in the Eucharist, creating bonds of social cohesion at precisely the points at which the symbolic system emphasized social division.[20] But these diverse forms of kinship held the capacity to create friendship, across potential enmity, precisely in that they did *not* delineate the same group: they overlapped but were not the same. Their effect was to embed the family, in the more narrow sense of a group of parents and their children, within a wider and overlapping network of *friendship*. Or at least they had the potential to do so. That has been my argument.

Would civil society's antipathy to the traditional bonds of friendship not then have stripped the family from that setting? "Civil" society had no place for such mechanisms. That abjection began with the changes I have described taking place—often in the most tangible sense—in the seventeenth century, but in terms of the place of marriage within this nexus, the defining moment came in the middle of the eighteenth century, in 1753 with an *Act for the Better Preventing of Clandestine Marriages.* This was the largely the work of the lord chancellor Philip Yorke, the earl of Hardwicke, who with Henry Pelham and his brother the duke of Newcastle was part of the continuing Whig supremacy in England after 1743. The "clandestine marriages" that the act annulled were not necessarily clandestine in any literal sense of the term. They were the marriages formed by mutual agreement before witnesses that were England's direct inheritance from traditional society and the canon law of the medieval church.[21] The act of 1753 went far beyond the protection of the rights of guardians and parents to choose the marriages of their children (or of their children to consent to that choice). Its effect was to require a parochial form of marriage before an Anglican clergyman, with the calling of banns and a definitive entry in a parish register. The only exceptions provided were for Jews and Quakers. All other marriages were to be "null and void to all Intents and Purposes whatsoever." The familiar betrothal at the church door "facie Ecclesiae" was explicitly put aside, "any Law or Usage to the contrary notwithstanding." The need to include that explicit provision is a telling trace of how far the traditional bonds of kinship I have described had survived the reforming zeal of the Reformation, which can obscure their continuing presence to a later historian. The force of the act is underscored by the savage penalty of transportation that it introduced for its infringement, "to some of his Majesty's Plantations in America for the Space of fourteen Years, according to the Laws in Force for Transportation of Felons" (and the death penalty for the "falsely making, altering, forging, or counterfeiting any such Entry in such Register").

Its effect was to make void in English law the traditional customary forms for making a marriage that one can still see being familiarly employed at the opening of the eighteenth century, as one reads through the consistory court records for London in the account given by their historian Randolph Trumbach. Thus Henry Owen, a barrister and justice of the peace for Carmarthen, might wed Mary Scurlocke by reading together the marriage liturgy from the Book of Common Prayer and exchanging a ring. John Ramsey and Ann Raby wedded by contracting themselves as man and wife in a garden and by John's giving Ann a ring. William Frances and Mary Hallows did the same by breaking a piece of gold between them. Peter Durrand wedded Elizabeth

Bayley by drawing up a written contract and receiving Holy Communion with her family as a pledge of fidelity, and Margaret Rigby and her fellow servant Edward Turpin similarly sealed their union by receiving Holy Communion together. These are forms that would have been as readily intelligible in the fifteenth century—if not in the eleventh century—as in the eighteenth. They are also forms that visibly corresponded to those with which two sworn brothers or the members of a confraternity readily pledged their fidelity in the Eucharist; sworn brothers continued to do so into the seventeenth century.[22]

These gestures were rather *more* than less Christian for not requiring the officiating presence of a clergyman—the prayer book and the Eucharist are signs of that—part of Christianity's universal moral economy rather than of a specifically sacerdotal matter; and what the act of 1753 introduced was not civil marriage. It was rather a prescribed parochial form of marriage, requiring an officiating priest and a determining register, of the kind that had been introduced in Catholic countries by the decrees of the reforming Council of Trent. It represented a revolutionary change with the past, and it was in the terms of John Locke's civil society that it was defended and maintained, despite the voices of protest one can still read in the resistance it provoked.

> It follows then, that no Man, by entering into Society, can or ought to be presumed to have yielded up into the Hands of the Society, his natural Right to contract Marriage, as shall seem to him most expedient for the Security of his Virtue. He cannot yield it up. It is a Right unalienable … There can be no doubt but that all Societies have a Right to prescribe in what Form and Manner the Marriage Contract shall be made, in order to bring it under civil Cognizance. But it is carefully to be observed that the legal Form of contracting Marriage hath nothing to do with the Essence of the Contract as it lies before God.

That closely argued protest against the provisions of the act comes from the pamphlet published in 1754 by the Anglican clergyman Henry Stebbing. The contract of marriage was, as he put it, "a Contract which lies before God and Man, in which Society hath no Concern." Stebbing expresses with precision the principle that for centuries had enabled marriage to overlap with a multiplicity of other forms of kinship that might also be formed by ritual and promise.

History was not to be with Henry Stebbing, and the crushing answer that prevailed is that given in "A Vindication of the Power of States to prohibit

Clandestine Marriages under the Pain of Absolute Nullity" by another Anglican clergyman, James Tunstall, in the same year as Stebbing's pamphlet.

> In short, I observe once for all, that the Right of Marriage is a natural Right, but the Obligation arising from a Contract of Marriage is a positive Obligation. Now all positive Obligations whatsoever are both subsequent and inferior to the Obligation arising from the original Contract of Society.

The point of that chopping logic was Tunstall's crushing judgment: that there is a

> Limitation then of the natural Power of contracting Marriage, in every Subject of a Civil State, to the Solemnities and Circumstances of Marriage, which the Civil State has, upon just and cogent Reasons, thought fit to appoint as necessary, being implied in the original Contract of Civil Society.

On the one hand, "the Essence of the Contract as it lies before God . . . in which Society hath no Concern." On the other, "[t]he original Contract of Civil Society." These are the parameters of two fundamentally opposed understandings of the basis of human friendship: the one individual, specific, *chosen;* the other rational, objective, universal, and *obligatory.* It was the latter that would prevail. It could not, of course, touch those other forms of sworn kinship beyond marriage that this book has described. These had never been the creatures of any such "civil" society, but it could and did divorce them from marriage, a divorce of which modern society was to be the inheritor: and in doing so it was to remove the family from the traditional setting that this diverse and complex world had created. "Friends" could still negotiate marriage and did, but friendship was no longer to be created in relations that overlapped with it and were akin to it.

Let me now set beside this argument—about the family and its setting—the argument about the body of the friend. Were their fates intertwined? My conclusion has been that the immediate social context for what I have called the gift of the friend's body in seventeenth-century England and in the centuries before was the greater extent to which in that culture, in comparison to our own, the life of the body—in the daily cycle of working, eating and drinking, the bodily functions and sleeping—was carried on outside the marital home. Because of this wider currency, bodily intimacy became an instrument by which social relationships could be established and given meaning. It was the equivalent in directly corporeal terms of those bonds of formal friendship in which the family had been set, and within that symbolic system the good-humored homoeroticism we sometimes see in the gift of the friend's body signaled beyond itself, to the place of comforting security that those bonds afforded in an insecure world. As both fell away, did the body *within* the marital home necessarily acquire a greater symbolic force? One can put the question more sharply. Did the loss of that setting then place on the sexual bond between husband and wife a burden of social meaning that before it had not been required to carry alone?

Was that burden of meaning the reason why the gift of the body came to be acknowledged in this society—"society" in John Locke's sense— only as a sexual gift between men and women? That this may indeed be the explanation for the ending of the symbolic world I have described is reinforced by a fundamentally parallel phenomenon. It is at this point, toward the end of the seventeenth century, that one can see a radically different attitude to homosexuality. It is at this point that the images of the masculine "sodomite" lost the alien associations that had kept it at such a distance from an image that one might normally apply to oneself, to one's neighbor or one's friend. The change gave the "sodomite" a new actuality and was quickly evident in violent action directed against homosexuality on a scale without precedent in English history. In 1699, 1707, and 1726 one sees large groups of "sodomites" being arrested, a profile markedly different than the isolated individuals one sees in court records in England before this point, where several years could pass without any prosecutions at all. When they do appear, they characteristically involve a breach of the peace or a breach of the social order in some other respect also.[23]

What this misses is that, in this new conception of the sodomite, homosexual desire was not represented as an alternative sexuality, a different but in some way logically symmetrical choice to heterosexuality: it was a perversion of something else. That assumption is encapsulated in the title of a broadsheet containing a sensational account of the arrest of one of these groups of sodomites in 1707, *The Women-Hater's Lamentation:* characterizing masculine "sodomites" not in terms of men but in terms of the women they supposedly spurned. It would be easy, too easy, to attribute the diminishing of what was signified by the gift of the body to the greater actuality of the "sodomite." This would be to collude with a cultural displacement. An asymmetry as pointed as this gave these new conceptions of the sodomite an unspoken affinity with the burden of social significance now placed on heterosexuality. The new conception of the sodomite rather shored up the new burden of sin. Does the perversion of heterosexuality in the one appear then culturally as the evidence for the naturalness and inevitability of the other?

These two phenomena are two sides of the same newly minted coin and together constitute a change fundamental enough to have buried a symbolic world that had subsisted across the centuries. The quotations from the two poems at the head of this chapter, separated by something more than time, are perhaps a measure of that change. I am inclined to think that it is indeed here that the explanation lies for that seismic change. But whether or not I am right in suggesting this explanation, as the older meaning that had once adhered so powerfully to the desire for the body of the friend slipped finally away, the new sexual culture of eighteenth-century England was ready to provide it with a new and radically abjected meaning. The world about it had changed, and the body of the friend seems lost.

It is tempting, at this point, to put a full stop and to draw the story to its close, yet however tempting that closure may be, the evidence troublingly resists it. "Civil" society would indeed quickly turn its face from the traditional forms of friendship. The few traces of their presence are hardly visible among the records left by civil society, but there are moments into the eighteenth and nineteenth centuries when—if one looks very closely—its forms can suddenly take shape and, against all expectations, become visible again. The road now to be followed is no longer the broad highway on which this book set out, four centuries before at the opening of the fifteenth century. It has dwindled to a neglected bridlepath. It goes across a wintry landscape where the evidence of its trail is hard to see, little more than a rock or a signpost that seems to mark a continuing way. Yet if we follow the stages that might mark its path, there is a growing realization that it does not disappear. That it is leading somewhere.

Marylebone Church, September 1680

One of these stages may be the explanation for a puzzling set of records. It is perhaps the first of these markers. On 12 September 1680 in Marylebone Church, then set almost in the open country north of the road to Oxford, James Howard married Arabella Hunt, a charming and engaging young woman of eighteen who lived with her widowed mother, Mrs. Elizabeth Hunt. Later Arabella Hunt would become a talented and successful musician—a soprano and a lutenist—associated with the court of Queen Mary. In 1680 their home was among the new houses that had sprung up on the grazing fields west of the city after the Great Fire of 1666, in the parish of St. Martin in the Fields, which no longer then quite justified its name. Her mother, Mrs. Elizabeth Hunt, had invited her friends, Sara Cunningham and Phoebe Horton, both neighbors in her parish, as witnesses to the marriage; and the wedding over, the party traveled on to Kensall Green, where Phoebe

Horton had lodgings, for the night. Cunningham and Horton were there the traditional witnesses to Arabella and James Howard's sharing their marriage bed, the same ritual that would have been represented by the blessing of the marriage bed in their ancestors' Catholic past. These were familiar rituals. They had taken place innumerable times, and the mundane entry in the parish register would have passed unnoticed were it not for the petition from Arabella Hunt heard some two years later in 1682 in the consistory court of the diocese of London for the marriage to be annulled. James Howard—it appears from these documents—like Arabella Hunt was a woman.[24]

"James Howard" was the name taken by Mrs. Amy Poulter, who in 1672 had married Arthur Poulter, the eldest surviving son of a prominent Hertfordshire family. Arthur Poulter died in January 1681, but he was still living at the time of Amy Poulter's marriage to Arabella Hunt; and during the annulment proceedings Amy Poulter defended her part in the marriage as having been carried out "not seriously but rashly and unduly and in a frollick jocular or facetious manner," as the stiff legal formulas in her formal response put it. Mrs. Hunt's friend Phoebe Horton confirmed in her evidence that Amy Poulter had worn men's clothes at the wedding Horton had witnessed in 1680.

The formal explanation submitted to the court was that Amy Poulter's deception had been carried out not seriously but in a merely "frollick jocular or facetious manner," yet the case is full of difficulties. If the wedding was a "frolic" on Poulter's part, why was Arabella Hunt taken in by it? Indeed, was she? Arabella Hunt never directly claimed in her petition that she had been deceived about Poulter's gender. This certainly would have been difficult to believe, for several reasons. As Sara Cunningham gave evidence to the court, Arabella Hunt had lived with Poulter for some six months after the wedding: "as Man and Wife at Bed and Board," as the deposition of Mrs. Hunt's servant Jane Jones puts it. Jones also gave evidence that Poulter had dressed not as a man but as a woman when she visited the house to court Arabella. Sara Cunningham's deposition adds that after the marriage Poulter "went most . . . in womans Apparrell, and especially when she went into the City."

Each of these witnesses assured the court that they had believed the female dress to be a disguise but did so without being able to adduce what was its purpose and were not pressed on this. One might wonder what was in the court's mind as it exercised this restraint. The alterations and additions in these documents and the guarded legal formulas they employ suggest that one important objective in the mind of the officials who drafted these documents was to ensure that they did not start any hares that might leave the court itself open to criticism. There are several points where the doubts one might entertain about Amy Poulter's explanation seem to have been shared by the officials of the court. The depositions (the evidence of the witnesses) are not verbatim accounts but rather written up by the registrar (or his deputy), from memory or from notes. He evidently would review the drafts and alter them before handing them to the witnesses for signature (or in the case of Jane Jones and Phoebe Horton, for their mark). Among them is a suggestive alteration by the registrar at the point in Jones's deposition where it confirmed the claim in Arabella Hunt's formal petition (or "libel") that Arabella Hunt left Poulter's company as soon as she "had by some meanes or other discovered that the sayd person was not a perfect man but an Hermaphrodite," as the deposition initially put it: scarcely a credible claim in the face of the evidence of the midwives who examined Poulter for the courts, that she was "a perfect woman in all her parts." When the official reviewed the document before passing it to Jones to make her mark, he prudently added the saving phrase "or at least suspected," above the line after the word "discovered": an alteration evidently of his own making that rescued the evidence for Arabella Hunt's petition.

The same cautious awareness that the full facts might not be set out seems to have been shared by the notary who acted as court proctor in drawing up Amy Poulter's formal response (her "personal answers") to Arabella Hunt's petition. The formula that I quoted above—that the marriage had been carried out "not seriously but rashly and unduly and in a frollick jocular or facetious manner"—came after two amendments by the notary. The first was the careful alteration of "and" to "or," which made the claim less vulnerable, but more importantly the notary had second thoughts about the phrase that he had added at the end of this formula, perhaps as a familiar reflex: "(and not other wise)." Was it precisely that "other wise" to which he had no wish to draw attention?

A trace of the court's enabling hand lies not only in these alterations but also in what was *not* there: no evidence was given—or apparently sought—from Arabella's mother, Mrs. Hunt, although it was she who had made the arrangements for the wedding: Phoebe Horton makes it clear in her deposition that it was *Elizabeth* Hunt who asked her to be present. It was to the advantage of a smooth handling of the annulment that Mrs. Hunt did not have to provide a deposition, for there were two questions that she might have had some discomfort in answering.

The first would be this. If there was no serious motive on Amy Poulter's part, if the wedding was merely a "frolic," why did this not become apparent when Mrs. Hunt made the usual inquiries of the family and "friends" of her daughter's suitor? It comes as a jolt in this regard to read in Phoebe

Horton's deposition that, although Amy Poulter used the name James
Howard at the marriage in Marylebone Church, at the house of Mrs. Hunt
it was "by the Name of Madam Poulter" that she went. The Poulters were
one of the leading families of Hertfordshire. Amy Poulter's father-in-law
had been the sheriff of the county earlier in the century, and the family had
been known in London since the fifteenth century, where the founder of its
fortunes, John Poulter, had been a London merchant. Hertfordshire is near
London, only a day's journey away: the name "Madam Poulter" alone would
have been enough to identify who Amy Poulter was—to Mrs. Hunt and to
her neighbors.

It is then unsurprising that neither Arabella nor her mother ever make
an outright claim to have been deceived about Amy Poulter's gender. A second question that Mrs. Hunt would not have wished to have been asked—
a detail that would immediately have stood out from the facts as a signal to
the officials of the consistory court, if not now to us—is why she arranged
for the wedding of her daughter to take place in Marylebone Church. To
ask that question in 1680 arguably would be to answer it, for the church of
"St Mary le Bone" had a distinct reputation. Its remote setting made it a
convenient spot for hasty, secret, or otherwise questionable marriages, in
which its officiating clergy would evidently quietly collude. The church has
disappeared, demolished in 1949; and its site is now the garden at the top of
the present Marylebone High Street: but its interior can still be seen in the
print of William Hogarth's *Rake's Progress*, where it is the setting for Tom
Rakewell's disreputable marriage. In this setting two lovers might have
arranged a hasty wedding, before their families and friends could intervene.
The motives for a wedding beyond the boundaries of the parish could be
many (and various); but in choosing this church for her daughter's wedding,
well away from her own parish, Mrs. Hunt had chosen a church where the
name "James Howard" would be accepted without demur and the officiating clergyman could be trusted not to look beyond Amy Poulter's masculine clothes. In fact as, piece by piece, one lays the matter out, it begins to
seem as if everyone understood what was going on: family, witnesses, court
officials, even officiating clergy—everyone, it would seem, except us.

What are we to make of it? As matters stand, these records potentially
point to a wider implication that might take one aback. Historians have assumed, not unnaturally, that in this respect at least the entries in English
parish registers are to be taken at their face value: if they record a man and
a woman being married, then that is what they were. But what are we to
make of that assumption—however reasonable—in the face of documents
such as these? If the masculine name "James Howard" in the terse entry in

the Marylebone parish register was a fiction—"Marriages. September 1680 ... James Howard & Arabella Hunt ... 12"—how many more such were there? The sharp point is that it is only because the parties were later given an annulment that here we know otherwise.

There is another possible explanation that would not carry so radical an implication. An earlier chapter of this book glimpsed the friendship of Ann Chitting and Mary Barber in their burial by each other's side early in the seventeenth century in the church of St. James in Bury and in the verses on their tomb. Like Amy Poulter, both Ann Chitting and Mary Barber were married, and Roger Barber, the husband of Mary Barber, was also buried by her. The friendship between Ann Chitting and Mary Barber evidently had a sufficiently formal and objective character for them to be buried together: "Henry her sonn her body here did place / next to her freind whose soules in heave' imbrace." My commentary was that that embrace was the kiss of peace, which could unite two families as well as two friends. We know of the monument (now lost) because of the manuscripts of the Suffolk antiquary Henry Chitting, Ann Chitting's son, circulated by him among the county gentry to celebrate their family connections. To this degree, the character of this friendship was one that overlapped with the bonds that could be created between two families by marriage and shaded into them. To Henry Chitting's family they counted for a great deal: Mary Barber was the niece of Francis Boldero, the servant and official of the lord keeper Sir Nicholas Bacon, the Chitting family's patron. It was here that the wider significance of the friendship of these two women lay—and that of their tomb, and that of Henry Chitting's manuscript.

As one moves across the seventeenth century, into the eighteenth and beyond, the presence of women in the historical record becomes easier to discern and will from this point begin to figure more visibly in this book. Does it provide a frame here? The tomb monument of Ann Chitting and Mary Barber—and the evident significance it carried for their families—suggests an intriguing possibility. Did Mrs. Hunt understand her daughter to be forming a relation with Amy Poulter of the same kind as Ann Chitting and Mary Barber had had? Mrs. Hunt was a widow and, judging by the friends at her daughter's wedding, her worldly connections appear very limited. Would a connection to Amy Poulter's family have lifted them? Could the connection in effect have provided the patronage that would be needed by a talented young woman with few connections embarking on life as a musician? The Poulters were a substantial county family, but perhaps more importantly for Mrs. Hunt the Poulters had been connected by marriage to the family of the earl of Marlborough, in that Arthur Poulter's father had married Lady Hester Ley, one of the heiresses of Sir James Ley, the first earl of Marlborough. Did Mrs. Hunt hope that the connection with Amy Poulter would bring Arabella the patronage at court that she needed?

If she did, then the annulment through which we learn of the wedding in 1680 may not have been the accident that it otherwise seems to be. An alliance of this kind would be fraught with difficulties, not least the slender thread of the immaturity of Arabella herself—that and a county family that might not share Amy Poulter's regard for this charming but perhaps unconnected young women (a recognizable dilemma that I will return to). Did Mrs. Hunt hope that Arthur Poulter, Amy Poulter's husband, would act for Arabella? If so, his death shortly before Amy Poulter and Arabella parted would have ended that expectation. But a connection such as this could not be entered into lightly or easily broken. Friendship in the world I have described constrained as well as enabled. Covenants bound. Did the wedding in 1680 provide the possibility of a way out at need? If the friendship between Arabella Hunt and Amy Poulter was of the kind that bound Ann Chitting and Mary Barber, then its ties overlapped with those that could be created between two families by marriage: and if an annulment released the one, then it also released the other. The English people, set in this respect apart from many of their continental neighbors, preserved their church courts largely intact into the eighteenth century because these courts served their needs. Sometimes they did so by squaring the circle. From the glimpses one catches of the workings of these courts, one can at points see them creating grounds for untying bonds of kinship and marriage, which allowed the parties with some integrity to walk away from relations that patently had broken down.[25] The question I am asking is whether this kind of official might still have been found at the consistory court of the diocese of London in the 1680s? It seems very probable that they were.

Did the wedding in 1680 provide a possible solution of this kind, held in reserve if the need arose? If an annulment were sought, it would have been granted: that could be relied on. The prospect of a way out, with some dignity, might have helped all involved to take those first steps in a friendship that could find itself treading a difficult road. If I have the measure of the officials of the English church courts right, then they were the sort of figures who knew that the gaps—and the overlaps—between one thing and its other had their utility: something that a nice and fastidious imagination cannot always grasp.

The scholarly first editors of these documents, Patricia Crawford and Sara Mendelson, shared the doubts one might entertain about the formal submission to the court on Amy Poulter's behalf, that she had no serious intent, and regarded her motives as enigmatic. The speculation that they make in their paper was that of a sexual desire on Amy Poulter's part, who they suggest may have fallen in love with Arabella: either deceiving her about her true gender or creating the circumstances for a lesbian love affair that foundered. Amy Poulter, in the male guise of James Howard, on this account would then have succeeded in passing herself off to Arabella Hunt's family as the kind of marriage match that Arabella would need; a suggestion that would also extend to the evidently covert nature of the wedding ceremony, if "James Howard" was then presenting himself as marrying his social inferior, for love, without the knowledge of his family: presenting them with a fait accompli. This spectacular deception (reminiscent of the Restoration stage) is certainly possible, despite its difficulties, including the mundane circumstance here that Amy Poulter was known by her real name of Madam Poulter at Mrs. Hunt's house.

In probing Poulter's possible motives and the nature of her physical relationship with Arabella Hunt, one would of course be confronting matters that cannot now be more than speculations. What I have attempted here is the more accessible alternative of seeing the wedding in 1680 through the eyes of Arabella Hunt's *family*. One cannot know whether Mrs. Hunt did believe Poulter to be a woman, or perhaps suspected it, or entertained the possibility that "Madam Poulter" might indeed be Madam Poulter. But what is striking in this wider context is that, if a relation like that of Ann Chitting and Mary Barber *was* still possible at the end of the seventeenth century, how little difference—in that wider context—would have been made by whether this figure was indeed Madam Poulter or the clandestine suitor James Howard: both potentially offered Mrs. Hunt the family connections her daughter might need.

If the bond between Arabella Hunt and Amy Poulter did provide such a link between families as Ann Chitting and Mary Barber had, then the provision of a way out of that bond at need was hard-headed but would prove to be realistic. In the event Arabella Hunt did not need Amy Poulter. By the time Arabella Hunt died in 1705, a quarter of a century after these events, she had become a celebrated musician at the royal court, her singing captured in Congreve's delicious lines.

> While we, charmed with the loved excess,
> Are wrapped in sweet forgetfulness
> Of all, of all, but of the present happiness,
> Wishing for ever in that state to lie,
> For ever to be dying so, yet never die.

She was a pensioner of Queen Mary, at the side of Henry Purcell and John Blow, and when she died, she left all her estate to her mother.

> Were there on Earth another Voice like thine,
> Another Hand so Blest with Skill Divine!
> The late afflicted World some Hopes might have,
> And Harmony retrieve thee from the Grave.

That was the epigram Congreve composed for the painting by Kneller of the beautiful Arabella Hunt seated on a bank with her lute.[26]

Perhaps, however, Amy Poulter had needed Arabella Hunt. For Amy Poulter things would not be the same. The court pronounced her marriage to Arabella Hunt null and void in December 1682. By the end of the following month Amy Poulter was dead, buried at the church in Cottered in Hertfordshire. Was the release from the promises that freed the one, too much for the other to bear? There is one fact in all of this that cannot be gainsaid. On a September day in 1680 she had indeed made those promises and received them.

Westminster Abbey, 1710

But *was* it possible at the end of the seventeenth century for Arabella Hunt and Amy Poulter to have had the same kind of friendship that Ann Chitting and Mary Barber had had? In 1680 we are at the other side of an England that was being transformed by the civil society that John Locke defined with such clarity, although he did not create it. In that world a covenant, however solemnly entered into before God and man, was subservient and inferior to that great abstraction, the Original Contract of Civil Society. Would the kind of dilemma that might have been foreseen for Arabella Hunt still have signified in that world?

Thirty years after Arabella Hunt's marriage, a monument would be placed in Westminster Abbey that arguably addresses that question. It can still be seen today in the quiet enclosed chapel of St. John the Baptist that opens off the ambulatory around the sanctuary of the abbey, set on the wall just within the gateway to the chapel. It marks the burial there in 1710 of Mrs. Mary Kendall and is one of the most beautiful of the abbey's many monuments (see fig. 8). An alabaster figure depicts Mary Kendall kneeling in prayer, in the contemporary dress of a lady, flanked by two Corinthian columns of red-veined marble, supporting entablatures and an open semicircular pediment of veined blue and gray marble. The monument (set out from an arch of honey-colored

Figure 8
The monument of Mary Kendall, Westminster Abbey.

and blue-veined marble) is surmounted by a cartouche of arms. Below is the name of her cousin Charles Kendall, her residuary legatee.

> This Monument was Erected by Capt. CHARLES KENDALL

The designation "Mrs." with which the inscription opens is a matter of social rather than marital status, as she died unmarried, judging by her will.

Mrs MARY KENDALL,

Daughter of Thomas Kendall Esqr,
And of Mrs Mary Hallet, his Wife,
        Of Killigarth, in Cornwall,
Was born at Westm^r. Nov.8.1677.
And dy'd at Epsome, March 4.17%.
Having reach'd the full Term
Of her blessed Saviours Life:
And study'd to imitate
His spotless Example.
She had great Virtues,
And as great a desire of Concealing them:
Was of a Severe Life,
But of an Easy Conversation;
Courteous to All, yet strictly Sincere;
Humble, without Meanness;
Beneficent, without Ostentation;
Devout, without Superstition.

These admirable Qualitys,
In which She was eqall'd by Few of her Sex,
Surpass'd by None,
Render'd Her every way worthy
Of that close Union & Friendship,
In which She liv'd, with
The Lady CATHARINE IONES;
And, in testimony of which, She desir'd,
That even their Ashes, after Death,
Might not be divided:
And therefore, order'd her Selfe
Here to be interr'd,
Where, She knew, that Excellent Lady
Design'd one day, to rest,
Near the Grave of her Belov'd
And Religious Mother,
ELIZABETH Countess of RANELAGH.

Was that "close Union & Friendship" a settled friendship of the same kind as had linked Ann Chitting and Mary Barber at the beginning of the century—and perhaps had been designed for Arabella Hunt, who lived in the same social world as Mrs. Mary Kendall and died in the same decade? That word "Union" is a strong expression even without the adjective, sufficient for Lady Catharine Jones when she died in 1740 to be buried here by Kendall. Kendall's wish "That even their Ashes, after Death / Might not be divided" repeats and amplifies that on the tombs of Chitting and Barber; the one seen from this world, the other from the next.

> Henry her sonn her body here did place
> next to her freind whose soules in heave' imbrace
> They lived and loved like two most vertuous wights
> Whose bodyes death wold sever he unites

But the friendship of Chitting and Barber was instrumental in uniting their two *families*, and it is there that I have suggested the context might have lain also for the hopes and plans of Mrs. Hunt for her daughter. Was this the case also here? The friendship of Mary Kendall and Lady Catharine Jones lies plain on the beautiful surface of this monument, but as one examines its details—and its setting—other figures also step forward. One of course is the figure of Lady Catharine Jones's mother, who closes the inscription. It is in terms of where *her mother* would lie that the visitor's attention is drawn to the setting of the monument: "Near the Grave of her Belov'd / And Religious Mother, / ELIZABETH Countess of RANELAGH." If the inscription draws attention to the family of Lady Catharine Jones, then the heraldic arms draw attention to the family of Mary Kendall. But so does another such detail: "This Monument was Erected by Capt. CHARLES KENDALL." Set in an emphatic position above the inscription (and indeed closer to eye level), it is *his* name that first draws the viewer's attention— and one might wonder why.[27]

As historical records, the funerary monuments in Westminster Abbey do not stand alone, because of the accompanying burial register maintained by the abbey (now in its muniment room). We know from this, for example, that Lady Catharine Jones was later buried here, and as one looks through its entries, one can see also that the chapel of St. John the Baptist was the burial place of the family of the first earl of Ranelagh. In 1695 the countess of Ranelagh was buried here, the earl in 1712. After Lady Catharine Jones's burial in 1740, her sister was buried there in 1758. The burial register does not indicate where her young brother had been buried in 1678, beyond that it was in the abbey, but it seems probable from these entries that he was buried there also. The burial place one might have expected of the Kendalls seems to have been in the south aisle of the abbey, where Mary Kendall's uncle, the M.P. James Kendall, was buried. By being buried with Lady Catharine Jones in the chapel of St. John the Baptist, Mary Kendall was lying in death with her friend as they might have lain together in the household of the earl of Ranelagh and his wife, the countess Elizabeth: that is the significance of this setting.[28]

Though this monument *is* beautiful it figured in a wider world of power and place—as Captain Charles Kendall would have been fully aware. Charles Kendall was the son of a merchant, and the magnificent monument he was able to erect in the chapel of St. John the Baptist is an eloquent testimony to the potentially influential connection of his family with that of the earl of Ranelagh. Richard Jones, the first earl of Ranelagh, was a colorful and controversial figure, famously described by the eighteenth-century historian Thomas Carte as "a man of good parts, great wit, and very little religion."[29] His life was marked as much by financial scandal (and indeed disgrace) as by the influence he continued to hold at the court of William and Mary, and that of Queen Anne when she succeeded them. The exquisite garden at his house in Chelsea, which Lady Catharine Jones inherited when he died in 1712, was the essence of good taste and art: quite simply, fit for a prince. When Captain Charles Kendall commissioned this exquisitely beautiful monument for the burial place of the earl of Ranelagh and his family, he was offering a gesture that had been chosen with care; its great beauty is precisely what made it apposite here to the family of a man with the tastes of the earl of Ranelagh. It is a persuasive trace of the power a settled friendship could still possess in the opening years of the eighteenth century to join not only two friends but also two families.

Launceston, Cornwall, 1731

The power to connect families was evidently contained in the friendship of two men as well as that of two women. The placing of the monument to Granville Piper and Richard Wise in the church of St. Mary Magdalene in Launceston illustrates that continuing role. It also points to why it held its own. It is perhaps another marker on this apparently continuing way. Granville Piper died in 1717, while in Bath, and was buried by Richard Wise in the abbey church there. When Wise died in 1726, he left instructions for his remains to be interred by those of his friend in Bath and for this cenotaph to be erected in the church in Launceston as "Monumentum mutui eorum Amoris" [a monument to their mutual love], as the inscription puts it (see fig. 9). The choice of the setting for the cenotaph in the north aisle of the church placed that friendship, in the most concrete of terms, within the context of the Piper family: its setting in the north aisle of the church was where the Piper burial place and the family pew were situated. When it was erected in 1731, it would have stood near the magnificent monument to Granville Piper's grandparents, the celebrated local figure of Colonel Sir Hugh Piper and his wife Sibella Piper that occupied a commanding position at the end of the north aisle. Their monument now survives only in fragments, but the stone tablet standing by the foot of the cenotaph marked their grave and today still reflects the setting of the Piper burial place.

The opposition to the erection of the monument (which I mentioned earlier in this chapter) was something new in 1731, but it is significant that it did not succeed. As one looks closely at the details of this monument, it begins to become apparent why it did not. The monument rises in four tiers that reach from the floor to the ceiling of the aisle. The base is a tall plinth of black-and-white-veined marble, and above is set the central inscription, surrounded by a decorative border and flanked by two symbolic female forms. To one side is Fortitude, grasping a sword and looking steadfastly forward. To the other is Wisdom in a state of composed reflection, with her

Figure 9
The monument to Granville Piper and Richard Wise in the church of St.
Mary Magdalene, Launceston, Cornwall. They are buried together in Bath.

symbol of a serpent entwined about her arm. On the tier above are the alle-
gorical figures of Faith, Charity, and Hope. Faith is depicted as the Magdalene, to whom the church is dedicated, holding her alabaster jar and gaz-
ing upward. Hope holds her symbol of the anchor and looks down to the
viewer below. The central and commanding position is given to Charity, depicted as a mother with her baby in her arms and her children by her, holding on to her. Pillars of finely polished marble forming frames enclose the
inscription and each of the figures, surmounted by a sculptured cornice on

the fourth and topmost tier, on which are placed busts of the two friends in their robes of office as alderman and mayor. The heraldic arms of the Piper and the Wise families are displayed below. Linking the busts and the heraldic arms is a flaming funerary urn depicting the Resurrection of Christ, set directly above the central figure of Charity and the inscription below.

The personification of the virtues is a repeated monumental device and has been admirably characterized by the architectural historian Jean Wilson.

> The Seven life-giving Virtues are Faith, Hope, Charity, Prudence, Temperance, Fortitude and Justice. The first three are the Theological Virtues— those inner qualities which are aspects of the Christian Faith and which define our relationship to God, the mood in which we live our lives, and our attitude to other people. The Four Cardinal Virtues, while essential to the Christian, are Platonic in origin, and define, not so much our general attitude to the world—Charity—as the moral strategies we should adopt in living the virtuous life and forging an equitable society . . . Taken together, the Virtues give a programme for the exemplary life, but they do not define the sphere in which that virtuous life is to be lived, or the earthly rewards to which such a life may lead.[30]

In this context, the inscription that I quoted earlier in this chapter identifies Piper and Wise's *friendship* as the sphere in which these two men expressed these virtues, "Fidissimum Amicorum Par" [most faithful pair of friends].

Jean Wilson's succinct analysis is entirely to the point but does not exhaust the monument's significance. It rather opens to view the significance of the setting within the church. Why are only two of the four cardinal virtues depicted—and why *these two*, Wisdom and Fortitude? The source of the three theological virtues that accompany them—Faith, Hope, and Charity—is St. Paul's first letter to the Corinthians: "And now abideth faith, hope, charity, these three; but the greatest of these is charity." Earlier in the same letter, Paul identifies the two cardinal virtues depicted here in *christological* terms: that is, as revealing not only the attributes of a Christian, as in Jean Wilson's commentary, but also the human and divine natures of Christ himself: "Christ the power of God, and the wisdom of God."[31] In Pauline terms then, Christ is present in the imagery on this tomb: not only in his Resurrection depicted on the funerary urn above the inscription, but also in the virtues of Fortitude and Wisdom that flank it. They too represent Christ. So too the three theological virtues point to Christ, and the link between them in this respect, in Pauline terms, is the Resurrection. In the same terms of 1 Corinthians, Christ's Resurrection prefigured the general resurrection at his future coming: "But now is Christ risen from the dead, and become the firstfruits of them that slept . . . Christ the firstfruits; afterward they that are Christ's at his coming." The context of the Pauline reference to the three virtues picks up this eschatological context: that is, one that looks to the end of the age and the general resurrection at Christ's second coming, "For we know in part, and we prophesy in part. But when that which is perfect is come, then that which is in part shall be done away . . . For now we see through a glass, darkly; but then face to face: now I know in part; but then shall I know even as also I am known. And now abideth faith, hope, charity, these three; but the greatest of these is charity." It is in that frame that Faith, Hope, and Charity in 1 Corinthians "now abideth" and, like Christ's Resurrection, prefigure his final coming.

The viewer envisaged for this monument is one who knows that this is the Piper family burial place and recognizes the Piper family pew close at hand, as indeed that memory has remained today in Launceston. In this setting in the north aisle of the church of St. Mary Magdalene, the three theological virtues (in St. Paul's terms) anticipate the general resurrection that the Piper family await for their dead lying there. If in these terms the monument is directed to the Piper burial place, then it is also directed to the Piper family pew. In terms of Paul's letter to the Corinthians the general resurrection is anticipated not only in Christ's Resurrection and in the three theological virtues but also in the Lord's Supper.

> For I have received of the Lord that which also I delivered unto you, That the Lord Jesus the same night in which he was betrayed took bread: And when he had given thanks, he brake it, and said, Take, eat: this is my body, which is broken for you: this do in remembrance of me. After the same manner also he took the cup, when he had supped, saying, This cup is the new testament in my blood: this do ye, as oft as ye drink it, in remembrance of me. For as often as ye eat this bread, and drink this cup, ye do shew the Lord's death till he come.

"Till he come": that, in the Pauline terms of this monument, is the point. The dead of the Piper family await Christ's return and the resurrection in their family burial place, the living at the Lord's Supper in their family pew; and the monument to Granville Piper and Richard Wise enfolds their friendship in death within the Piper family burial place, as in life they received Holy Communion together in the Piper family pew, at the Lord's Supper in Launceston church.

I have analyzed the significance of this tomb at such length not solely to recover the theology it expresses, for this is the same theology of friendship that I explored in my chapter on families and friends, in the iconography of the tomb monument of John Bloxham and John Whytton and explicitly in the hymns to St. John as Christ's friend and in the preaching that employed them. The point I have sought to make is more historical and more immediate to the questioning of the influence of civil society I have essayed in this chapter. Can one really take such a monument, so confident and forceful as this, as the trace of a world that was vanishing? If I have read this monument aright, it suggests that, although traditional religion of the kind represented by St. Mary Magdalene's church bowed to the new forces of civil society, they had not entered its spirit. On its own ground and in its own terms, it could and did resist them.

Hereford Cathedral, 1746

In such a context, a settled friendship evidently retained the power to unite two families, within a traditional view of religion's role that stubbornly maintained itself in Launceston's church. That view also allowed a quarrel to be laid down with dignity. In Hereford Cathedral there is an eloquent trace of that continuing role, also.

In 1746 Lord James Beauclerk became the bishop of Hereford, and his magnificent fourteenth-century bishop's throne can still be seen in the choir. It now stands as an eastward extension of the choir stalls, but in 1746 it stood apart, as it had since the fourteenth century. The medieval bishops of Hereford did not sit in choir like canons of the cathedral, singing the psalms; they were great lords, and the throne with its canopy formed a private booth that shielded them and looked across the sanctuary to the high altar. But as Bishop Beauclerk looked from his throne toward the altar, what he saw on the pavement immediately beside his throne was a monument: to the friendship of the two men buried beneath the ledger stones that were laid side by side there (see fig. 10). Each displayed the appropriate heraldic arms, and the stones were joined by a depiction of two hands reaching from one to the other, meeting in the handfast.[32] Below them was the inscription, which ran from one stone to the next. "In Vitâ conjuncti," the inscription begins, and it continues on the other stone "In Mortê non divisi" [In life united: in death not divided]. The second part of the inscription is from David's lament for Saul and Jonathan in 2 Samuel: in the Latin, "in morte . . . non sunt divisi." The term in that first part—"In Vitâ conjuncti"—is the sworn brotherhood of Amys and Amylion, "Quos Deus sicut unamini concordia et dilectione in vita conjunxit, ita et in morte eos separari noluit" [God did

Figure 10
The tombstones of Herbert Croft and George Benson, respectively bishop and
dean of Hereford Cathedral, where they lie. (Copyright The Dean and
Chapter of Hereford and the Hereford Mappa Mundi Trust)

not wish to divide in death those whom in life he had joined as one in unity
and love].[33]

This monument echoes and repeats that of the friends who have peopled
this book, from the tomb monument of William Neville and John Clanvowe in the fourteenth century with which it opened, and were it not for
the memorial inscriptions on the monument, one might have taken it for a
relic of such a distant past. As Bishop Beauclerk was only too well aware, it
was not. The inscriptions on the ledger stones identify the two figures
buried below them as Bishop Herbert Croft, a recent predecessor of Beauclerk as bishop of Hereford, and Dean George Benson, the dean of the

cathedral in his time. Each had died and been buried here only a generation before, in the 1690s. This, for Bishop Beauclerk, was a *modern* monument.

Herbert Croft and George Benson were born in the early years of the seventeenth century and lived through its wars and religious divisions, an experience that profoundly shaped their friendship. Croft had become dean of the cathedral in the midst of the civil war in 1644, in an area with strongly royalist sympathies, taken and lost by the parliamentary forces: until in December 1645 Colonel Birch definitively took control of the city for Parliament. Here the forces of religious zeal had none of the restraint they had in Oxford. The cathedral library was looted, monuments were defaced and destroyed, and Croft came close to being murdered by Colonel Birch's men, who trained their guns on him when he attempted to stop the iconoclasm and destruction in the cathedral. Subsequently he was ejected from his post as dean and from his house and the canons from theirs. With the Restoration of Charles II, Croft returned in triumph in 1662 as bishop of Hereford. George Benson had been part of the cathedral clergy with Croft and had suffered with him. With the Restoration he too returned to the cathedral, and in 1672 he became its dean.

Croft's decision to be buried with a memorial that did not mark his marriage to his wife Anne (the daughter of his predecessor as dean of Hereford) but rather his friendship with Benson reflects something of the closeness of the bond between them. But *does* that wholly account for this monument? Let me go back to Bishop Beauclerk—and that placing of this monument beside the bishop's throne. Their joint tomb has memorialized Croft and Benson in the cathedral for their friendship, but they are remembered there for something else also—which might have come immediately to mind at the sight of this monument. To appreciate it requires some acquaintance with canon law and the history of Hereford Cathedral: on 16 April 1677, Bishop Herbert Croft began a visitation of the cathedral without protest or objection by its canons—and in doing so ended a long and bitter quarrel.[34]

The medieval bishops of Hereford were great lords, but they were not the lords of the cathedral clergy: not in the view of its canons, at least. From their earliest days the canons of the cathedrals had claimed independence from episcopal control. The thirteenth and fourteenth centuries would see this freedom challenged and worn down. This freedom was not lost without resistance, sometimes employing force, as occurred when the archbishop of York attempted to hold a visitation of his cathedral in 1328. The bishop's detailed visitation of the cathedral and its affairs was both the symbol and the effective instrument of that contested lordship. Determined though the resistance often was, history and the forces of church reform were not on its side. The canons of Lincoln Cathedral capitulated in 1246, Wells in 1338, Salisbury in 1393. Hereford alone stubbornly held out, despite appeals to Rome and repeated but vain attempts by the bishops of Hereford, up to the eve of the Reformation.

To this quarrel the coming of a reformed religion would make little difference. In 1559 the accession of Queen Elizabeth brought Bishop John Scory to Hereford, a man whose zealous determination to root out the Catholicism of his diocese was equaled only by his determination to resume its old quarrels. He would have his visitation. The cathedral claimed its ancient privileges and succeeded in having none of it. The dispute raged on for several years and is marked by a letter full of exasperated venom from Bishop Scory to William Cecil, the powerful secretary of the queen.

> The disorder of the cathedral church of my bishoprick is such that it may be justly accompted a verie nursery of blasphemy, whoredom, pryde, superstition and ignorance, and yet no power in me to reforme yt, the same being exempt of my jurisdictyon, contrary to the usage in all other like churches, to Godes high displeasure and my great griefe and hartye sorrow.

He complained to Cecil that he "dare not without a great guard move out of his lodgings," which was quite likely true: but more likely it was the effect of the substantial fortune that the reform of his diocese had given him, by plain simony and extortion, than the opposition of the cathedral clergy. But these were menacing words in Bishop Scory's letter, although the queen had not yet been excommunicated by the pope and martyrdom still lay in the future of seminary priests like Robert Morton, whom we met earlier in this book. Words like "superstition" and "ignorance" were code words in Elizabethan England for popery, and the burnings of heretics under Mary were still fresh in the memory.

Where Bishop Scory did not succeed in enforcing an unopposed visitation by the bishop of Hereford, his successors in the Jacobean and Caroline churches fared only minimally better. Although they made inroads, it was not without protests and resistance. With the restoration of the Stuart monarchy and an established religion in 1660, the quarrel wearily resumed. But how tenable was it now? A reformed but still episcopal Church of England had withstood a rebellion and fought a civil war to uphold episcopacy. Dean Croft had nearly been martyred for its forms in his own cathedral. If the clergy of the cathedral now abandoned their stance, would they not lose face—and status and authority with it? The problem, of course, was that this quarrel had been going on for nearly *five hundred years.*

The friendship of Bishop Croft and Dean George Benson allowed a way out with dignity. One cannot be sure what degree or form their friendship took without more evidence, although the echo of Amys and Amylion on their tombs suggests the awareness of a friendship bound by oath and obligation like theirs (as does the handfast it depicts). There may also be a trace of its confirmation in the Eucharist (as there is with the monument to John Finch and Thomas Baines) in the description given by the antiquary Browne Willis in 1730, that the setting of their monument lay within the communion rails, a possibility strengthened by the choice of 16 April 1677 as the commencement of the visitation: the day immediately following Easter communion, when the Lord's Supper would have been celebrated in the cathedral. If Bishop Croft and Dean Benson had received Holy Communion at the general Easter communion at the cathedral, the sacrament of union that day would have marked a momentous and historic resolution of an old quarrel. The rhetoric on this monument is something one can recognize. The close union and friendship to which it corresponds, in rhetoric at least, transcended the quarrels of the past: within its terms *this* dean of the cathedral and *this* bishop of Hereford knew no difference between them; and the dean and chapter of the cathedral were now free with dignity and grace to accept the episcopal visitation that they had so long resisted.

Bishop Herbert Croft owed Dean George Benson and the cathedral clergy a great debt for that acquiescence, and this monument appears to have repaid it, or rather passed it on to his successors. The ecclesiastical and scholarly Latin of the inscription appropriately veiled its terms, but not from the learned or from any future bishop of Hereford; and the placing of the monument beside a successor's throne would leave him in no doubt, however elegantly this was expressed, of the debt of gratitude he owed to Benson and the cathedral clergy of Hereford. In 1765 Bishop Beauclerk would hold his own visitation of the cathedral. It was done with dignity and served its purpose, but not all were overawed by their diocesan. Relations between Beauclerk and his dean and chapter were never good. They began frostily and became worse, and his dean and chapter had no hesitation in pointedly, if politely, reminding the archbishop of Canterbury when asked to intervene that the bishop's right of visitation at Hereford was a gift and no ancient right. During his long incumbency and to his last days, Beauclerk quarreled with his dean and chapter. But the eloquent gesture of Benson and Croft had done the work they envisaged for it, and as Hereford slipped into its eighteenth-century slumber, no one was leveling their guns at anyone or hinting that uncooperative cathedral clergy might conveniently be hanged. This was now only a family quarrel.

Holy Trinity, Goodramgate, 1834: Easter Day

The middle years of the nineteenth century would see a radical restoration of Hereford Cathedral, under its energetic new dean, the antiquary and scholar John Merewether. During this reordering the ledger stones marking the graves of Dean George Benson and Bishop Herbert Croft would be taken up and put aside in the graveyard within the cathedral close, when a new floor was laid in the east end of the choir. In 1867 they were repaired and restored to the cathedral; they were not returned to their original place, beside the bishop's throne, but rather to a quiet spot in the southeast transept, where they can still be seen today.[35] Can one trace a changing context in that removal? It is difficult to judge that question: the significance of their original setting may have seemed no longer apposite, or necessary; or it simply may have been forgotten. The difficulty in making a judgment lies in that loss of a clear context that one had for a moment in the early part of the eighteenth century. The question can perhaps be put more widely in this way. England did not change suddenly and systemically, at some point toward the end of the seventeenth century with the coming of civil society. But was the world I have followed, the traces of which are still visible if one looks for them, nonetheless slipping away across the century that followed? Is that why the evidence is so fragmentary: do these voices, in effect, diminish and grow fainter as their world disappeared? Or is it simply that they are becoming more difficult to hear? Are they fading, or is it only their *audibility* that is fading in the evidence that remains? The commonsense answer is perhaps the former, but it is an argument from silence, that most dangerous of all the arguments that a historian can employ.

Seductive though that answer is, it is radically undermined in the early years of the nineteenth century by a diary kept about a mile northeast of the mill town of Halifax, in a country house beyond Beacon Hill. This is the diary of Anne Lister, who until her death in 1840 was the mistress of Shibden Hall, after the death in 1826 of her unmarried uncle James Lister. The Shibden Hall that Anne Lister inherited was a house of the fifteenth century that sat above Shibden Dale, close by the road that in Anne Lister's day led eastward toward York and a wider world. Shibden Hall today is still largely as Anne Lister left it. The industrial architecture of Halifax below recalls the formidable place the town once occupied in the textile industry, which drew on the rivers of these isolated valleys in Calderdale and the skills of its people.

Lister's diary is, by any standard, an astonishing historical record. It consists of twenty-seven quarto-size volumes containing some four million words written in Lister's abbreviated hand (sometimes in a code of her own devising), which recount in close detail her life, that of her family, the business of her estate, and the effect on them of the politics and the industrial and scientific changes of the time. Even the diary itself is only a small part of the manuscripts of Shibden Hill, including nearly a thousand of Lister's letters, set among documents stretching back to the thirteenth century.

Any discussion of Lister's diary—including the one that follows—relies to a very great extent on the labors of the editors of the Anne Lister manuscripts that I discuss in the afterword to this book. In 1988 an important pioneering study by Helena Whitbread made extensive extracts from the diaries readily available for the years 1817 to 1824. Most recently Jill Liddington has edited—and most importantly contextualized—with meticulous scholarship detailed extracts from the later years, especially 1833-1836. The contribution to this work that I propose to attempt in this chapter is not to add to the transcriptions and editing already carried out, but rather to place Anne Lister within the wide historical perspective that this book arguably provides in one important respect, the connection I believe one can grasp between Lister's friendships and her religious beliefs.[36] Among the wealth of contextual detail in these manuscripts, there stands out in unmistakable detail the degree to which a settled friendship could still be comprehended by family and friends in the 1830s as creating bonds that overlapped with and shaded into those created by a marriage: the story this book has told, precisely what one might have assumed had disappeared across the eighteenth century. Lister's diary demonstrates with telling force how far they had faded *only from view.* The considerable problem these entries present is *how* these forms had survived, when they had long ceased to signify in civil society. That is the question I propose to pursue, and I make no apology for a task that will take some time. These entries are not the fragmentary evidence on which this chapter up to this point has had to draw: they still lie in their first context, but that context in Lister's life will not easily open itself to view. Lister did not write her diary for us: here we are in someone else's house and at best as guests. In particular we need to be alert to the possibility that *why* something matters is not being explained to us—that, to Lister as she wrote her diary, its importance was self-evident, as it is not to us.

There is also a second reason why I shall ask the reader to bear with me in looking in close detail at this evidence, which comes so late in the day, or rather two reasons. One is that, if what we are seeing in Lister's diary was qualitatively the same as the forms of friendship that I have described in this book, that past should provide pointers to some of the contexts tantalizingly left open by Lister's diary. The second is that the wealth of the detail there could provide a unique opportunity to draw close to these forms: to provide a light over the path I have followed and to answer questions in modern terms that the lack of evidence has obstructed. But *are* these the same forms of society? That is the pivotal question. So let me turn to it first.

The evening of an autumn day in September 1832. Anne Lister is sitting with her aunt Anne in a small parlor at Shibden Hall, and she confides to her the decision she and her friend Ann Walker (the heiress of a neighboring estate) had made to settle as companions for life. Their friendship, Walker had said, "would be as good as a marriage." "Yes," Lister had replied, "quite as good or better."[37] This evening Lister took her aunt into her confidence.

> Telling her my real sentiments about Miss Walker and my expectations that the chances were ten to one in favour of our travelling and ultimately settling together. My aunt not to appear to know anything about it, even to Miss W——, till I had mentioned it to the latter. My aunt ... seemed very well pleased at my choice and prospects. I said she had three thousand a year or very near it (as I had understood some time since from the Priestleys). She thought my father would be pleased if he knew and so would both my uncles.[38]

By February 1834, she was able to confide more to her.

> With my aunt from 8¾ to 9 50/"—talked of my journey to Paris & taking Miss W——. Letter from her ... says very little alluding to our union but yet enough to show me she thinks of it as fixed ... Talked to my aunt tonight as if the thing was nearly done, but I should know better in York—tacitly meaning that I should then make her give me a ring & bind herself by a decided promise.[39]

In the spring of that year Anne Lister and Ann Walker visited York and made that decided promise. Its form recalls directly and in the most concrete terms the forms this book has followed. On Easter Sunday, 30 March 1834, Lister and Walker solemnized their union by receiving Holy Communion together in Holy Trinity Church in Goodramgate, near York Minster—as two sworn brothers out of the fifteenth century might have done, like Nicholas Molyneux and John Winter at the church of St. Martin at Harfleur, or as King James I and the duke of Buckingham had planned at the communion at Christmas 1624, making "a new mariage, euer to be kept hearafter." Or indeed in more mundane circumstances, as Margaret Rigby and her fellow servant Edward Turpin and others like them were able to wed in customary forms such as receiving Holy Communion together before the Marriages Act of 1753.

So much is at stake for Anne Lister in this passage that, as Jill Liddington points out, her coded writing becomes uncharacteristically confused.[40]

> Three kisses—better to her than to me . . . At Goodramgate church at 10 35/″;
> Miss W— and I and Thomas staid the sacrament . . . The first time I ever
> joined Miss W— in my prayers—I had prayed that our union might be
> happy . . .

To that, Lister adds "she had not thought of doing as much for me": a comment that would prefigure the anxieties in later years about Walker's nervous and anxious personality. Walker had indeed not been her first choice. Lister was now a mature woman of forty-one, and her choice had first been the daughter of a York doctor, Mariana Belcombe, whom Lister had met in 1812 when Lister was 21. Mariana Belcombe would marry Charles Lawton, a man who was wealthy enough to have given her a comfortable lifestyle. Lister continued to hope after her marriage that Mariana would settle with herself, and indeed they would remain attached to each other throughout Lister's life; but as Mariana came to accept the pragmatic compromise she had made in marrying Charles Lawton (and he perhaps also), Lister turned her thoughts elsewhere, toward Ann Walker.

In those early years Lister had evidently thought of a union of the same kind that she would later form with Walker, as one can see from an entry in her diary in July 1821, when Lister and Mariana had paid a visit to Mariana's brother and his family in Staffordshire.

> We talked all last night & only closed our eyes to dose about half-hour, just
> before getting up . . . & then bound ourselves to each other by an irrevoca
> ble promise for ever, in pledge of which, turned on her finger the gold ring
> I gave her several years ago & also her wedding ring which had not been
> moved off her finger since her marriage. She seems devoted to me & I can &
> shall trust her now.[41]

Five days later she adds,

> M— & I talked matters over. We have agreed to solemnize our promise of
> mutual faith by taking the sacrament together when we next meet at Shib
> den, not thinking it proper to use any still more binding ceremony during
> C—'s life.[42]

"C" is Mariana's husband, Charles Lawton. The "still more binding ceremony" would presumably have been a form of marriage of the kind that one
sees in the consistory court records that I mentioned earlier in this chapter,
such as reading together the marriage liturgy from the Book of Common
Prayer—although these could be an exchange of rings or the reception of
Holy Communion together as Lister and Walker would later do. On a cold
night at Shibden Hall in January 1822, sitting alone in her study upstairs,
Lister wrote a melancholy note after Mariana had left the house earlier that
day: the carriage had been at the door just after nine that morning.

> How dull without M—, my wife & all I love . . . Felt very low & dull. Oh,
> that M— & I were together. Had a fire at night contrary to my usual cus-
> tom. It cheered the room a little but everything looked, & I felt, desolate.[43]

An earlier entry:

> She is my wife in honour & in love & why not acknowledge her such openly
> & at once? I am satisfied to have her mind, & my own, at ease. The chain is
> golden & shared with M—. I love it better than any liberty.[44]

Several years later Lister exchanged wedding rings with Walker as she
had done with Mariana Lawton. In the month before that Easter Day at
Holy Trinity Church, on 12 February 1834, she noted in her diary (with the
first words underlined): "*She is to give me a ring & I her one* in token of our union
as confirmed on Monday."[45] They did so a few days later, on 27 February.

> I asked her to put the gold wedding ring I wore (and left her sixpence to pay
> me for it). She would not give it me immediately but wore it till we entered
> the village of Langton and then put it on my left third finger in token of our
> union—which is now understood to be confirmed for ever tho' little or
> nothing was said.[46]

The uncanny presence of these traditional forms does not diminish as
one looks closely at the language Lister employs in these passages, but rather
grows. The term "union," for example, which Lister employs in recounting
Ann Walker's letter—"says very little alluding to our union but yet enough
to show me she thinks of it as fixed"—is the same term employed in the monument to Mary Kendall and her friendship with Lady Catharine Jones in 1710:
"that close Union & Friendship, In which She liv'd, with The Lady CATHARINE
IONES." Lister's "wedding" and "wife" echo James I's description of his

friendship with the duke of Buckingham as a "marriage," a century before—
and the "wed" or "wedded" brothers of the Middle English Brut chronicle
or the romance of Athelston, where the same term is used interchangeably
for a "weddyd" brother or a "weddyd" wife. Arguably most telling in this
respect is the antiquity of Lister's expression that such a union was a "promise of mutual faith." That expression—and in this context—would have
been immediately intelligible across the centuries this book describes, strikingly echoed in the fifteenth-century register of Oseney Abbey that I discussed in my first chapter and its opening invocation of two sworn brothers from the eleventh century: "It is to be minded that Robert D'Oilly and
Roger D'Ivry, sworn brothers and i-confedered and i-bound everich to other
by faith and sacrament, came to the conquest of England with King William
Bastard." "Sacrament" here does not mean the Eucharist, but is the Middle
English term corresponding to Lister's "promise" (as "wed" in Middle English also means a covenant or a promise). Her adjective, "mutual," is the
register's "i-confederyd or i-bownde euerich to other"; and in each case that
central and crucial term "faith" is the same: our *promise of mutual faith* "by
feyth and *sacrament.*" Yet that Middle English version is only a translation—
already two centuries old—of the resonant Latin that Abbot William de
Sutton had given his register in the thirteenth century. The thirteenth-
century register itself takes us back to those two men who lived in the
eleventh century. "Memorandum quod Robertus de Olleyo & Rogerus de
Iuereyo, fratres iurati & per fidem & sacramentum confederati, venerunt ad
conquestum Anglie cum rege Willelmo Bastard": "per fidem & sacramentum confederati," "our promise of mutual faith"—it is the same term. It is
as if one had found the fifteenth century, alive and well, living in the large
and prosperous parish of Halifax.

These do indeed appear to be the same forms that this book has followed. However difficult to explain, the precision of these terms directly recalls a distant past. So does Holy Trinity Church in Goodramgate. On a
snowy day in January 2001, I visited York to see the church where Anne Lister and Ann Walker had sealed such a promise of mutual faith in the Holy
Communion that Easter Day. To come to this church, across the long path
of this book, is a curiously uncanny experience, and not only because it remains today largely as Lister and Walker saw it (see fig. 11). The church remained untouched by the Victorian restorers; and it still contains, crowded
into it, the eighteenth-century box pews that Lister would have seen, the
same communion table with the same paten, cup, and flagon, the same em-
broidered frontal to the communion table, the same communion rails with
their distinctive bowed opening, so that bride and groom could kneel

Figure 11
Holy Trinity Church, Goodramgate, where Anne Lister and Ann Walker took
Easter communion together, as it appears today.

together looking directly at each other and into each other's eyes. But the
breath-taking culmination is the great east window above the communion
table: the glowing detail of its fifteenth-century glass sets out that traditional world of kinship and friendship at the heart of religion's role that this
book has followed.

Even the most sober of historians might be forgiven for perceiving this as
evidence that one had not lost one's way. So too (but less rationally) seemed
the rediscovery of Lister's gravestone a short time before I visited Halifax
Parish Church that winter's day to search for it. These are not perhaps the
thoughts of a detached, objective, and scientific historian: I will nonetheless
return to them, but for the moment they must be put aside. The great east

window of Holy Trinity, Goodramgate, serves a more immediate purpose. It lays out and rehearses the thesis of this book, on the role that religion played in traditional society: in creating kinship and friendship, confirming it in the Eucharist. Before I turn to the survival of that role in the world of Anne Lister, let me allow it to recapitulate what that role was, to set out, as it were, the scale of what needs to be explained. This explanation will quickly take me beyond what Lister could have made explicit. The ritual with which she solemnized her union with Ann Walker would indeed have been familiar to that world; the terms she used are theirs; but their import was something, I think, that for her needed no explanation, as familiar to her as the paths and bridleways across Calderdale. She took them for granted. It is rather we who need carefully and meticulously to unpack them.

There is a crucial difference between the intent of this window and that of Lister's diary, which this window might address. Lister does not tell us *why* she solemnized her union with Ann Walker in the Eucharist, because she did not write her diary for us—it was not left as a message for us to read. This window was. I do not think that Lister and Walker could read all its details, but I do think they understood—as I shall explain—that what they were doing that Easter Day had an immense antiquity: and they were right.

Looking Back: "Of Spiritual Friendship"

That antiquity relates directly to the first of the two considerable ends that I earlier suggested might be met by reading Anne Lister's diary together with the history this book has followed. One was that to do so might answer some of the questions her diary tantalizingly leaves open. I propose now to pause, to take this first glance back into the past. The guide lies in Lister and Walker's decision to solemnize their union in the Eucharist, which so strikingly echoes the forms I have followed; and there is perhaps a ready place to begin to explore that tangible link with the past. Was that ritual gesture already set out in its great east window? We may have difficulty now in grasping the import of Lister's communion with Walker and how it sealed their promise of mutual faith, but its builders I think would have understood it: and in this window they left a message for us (see figs. 12 and 13).

Holy Trinity Church is kept open by the determined efforts of the Churches Conservation Trust, who can afford neither to heat nor to light it. The day of my visit their resolute representative lit the candles for me so that I could find my way around the church; and wrapped in an overcoat and muffled in gloves and scarf, I sat down before the east window, as the

Figure 12

The east window of Holy Trinity Church as it appears today. (Photo by Paul Barker; courtesy of The Churches Conservation Trust)

	Arms of John Walker?	Arms of Archbishop George Neville	Arms of Archbishop John Kempe	
St. George	St. John the Baptist	Corpus Christi	St. John the Evangelist	St. Christopher
St. Mary Cleophas, Alphaeus, and their children	St. Joachim and St. Anne with Christ	Coronation of the Virgin Mary	Salome and Zebedee	St. Ursula
Domina Mundi	Regina Coeli	Sancta Maria	Mater Ecclesiae	Imperatrix Inferni
St. Paulinus	St. Aidan?	St. John of Beverley?	St. William of York	St. Wilfrid?

Figure 13

The east window of Holy Trinity Church in its original layout.

sun shone through its glass and down onto the communion table below.
What then does one see?[47]

At the center of the window is a man of the fifteenth century, kneeling
before the depiction of the Holy Trinity in the central panel. His tonsure
marks him as a cleric, and his prayer is set out on the scroll issuing from his
mouth: "Te adoro te gl[o]rifico o beata trinitas" [I worship Thee, I glorify
Thee, O Blessed Trinity]. The verses set across the central panels recover
his name: John Walker, the rector of this church and the donor of this window at some point around the year 1470. "[W]alcar rectoris a(n)i(m)ae
miserere ioh(annis)."[48] The verses begin in an elegant Latin construction
that opens with his last name, "Walker," and ends with his first, "Johannes."
John Walker's will is in the Borthwick Institute in York and contains a provision reminiscent of one I mentioned earlier in this book: the provision that
William Jekkes made in his will in 1499 to be buried with his friend and fellow priest Simon Bulleyne in the church of Salle in Norfolk. A testamentary
provision of this kind would seem also to have been made for the priests
buried or commemorated together in Merton College chapel, first John Bloxham and John Whytton and later Ralph Hamsterley and Thomas Harper,
near the time when this window in Holy Trinity Church was constructed.
John Walker's provision in his will (in translation) is this. "I leave ... my
body to be buried in the churchyard of the parish church of All Saints, Berkyn,
by the Tower of London, namely within and near the south door of the said
churchyard." The precision of that instruction suggests that it was made so
that Walker could lie near the grave of someone already buried there; and
the most likely figure for this is the figure mentioned later in his will and
linked with him there in a joint chantry in All Saints Church (as Ralph
Hamsterley appears to have provided a chantry for himself and Thomas
Harper at the altar by their memorial). "*Also I will*," continues Walker, "that
my executors, immediately after my decease, make provision for having a
chaplain to celebrate divine service daily for my soul and for the soul of
Thomas Broune in the said church of All Saints for half a year."[49] As far as
I am aware, the evidence ceases here. We cannot know if John Walker and
Thomas Brown were formally sworn brothers (like the monk and the merchant in Chaucer's *Shipmannes Tale*) or, if so, whether the bond between them
was solemnized in the Eucharist: the form that Juvénal des Ursins described
as customary in the fifteenth century. But if the Eucharist lay fittingly at the
conclusion of their lives, would it not have lain also fittingly at its onset?

Indeed, is it perhaps still present in the imagery of this window—in the
image of the Corpus Christi [Body of Christ] at its center? Is this in effect
a reference to the Body of Christ in the Eucharist at the altar below? The

window as we see it today consists of three tiers, of five lights each, which open out from the central panel depicting the Holy Trinity. The figure of John Walker is on a minute scale beside this depiction of the Trinity before which he kneels, the same image as in the sixteenth-century altarpiece in the English college in Rome, described earlier in this book in the monument to Nicholas Morton and John Seton and recording their wish to be buried together. In this image, God the Father holds the body of the crucified Son—the Corpus Christi—with the Holy Spirit descending. The marks of the scourging are visible on the Son's body in the Holy Trinity window, and blood flows from his wounds.

By this scene, in the panels to each side, are set the figures of St. John the Baptist and St. John the Evangelist and beyond them, in the outer panels on the same tier, St. George and St. Christopher. The lights in the central tier are larger than either those above or those below, and the figures in them with the Corpus Christi at their center dominate the window. But why *these* four saints? The answer, I would suggest, is that—although they tower far above the tiny figure of John Walker at their center—they are here because they are his kindred and his friends. "Walcar rectoris animae miserere Johannis": the evidently carefully chosen construction emphasizes the last word—"Johannis"—and gently points the viewer to the name that John Walker shares with St. John the Baptist and St. John the Evangelist. In the terms of the fifteenth century, in doing so it points to their spiritual kinship with him. In the monument to John Bloxham and John Whytton, St. John the Baptist appears there, I suggested, as their *patrinus*, their godfather in spiritual kinship; and the clue to that—as evidently here also—was the attention drawn by the monument to their first names, conventionally the name of a godparent in the fifteenth and fourteenth centuries. St. John the Baptist and St. John the Evangelist here watch over John Walker with the loving care of his *patrini*, his spiritual kin. With them, St. Christopher and St. George stand as his *patroni*, his friends at the court of heaven, for these two saints were the patrons of the York guild of St. Christopher and St. George, of which Walker was a member—as he was a member also of the prestigious York guild of Corpus Christi. The figures on the central panel of this window set the *patroni* of his guilds by the celestial *patrini* who watch over him.

With Walker's heavenly patrons are set the heraldic arms of his earthly patrons: John Kempe, the bishop of London, and George Neville, the archbishop of York and a fellow member of the York guild of Corpus Christi. The heraldic arms above the depiction of the Corpus Christi are those of Archbishop Neville, "impaled" with those of his diocese (like the arms of a husband and wife), as the arms of William Neville—also with the Neville

saltire—were impaled with those of his friend John Clanvowe on the monument above their tomb that opened this book. On the topmost tier two
other sets of heraldic arms flank those of Archbishop Neville: probably the
dexter ones are those of Walker himself while on the other side are those of
Bishop Kempe, in whose diocese Walker had a living.[50]

Spiritual kin, spiritual patrons, earthly patrons: set around the Corpus
Christi, both here and perhaps on the altar below. Although that last is yet
to be established, in this design the friendship that subsists between earth
and heaven is a model for the friendship and the kinship that properly
ought to subsist on earth: whether between a bishop and the priests of his
diocese, as between the brothers and sisters of a guild, or between two friends
who might at the end lay together in the same tomb. The images become
arguably here a model also for the friendship that ought to subsist between
two nations. In the tier below the Corpus Christi and the four saints who
stand as Walker's *patroni* and *patrini* is an image of St. Ursula, with the figures associated with her sheltering under her cloak and the arrow (the
instrument of her martyrdom) that identifies her. An image of St. Ursula
is no unusual sight in York. There are several among its medieval stained
glass, and they point with a proud catholicity to Cologne and St. Ursula's
great church there, which would have been a familiar sight to the trading
merchants of York.[51] This element too possibly points to John Walker,
who may have belonged to a merchant family, but as the viewer turns to
look at the other panels in the tier below, the design opens into another
world. The figures one sees there are not the family and friends of Walker
but those of the Corpus Christi, of the incarnate Son of God.

In the central panel of this tier, Mary the mother of Christ is presented being crowned by the Holy Trinity, an image that corresponds directly to that
of the scourged and bleeding body of her crucified son immediately above.
In the one the focus is the body of the Son, in the other that of his mother:
the scene this panel depicts is the coronation of the Virgin at the end of her
earthly life, after her body has been assumed uncorrupt into heaven. The corporal reality of the body of the Mother of God glorified in heaven—as with
the body of her Son that still bears the signs of his passion—is reemphasized
by the lights to each side. In the dexter light Christ appears in the family of
the Virgin, with her parents St. Joachim and St. Anne. In the panel beyond
appears St. Mary Cleophas, the Virgin Mary's sister, and her husband Al-
phaeus and their children, the four brothers (three of them future apostles).

But why then the light on the other side, in which Salome and Zebedee
appear, the parents of St. John the Evangelist depicted in the light above,
with St. John as a baby in Salome's arms (and originally his brother James

below)? Does this light also point to the Corpus Christi? This window is not alone in aligning these married saints and their families, and there is some suggestion that devotion to St. Anne in the fifteenth century may have assimilated Salome as a second sister of Mary with Mary Cleophas mentioned as Mary's sister in the fourth Gospel at the foot of the cross.[52]

Another possible explanation for the presence here of Salome and Zebedee, which does not exclude the first, turns on that scene at the foot of the cross. In the design of the great central panel, the figure of John appears by the body of the crucified Son. The wooden "rood" screen before the altar in Holy Trinity, Goodramgate (now lost), repeated the same scene, St. John standing with Mary on either side of Christ on the cross.[53] The scene recalls St. John's Gospel, in which the dying Christ entrusted his mother to St. John. In the fifteenth-century carols to St. John as Christ's friend and in the preaching that employed them (which I discussed earlier in this book), St. John is translated by this scene into Christ's sworn brother, taking on a sworn brother's charge to care for his dying friend's family.

> "Modir, be noþinge desamaied . . . Ion, Myn owne der' broþere . . . schal rule
> þe & loke to þe as to his owne modir"

> As he in his passion to his dere moder
> Toke the for her keper, her son, and his brother,
> Pray that owr hartes may most of all other
> Jhesum semper amare.

If in this alone, John is made Christ's kin as his friend and sworn brother, and the point is engagingly emphasized by the lily that Salome holds—usually held only by Mary—and by the letter X—for Xristos or Christ—that appears on the robe of the infant St. John. In the words of Christ on the cross in St. John's Gospel, "'Mother, there is your son' . . . and to the disciple, 'There is your mother.'" But the Corpus Christi that hung on the cross was also the body that enfolded John when he lay in Christ's bosom, at the institution of the Eucharist at his last supper with his disciples: when he blessed the bread and said, "This is my Body."[54]

I shall return in a moment to that Eucharist (and the path that leads from it to Anne Lister and Ann Walker). But to respond fully to that possibility one needs to look below and beyond this apparently final tier of the window. Below the window we see today is a finely polished wooden reredos with the Ten Commandments set out in English on the two central panels, with the Lord's Prayer to one side and the creed to the other. This is not how the window looked in the fifteenth century. Below the three tiers we now see, the design of the window was completed by two others extending down to the altar below. Their loss was not the product of the reforming zealotry of the sixteenth century; when they were removed around the turn of the seventeenth century, its iconoclasm was only a memory. Their excision was rather a product of that same "civil" instinct that had swept away the glass in Merton College chapel and that, as in the lost inscriptions here, comprehended the dead in the friendship of the living by their prayers that the inscriptions sought for them. Fragments of the lost windows can still be seen in the lights at the east ends of the north and south aisles: haunting fragments in which one glimpses for a moment a book, a jeweled glove, a saint's name, or a lady of the fifteenth century, and at one point almost complete (in the middle light of a window in the north aisle) an image of Sancta Maria, Mary as the Mother of God, holding in one hand a scepter and in the other the Christ child.

The design of these windows is not wholly lost to us. As Pauline Sheppard Routh has shown, the design can still be recovered from a description by the antiquary Roger Dodsworth in the earlier part of the seventeenth century and from the drawings made around 1670 by Henry Johnston for his brother the antiquary, Nathaniel Johnston, both now among the manuscripts of the Bodleian Library.[55] The lost lights were also seen, shortly before their destruction, by the eighteenth-century antiquary Thomas Gent and later described by him. The design of the window unfolds in these accounts: first, a row of lights below the window we see today, composed of images presenting the Virgin Mary as in her titles set on the scrolls above them. "Domina Mundi" and "Regina Coeli" appear to one side. "Mater Ecclesiae" and "Imperatrix Inferni" to the other. But in the center of the tier—below the triumphant image of the coronation of the Virgin's uncorrupt body and, towering above that, the body of her crucified Son—was the crowned image of Sancta Maria as the Mater Christi, the Mother of Christ that one can still see in the light at the end of the north aisle, set within a blazing rayed aureole, one hand holding her royal scepter and the other holding aloft the body of the newly born Christ.

In the tier below, that triumphant celestial vision blended into the recognizable and homely world of the fifteenth century. In this final tier it seems that four married couples knelt by the venerated local saints of the north: Paulinus, Aidan, John of Beverley, William of York, Wilfrid. An ecclesiastic they would have known joins them. The "chaperone" hat of a prosperous figure sits casually on his shoulder. At one point is a lady's veiled headdress, at another a miller's wife in a "blewn gown with a girdle." We are back with the fifteenth century and John Walker, kneeling by the image of the Trinity and offering his prayer. The donors of this window were evidently members with Walker of the guild of Corpus Christi, husbands and wives being admitted to membership together. Some of the figures in the window and referred to in the inscriptions can be still be identified with some degree of probability: William Egremond, a shipman and freeman of the city; his son William, a bishop and the donor of this window in his father's memory; John Billar, a miller and baker; his wife Isabella; his son William, who became a public notary and a man of the law; William Thorpe, a merchant and at one time sheriff of York; and his wife Isabella. The almost tangible presence of these figures prompts the viewer to envisage these figures and others like them kneeling in the congregation around the altar, and in doing so it draws the eye to the altar below. The window lifts the image of the Corpus Christi high above the congregation in the church for all to see, as the priest at the altar would have elevated the bread blessed and broken in the Eucharist, the Corpus Christi—"This is my Body"—held aloft in his hands. It is before this that these figures are kneeling, both in the design of the window and in the congregation gathered below. In its original form the point would have been evident to view: in this window the guild of Corpus Christi and the parish of Holy Trinity, Goodramgate, have joined John Walker at the Lord's Supper in the Eucharist, as they might have done in the general communions on Easter or Christmas Day. There they have been joined by their neighbors, their patrons, and their kindred, in heaven as well as on earth.

Anne Lister and Ann Walker would not have used their language of transubstantiation. Nor would they have been able to read the detail in the design of this window. But unlike us they did not need to. A traditional-minded Anglican like Lister still believed that she and Walker were, in the words of the Prayer Book, partakers of the Body and Blood of Christ; and she evidently shared the conviction, so powerfully evident in this window, that the Eucharist could mark the kinship of those who shared that supper. With that realization the bridge that links this fifteenth century world to that of Lister and Walker becomes visible. I shall come in a moment to the means by which Lister might have inherited such a conviction, but before walking back over that rainbow bridge to the nineteenth century, one can now see Lister and Walker's gesture in a wider field and begin to draw the threads of this book together. How would a priest of the fifteenth century like John Walker have understood Anne Lister and Ann Walker's gesture? How would it have been understood by those merchant families and their neighbors that made up the guild of Corpus Christi?

To them one must add the more boisterous and popular confraternity of St. Christopher and St. George. On St. George's Day in Mary's reign they revived, "accordyng to the ancient custome of the citie," their noisy procession: the drums and musical instruments coming first, St. George impersonated on horseback with his dragon made of painted canvas and filled out by hoops, and the giant figure of St. Christopher carried with him through the streets. The civic records defiantly recorded that the figure of St. Christopher was mended by "a great nale," but they also added as clearly that a celebration of the mass should be the climax of the day—and a sermon.[56] How might John Walker have explained in such a sermon the nature of the kinship among the members of the confraternity solemnized that day in the Eucharist?

The advantage of asking the question in the context of the fifteenth century is that on the shelf are books that will allow one to essay that question, works that the "civil" culture that John Locke defined with such clarity would cut off. Works like these are not merely a mirror of their culture, even less its origin: these are rather individual voices, at precise historical moments, that inhabit that world and respond to it. In that sense they still give access to it. There are two works that I propose to take down, as it were, from a shelf in the fifteenth century. Both are products of the wide reforming movements in the church that spread in the eleventh and twelfth centuries from Rome. A central place in these new intellectual currents would be occupied by their concern with the nature of friendship and of kinship. One is *De Spiritali Amicitia* [Of spiritual friendship] by Aelred of Rievaulx, the other the treatise written in the generation before by Anselm of Canterbury, *Cur Deus Homo* [Why did God become man?]. The argued explanation they give is what one can then take back to the nineteenth century and use to unlock the traditional significance that lay behind Anne Lister and Ann Walker's gesture.[57]

The imagination of Aelred was easily caught as a young man by the monasteries in Yorkshire that were being founded in the early, heroic years of the Cistercian movement in England. His *De Spiritali Amicitia* was written in the later years of his life when he was abbot of the Cistercian monastery of Rievaulx, a day's journey to the east of York, around the year 1160. Part of the force of Aelred's book comes from its personal cast (the literary model here is Augustine's *Confessions*), but the word "spiritual" in the title is not a term restricted to the monastery: the "spiritual" kinship created by baptism, for example, would be a source of friendship available to all. Aelred's term "spiritual" is a comprehensive one, a life lived according to the virtues available potentially to all; and Aelred's book arguably represented a critical engagement with the ethics of those bonds of friendship that were coming to mark the increasingly confident and expanding culture of Europe in the eleventh and twelfth centuries. The patristic sources of Christianity at several points dealt with the ethics and nature of friendship, but Aelred's book was the first sustained treatise on friendship in the Latin tradition. In it Aelred created an original and distinctive fusion of classical humanism with Augustinian theology that would give it a lasting influence: the one a luminous confidence in the potential for good in human friendship: the other Augustine's sharp awareness of friendship's frailty in a fallen world.

The culminating vision of Aelred's book catches the design of the east window of Holy Trinity, Goodramgate.

> Quid ergo? Nonne quaedam beatudinis portio fuit, sic amare et sic amari; sic iuuare et sic iuuari; et sic ex fraternae caritatis dulcedine in illum sublimiorem locum dilectionis diuinae splendorem altius euolare; et in scala charitatis nunc ad Christi ipsius amplexum conscendere, nunc ad amorem proximi ibi suauiter repausaturum descendere?

> [What then? Was it not a foretaste of bliss to love thus and thus to be loved; thus to help and thus to be helped; and thus to fly upward from the sweetness of fraternal charity to the more sublime place of the Divine love, now to rise by the ladder of charity to the embrace of Christ himself, now to descend to the love of neighbour, to rest there happily?][58]

The term "proximus" that Aelred employs here for "neighbour" is the generic term used in the second part of Christ's summary of the Law: "Diliges proximum tuum, sicut teipsum" [Love your neighbor, as yourself] (Matthew 22:39; Mark 12:31). The immediate context is Aelred's memory of the two friends, both now dead, who had shaped his life: one the love of his youth, almost certainly his beloved Simon, the lament for whom breaks into Aelred's *De Speculo Caritatis;* the other the "baculus senectutis meae" [staff of my old age] (in the words of the book of Tobit), whose name is not identified by Aelred.[59] Aelred's "proximus" here extends beyond this immediate context to the final crucial argument of Anselm's *Cur Deus Homo.* So also does the window of Holy Trinity Church.

We met Anselm earlier in this book in his monastery in Normandy, dispatching his formal familiar letters of friendship in the cause of the progress of the Gregorian reform. Later he would become the archbishop of Canterbury under the Norman kings. Perhaps his greatest theological work would be his treatise *Cur Deus Homo,* which he completed by 1098. In it he expresses with a careful, theological precision the logic of the communitarian vision in the great east window of Holy Trinity, Goodramgate. Anselm's treatise is a dialogue between himself and a pupil named Boso. Boso is no mere vehicle. Anselm keeps his best wine until the last, and Boso's questions reveal the provisional nature of Anselm's developing argument. As the book draws to its close, Anselm summarizes the argument he has made up to that point on the limitless value of the offering Christ made on the cross, which the Eucharist presents—an argument that Anselm knew had a potential flaw.

> Quibus convenientius fructum et retributionem suae mortis attribuet quam illis, propter quos salvandos, sicut ratio veritatis nos docuit, hominem se fecit, et quibus, ut diximus, moriendo exemplum moriendi propter iustitiam dedit?

> [To whom could he more fittingly assign the fruit of, and recompense for, his death than to those for whose salvation (as the investigation of the truth showed us) he made himself man, and to whom (as we said) he in dying gave the example of dying for righteousness' sake?]

Anselm then turns to the problem that lay hidden in his argument, and it is this that links Aelred's book on friendship with Anselm. Infinite though Christ's offering might be, how could it be offered *for others*? "Frustra quippe imitatores eius erunt, si meriti eius participes non erunt" [In vain, however, would they be imitators of him if they were not sharers in his merits]. But *were* they others, in this sense? Anselm's argument is this. By becoming man Christ made those he would save his *kin*. "[Q]uos iustius faciet haeredes debiti quo ipse non eget, et exundantiae suae plenitudinis, quam parentes et fratres suos?" [Whom could he more justly make heirs of a debt of which he himself has no need, and of his own abundance, than his kin and brethren?] God became man in Anselm's argument so that humankind could become *his* kin and *his* brethren: thus they could inherit the debt due to him—and all the boundless riches he possessed. Aelred's ladder of charity and the east window of Holy Trinity alike depict, in Anselm's terms, the moral universe that act created; in the latter case, through the eyes of a single individual, in which the kin and friends of John Walker become inseparable from those of Christ.[60]

The ethics that theology required (and made possible) are the subject of Aelred's book. His preface to them are the questions that beset him in his youth.

> Itaque inter diuersos amores et amicitias fluctuans, rapiebatur animus huc atque illuc et uerae amicitae legem ignorans, eius saepe similitudine falle-

batur. Tandem aliquando mihi uenit in manus, liber ille quem de amicitia
Tullius scripsit; qui statim mihi et sententiarum grauitate utilis, et eloquen-
tiae suauitate dulcis apparebat. Et licet nec ad illud amicitiae genus me
uiderem idoneum, gratulabar tamen quamdam me amicitiae formulam
reperisse, ad quam amorum meorum et affectionum ualerem reuocare dis-
cursus.

[So it was that my spirit was tossed about, oscillating between various loves
and friendships, and, unaware of the law of true friendship, was frequently
misled by its semblance. Finally at some stage the book of Cicero on friendship came into my hands, and I found it both worthwhile for the serious-
ness of its ideas and attractive for its appealing style. And although I did not
consider myself fit for the kind of friendship he recommended, still it was
a relief to have come across some ideal of friendship to which I could relate
the internal debate of my loves and affections.][61]

Cicero's *De Amicitia* transmitted to Aelred the classical humanism that in
this book he united with Augustine. As James McEvoy has elucidated this
passage, the term "similitudo" Aelred uses here—"saepe similitudine fal-
lebatur" [frequently misled by its semblance]—resonates in Augustine's
vocabulary with terms such as "imago" and "vestigium." The rationale of
these exemplaristic terms is that all things refer to their origin and ideal in
the mind of God, and that among them the only substance we might find
in this world of shadows in this way is God himself. At the end of the first
book of Aelred's treatise this becomes his spectacular formulation, "Deus
amicitia est" [God is friendship].[62] Here Aelred had drawn on and widened
a passage in Augustine's *Confessions:* "Beatus qui amat te et amicum in te"
[Blessed is the person who loves You and his friend in You], to which Augustine added "et inimicum propter te" [and his enemy because of You].[63]
Friendship in this view is not part of the world of shadows, but in its true
law has its origin in the mind of God himself.

Such a conclusion necessarily touches closely the nature of that "formula" of friendship, the "verae amicitiae lex" [law of true friendship] that
Aelred found in Cicero's *De Amicitia.* Although Aelred's treatise contains
much (sometimes homely) advice on how to sustain friendship, the "formula" he refers to here is not reducible to a set of rules.[64] It is an *ideal,* which
has its origin within God himself, and which through God's grace can loosen
the chains of sin and frailty that bind the human will. That implication
is rhetorically present in *De Spiritali Amicitia* in the opening words of the
first book in which, apparently casually but with a blessing, Aelred greets

Ivo, the troubled and thoughtful monk with which his dialogue will begin. "Ecce ego et tu, et spero quod tertius inter nos Christus sit" [You and I, then, here: and I hope that Christ will be a third among us].[65]

The expression is a reference to Christ's promise that, where two or three are gathered together in his name, "ibi sum in medio eorum" [I am in the midst of them there] (Matthew 18:20). The second book of Aelred's treatise opens some years after Ivo's death and Aelred's discussion with him in the first book. Aelred shapes the rhetoric of his treatise in its final form in this way around the fact of death, and it is in the face of death that the distinctive difference between an understanding of friendship such as Aelred's and a "civil" Kantian understanding most clearly emerges. The point is worth looking at closely, for at the end of the twentieth century, when Jacques Derrida marked his radical questioning and rereading of a Kantian view of friendship, in his *Politics of Friendship,* he did so in the same terms: terms that he recognized had an intellectual echo in Augustinian Christianity. The monuments to the dead that have punctuated the argument of my book are not fortuitous to a history of friendship. They are its fault line.[66]

Let me unpack that claim. Aelred's expression moves toward a universalizing gesture yet at the same time refuses to commit the friend to it. On one side, if God is friendship, then the friend is in fact nearest to us, not in the flesh, but when he or she comes into our very hearts as spiritual beings when they are removed from us.

> Equidem carissimi mei recordatio, immo continuus amplexus et affectus, ita mihi semper recens est; ut, licet ex humanis exemptus, conditioni satis dederit, in meo tamen animo numquam uideatur obiisse.

> [Indeed, the memory of my beloved Ivo, yes, his constant presence and affection are, in fact, always so fresh to my mind, that, though he is buried and taken from the world of the living, yet to my spirit he seems never to have died].[67]

Aelred's final speech in *De Spiritali Amicitia* begins (echoing Cicero) with his memory of his beloved Simon and of the friend of his old age, both now dead. "Recordor nunc duorum amicorum meorum, qui licet exempti praesentibus, mihi tamen uiunt, semperque uiuent" [I remember now two friends, who, although they have passed from this present life, live to me and always will live].[68] Yet as he moves in this way toward a universalizing gesture that Kant would have recognized, the agonized lament for the loss of Simon that breaks into Aelred's *De Speculo Caritatis* refuses to commit the friend to the gesture and insists on the irreplaceable nature of the loss.[69] The conviction would later become Montaigne's, and it is there that Jacques Derrida found it: "If you press me to say why I loved him, I feel that it can only be expressed by replying: 'Because it was him: because it was me.'"[70]

The point can, indeed in time must, be put in more concrete terms. The scriptural basis for Aelred's lament is David's for Jonathan and Saul (which formed the basis for the epigraph for chapter 1), but it ends with this prayer for Simon.

Et tu pater Abraham, etiam atque extende ad suscipiendum hunc pauperem Iesu, alium quemdam Lazarum, manus tuas, aperi gremium tuum, expande sinum, et a uitae huius miseriis reuertentem pie suscipe, foue, consolare. Mihi quoque misero, qualicumque dilectori suo, in ipso sinu tuo cum ipso aliquando locum quietis indulge. Amen.

[And you, O Father Abraham, stretch out your arms to this poor servant of Christ, this other Lazarus. Open your bosom, make wide your embrace, and lovingly receive this weary traveller returning to his home. And to me, a wretched man, but his beloved friend, grant a quiet place wherein to abide with him some day. Amen.][71]

Is the "quiet place" where they will lie together an idea of heaven or of the shared grave in which Aelred and Simon will together await the resurrection? In either, it is a place he will share with Simon. The most radical, the most unmistakable insistence on the unique and irreplaceable nature of friendship is the shared grave of two friends that has punctuated the course of this book: that even in death, especially in death, still "Ecce ego et tu" [You and I, then, *here*].

The distinction between this and a universalizing view of friendship—which I have characterized as Kantian—could not be put more graphically than in the gesture of the shared grave. But the formula is still "Ecce ego et tu, et spero quod tertius inter nos Christus sit" [You and I, then, here: and I hope that Christ will be a third among us]. The gesture of the shared grave refuses to commit the friend to a universalizing ethic; it insists on the irreplaceably rooted nature of a friendship, however ethically troubling that may be: the love of the shared and the same. But the formula also entrusts it to a gaze that insists equally on looking out from it. Set within Anselm's logic, this "third" draws the eye beyond that eternally appealing prospect of "You and I, then, here," beyond the individuals for whom a friendship is made, to Christ and to *his* kindred and *his* brethren. In Aelred's graphic vision the ladder of charity rises toward Christ himself and comes down to the love of neighbor.

In the centuries after Aelred, the Eucharist would increasingly convey that conviction about the ascent and descent of charity. The promulgation of the feast of Corpus Christi in 1264 and its widespread popularity marked a visible stage in that process. Another was the growing practice of the general communions at Christmas, Easter, or the other quarter days, delayed so that parishes and communities could make their communions together, reaffirming the bonds that bound them and laying down with some dignity their quarrels. The confraternities of Corpus Christi were a small part of that process, as was the design of the east window of Holy Trinity Church. It reflected a set of beliefs that this book has argued would not be abandoned, or only hardly, by traditional-minded believers on both sides of the Reformation divide. The kinship one sees in the east window of Holy Trinity began with the friendships, the households, the confraternities, and the kin represented there—its terms could hardly make that clearer—but in the bread and wine in the Lord's Supper below, it was transformed into a universal sacramental sign that knew no boundaries and no limits. It was that sign that was offered and received in Holy Communion and depicted in the Corpus Christi of this window.

The practical form of such ethics is caught by a passage in *De Spiritali Amicitia*, in which Aelred discusses the ritual kiss. One kind of corporal kiss in Aelred's account is a "signum reconciliationis, quando fiunt amici, qui prius inimici fuerant ad inuicem" [a sign of reconciliation, when they are made friends who had been enemies to each other]. Another was "signum pacis, sicut communicaturi in ecclesia interiorem pacem exteriori osculo demonstrant" [a sign of peace, as those who are about to receive Holy Communion in church demonstrate an inward peace by an exterior kiss]. A third was "signum dilectionis, sicut inter sponsum et sponsam fieri permittitur; uel sicut ab amicis, post diuturnam absentia et porrigitur et suscipitur" [a sign of love, as is allowed between the betrothed or offered and received from friends after a long absence]. A fourth was "signum catholicae unitatis, sicut cum hospes suscipitur" [a sign of Catholic unity, as when a guest is greeted].[72] When given and received solemnly (and before witnesses human and divine), such signs shored up the frailty of human nature. Externally, the witness of one's neighbors held them, internally, a code of honor did. They determined who and what you were. This was not a universalized solution to the ethical uncertainties of friendship. It subsisted rather in the concrete and the actual, and it sought to confront and transcend its ethical uncertainties there, eye to eye and face to face, in signs offered and received.

Such signs did not stand in the place of ethics, but they could enable them to begin. It is the stubborn persistence of that ethic—and its association with the sites of a traditional Christianity—that we are still seeing across the terrain this chapter has traversed.

If this is indeed the ethic that still lay behind Anne Lister and Ann Walker's gesture that Easter Sunday in 1834, then a conclusion has crept upon us with the widest implications. *Was* the union they solemnized that day only between these two friends? If this is the ethic that gave meaning to their gesture, then we are missing the point—a point that would have been self-evident to them—if we look *within* their friendship alone for its rationale. To find what it would hold, we must also look beyond it. But where?

Anne Lister's Religion

How then did this ethic reach Anne Lister? The answer to that question might provide a guide to this wider question also. One possibility and its corollary can, I think, be quickly discounted: that Anne Lister found it through her reading and that it would be readily evident in her mind. Her reading was indeed wide, and she mastered Greek and Latin, as well as algebra and rhetoric, even after she left her school in York: but an incident she recorded in her diary in April 1835 reveals how much her religion came from outside that world of books. It takes place late in the year that followed her Easter communion with Walker in York. The "Mr Musgrave" in this entry was the vicar of Halifax, who had come to administer the Order for the Visitation of the Sick in the Book of Common Prayer for Lister's beloved aunt Anne. Lister may have been concerned for her aunt's life and asked Mr. Musgrave whether the absolution of sins given in the order of service really gave full absolution, in the sense that a Catholic would have understood it. He reassured her.

> Mr Musgrave came to administer the sacrament to my aunt . . . Mr Musgrave did not wait 5 minutes but began the service as immediately as possible—seeming not meaning to stay long, till I got him on his own subject & he then sat talking till 2¼. I referred to our sick service—Mr M— owned that our priest did really give absolution in the same sense as it is understood to be given by the Roman Catholic priesthood—then referred to the Catechism . . . Asked M— if there was any one work which gave a succinct but clear exposition of the faith of the established Church of England—I always regretted that it was so little in my power to give a reason for the hope that was in me.[73]

"So little in my power to give a reason for the hope that was in me." Despite her wide reading, Lister's religion was evidently something more direct, and the clue that she herself gives points elsewhere. It was her aunt Anne, she once wrote, who "lifted me within the pale of Christianity."[74] The reader will perhaps have noticed a small detail that might now signify: Anne Lister shared the same name with her aunt. Her aunt Anne was her godmother, and in the traditional manner, Anne Lister was given her godmother's name at her baptism as she was lifted by her from the font. In terms of spiritual kinship, her aunt Anne was indeed her *mother*.[75]

The other figure to which we might look is her uncle James, who was her godfather, and the role was evidently in his mind when he included his newly born goddaughter in "Genealogy of the Lister Family at Shibden Hall," which he drew up carefully in his own hand. "Anne Daughter of Jeremy Lister was born at Halifax on Sunday April 3d 1791, and was baptized on Monday September 12th following, she is now living."[76] The point of that last phrase—"she is now living"—is that Anne Lister was at this point the apparent heir of the Shibden Hall estate, where her unmarried uncle James lived with her aunt Anne. The link between Anne and her godparents was particularly close as well as dynastically important, and in 1815 when she was twenty-four she went to live with her godparents at Shibden Hall. One can still see her portrait in the great hall there, between those of her uncle James and aunt Anne. A clear measure of the bond between them is the will her uncle made in 1822, which appointed his niece as his heiress, without entailing the estate to ensure that it did not pass out of the family after her death or appointing trustees to protect it in the event of her marrying, provisions that would have been quite normal when leaving an estate to an heiress. In this respect he evidently trusted the judgment that would be exercised by this remarkable niece and goddaughter.[77]

Anne Lister evidently greatly loved her aunt Anne and her uncle James. That evening in September 1832, when Lister confided in her aunt, is one of many illustrations of the closeness between them that pervades Lister's diary. Was it through her godparents that Lister acquired her religious faith?

> Then shall the Priest speak unto the Godfathers and Godmothers on this wise ... "this Infant must also faithfully, for her part, promise by you that are her sureties, (until she come of age to take it upon herself,) that she will renounce the devil and all his works, and constantly believe God's holy Word, and obediently keep his commandments ... ye must remember, that it is in your parts and duties to see that this Infant be taught, so soon as she shall be able to learn, what a solemn vow, promise and profession, she hath here made by you."[78]

The closeness between Lister and her godparents suggests that her uncle James and her aunt Anne did not take their part and duties in this lightly.

If Lister first learned her faith through the family of her aunt and uncle at Shibden Hall, then Shibden Hall itself will have played a part in giving her faith its markedly traditional character. In a letter to Mariana Lawton a few weeks after her Easter communion with Ann Walker, she described Shibden Hall as "my own place where my family had lived between 2 & 3 centuries, I being the 15th possessor of my family and name." It was in fact two centuries rather than three, but my point is perhaps all the sharper for Lister's careful imprecision.[79] The New Year's gifts for the servants and the men on the farm would have been as intelligible in the seventeenth century as they were in the nineteenth century, and the livery of the male servants in the fifteenth.[80] The ways of the Shibden Hall estate were a real link with that past.

As one walks around Halifax Parish Church, it is easy to grasp how readily Lister's Anglican religion and the Calderdale families were mapped one in the other, in the most concrete of terms. Halifax Parish Church is a building largely of the fifteenth century; its north and south chapels were added early in the sixteenth century, originally as chantry chapels.[81] The masses for the dead probably ceased there with the Reformation, but the chapels themselves continued to be the burial places of the Calderdale families. Burial within the church continued into the nineteenth century, and the introduction of family pews added to the identity of particular parts of the church with individual families. The Waterhouse family, for example (who preceded the Listers at Shibden Hall), still commemorated their dead in the north chapel in Anne Lister's time (and would continue to provide for the restoration of the chapel early in the twentieth century). The Listers were also a local family, their burial place in the south chapel, at the west end, next to the constables' pews; one can still see the monument to James Lister and his wife Mary (who died in 1729 and 1750) at the southwest corner of the south aisle.[82] In 1826 when her uncle James died, Anne Lister laid his remains there in the same way as he had lifted her from the font at her baptism. In 1836 she buried the remains of her aunt Anne there when she died. Their family pew was probably nearby (possibly in the gallery above). In Anne Lister's day the layout of her parish church still replicated the human geography of the families of Calderdale.

Her godparents, Shibden Hall, Halifax Parish Church—these were the contexts through which Lister acquired her markedly traditional faith, that "hope that was in" her, as she put it. To this one must add the Anglican Book of Common Prayer, envisioning its role not as a book on her shelves

but one carried with her to church and heard there Sunday by Sunday, until its cadences and its injunctions became as familiar as the voices of her uncle James and her aunt Anne. In these terms it provides the direct clue to
that decision to solemnize her union with Ann Walker in the Lord's Supper at Easter 1834. Set alongside this the numerous references in her diary
to her having "staid the sacrament," as she puts it, and particularly a telling
entry of this kind for Sunday, 30 March 1823, also Easter Day. To "stay the
sacrament" was Lister's shorthand for remaining in the church after the service of Morning Prayer to receive Holy Communion when (in Halifax generally once a month) the minister administered the Order of the Administration of the Lord's Supper or the Holy Communion from the Book of
Common Prayer.[83]

Now, Lister was meticulous in recording the smallest of details, but the
significance of her having "staid the sacrament" was no such detail. The Listers of Shibden Hall had position rather than fortune. Uncle James was content to live off his rents, and he had not sought to develop the estate as some
of his neighbors with greater wealth (but to the Listers' mind less rank) had.
They were conscious of their position and might not visit "new" families.
But they did make their communions with them around the Lord's Table,
especially at the general communions at Christmas and Easter Day. When
Lister recorded that she had "staid the sacrament" she was recording that
she had fulfilled that obligation of Christian friendship to her neighbors.

The weight of that duty is conveyed by this entry for Easter Day in 1823.
Here the Friday she mentions would have been Good Friday in preparation
for Easter.

> Having gone to the new church, did not stay the sacrament either today or
> Friday. I doubted whether to stay today. Felt remorse at not having fulfilled
> this sacrament & afterwards, in bed at night, prayed to be pardoned in this
> thing.[84]

Lister read prayers at home on Sundays, and her reluctance to receive the
communion along with the large and trying congregations at Easter time
was not due to distractions or business. The entry is a telling indication of
how much the Eucharist remained for Lister a communal rite, in which the
bonds of friendship between neighbors could be affirmed and their tensions
laid down. The offense for which she prayed to be pardoned was not only
an offense against God but also against her neighbor. We are back with the
east window of Holy Trinity, Goodramgate.

This ethic, one might say this moral tradition, would have been as read-

Figure 14
Monument marking the tomb of Anne Fleming and Catherine Jennis, church
of St. Mary the Virgin, Wiveton, Norfolk.

ily intelligible in the fifteenth century, even in the eleventh. By the eighteenth
century it no longer stood on the intellectual high ground that it had occupied in the fourteenth century, when students of theology and canon law at
Oxford studied *De Spiritali Amicitia*. It survived in a traditional-minded religion that stubbornly persisted in identifying Christianity first with the often
difficult demands of friendship to one's neighbor and one's kin. The persistence of that ethic across the eighteenth century is caught by a monument
in the parish church of St. Mary the Virgin in Wiveton, Norfolk, reminiscent of Anne Lister and Ann Walker (see fig. 14). Now placed by the door
is a fine classical monument from the very end of the eighteenth century.
The inscription is set in an oval of white marble, offset from a solemn background of veined gray and black stone, supported by ornamental leaves or

fronds suggesting perhaps mortality and surmounted above by a single funerary urn with a suggestion of the resurrection.

Near this Monument
and in the same Vault
with the Remains
of
her much respected Friend
M^{RS} *CATHERINE JENNIS*
is interred the Body
of
M^{RS}. ANNE FLEMING Spinster
Daughter of JOHN FLEMING Gent~:
and SARAH his Wife
late of Great Snoring.
She died Jan^{ry}. 16th. 1795 Aged 73.
In her were united
the true Characters
of
a pious and charitable Christian
and
a kind and sincere Friend.

"Mrs." here denotes social rather than marital status.

Their vault is by the steps leading up to the communion table, still indicated by an inscription on the floor: set among the monuments that cluster in
this part of the church, which trace a continuity among families and friends
and across time. Nearby, under the chancel arch, William Bisshop, a pre-
Reformation rector of the church (who died in 1512), is depicted on the monumental brass above his tomb, dressed in the eucharistic chasuble and holding in his hands the consecrated bread and wine of the mass: the inscription
on his brass seeks the prayers of the living for his soul. Nearby, in the central aisle, a brass commemorates Thomas Brigge, whose wife Joan presented
William Bisshop to the rectory of Wiveton in 1475, on the death of her
brother-in-law William (during whose incumbency the present church was
built). Near the pulpit, Thomas Brigge's great, great grandson George Brigge,
who died in 1597, is commemorated on his brass with his wife Anne. Almost
a century later, in 1671, the stone slab carrying the indent for William Bisshop's brass was incised with an inscription in Latin capitals that commemorated that there "quo[qu]e" [also] now lay buried the remains of

Robert Lowde, described as a priest "eccl[es]iae anglicanae" [of the English Church] together with the remains of his wife Anne. Was Rev. Robert Lowde (or perhaps his wife Anne) a later relation of William Bisshop? I do not know; but that easy, almost familiar use of "also" is redolent of an easy companionship with the past.[85] The connections among these tombs find a gentle reflection in the connections made by this inscription, punctuated by the lineation and the emphasis it gives. The "Remains" of the one are interred with the "Body" of the other; on the one side the "Friend," on the other the "Daughter." What, within the design of the inscription, makes these connections possible is the emphatic parallel of its conclusion: between a "Christian" and a "Friend." "Deus amicitia est" [God is friendship]: that conviction is not out of place in such a context.

Looking Back: *The Book of Gomorrah*

Let me now summarize my argument thus far. The symbolic system that centered on the body of the friend seemed to be lost in the landslide of cultural change that accompanied the civil society that emerged in seventeenth-century England. Yet this chapter has persisted in following the continuing way into the nineteenth century that leads from that point, however fragmentary the path becomes. It is easy to miss. The markers that I have followed lay within the bounds of a moral tradition and a view of religion's role that did not occupy the center stage and is now not readily visible. The well-appointed record offices or the university libraries are more likely to attract a modern social historian than the chapels and transepts of the English cathedral churches after Evensong, or the winding country bus that takes one from Plymouth to Launceston. But the markers that trace the continuing vitality of that ethic are more likely to be found now in such places: in a church in rural Cornwall, or in a family chapel in Westminster Abbey, or by the communion rails of a cathedral in the West Country—or with two friends, such as Anne Lister and Ann Walker, solemnizing their friendship and their kinship by receiving Holy Communion together in such a setting.

That gesture and its setting directly recall the continuing association of that moral tradition with the sites and rites of a traditional-minded Christianity. The evidence for its continuing strength was underlined as I looked closely at the terms that Lister found to hand to convey that ethic and how it had been transmitted to her. I have argued that this ethic confronted the ethical uncertainties of friendship in the concrete and the actual, eye to eye and face to face, as I put it, in signs offered and received, however problematic that ethic might seem from the viewpoint of a "rational" and Kantian ethics, in a rhetorical gaze that looked beyond the good of the friends for whom a friendship was made.

I propose now to pause and, shortly, to take a second backward glance into the past from this vantage point. I suggested earlier that there were two substantial, but contrasted, reasons why Lister's diary might be read together with the history this book has followed. One was that this history might provide answers to some of the questions tantalizingly left open by Lister's diary, which was to form the basis of the glance back I have already taken, to the ethics implicit in her Easter communion with Ann Walker. I propose now to take the second of these two backward glances. Does the wealth of detail in Lister's diary cast a light over this history itself? Lister's diary is the vantage point that this book needs as it draws toward its conclusion.

The diary arguably casts a light over this history in one important respect that has repeatedly challenged the parameters of this book. The unifying symbol across the world I have described was the body of the friend. It shaped the central chapter of this book, and the symbolism one sees there was not a metaphor. It embraced; it shared a common bed, a common table. It had a mouth, hands, arms. But did it not also have the body's genitals? Did its symbolic significance stop short there? The laughter that closed an earlier chapter suggested that it did not. Yet the sexual potential in these gestures has repeatedly come into view only to slip away again. First, it came into view with the "sworn" brother. "In vitio sodomitico nimium delectabat" [He particularly delighted in the vice of sodomy]: that was the judgment of the Meaux chronicle on Edward II, whose "wedded" brother was Piers Gaveston. But how can one distinguish such an erotic motive from others that lay alongside it equally well attested, if not more? It returned with the body of the friend, its homoerotic humor easy to find, in turns rough and cruel, teasing, charming. But how could one distinguish this from a masculine humor that was also about a body that was indicatively male? It returned again, insistently, pressing on my account of the friend as enemy. The charge there of being a "sodomite" was a fearful weapon when its victim was vulnerable and its ground those very conventions of intimacy that elsewhere seemed protected. But why should one *believe* a charge so cunningly made?

This is not, of course, to say that the erotic has not been part of this history. But sexuality in a more narrow sense has eluded it whenever it has come into view. With the diary of Anne Lister that problem falls away. Lister's relationship with Ann Walker was unquestionably sexual. So also had been her relationship with Mariana Lawton. The passages from her diary deciphered and transcribed by Helena Whitbread in 1988 in *I Know My Own Heart*, left no one in doubt of this (nor did Jill Liddington's edition of later entries in the diary). Directly and simply, Lister left a record of the kind of intimate sexuality that historical evidence rarely affords. The kisses that preface Lister's Easter communion with Walker, "Three kisses—better to her than to me," were indeed sexual kisses.

Does this evidence provide a vantage point in this respect also? Let me unpack the evidence on this point, into two parts. The first half is my conclusion that Lister's Easter communion with Walker is a product of the history I have described and that that history was not a specifically sacerdotal matter but, as I put it, was a part of the moral economy of Christianity. The terms in which Lister apparently understood that day, which we see cross the diary after her friendship with Mariana Lawton, are those of that history; and the evidence—from whatever angle one approaches it—takes one back, repeatedly, to that conclusion. The other part is that the sworn friendship one sees here between Lister and Walker did have a sexual potential—even in the most narrow genital sense. If Lister is representative of this history, does her diary address these unanswered questions? The problem with that way of formulating the question, of course, is whether Lister *is* representative. So let me rephrase it. Within this history, would a sexual *potential* have stood in the way of the confirmation of a sworn friendship in the Eucharist? The answer must be that it would not, in that it evidently did not do so here. Nothing that I have left to say will detract from that conclusion. My task as a historian is to point to the evidence and to insist on it. But my task as a historian is also to probe the significance of that conclusion. As Lister's diary addresses this question, another question swims into view that the historian, at least, cannot gainsay. How much does that answer tell one? I have written this book for those interlocutors who are willing to ask that question.

Let me go back again to that September evening, when Lister confided her real sentiments about Miss Walker to her beloved aunt Anne. First, how much does this answer tell one about how their friendship was perceived by her family: by her aunt Anne and by her father and her uncles, to whom her aunt's thoughts immediately turned? We know of the sexual nature of Lister's relationship with Walker because of the entries in the diary. Her aunt Anne did not. This is underlined by an entry Lister made in her diary in August 1821, when Mariana Lawton had apparently transmitted to Lister a sexually acquired disease, acquired from Mariana's husband, Charles Lawton. Lister confided in her aunt Anne, who apparently thought that the illness had been taken from a cup or the stool. It evidently never occurred to her that it might have been acquired from Mariana Lawton (and her husband). "How little she dreams what is the matter."[86] Shibden Hall is an intimate building, the bedrooms are not distant from each other. If Anne Lister's aunt did not know of the sexual nature of her niece's friendships, how likely was it that anyone else would have?

What her aunt and the rest of the world *might* have made of her friendships is of course a different matter. A satirical piece in 1835 in the Leeds *Mercury* about Anne Lister and Ann Walker may have implied as much, as may a disturbance (akin to a shivaree) directed against them in Halifax the following year. Both had other immediate contexts: the one, Lister's part in the bitterly contested Halifax borough election of January 1835; the other, the resentment aroused by Walker's commercial developments in the poor Caddy Town area. The context and timing (as Jill Liddington has argued) suggest that the sexual innuendo was being employed to warn Lister and Walker off their *political* and public activity, rather than vice versa.[87]

Is it possible that Lister's aunt Anne understood her niece's relationship with Walker in terms similar to the closeness of the relationship she herself had had with her beloved sister Martha, who had died in 1809? In the years after Martha's death Anne would wear a pearl ring enclosing a lock of her sister's hair.[88] As she had gradually taken over from her sister the responsibilities for running the household, so her niece would gradually take these over from her. Did her aunt see Lister and Walker as in effect sisters to each other?

The point is not, however, only in how *others* understood Lister's relationship with Walker. The question is also how she understood it herself, and there are two passages in Lister's diary that reveal the caution this question needs. The first is a passage in August 1822, which follows a visit Lister made to Lady Sarah Ponsonby and Miss Eleanor Butler in Llangollen, the two upper-class Irish women who formed a lifelong household there together.[89] This passage, unusually, casts a direct light on Lister's view (and that of Mariana Lawton) on the sexual ethics of female friendship, which other passages take as read. It includes a letter from Mariana.

> The account of your visit is the prettiest narrative I have read. You have at once excited & gratified my curiosity. Tell me if you think their regard has always been platonic & if you ever believed pure friendship could be so exalted. If you do, I shall think there are brighter amongst mortals than I ever believed there were.

Lister's comment in her diary is this.

> I cannot help thinking that surely it was not platonic. Heaven forgive me, but I look within myself & doubt. I feel the infirmity of our nature & hesi-

tate to pronounce such attachments uncemented by something more tender still than friendship.

The point here is not only, or principally, that both Lawton and Lister appear to take it that an exalted ideal of female friendship would be a platonic friendship. The point is also in that phrase "I feel the infirmity of our nature." This is the Book of Common Prayer: the collects that closed the litany that Lister would have heard Sunday by Sunday after Morning Prayer and those for the Sundays after Epiphany: "Almighty and everlasting God, mercifully look upon our infirmities . . . the frailty of our nature."[90] The point that I am making is that the sentiments here are a commonplace that one could have found by taking down the Book of Common Prayer from the shelf.

The second passage I have in mind is a brief passage for a Sunday in February 1834, although to grasp its significance one needs to be as familiar with the text of the New Testament as Lister was.[91]

Walked to church & back with my father . . . Mr Musgrave preached 3 minutes, good sermon from Romans i. 22.

The text from Romans 1:22 on which Mr. Musgrave preached that morning is "Professing themselves to be wise they became fools," but that is only the beginning of the sentence, which continues "And changed the glory of the incorruptible God into an image made like to corruptible man" and draws this conclusion: "For this cause God gave them up unto vile affections: for even their women did change the natural use into that which is against nature." The "natural use" as the context makes clear is sexual. This is arguably the one (and only) explicit condemnation of lesbian sexuality in the Bible. Yet Lister's entry reflects none of this. She merely says that this was a "good sermon."

The fear and horror of the "sodomite" that I recounted in my earlier chapter on the friend as enemy had not lessened by the nineteenth century. Indeed, the spectacle of mass arrests and executions in England is a characteristic of the civil society of eighteenth-century England rather than of the centuries that preceded it. Nor were women exempt. When the Bradford antiquary Arthur Burrell and John Lister deciphered the code employed by Anne Lister and read the sexual passages, Burrell argued that the diaries should be burned (in their entirety).[92]

Anne Lister's entry is no eccentricity. Her response is as familiar in the world I have described in this book as the social ethic that lay at the heart of her Easter communion with Ann Walker. More than three centuries before in fifteenth-century Venice, Marin Sanuto, another diarist, noted a sermon he had heard preached by a Franciscan friar in the church of San Marco on Christmas Day 1497. The preacher inveighed against the "societies of sodomy," who had brought the plague on the city. One might have expected an uneasy response in Sanuto's diary. A report by the Mantuan ambassador notes that Marin Sanuto was "famous in the profession" of being a sodomite in Venice: that he had sexual relations with one of his male servants and indeed "when he has spoken with one a few times he comes upon one as if to impale one." Evidently it did not occur to Sanuto that he was one of those sodomites that had brought the plague on the city. His diary merely notes that it was a "good sermon."[93]

Sanuto may have enjoyed the merit of the sermon as a piece of rhetoric, well confected, as indeed it may be that on that Sunday morning Anne Lister wished to brush aside the rest of the famous passage from Romans 1, but to say this merely is to restate the problem in another form: *Why* were they able to do so? Lister's reaction is not unintelligible. St. Paul's point in this opening passage in the Epistle to the Romans is that the sexuality he condemns (and he includes sexual relations between men) is a product of idolatry: they "changed the glory of the incorruptible God into an image made like to corruptible man." It is not difficult to understand that Lister might not have applied that passage to herself. Paul's strictures on the consequences of idolatry might have applied to the "Hindoos" or the "Booddhists" (or even perhaps to the popish Irish). But could a respectable county Tory lady like Lister have thought of herself as an *idolater*? The notion was unthinkable, absurd. How could Paul's conclusion have applied to her?

Marin Sanuto's reaction became increasingly familiar to me during the research for my book *Homosexuality in Renaissance England*. The origin of that book, written some twenty years ago, lay in the degree to which, as it seemed to me, the language of "sodomy" could be suspended from the physical intimacy that pervaded the culture of sixteenth- and seventeenth-century England. This appeared to be the detective story where the clue was that the dog did *not* bark. My chapter on the body of the friend revisits that lacuna, in the degree to which exotic images of the "sodomite"—that "most dangerous and infectious beast"—seemed to leave untroubled the homoerotic humor that accompanied masculine friendship. There was a potential common ground between the "sodomite" and the shared beds and close bonding of its male companionship, but the point of the joke was the evident unwillingness to take it seriously.

In my book the context was masculine friendship, but the work of Valerie Traub shows what appears to be a comparable mechanism at work in female friendship, and indeed in the same contexts, the shared bed and the embrace of friends. It was more than a decade before the intellectual origins of a reaction like that of Marin Sanuto was opened up, by the publication in 1997 of Mark Jordan's *Invention of Sodomy in Christian Theology*. Jordan is a scholar of Thomas Aquinas, but his book drew attention to the originary importance of the eleventh century (rather than among the scholastics of the thirteenth century such as Aquinas) and the creation there of the notion of "sodomy" as a tool of theological epistemology: at the point when the world described in this book was taking shape.

That enduring creation is the starting point for this second backward glance over this book and the history it has covered—a glance very different than the first. One response to the ethical uncertainties of friendship in this culture was Aelred's *De Spiritali Amicitia*, which should be read in this context with Anselm's *Cur Deus Homo*. A radically different option would be offered in the treatise by Peter Damian, entitled in some of its early manuscripts the *Liber Gomorrhianus* [The book of Gomorrah].[94]

Peter Damian was the prior in the eleventh century of the monastery and hermitage of Fonte Avella in central Italy. He was later for a time (and rather against his will) cardinal bishop of Ostia, and he played a prominent part in the same forces of ecclesiastical reform that, in the two generations following, would touch first Anselm and then Aelred. It seems that his *Liber Gomorrhianus* (composed around the year 1050) first coined the term "sodomia" [sodomy], in an analogy with "blasphemia" [blasphemy].[95]

> Illud etiam addimus, quia si pessima est blasphemia, nescio, in quo sit melior sodomia. Illa enim homines facit errare, ista perire. Illa a Deo animam dividit, diabolo ista coniungit. Illa de paradiso eicit, ista in tartarum mergit. Illa mentis oculos cecat, in ruinae voraginem ista precipitat.

> [We add this also: because if blasphemy is the worst, I do not know in what way sodomy is better. The first makes men to err, the latter to perish. The former divides the soul from God, the latter joins it to the devil. The former casts out of paradise, the latter plunges into Tartarus. The former blinds the eyes of the mind, the latter casts into the chasm of ruin.][96]

There are several critical aspects to the formulation Peter Damian makes here, which would have a long genealogy over the centuries that followed. The one that relates most directly to the history of friendship is that apocalyptic assertion: "sodomia ... homines facit ... perire" [sodomy makes men perish]. "Sodomy" here is not a form of sexuality; indeed, it is not a "thing" at all but its undoing. It signifies precisely nothing, a potential for confusion and disorder that knew no bounds. If "sodomy" undermined the coherence of men's identity, as the formulation implies, would it not also by the same token undermine the bonds of society and alliance wherever the "sodomite" figured? It would also cast them "into the chasm of ruin." Peter Damian's formulation provides a radical basis for the readiness to apprehend the "sodomite" in apocalyptic and *political* terms: as the traitor, the betrayer, the false friend.

The second point is more specifically about the history of ethics and is the one Mark Jordan makes about this passage: "what is new in this sentence is the abstract noun, the abstraction of an essential sin. To assert that there is an essence, 'Sodomy,' is to imply that there is one intelligible formula that captures a previously unspecified range of human acts, activities, or dispositions." "The abstractive power of the word abolishes motives and circumstances."[97] This is precisely what Aelred does not do in *De Spiritali Amicitia.* The point at which the notion of "sodomy" might have appeared in Aelred's book is the section in which he discusses how lust can obscure the true character of friendship.[98] The term he uses here, "concupiscentia," does not necessarily connote sexual desire; but the close echoes from two corresponding passages in Augustine's *Confessions* at this point, where the word does have that connotation, places it on the agenda here also.[99] In contrast to Peter Damian, Aelred has no recourse to Peter Damian's notion of "sodomy": his discussion is about the influence of virtue—and of the corresponding vices that detract from it—set between a friendship governed (or rather not governed) by emotion at the one pole, by reason at the other. It reintroduces precisely those motives, circumstances, and actions that Peter Damian's apocalyptic abstraction excludes.

> Eapropter primordia amicitiae spiritalis, primum intentionis habeant puritatem, rationis magisterium, temperantiae frenum; et sic suauissimus accendens affectus, ita profecto sentietur dulcis, ut esse numquam desinat ordinatus.

> [For that reason the beginnings of spiritual friendship ought to possess, first of all, purity of intention, the direction of reason, the restraint of moderation; and thus when the desire is kindled with such delight, then it will taste so sweet, so that it will never cease to be properly ordered.][100]

The third point (and arguably here the critical one) about Peter Damian's formulation that directly addresses the historical question itself is the transition he makes from "sodomy" to "sodomite." The origin of "sodomite" is the biblical city of Sodom, destroyed by fire in the account in *Genesis*, but in Peter Damian's treatise the "sodomite" becomes an eternal potential and an inhabitant of Peter Damian's eleventh century. "Sed iam te ore ad os quisquis es, sodomita, convenio" [But, now, I come face to face with you, sodomite, whoever you are]. "Face to face" is graphic in the extreme, literally "mouth to mouth": as if they were exchanging the kiss of peace, in the most solemn form.[101] The term "sodomy" evidently was not taken up in England until the fourteenth century. It was rather as "sodomite" that it arrived in England, at the beginning of the twelfth century.[102] The priority is entirely comprehensible; indeed it is what one might have expected. "That transition from acts to persons is perhaps what an essence does best," as Mark Jordan puts it. "By coining an abstract term to group together a series of acts, Peter Damian has made the inference from acts to agent almost automatic . . . The unity of the abstract essence, Sodomy, points back to the unity of the identity in Sodomites." Here lies most clearly the radical asymmetry between the "friend" and the "sodomite." Let me put it this way: one cannot write a history of "sodomites." "Being a sodomite is not the kind of fact or datum, the kind of condition or disposition or event, about which it makes sense to speak of reliability. Within this theological epistemology, no evidence is simply reliable—and almost any datum can be suggestive." That suggestibility was the subject of my chapter on the friend as enemy. The specter of the "sodomite" repeatedly comes into view in a history of friendship, as it has done in this book, only to slip away again. An objective, *historical* study of the "sodomite" becomes an impossibility.

Peter Damian's terms would come to be used far beyond his concerns in the eleventh century. They acquired an enduring place in Catholic canon law in "casuistry"—the judgment of ethical cases—and they would ultimately play their part, in a dramatic reversal, in shaping the modern "homosexual" identity. They were part of the many unacknowledged inheritances that England retained from the imagination of its Catholic past. By a reversal it would be transformed into the sodomitical "papist." The sodomitical traitor—and the haunting fear of the false friend—would be the subject of the deadly fantasies that my chapter on the friend as enemy explored. Directed without, it made persuasive propaganda: within, a beguiling distraction—or simply a weapon to use against a beaten opponent, when he was down and vulnerable.

Peter Damian's claim to come face to face with the "sodomite" was always a fantasy, but the fantasy required that any charge imply a fantastically *suspended* sentence. One of the first clues to this in *Homosexuality in Renaissance*

England was the years that might pass between charges of sodomy in the as-
sizes or a magistrate's court. When a charge was brought, it is equally telling
how frequently it would turn on a breach of the social order in some other
respect also. England was not unique in this: similar patterns later became
apparent in studies of Holland, France, and Germany.[103] The asymmetry
of friendship to "sodomy" necessarily lay in a critical difference. "Sodomy"
signified enormously, but it did so in the measure of how little it referred to
a datum that could actually be verified or refuted. It was that that made its
implications so suggestible. Friendship both signified and referred. Its
terms were not, could not, be held apart from the difficult distinctions that
shaped these boundaries and limits. Its ethics recognized them, and its conventions negotiated them through rather difficult and dangerous demands.
The ethics were the subject that my chapter on family and friends explored.
The conventions were the symbolism of the body and the tactfully enabling
rhetoric of the friend, which shaped the chapters that followed.

Aelred and Peter Damian are individual voices at particular moments in
time, but they are also the two poles that span the possible response to the
ethical uncertainties of friendship: one a retreat from those uncertainties
into fantasy and abstraction, the other the readiness to confront them con-
cretely and—truly—face to face. In the actual world, friendship could not
be an unreserved good, other than in an enabling rhetoric. It could be a great
evil, as it could be a great good. The ethics and rituals of friendship provided a frame in which men and women could begin to confront that diversity of motives, of circumstances, and of acts that the notion of "sodomy"
looked clean through. The specter of the "sodomite" was a fearsome weapon,
and it was to hand, but as a instrument of *ethics* it was useless.

I earlier suggested the truism that the sources of intellectual history were
not merely a mirror of their culture, even less its origin. Peter Damian's
"sodomy" is perhaps an extreme example of that truism. Men and women
might employ the specter of the "sodomite" when it suited them, but beneath the polemics of the Reformation and the compilations of canonists,
how seriously did they ever take it? The laughter in Shakespeare's twentieth
sonnet proved to be a laughter one can hear over and again in that world,
and it gives its own answer: Whether someone was your "friend" mattered
in a measure quite as vast as whether someone was a "sodomite," but friendship could be verified or refuted. It was established by covenants given and
received, held within tight codes of honor, with clear evidence of where it
had its boundaries and its limits, its circumstances, motives, and actions.

Let me clarify as much what I am *not* saying here as what I am. I am not
saying that Peter Damian and Aelred would have come to different judg-

ments about what we now call homosexuality. My point is rather that the foundations of their response are fundamentally incompatible: one an abstraction away from the diverse acts, circumstances, and motives that for the other were the very ground of ethics. Nor am I saying that the priests who presided over the rituals of friendship that I have described in this book were engaged in a pretense. My point in analyzing the shape of these rituals is more fundamental: no liturgy can be an unreserved endorsement of a necessarily uncertain human reality—not these rituals, not marriage, not the Eucharist. The shape of these liturgies was designed to negotiate—with integrity—the dangers of mutual appropriation always present when church and world come together. Finally, perhaps most important, this is not to say that the individual Christians who took part in these rituals or stood as witnesses to them were preoccupied with the ritual alone. The point I have sought to make is that the potential good to which they were responding lay for them self-evidently *beyond* the individuals for whom a friendship was being made. There and there alone was it truly good.

Anne Lister's Family

Where then did that ethic lie for Anne Lister and Ann Walker? The answer I would suggest is that it lay in the same context that had transmitted it to them: with their families and the obligations they held to their neighbors among the hills and valleys of the parish of Halifax. It is perhaps not easy now to empathize with these values. They were first (and at times also last) a matter of property and what it signified. To view them from within the world of Anne Lister one needs to see them through the eyes of a county Tory gentry: locked out of substantial political power across the eighteenth century but with an immovable dislike of Whigs (perhaps Hanoverians also) and a fierce commitment to what they saw as the values of their communities. Such values are unlikely to catch our imagination now. Yet they were ethics that looked beyond the good alone of Anne Lister and Ann Walker, and there is at the end a detail, a fragment, that might open up that ethic again and show where, at its best, it pointed.

The trace of these ethics is the easy transition in Lister's diary from her love for Walker to property. Tuesday, 7 January 1834:

> Long talk—she will employ Mr Gray in York to make her will—meant to leave me and Captain Sutherland executors and secure all to the children. She seems quite decided to take me and leave me all for my life and I said then I would do ditto.[104]

A month later, Monday, 10 February 1834:

> [B]etter make up her mind at once, or what could I do? She agreed it was un-
> derstood that she was to consider herself as having nobody to please, & be-
> ing under no authority, but mine. To make her will right directly—and, on
> returning from France and on my aunt's death, then to add a codicil leaving
> me a life estate in all she could and I would do the same to her. Well, then,
> is it really settled or not? I am easy about it & shall prepare for either way.[105]

The friendship on which Anne Lister and Ann Walker were embarking was
as much a settlement of property as of affections. The anxious calculations
one sees in these entries preceded her joyous note two days later, underlined
by her: "She is to give me a ring and I her one."[106]

Is the most tangible trace of this context the diary itself? Lister's diary
cannot be understood apart from the vast archive of her papers that remained at Shibden Hall and the implications they hold for *why* she kept her
diary. A substantial clue lies in the close relation between her diary and her
business correspondence: she noted in her diary the letters she sent and received, making transcriptions. Was it her letter book? As Jill Liddington
has put it, Lister was her own archivist, and as anyone who has maintained
a working archive knows, the problem is not filing papers away—that is deceptively easy—the problem is finding them again. As Lister managed her
estate and conducted her business, her diary provided a key to that retrieval:
it showed her where to look.[107] That the evidence of her love for Ann
Walker is to be found here is a revealing trace, in the most material sense,
of its context—"she is to give me a ring," the kisses, the words of love and
affection, the whispered entreaty in the early dawn: that these are *here* speaks
eloquently of how much the body of the friend could still signify for Lister
in a world of property and place.

Her friendship with Walker was a marriage of rank and fortune. "She
has money and this might make up for rank . . . The thought as I returned
amused and interested me."[108] That was Lister's note on a day in that summer of 1832 in which she would fall in love with Walker, and there was indeed a sharp contrast between their families. The honorable but somewhat
threadbare gentility of the Shibden Hall estate was in marked contrast to
the nearby Crow Nest estate of the Walkers. Ann Walker's grandfather,
William Walker, in the eighteenth century had made a fortune in Halifax's
worsted manufacturing industry. The Piece Hall in Halifax is still a magnificent testimony to the wealth that industry could produce. Ann Walker
would become the coheiress to the Walker fortune through the unexpected

death of her brother John in 1830, and Lister saw in Ann Walker's wealth
the instrument for which she had longed: it would enable her to restore the
Lister family and her beloved Shibden Hall estate to their rightful place.

After their union in Holy Trinity, Goodramgate, Lister and Walker
turned to the task of revising Walker's will in Lister's favor (and Lister's in
hers). The first of these was no small task. It would need to circumvent the
complex and detailed provisions in the will of Walker's father that were designed to protect her and the Crow Nest estate from the attentions of a
fortune-hunting husband. The winter evenings of 1834 would be occupied
in that task.

All this evening besides till 11 25/" reading over A——'s father's will—65
foolscap pages of her copying.[109]

The attention of Walker's family would soon be aroused. So also the
alarm of Walker's brother-in-law Captain Sutherland of the 92nd High-
landers, who had married her sister Elizabeth. The point touched him
closely, as under the terms of the will of John Walker, Ann's father, Captain
Sutherland's son would inherit Ann's share of the estate if she were to die
childless, in addition to that of his mother. Captain Sutherland's alarm
greatly increased when it became apparent that Anne Lister had removed
the Walker deed box to enable the detailed plans she and Ann Walker were
now engaged on. There was little he could do about it, however, and in the
event it became apparent that the provisions in John Walker's will could in
large measure be circumvented. The bulk of Ann Walker's estate would remain entailed to the Walker heir, but Ann Walker was able to redraft her
will to leave Lister her *un*entailed property; and crucially, there was no effective bar to Walker's diverting her *income* to the restoration of the Lister estate. So it was to be. Many of the developments that Lister organized are
not now readily visible on a visit to Shibden Hall, such as the sinking of a
coal pit for the expanding industrial needs of Halifax; but one can still see
the transformation that Lister's management brought to the estate, perhaps
most memorably now in the Gothic tower and the present great hall. The
scale of the developments on which Lister embarked is evident in the beautiful watercolors prepared for her by the young architect John Harper, who
played a major part in preserving medieval York. The scale of these plans
sets out graphically what in Lister's mind lay in the future through her marriage to Walker.[110]

Are the prospects this settled friendship opened up for her family the
reason that her aunt greeted them as she did that evening in September?

Twelve years before, Lister's union with Mariana Lawton would have been the union of two families also, and the contrast in the reaction then is striking. When Lister and Mariana Lawton had exchanged their promises in 1821, Lister turning on Lawton's finger the gold ring she had given her, that same day they solemnized their union in church, as Lister and Walker would do in 1834: but while the setting in 1834 was that of the Eucharist, in 1821 the setting was rather the traditional kinship created by baptism: a kinship between families. Later that same day they stood together as sponsors, godparents, at the baptism ("christening") of the daughter of Stephen Belcombe, Lawton's brother, and his wife in Staffordshire.

> About 1½, Mr & Mrs Meeke (she Harriet's sister) arrived for the Xtening from the Broomes', near Stone. At 2, we all went to the parish church . . . Mr Goldsmid, & M— & myself being the sponsors for the little Mariana Percy Belcombe called at my request after M—.[111]

In traditional terms that act created between Lister and Lawton a tie of spiritual kinship. But *Mariana* Belcombe? The child was given Mariana's name, and Lister's explanation is that she was "called at my request after M—." Does the explanation Lister adds imply that the intended name had been Anne?

An unspoken norm must be read within this entry. "Civil" society did not succeed in putting aside the attachment to the naming practices associated with the wider friendship created by baptism (which I looked at in my earlier chapter on friendship and the family). There is a telling illustration of that persistence at work in the parish register of Hanwell, in Middlesex in 1731, the kind of exceptional entry that makes explicit the continuing norm, here made explicit by a mistake. "Daughter. Thomas, Son of Thomas Messenger and Elizabeth his Wife, was born and baptized Oct. 24, by the midwife at the Font called a boy, and named by the godfather Thomas, but proved a girl." Naming was not the preserve only of rural midwives. An entry for 1720 in the register of St. Margaret's, Westminster, records the baptism of the son of the marquess of Annandale and carefully notes the godparents, not surprisingly in that one of them was King George I. The child was called George.[112]

If Lister had given the little Belcombe child at her baptism the name of *Anne* Belcombe, she would have been giving her not only her own name but also the name she had inherited from her own godmother, her aunt Anne: a name that would have signaled the union of the two families, in spiritual kinship at least. Lister's standing as godparent to the little Belcombe daugh-

ter created a bond between the two families, and it was not created lightly
or forgotten: nearly twenty years later (in 1841) after Lister's death, it was still
in Ann Walker's mind when she altered her will to leave a bequest to two of
Lister's goddaughters, including Mariana Belcombe, now a young woman.[113]
There was a considerable social disparity between a family like that of the
Listers and the Belcombes, the family of a York doctor with little social significance (and less money). In this entry Lister presents the naming, rather
carefully, as a compliment to Mariana Lawton. But was it also a tactful gesture to her godparents not to press that point? An incident in Shibden Hall
in 1822 when Lister altered her will in Lawton's favor strengthens that view,
through the reaction we see there of her aunt and uncle.

> Went downstairs & staid with my uncle & aunt till near 9. They both wit-
> nessed my will in favour of M——. My aunt very low. My uncle carried it
> off better than I expected but I fear they will be dull & somewhat desolate
> at first.[114]

In 1822 the prospect of Shibden Hall being united to the Belcombes left Lister's godparents disheartened, but the prospect of its union to the estate of
the *Walkers* was clearly a different thing.

Let me now pause for a moment again. I have sought to reconstruct Lister's friendship with Walker not directly or only through Lister's eyes but
also through those of her family—from the view, one might say, of that *other*
Anne Lister who was her aunt and godmother. This reconstruction is not
to suggest that there was no difference between the England of Anne Lister
and the world of kinship and friendship one sees in the fifteenth century.
The differences were tangible and real. To an inhabitant of the fifteenth
century the most striking absence from their Easter Sunday ritual in 1834
would have been the lack of the kiss of peace, exchanged at the church door
for all there to witness. The Thomas who accompanied Lister and Walker
that day was a servant to carry their prayer books, not a witness to their
union. There was still, of course, that day a witness to their promises, and
one enough: Christ, who would hold their promises in his keeping. But it
was a matter between them and God. Their promises did not now signify
in a *civil* sphere outside that relation, however binding it might be to their
consciences. Four centuries before, the Listers and the Belcombes might have
become "perpetual gossips" to each other, families that were linked by spiritual kinship despite social difference: indeed, because of it. In nineteenth-
century England such kinship did not, could not, signify in "civil" society.
But was this not a state that suited the needs of the Listers? If Lister had

been a man and able to marry Walker within the terms of civil society, with the marriage would have come a marriage settlement and the appointment of trustees to protect the Walker estate. We could be quite sure that Captain Sutherland would have been one of them. Civil society may not (indeed did not) recognize Lister's union with Walker in Holy Trinity Church, but it would have had no hesitation in employing the traditional devices still available against a fortune-hunting husband if Lister had been a man and marrying Walker. But what opportunity was there for a settlement and trustees here?

Some time ago I posed a question that I allowed to drop from sight, as I knew that unraveling it would be no quick or easy business. *Why* did the forms of traditional society described in this book survive into nineteenth-century England, when they had so long ceased to signify in civil society? It now seems possible to answer that question. Or rather, it becomes its own answer. Precisely because civil society did not comprehend these customary terms of friendship, they had the power to challenge and circumvent it. A state of affairs that suited the Lister family very well indeed.

Halifax Parish Church, 1841

As the parishioners of Halifax Parish Church were removing the pews at the west end of their church at the close of the twentieth century, more than a century and a half after Anne Lister's death, a broken gravestone came to light beneath the Victorian floor.

Only a fragment of the inscription survives, barely legible to identify it as the low gravestone of Anne Lister. "... S[hib]den-Ha[ll] [w]ho died 22nd [September 1840] ... Koutai[s] in Georgi[a] ... interred here 29 April 1841 ..."[115] The import of the stone is not the information it gives, for this was already known: it is *that* it is there. If the way I have, as it were, turned the diary of Lister around has allowed me to recount her story from the viewpoint of her family, at its end it allows me to tell it again—and in this fragment in the smallest of compasses—as Ann Walker saw it. In it she can step forward and speak in her own voice.

It is not an easy voice to hear. The anxiety and nervousness that Lister saw in her that Easter Day in 1834 recurred across their lives. After Lister's death, Walker became the mistress of Shibden Hall. With aunt Anne and uncle James dead, there were no hands to help her or to fight off the spurned and returning ghosts. In 1843 her sister and her brother-in-law Captain Sutherland succeeded in having her forcibly removed from Shibden Hall and placed in a private lunatic asylum near York, with the assistance of Dr.

Belcombe (the brother of Mariana Lawton). Walker died impoverished in 1854. Captain Sutherland died in 1847, at Shibden Hall, by then a wealthy man. The Listers returned to Shibden Hall on Walker's death, through the distant branch of the family in Wales, and their heir John Lister found Anne Lister's diaries and began their unraveling.[116] But Walker's sad end is not, I believe, how we should part from her.

In 1839 Lister and Walker set off on a journey across Europe that fifteen months later took them to the remote area of Koutais in Georgia. There Lister died from a fever, on 22 September 1840. Left in Georgia, Walker found the strength to have Lister's body embalmed and to bring it back to Halifax, in what must have been in this remote area and so far from home a harrowing journey, which took six months. Also on that journey was at least part (if not the whole) of Lister's diaries. This journey perhaps most of all reveals the hidden strength of Ann Walker.

But *why* did she do it? Why this terrible journey? Why not bury Lister's body on a quiet and beautiful mountainside in Georgia where she died? The answer lies in that family burial place in Halifax Parish Church. Walker brought her friend's body back so that she could lie there with her ancestors, with her uncle James and her beloved aunt Anne: so that at the last day she could rise with them, at the resurrection of the dead, in Halifax Parish Church. Did Walker plan to lie there also with her? I do not know, but that gesture suggests that she did. To see the love Lister had for Walker and to understand it, one must see Shibden Hall, still as Lister transformed it. But if you wish to understand Walker's love for Lister and the family she joined, you must go down the hill into Halifax, to its parish church. Walk around it. Look for the burial place of the Listers in the south chapel. Find the gravestone of Anne Lister there. It speaks with a greater eloquence than I might ever muster.

Dorset, March 1834

The conclusion of this chapter lies in the wide world beyond Shibden Dale. If you walk west out of Halifax, across Soyland Moor to stand on Blackstone Edge, you can see to east and west the influence of the industrial towns that in the 1830s were feeling their growing strength: Huddersfield, Bradford, Rochdale, and Manchester stretching away to the horizon. From Blackstone Edge you can also glimpse those isolated valleys where an old ethic and moral tradition had retained a stubborn vitality. But had it also survived here among the laboring classes creating the world's first industrial nation?

Among working people I know of no equivalent to the diary of Anne

Lister, but there are moments in the evidence that ought to make one wary of assuming that what had survived in Shibden Dale had not survived among them also. The most persuasive evidence of sworn friendship among the common people at any point is its place in that common stock of stories that they possessed, a place one can trace in a ballad like *Bewick and Graham*, which continued to appear in cheap chapbooks printed around Newcastle into the nineteenth century. This story of the two sworn brothers whose friendship foundered on the quarrel of their fathers had the capacity to articulate resentment against authority, and in doing so to lend itself to other ends. Its setting was in the same border country as Newcastle, but it is a variation on a tale as old as *Amys and Amylion*. Walter Scott described it as still being part of an oral culture in the early decades of the nineteenth century when he was editing his *Minstrelsy of the Scottish Border*.[117] One needs to treat with a proper caution his claim to have corrected a version taken down by his friend William Laidlaw (where the performer "professed to have forgotten some verses") and his claim to have corrected it, in his 1839 edition, from the recitation of a hostler—a stableman—in Carlisle. But what is telling in this respect is the dialect term "bully" that the ballad employed for a sworn brother, where the historical ground is certainly firm.[118] At the close of the eighteenth century the same term had been recorded by the antiquary John Brand, when he was preparing his history of Newcastle and the coal trade, as "a common appellation among the people concerned in the coal works for brothers." John Brockett noted the word again when he was preparing his *Glossary of North Country Words* (published in 1829), glossing it there as a term used among the pitmen and the keelmen—the men who worked the barges—designating both a brother and a friend. Intriguing though these details are, they are fragments, preserved by a curious folklorist or antiquary: but on 19 March 1834, in the Crown Court at Dorchester, the sworn brotherhood of the laboring poor was seized upon in events that would reverberate across England. Suddenly the light becomes very bright.[119]

With it one steps unmistakably into the wider world emerging around Anne Lister's Shibden Dale. As Lister and Walker were solemnizing their promises of mutual faith that Easter Day in York, large and angry crowds were beginning to gather in those very industrial towns one can glimpse from Blackstone Edge. On 4 April 1834 a large crowd gathered in Bradford. As the month wore on, other such crowds made their voices heard, in nearby Huddersfield and on Hunslet Moor near Leeds. There William Rider, a Yorkshire stuff-weaver and later a prominent Chartist leader, urged the crowd to protest against a blow directed at the whole body of working people.[120] Other angry demonstrations gathered in Newcastle and Manchester. The threatening climax was a large and menacing gathering of forty to fifty thousand protesters that confronted the Home Office in London and the Whig government there.

The cause of this anger was the savage penalty of transportation imposed in Dorset on six agricultural laborers: George Loveless and his brother James, Thomas Standfield and his son John, James Hammett, and James Brine. In the martyrology of trade unionism they came to be known as the Tolpuddle Martyrs. In October 1833 they had organized the Friendly Society of Agricultural Labourers at a meeting in Thomas Standfield's cottage in Tolpuddle, with the intention that the society would later be incorporated into the Grand National Consolidated Trades Union. The event on which the authorities would seize in the subsequent prosecution took place on 9 December 1833, in the upper room of Thomas Standfield's cottage, when the first members were initiated by oath. This ceremony formed the basis of the subsequent prosecution under the Unlawful Oaths Act of 1797, a law created in the wake of the fears aroused by the French Revolution.

These six men were already linked by close ties of work, of kinship, and of religion, and the ritual they employed in December 1833 was evidently not of their own devising. At the trial in 1834 the prosecution did not bring forward a full description of the ceremony, beyond a few scraps of evidence remembered by informers; but the Home Office files contain a description by two informers of such a ceremony carried out in Yorkshire and document the influence on these Dorset laborers of industrial agitation emanating from Yorkshire. There are also two other accounts that one can compare. One is a detailed description of such a ceremony attributed to a Yorkshire union in a hostile account published in 1834. The other is a description at an inquest, reported in December 1832, on a young Irish blackleg who was murdered by unidentified assailants at Farsley near Leeds. The first of these ceremonies is attributed to the "cordwainers" union—a union of leather workers or shoemakers—the second to a union of wool combers in the Yorkshire worsted industry, and the third to a clothiers' union.

There is again as one reads through these accounts that same uncanny sense of a distant past still alive in the nineteenth century that one has with the diary of Anne Lister. All six men were practicing Christians. James Hammett and James Brine were members of the Church of England. George and James Loveless and Thomas and John Standfield were devout Methodists. The forms and language of the kind of traditional Christianity I have followed in this book reappear in these accounts. The wool combers' ceremony began with a collect for peace that echoes the wording of the Book of Common Prayer.

O God, who art the author of peace and lover of concord, defend us in this
our undertaking, that we may not fear the power of our adversaries, through
the merits of Jesus Christ our Lord. Amen.

Sworn brotherhood, friendship and promises of fidelity shaped the ceremony one sees, set amid hymns and prayers.

Then amongst us, you will shortly be entitled to the endearing name of
brother . . . We are uniting to cultivate friendship, as well as to protect our
trade . . . Hoping you will prove faithful, and all encroachments on our
rights withstand, As a token of your alliance,—give me your hand.

At its end, the rubric that the participants "then salute"—and repeat together the opening collect for peace—suggests a closing gesture akin to the
old kiss of peace (in the nineteenth century the phrase could still imply the
exchange of a formal kiss or embrace as well as the handfast).[121] One source
of these ceremonies was the Book of Common Prayer, another the hymns
of the Methodist tradition, and a third was the Bible. In 1831 one of the first
expenses of the Huddersfield branch of the engineers' Old Mechanics
union was a Bible.[122] This was undoubtedly used for swearing oaths, but it
would be crass not to understand it as also being read aloud, as it apparently
was (according to one of the prosecution witnesses) in the ritual in the upper room of Thomas Standfield's cottage in December 1833.[123] The Bible
provided a powerful source of socialist rhetoric, whether from the New
Testament in Mary's hymn, "He hath put down the mighty from their seats,
and exalted them of low degree. He hath filled the hungry with good things;
and the rich he hath sent empty away" (Luke 1:52–53), or from the Old Testament in psalm 94, that angry cry for vengeance against the proud who op-
press the weak and the poor, read at the ceremony described at the inquest
in Farsley in 1832.

O Lord God, to whom vengeance belongeth; O God, to whom vengeance
belongeth, shew thyself. Lift up thyself, thou judge of the earth: render a reward to the proud . . . They break in pieces thy people, O Lord, and afflict
thine heritage. They slay the widow and the stranger, and murder the fatherless.

This was the church of the poor. The secrecy and the savage penalties
doled out to the Tolpuddle laborers make all too clear that this was in

earnest. The years 1833–1835 saw a rising wave of industrial agitation that—for the moment—broke against the ferocity of the Whig government and the lockouts of the employers. When Sidney and Beatrice Webb were collecting material at the end of the nineteenth century, every old union had its memory of the secrecy and suffering of these early days.[124] It was in such earnest terms that George Loveless described that meeting in Tolpuddle in October 1833: "The names of God and Jesus Christ were introduced into the Declaration . . . it was a sort of form of Prayer, calling upon God to keep us steadfast in what we had engaged."[125]

These events in a Dorset village would later echo around the world. They provide a frame in which to judge that bright light that for a moment is also cast by Anne Lister's diary on the path I have followed. At the end of the seventeenth century the "Civil Society" of John Locke might easily appear as the only marker that pointed ahead: to its own, triumphant, version of modernity. Yet in the England of the 1830s the presence of that other continuing path is suddenly made plain again. The world Anne Lister and Ann Walker inhabited was no traditional idyll. In social terms, a laborer's cottage and two Yorkshire gentry in a box pew in church are at the opposite ends of that world. These were precisely the landed gentry that a union of agricultural laborers would confront, and the paternalist conventions of Lister's Shibden Hall estate fit all too easily with the suffering and exploitation in her mines. Friendship and enmity lay potentially close at hand in this world and always had. Yet the events that took place in this Dorset cottage and in Holy Trinity Church, Goodramgate, would have been equally intelligible four centuries before to the parishioners of Holy Trinity and the members of York's confraternities—far more so than the claims of Locke's "Civil Society."

These were oaths that, in Henry Stebbing's redolent terms, lay before God, in which "society" had no concern at all: the one a solemn prayer calling upon God to keep those who made it steadfast in the alliance on which they had engaged, the other a union confirmed in the Eucharist. Although Lister and Walker and these six defiant Dorset laborers were at the opposite ends of their world, it was a world common to each. What they shared was a fierce contempt for the economic individualism of the Whigs. Civil society had not entered their soul. Possessed of a traditional view of religion's role, they stubbornly continued to stand outside the "civil" view of the world and defied it. Lister's diary and the ceremonies of the laboring poor alike demonstrate the continuing vitality of that traditional religion into the nineteenth century, and they demonstrate *why* it survived. The sworn

CHAPTER 7

Coda: The Lickey Hills, August 1890

When once the last Funereal Flames ascend,
No more shall meet, *Achilles* and his Friend,
No more our Thoughts to those we lov'd make known,
Or quit the dearest, to converse alone.
Me Fate has sever'd from the Sons of Earth,
The Fate fore-doom'd that waited from my Birth:
Thee too it waits; before the *Trojan* Wall
Ev'n great and god-like Thou art doom'd to fall.
Hear then; and as in Fate and Love we joyn,
Ah suffer that my Bones may rest with thine!
Together have we liv'd, together bred,
One House received us, and one Table fed;
That golden Urn thy Goddess Mother gave
May mix our Ashes in one common Grave.
　　—*The Iliad*

On the Lickey Hills south of Birmingham is a house and chapel close to the village of Rednal that have belonged to the fathers of the Oratory of St. Philip Neri since the nineteenth century. It is also their burial ground, and among the graves, in that quiet spot, is one of two friends who were buried there together: the first in 1875, his friend in 1890. A handwritten notice on the gate informs the visitor when visits "to the grave" may be made. With a characteristic English reserve it says no more: anyone who has found their way here already knows whose grave this is.

　　The path is an unassuming track set among trees and plots of vegetables, and the grave in the burial ground is marked by a simple memorial, in the form of an encircled Latin cross. In the upper part is the name, still clearly

Figure 15
The gravestone of John Henry Cardinal Newman and Ambrose St. John,
graveyard of the Oratory of St. Philip Neri, Rednal, Warwick.

legible, of the first of the two friends who were laid there together: "Ambrose St John," it reads, "died May 24 1875." Below, and in the center of the cross, is the name of his friend whose remains were laid in his grave in 1890: John Henry Cardinal Newman (see fig. 15).

Their burial in the same tomb was the emphatic wish of Newman, expressed in a note he wrote on 23 July 1876, the year after the death of Ambrose St. John, for Father William Neville in a notebook that he had begun in 1864 of instructions for his executors. Neville was a priest of the Oratory in Birmingham to which Newman and Ambrose St. John belonged, and Newman's literary executor. The note was included by Neville in the unpublished papers that he arranged and published in 1893, as the *Meditations and Devotions of the Late Cardinal Newman*. The text of the note is below; but let me pause here for a moment to emphasize the name of Father Neville, whom we shall meet again: he is, as we shall see, the witness.

This is the note Newman left.

> I wish, with all my heart, to be buried in Fr Ambrose St John's grave—and I give this as my last, my imperative will.[1]

The note then turned to his requiem mass and funeral and to the inscription for his memorial stone at the Oratory at Birmingham. "If a tablet is put up in the cloister, such as the three there already, I should like the following, if good latinity, & if there is no other objection." In 1881, he added in the margin "e.g. it must not be, if persons to whom I should defer thought it sceptical." The inscription he gave is this:

JOANNES HENRICUS NEWMAN

EX UMBRIS ET IMAGINIBUS

IN VERITATEM

DIE—A.S. 18

Requiescat in pace

"Ex umbris et imaginibus in veritatem" [from shadows and images into truth]. "Umbris" is the ablative plural of "umbra" [shadow], "imaginibus" of "imago" [image]. Newman adds some notes on the appropriateness of that word "umbra."[2] "My only difficulty is St Paul Hebr x. 1, where he assigns 'umbra' to the Law—but surely, though we have in many respects an eikôn of the Truth, there is a good deal of skia still, as in the doctrine of the Holy Trinity." Twice in the years that followed, he returned to this note. The first time was in February 1881, when he added to his "last, my imperative will" to be buried in St. John's grave these emphatic terms: "This I confirm and insist on." The second and last was at some later date: above the line—and underlining the last word—he added "and command."

The question I propose to follow here is *why* Newman was so emphatic—so insistent—in these instructions on his burial. His burial was a personal matter and clearly to be honored, and Newman and St. John are not alone in lying in a shared grave at Rednal; they lie here with other fathers of the Oratory who were buried together evidently because they were brothers. What then prompted Newman in this note to insist on his burial with St. John in these emphatic terms, that this was his "imperative will"? Why indeed did he return to these instructions several years later—and there "confirm," and "insist," and "command"?

It is possible—albeit only a speculation—that Newman's insistence reflects his concern that his successor might respect his remains by building a mausoleum for them at the Oratory church in Birmingham. His repeated return to his instructions reflected the deaths of those in his community that he might rely on to prevent this. But this speculation, of course, only restates the problem. Why was it that Newman did *not* wish this? Why did he wish rather to lie in Rednal with Ambrose St. John?

Let us go back forty years, to the spring of 1841, when Newman seems first to have met Ambrose St. John. The setting was the consecration of Ampfield Church, in the parish held by Rev. John Keble, Newman's beloved (and revered) comrade in the "Oxford" movement in the Church of England (which in 1833 set out to restore Catholic belief and practice within it). In his diary Newman noted that one of those present that day was "Mr. St. John," and when many years later he made a fair copy of the diary, he underlined St. John's name, as though the meeting that day in 1841 held a special significance for him.[3] It is easy to grasp why. "From the first he loved me with an intensity of love, which was unaccountable," Newman later wrote. "As far as this world was concerned I was his first and last."[4] Newman's reservation—"as far as this world was concerned"—was that his expression echoes the words of Jesus in Apocalypse 22:13: "Ego sum alpha et omega, primus et novissimus, principium et finis" [I am Alpha and Omega, the *first* and the *last*, the beginning and the end]. He had come to him, Newman later wrote, as the Angel Raphael came to Tobias, as Ruth to Naomi.[5]

After that first meeting in 1841, they would be received into the Catholic Church at almost the same time: St. John on 2 October 1845, Newman a week later on 9 October. There is a painting of them from this time, sitting alone at a table in their study in Rome. The contrast between them is striking, Newman a mature man of forty-six, St. John a young thirty-two. "In 1847 at Rome they used to call him, as being fair and Saxon-looking, my Angel Guardian."[6] The gentle humor in that comment disguises much. It is difficult perhaps for us now to grasp how great a gulf Newman's reception into the Catholic Church created for him and how much it made an outcast of him in Victorian England. He would not meet John Keble again for almost twenty years, and the same was true of many of his friends and companions: he would never see his sister Harriet again. These losses created an enduring bond between Newman and St. John, which would never be broken.

Newman's love for Ambrose St. John shows most tellingly in the letters Newman wrote in the days following St. John's death. The calm with which

he first responded to his friend's death gradually gives way to an overwhelming grief, as he repeats over and again that same phrase: "This is the
greatest affliction I have had in my life": "or that I can have," he adds.[7] Toward the end of the month following St. John's death, he writes that "a day
does not pass without my having violent bursts of crying, and they weaken
me, and I dread them."[8] Father Tristram of the Oratory recorded the memory of Newman at St. John's requiem mass in his book *Newman and His
Friends* (231)."The utter misery of the expression on his face at the Mass of
Requiem remains still an unforgettable memory in the minds of those who
were present; he insisted on giving the absolutions himself, and as he did so,
he broke down continually." A phrase Newman used in one of these an-
guished letters of 1875 echoes Jesus' words in the Gospel of John (8:12)—
that he is the light of the world—as "first and last" echoed Jesus in the
Apocalypse. He was, he wrote, "my earthly light."[9]

> I have ever thought no bereavement was equal to that of a husband's or a
> wife's, but I feel it difficult to believe that any can be greater, or any one's
> sorrow greater, than mine.[10]

Their bond was spiritual. The evidence (if such is needed) is in a letter
Newman wrote in the days following St. John's death, recounting a conversation between them before St. John lost his speech in those final days.
He went through, he writes, "the history of his whole life, expressed his
hope that during his whole priestly life he had not committed one mortal
sin."[11] One needs to be cautious here, of course. Newman is writing in the
hagiographic mode, and at the heart of the ideal of the pure priest was this
aspiration: no mortal sin after ordination. But can one take this as historical evidence only of the sense of the message that Newman was piously conveying? If we restrict the question of historical fact to something Newman
himself came to believe, then for his time and culture the statement about
St. John is definitive. Yet they were not afraid to touch and draw close. This
is from the accounts Newman gave of his last moments with St. John:
"Then he put his arm tenderly round my neck, and drew me close to him,
and so kept me a considerable time." "I little dreamed," he later wrote, "he
meant to say that he was going." "At 7 P.M. when I rose to go . . . it was our
parting."[12] Their love was not the less intense for being spiritual. Perhaps,
it was the more so.

The simple explanation for Newman's "last, my imperative will"—and
surely the right one—is, then, the love each had for the other. But is it the
whole of the explanation? The depth of the bond between them—if that is

to be the whole of the explanation—would rather have made it the *more* than the less certain that his wishes would be followed. Is there something that this explanation passes by? That is the question that I want to press, and there is a clue to this possibility in a detail of the manuscript that might easily escape the eye. It is a small sketch placed close above the instructions Newman left for his burial with Ambrose St. John—a rough sketch in pencil, marked only by a few lines and some initials, which Newman appears to have added as he later returned to these instructions to insist and confirm them. Two of these vertical lines appear to be a sketch of St. John's grave— judging by the letters *a s j* above, evidently standing for "Ambrose St John." To each side, two other graves appear sketched in the same way: the one headed "e," the other "joseph." Their meaning becomes plain when one visits the burial ground at Rednal. A grave lies to each side of the grave Newman shares with Ambrose St. John: one of these is the grave of Edward Caswall, the other that of Joseph Gordon, part of that first generation of Oratorians with Newman at Birmingham. Both died before Newman: Gordon in 1853, Caswall in 1878. Does this sketch convey something more than the mere placing of Newman's grave? The unmistakable answer to that question lies in Newman's room in the Oratory at Birmingham, exactly as Newman left it when he died in 1890.

At the far side of the room is the altar where Newman (as a cardinal) said mass, with the pictures of friends that he would remember at his mass on the wall beside the altar. There one can see the pictures of Joseph Gordon, Ambrose St. John, and Edward Caswall. These were, as he put it, "the three who from the first threw in their lot with me, from the moment they could do so."[13] That is Newman writing in January 1878, shortly after Caswall's death. In a letter a few days later, he added this.[14]

> [T]hough I want to do many things before I die, it seems unnatural that those who are so much younger than I am, should be called away and that I should remain. Three great and loyal friends of mine, Frs Joseph Gordon, Ambrose St John and Edward Caswall now lie side by side at Rednall, and I put them there.

"I put them there": to grasp the implication of that stark testimony, one has to go back to the death of Joseph Gordon in 1853. Gordon was received into the Catholic Church in 1847 in the wake of Newman's own reception, and became one of the first generation of Oratorians at Birmingham and in the years that followed a critical source of strength to Newman. This became all the more necessary in the aftermath of Newman's indictment in the

Corn Exchange lectures of Dr. Giacinto Achilli, a former Dominican friar and a public lecturer in London (whose subject was the iniquities of the Roman Inquisition). Gordon was extensively involved in the defense of the ensuing action for libel against Newman, which seemed in antipapist England to threaten Newman with imprisonment. Gordon traveled to Italy to establish evidence that Newman could use in his defense. Newman came to believe that the anxieties of this time were the cause of Gordon's death. In a memoir to which he contributed, he refers to himself in the third person as "the Father."[15]

> On S. Cecilia's day, November 22nd, the Father was called up to London for judgement. It was too much for Father Gordon; faithful to his own loyal heart, on that very day he was seized with a pleurisy, and when the Father returned from London on the morrow with his process still delayed, he found him in bed. It was the beginning of the end. He languished and sank, got worse and worse, and at the end of nearly three months, on the 13th of February, 1853, he died at Bath. He is in the hands of his God. We all loved him with a deep affection; we lamented him with all our hearts; we keenly feel his loss to this day. But the Father's bereavement is of a special kind, and his sorrow is ever new.

The role that Gordon had played fell to Ambrose St. John and Edward Caswall, and in 1864 the prospect of his own mortality broke in upon Newman forcefully, a mortality that he would come to connect with the death of his companions. As he later wrote,

> My two dear friends, St John and Caswall, died one at 60, the other at a little past 60. I, when I was 60, was seized with an all overishness, which I could not analyze. I could not sleep—I could do nothing. This was my condition for several years and for a time I thought any thing might happen. My spirits were unaccountably low, and the very week before I began my Apologia I was so alarmed that I hastily wrote my last instructions about myself for my executors, as if I were to die.[16]

These "last instructions" form the opening of the notebook where, in 1876, he added his instructions to be buried in Ambrose St. John's grave. The writing of Newman's *Apologia pro Vita Sua*, which he mentions here, became a turning point in what he was to achieve in the decades that lay ahead: but Joseph Gordon remained powerfully in his mind, and when Newman's poem *The Dream of Gerontius* appeared in full in 1866—his narrative of a soul's journey into death and beyond—he dedicated it to Father Joseph Gordon.

At the close of the *Apologia* Newman names Ambrose St. John and Edward Caswall among the priests of the Birmingham Oratory, "with whom I hope to die," yet in what he says there, can one also glimpse another growing realization?[17]

> And to you especially, dear AMBROSE ST JOHN; whom God gave me, when He took every one else away; who are the link between my old life and my new; who have now for twenty-one years been so devoted to me, so patient, so zealous, so tender; who have let me lean so hard upon you; who have watched me so narrowly; who have never thought of yourself, if I was in question.

"Who let me lean so hard upon you . . ." In the light of Gordon's death is there here a glimpse that St. John—and Caswall also—might be taken from him in giving him everything as Gordon had done? That is what Newman would come to believe, and he may well have been right. On Gordon's death in 1853, Caswall and St. John together filled the place that he left. When they too died in their early sixties—St. John in 1875 and Caswall in 1878—the pattern that Newman had seen unfolding in Gordon's death was to his mind now plain. Newman would live to an old age, and the years until his death in 1890 would see his work came to its fruition. In Newman's mind these years were the gift of these three men on whom he had leaned. To them we should then add William Neville also, who would step into the place left by St. John and Caswall after 1878. Newman's determination to be buried in St. John's grave beside Gordon and Caswall acknowledges the immense debt he owed these men: "I put them there."

Let me clarify what I am proposing here—to avoid any easy misunderstanding. I am not arguing that Newman's love for Ambrose St. John was not preeminent and distinctive. It was in terms of St. John that he expressed his last, imperative will; and although he lies beside Gordon and Caswall, he lies with St. John in the same grave. The hope that gesture makes concrete—as it does with all the shared graves of this book—is not a hope of distant life in heaven, but a corporeal hope on this earth: that on the Last Day, at the general resurrection of the dead, the first figure his awakened eyes will see will be him. One cannot put aside the strength of that gesture. My point is rather that, in Newman's sketch of the graves that lie close beside the one he shares with St. John, there is a critical clue—which we should strain to grasp—that in his final gesture Cardinal Newman was expressing not only his love for Ambrose St. John but also the conviction that in that love he had perceived something of the nature of friendship itself.

The gesture was no singular or new thing. The shared monuments of friends buried together have punctuated this book across the centuries it has followed, and their context was a tenacious religious faith—the story of which this book set out to recover—in which kinship and friendship lay at the heart of religion's role. The question I propose is whether Newman shared that faith and whether his burial with St. John was designed to express it. Is *that* why his injunctions insist and command?

The answer that I propose is that indeed it was. But first one needs to draw together evidence that may seem disparate. The initial place where one should turn is Newman as a preacher and to the play of the terms "veil" and "shadow" that (as has been pointed out by Father James Tolhurst) make coherent his difficult and otherwise paradoxical assertions about the nature of friendship and love.

These terms of Newman are rich with exemplarist overtones: that is, that all things refer to their origin in the mind of God. Here is Newman in his sermon "The Invisible World."

> Bright as is the sun, and the sky, and the clouds; green as are the leaves and the fields; sweet as is the singing of the birds; we know that they are not all, and we will not take up with a part for the whole. They proceed from a centre of love and goodness, which is God himself; but they are not his fullness; they speak of heaven, but they are not heaven; they are but as stray beams and dim reflections of His Image; they are but crumbs from the table. We are looking for the coming of the day of God, when all this outward world, fair though it be, shall perish; when the heavens shall be burnt, and the earth melt away. We can bear the loss, for we know it will be but the removing of a veil. We know that to remove the world which is seen, will be the manifestation of the world which is not seen.[18]

That term "imago" that Newman uses in his note in anticipation of death is also an exemplarist term, akin to "veil" here and the "stray beams and dim reflections" from beyond it. It is taken from Cicero's *De Officiis*, where Cicero uses it in a similar manner to this exemplarist sense.[19] "Imago" can denote an illusion, but it also has these overtones of a resemblance, of a reflection in a mirror.

It is this exemplarist theology that makes coherent the paradoxical comments Newman makes in the gentle, tender letters he wrote to Henry Edward (later Cardinal) Manning in 1837 when Manning's wife was mortally ill.[20] If, he writes, in

> His great wisdom and love He take away the desire of your eyes, it will only be to bring her really nearer to you. For those we love are not nearest to us when in the flesh, but they come into our very hearts as being spiritual beings, when they are removed from us. Alas! it is hard to persuade oneself of this, when we have the presence and are without the experience of the absence of those we love; yet the absence is often *more* than the presence.

The emphasis is mine, but Newman returns to it and to the word "more"— as a paradox—in a letter to Manning a few days later: "The thought of the dead is more to us than the sight of the living, tho' it seems a paradox to say so."[21] "Thus," as Newman puts it in his sermon "On Mental Prayer," "the true Christian pierces through the veil of this world and sees the next."[22] Newman's point as he puts it here is equally that the world is a veil, and that its substance can be glimpsed *in this world.* His explanation is this, as he puts it in one of the meditations that would be published by Father Neville: "Thou art Thyself the seat and centre of all good, and the only substance in this universe of shadows, and the heaven in which blessed spirits live and rejoice."[23] Newman's assertion that those we love are rather the *more* with us than the less, when taken from us, becomes intelligible as such an exemplarist assertion: with its corollary, that in friendship one can experience in this world something of that substance—which is God—within this universe of shadows.

The point is one that the saintly English cardinal Basil Hume would later make explicitly. He added it, in the days following the death of a close friend, to a teaching document he had written some years before. "When two persons love," he wrote, "whether of the same sex or of a different sex . . . they experience in a limited manner in this world what will be their unending delight when one with God in the next."[24] These are fine pastoral words and heartfelt, but also good historical scholarship. Hume was a monk, and in the years following the Second World War he (as many others) read the historian Dom Jean Leclercq (himself a monk) and the Cistercian writings on friendship of the twelfth century. It was in such exemplarist terms that Aelred of Rievaulx in *De Spiritali Amicitia* (as I argued) was led to his spectacular formulation: "Deus amicitia est" [God is friendship]. It is that same theology one is seeing here, both in Hume and in Newman.[25]

A classical education in nineteenth-century England would readily have identified Newman's burial with Ambrose St. John as that of Achilles and

Patroclus. In Homer's *Iliad* the shade of the dead Patroclus implores his friend to bury their remains together in a single grave: the lines that stand as the epigraph for this chapter.[26] This famous passage—famous at least until the decline of classical education—is a measure of how ancient was the gesture of the shared grave that has punctuated the argument of this book. So too are the rituals of friendship and of ritual kinship that accompanied it. But in Homer's lines the gesture is an act of defiant pagan mortalism, a transcendence beyond death only in their mingled ashes. The story this book has told is the transformation of such rituals within a distinctively Christian ethic: the story of how friendship, the family, and religion fell in love. By the time of Aelred of Rievaulx's *De Spiritali Amicitia* in the twelfth century, that process was complete and would endure across the centuries that followed.

Seven centuries divide Aelred from Newman, but not in their theology. Yet an argument that Newman's burial with St. John represented the same traditional beliefs that this book has followed may require something more than this. To make a substantial connection between those traditional beliefs and Newman's own, one needs also to see in Newman two more concrete things. The first is the same eucharistic expression that I have argued became identified with that ethic during the second Christian millennium and that has been the evidence this book has followed. The second is that—arguably at least—one also needs evidence that Newman *knew* that his burial with Ambrose St. John was something that would have been recognizable across those centuries. The first is a good deal easier to achieve than the second, so let me turn to that first.

The place one might look is a small bound notebook among Newman's manuscripts at the Oratory at Birmingham, containing a list of his friends.[27] Like many of the documents I have drawn on in this book, we misunderstand this manuscript if we see it simply as a source of names and dates for the historian. It is a small book—measuring 13 by 11 centimeters—easy to handle, and bound in a cover of needlework made by Mrs. Pusey in her last illness. The presence of the cover is a trace of how much it was designed to be handled. It was something that Newman *used.* It is set out across the year, divided into months and days, and the names of the friends remembered here are assigned to a day with a note of the year of their death, sometimes the exact time. It is a trace of the altar in Newman's room at the Oratory in Birmingham to which it corresponds, surrounded by pictures of his friends from the past and their memorial cards. All of the people who, in this way, were present in the altar in Newman's room are included here, Ambrose St. John on 24 May, the day of his death.[28] This manuscript is a surviving trace—in the most material sense—of Newman at prayer in the mass. When in Newman's day the priest said mass and had consecrated the elements in Christ's words, he would silently mention names of the dead, with the prayer "Ipsis, Domine, et omnibus in Christo quiescentibus, locum refrigerii, lucis, et pacis, ut indulgeas, deprecamur" [To these, O Lord, and to all that rest in Christ, grant, we beseech thee, a place of rest, light, and peace]. What we are seeing in this manuscript is Newman praying, day by day, for his friends in the mass.

In this manuscript friendship and the Eucharist are inseparable, as they were to the traditional-minded Christians this book has described. Perhaps the most telling evidence of all lies in the events on the night that St. John died. Newman's early biographer Wilfrid Ward gave wide currency to the Romantic (even Gothic) story that "when Ambrose St. John died Newman threw himself on the bed by the corpse and spent the night there."[29] What appears to have taken place is recounted in a letter William Neville wrote a few weeks later, on 2 July 1875. Neville is a crucial witness here, as he was with St. John in his last illness and at the end, as Newman later explained in a letter.

> Father Neville, however, had kept his Rituale always open and close to him through the illness, and, when all of a sudden at 11 o'clock at night, after I have left him, he fell back on his bed and his countenance changed, at once he gave him absolution and began the prayers, and my dear friend passed away while he was reading.[30]

Newman was woken up at the Oratory in Birmingham at midnight and arrived a little before one o'clock. At that moment, he had the calm that the kindness of nature can give on bereavement, when things must be done, before the storm of grief breaks. Neville's account in his letter is that Newman, first, said the office of prayers for the dead beside the body of his friend. Then he went into the room below and wrote telegrams and letters "so calmly." It was now two in the morning—"the Aurora of St Philip's eve" as Neville puts it—and Newman was now free to do what his heart and his faith told him to do. It tells us everything about what friendship was for Newman. He went to the altar in the house and said the Mass of the Dead for his friend.[31]

With that gesture the centuries roll back. In it one can see clearly now, in a line stretching behind Newman, the figures across those centuries that this book has recounted. They did not have Newman's sanctity and that of his companions, but they were men and women who shared with him a tenacious traditional faith. They are John Bloxham and John Whytton, scholars and priests in the fourteenth century buried together in the choir of Merton College, under their great memorial brass at the steps to the high altar. They are their contemporaries, those two tough knights, William Neville and John Clanvowe, buried together in the Dominican church beneath a monument that depicts the kiss of peace in the mass. They are those fellows of Merton, Ralph Hamsterley and Thomas Harper, whose memorial brass lay with that of Bloxham and Whytton in Merton College chapel by the altar of St. Katherine, where Hamsterley provided for the mass to be said for them together on the eve of the Reformation. They are their spiritual inheritors in the later Catholic exiles, Nicholas Morton and John Seton, whose memorial stone in the Venerable English College in Rome records their wish to be buried together and draws the eye in its design up to the Corpus Christi at the altar. They are also those in the Reformed Church like John Finch and Thomas Baines, buried together by the communion table in Christ's College, with an inscription whose terms are picked up—and made universal—above the communion table: as the Eucharist continued to shape the burial of friends together like them, scholars such as John Gostlin and Thomas Legge, churchmen like Herbert Croft and George Benson, county gentry such as Granville Piper and Richard Wise, or Anne Fleming and Catherine Jennis, Anne Lister and Ann Walker.

But did Newman *know* this? Did Newman know that in his being buried with St. John these traditional-minded Christians over the centuries would have recognized the beliefs they shared with him and expressed in the same gesture? This second question is the more difficult one. Did Newman know that, in the final gesture of his burial with Ambrose St. John, he was conveying that faith to the future? That has been my argument.

Newman as preacher, Newman as priest: the place to find an answer to this question is Newman as historian. One of the most touching passages in Newman's writings is his farewell to Oxford in *Apologia pro Vita Sua*. One of the last to whom Newman said goodbye was Dr. Ogle, who had been his private tutor when Newman was an undergraduate.

> In him I took leave of my first College, Trinity, which was so dear to me, and which held on its foundation so many who had been kind to me both when I was a boy, and all through my Oxford life. Trinity had never been unkind to me. There used to be much snap-dragon growing on the walls opposite my freshman's rooms there, and I had for years taken it as the emblem of my own perpetual residence even unto death in my University.[32]

There is friendship in several ways in that passage, for in Newman's day a college fellow who married as an undergraduate gave up his fellowship. Newman's vocation was to friendship, not marriage. He would not see Oxford again for thirty-two years—except its spires from the railway.

Newman saw Oxford with the eye of a historian. There is a revealing picture of this in Newman's essay "Medieval Oxford" in his *Historical Sketches*, redolent of Anthony Wood's *History and Antiquities of the Colleges and Halls in the University of Oxford*, which he quotes.[33] But the point I want to follow— apparently a donnish detail—is that Newman's essay in *Historical Sketches* is a revised version of a long review he contributed to the *British Critic* in 1838, of the three volumes of James Ingram's *Memorials of Oxford*. In the first volume of Ingram's *Memorials* you will see John Bloxham and John Whytton's memorial brass above their tomb illustrated: they stand together under their canopies, like the saints in the fourteenth-century windows about them, as if sanctified by their friendship. Ingram's transcription of the inscription on their brass records their burial together below and indicates that their great memorial brass lay for two and a half centuries at the center of the choir of Merton College, Oxford.[34]

Newman would have taken Ingram's volumes down from the shelf again in 1861, when he saw the correspondence in the *Times* on William Butterfield's alterations in Merton—during which Bloxham and Whytton's memorial brass was returned to the choir, until a second stripping of their friendship from the altar in our own time: but I do not think Newman needed reminding of that memorial.[35] Nor do I think he saw it for the first time in Ingram's volumes. It would have been familiar to him since his days as an undergraduate, when he stayed in Oxford during the vacations, and he and his friend John William Bowden explored Oxford together. One might be forgiven for seeing an echo of them in Charles Reding and William Sheffield, the two undergraduates in Newman's novel *Loss and Gain*, walking out together and stopping to look inside a chapel.[36] When one has seen this monument, one does not easily forget it, especially a man like John Henry Newman. In Oxford and in this monument the past had left a message for Newman that he would one day find.

The gesture of his burial with Ambrose St. John was one Newman shared with a distant Catholic past, the faith it expressed was the same: and he knew it. Yet the monument to John Bloxham and John Whytton rather underlines how little in the end Newman's awareness of their monument from the fourteenth century mattered, for his gesture was no self-conscious Victorian Gothic. What impelled Newman's gesture was not the memory of Bloxham and Whytton but of Joseph Gordon, Edward Caswall, and

Ambrose St. John; and with that gesture one steps out of the history this book has recounted and into the contemporary world. Did Newman's conviction still subsist there? Did it, in a word, survive? Let me now turn back to that inscription to which Newman himself turned in his note in anticipation of death, after expressing his last, imperative will to be buried with St. John. In January 2001 the inscription was referred to and quoted in a letter that Pope John Paul II sent to the Catholic archbishop of Birmingham, Archbishop Vincent Nichols, to mark the second centenary of Newman's birth, at a time when John Paul was himself infirm and had his own death in prospect.[37] In his letter Pope John Paul drew attention to the importance of Newman's tomb in understanding his theology: this is the grave in Rednal that he shares with St. John; but in his letter Pope John Paul relates Newman's tomb to the inscription now on his memorial stone at the Oratory at Birmingham. The two are not distinguished in John Paul's letter, and the scholarship of that connection is impeccable, for it is the same connection that Newman himself makes, in the note he wrote in anticipation of his death.

If the Oratory in Birmingham is locked, you can walk around to the side of the church; there you will find the gate to the cloister. On the far wall is Newman's memorial stone. No one—perhaps not surprisingly—altered the inscription he set out in his note, whether for orthodoxy or latinity. The only alterations were to place his heraldic arms above the inscription and to add the word "Cardinalis," to record that when he died he was a cardinal of the Holy Roman Church. For the Oratorians in Birmingham, he is always "our Cardinal."

> JOANNES HENRICUS CARDINALIS NEWMAN
>
> EX UMBRIS ET IMAGINIBUS
>
> IN VERITATEM
>
> DIE XI AUGUSTI ANNO SALUTIS MDCCCXC
>
> REQUIESCAT IN PACE

> [John Henry Cardinal Newman
> From shadows and images into truth.
> 11 August in the year of salvation 1890.
> May he rest in peace.]

"From shadows and images into truth." Newman's explication was that in friendship we can see a stray beam or a dim reflection here in this world of what will be our unending delight when one with God in the next: thus it is that it can endure beyond the grave, as the tomb monuments in this book so graphically assert. On the one side his inscription. On the other his burial in the grave of Ambrose St. John. What one says in words, the other says in gesture; they signify the same.

In his letter Pope John Paul asked for prayers that the time could soon come when the church could beatify Newman: "can officially and publicly proclaim the exemplary holiness of Cardinal John Henry Newman." In Catholic belief, the process toward which that proclamation may point in Newman's eventual canonization is inseparable from the care of his relics, and it is likely that his relics will be brought into the Oratory Church in Birmingham to lie by the altar. The inheritors of Newman's faith should not separate them from his final gesture. Is it comprehensible that one could now credibly tear his remains from those of his three companions? From the remains of the friend who was also as far as this world was concerned his first and the last? That gesture was Newman's last, imperative command: his last wish as a man, but also something more. It was his last sermon.

My argument has been that Newman's burial with St. John cannot be detached from Newman's understanding of the place of friendship in Christian belief or its long history, but as one turns from the graveside in Rednal, does the story I have set out to tell come to its end? The ethic and moral tradition I have followed was designed to bring about reconciliation, kinship, and friendship in a divided world and to do so directly, face to face. The Enlightenment put aside this traditional ethic with contempt and put in its place a Fraternity that it claimed would be "universal," "rational," even "scientific"; but as the nineteenth century drew to its end, that experiment was terrifyingly failing and Europe was moving toward a war that would engulf the whole world, in fire and blood. As one stands by the grave of Cardinal Newman, one might well be forgiven for thinking that the light I have followed, across the terrain this book has covered for close on a thousand years, seems at last to flicker and go out. Yet there is another way to end this story, one that explains why it has been so resistant to its closure.

In the last months, as I was finishing this book, I began to talk publicly about my findings, and those monuments to friends buried together that punctuated my argument could prompt a telling response. At the talk's end I would frequently be approached by someone from the audience to tell me that they knew of another such monument, or had heard of one, or thought perhaps they had seen one. This underlined what I had already guessed, from the chance or grace that had led me to discover those monuments. There are many more. Why have these monuments played so little part in our understanding of the past? Why have we not *seen* them before?

The world I have described survived. It did so in two contrasted ways. To a western Christian, one way is far from home. In substantial part at least, it survived in the living Christianity of the East that was embraced by Pope John Paul II when he made his historic visit to the Syrian-Orthodox Cathedral in Damascus in the first spring of the new millennium. This followed by only a few months his letter on the significance, far to the West, of the tomb of John Henry Newman. In Damascus Pope John Paul spoke of his "fervent hope that Christians everywhere will once again open their hearts to the spiritual and doctrinal treasures of the Churches of the Syrian tradition."[38] One of these traditions is a surviving form of the rites I described in the Latin West.

It was set out in a homily by the Syrian-Orthodox archbishop in Jerusalem, Archbishop Dionysius Behnam Jajaweh, when two female American scholars sharing an interest in the Syriac-speaking Christianity of late antiquity were united by him in the rite in June 1985, in the Church of the Holy Sepulchre in Jerusalem. With Professor Robin Darling Young we walk back through the Old City and into the past.

> We followed the bishop and a monk through the Old City to a side chapel in the Holy Sepulchre where, according to the Syrian Orthodox, lies the actual tomb of Jesus. After the liturgy, the bishop had us join our right hands together and he wrapped them in a portion of his garment. He pronounced a series of prayers over us, told us that we were united as sisters, and admonished us not to quarrel. Ours was a sisterhood stronger than blood, confirmed in the outpouring of the Holy Spirit, he said, and since it was a spiritual union, it would last beyond the grave.[39]

The men and women who built the tomb monuments described in this book would have readily understood that homily. But the world I have described survived also in a more tangible, a more material, sense. Let me go back to that question these tomb monuments prompted for me, the question that continued to press itself upon me as I wrote this book. Why have we not seen them before?

One day that summer when I was finishing my book, I walked across the Norfolk countryside with a friend to Wiveton Parish Church to search for the monument to Anne Fleming and Catherine Jennis, which the medievalist Judith Bennett had alerted me to. The church door was unlocked, and although there was no mention of the monument in the guides by the door, it was not difficult to find, for someone—I do not know whom—had beautifully cleaned it, lifted it up, and placed it on the wall by the door.

AFTERWORD

Historians and Friendship

The introduction to this work sets out why a book about the history of friendship might matter: this afterword is more technical. It describes the place this book occupies within the specific concerns of historians: a guide as it were to the pipes and plumbing that lie beneath its surface. It is thus written for my fellow historians, and for those who, having followed the story this book has sought to recover, wish to stay with it a while longer and follow the reaction it is likely to prompt in the academic world. For the reasons I set out below, it is likely to have a stormy welcome.

I took the wraps off my findings in a lecture I gave at Newman House, St. Stephen's Green, Dublin, on 21 July 2001. Amid the many accounts of that lecture that followed in the press, the only "authorized version" was the summary that appeared in the Catholic weekly the *Tablet*.[1] But this is to anticipate.

The Politics of Friendship

The starting point for a description of this book's strictly academic context lies with the constitutional historians of Victorian England, who laid down the influential assumption that the friendship created by kinship has played little or no part in shaping the development of English government and society: the assumption this book challenges, in root and branch.

The history of friendship slipped from sight, as I argue, as the friendship created by kinship was obscured by that assumption. I begin with an anatomy of that assumption: with kinship rather than friendship. Later I turn to the impulses from which friendship pressed itself back into the historical account and on which this book has drawn; but this initial anatomy proves no easy or quick task, for much was at stake.

First to identify these historians: this group of Victorian historians included figures such as Frederic Maitland, John Green, and Edward Freeman, but the preeminent figure among them was unquestionably William Stubbs, whose *Constitutional History of England in Its Origin and Development* was to be immensely influential. Where the friendship created by kinship had obtruded on their accounts, its presence was glossed over as a form of "bastard feudalism," a term coined by Charles Plummer in 1885, obstructing the onward march of the royal administration. That onward march to the unique English constitutional settlement of their time formed the programmatic basis of their writings, but their underlying assumption that the friendship created by kinship was the pluperfect of history was retained by their Marxist critics when they reintroduced kinship into their description of English history, along with that notion of a recidivist "bastard feudalism."

In the 1950s these critics included Maurice Dobb, Rodney Hilton, Christopher Hill, and Eric Hobsbawm, who in the years following the Second World War were active in the Communist Party Historians' Group, the programmatic statement of which was A. L. Morton's *People's History of England*, operative in local branches across the country.[2] At this point much of the published work of these historians lay in the future and would take a markedly less schematic approach. Indeed, Eric Hobsbawn's paper on the culture of the tramping artisans later gave me a first inkling of the social context among the common people for the sworn friendship I describe in this book. But their viewpoint in the 1950s would be inherited and perpetuated by more recent historians who—although they did not inherit the political programs of their predecessors—retained their historical framework in this respect intact, historians such as Lawrence Stone in his *Family, Sex, and Marriage in England, 1500–1800* or later Anthony Fletcher in his *Gender, Sex, and Subordination in England, 1500–1800*. The kinship this reintroduced into the historical narrative was always composed of straw men, disappearing as English society passed into modernity: its character, its place in the narrative, was that it passed, as English society passed, into modernity, and the modern conjugal family emerged with it. The liminal status this gave to kinship was taken to its logical conclusion in the historians of the Cambridge Group for the History of Population and Social Structure, such as Alan Macfarlane, who has argued that there is no effective kin group to be identified in English society, at any point, beyond the conjugal group of mother, father, and children.

The thesis of this later group of historians is set out in a developed form in a large body of work that includes *Household and Family in Past Time*, edited by Laslett and Wall; Wrightson and Levine, *Poverty and Piety in an English Vil-*

lage; Laslett, *Family Life and Illicit Love;* Wall, Robin, and Laslett, *Family Forms in Historic Europe;* Smith, *Land, Kinship, and Life-Cycle;* Macfarlane, *The Family Life of Ralph Josselin, The Origins of English Individualism, Marriage and Love in England,* and *The Culture of Capitalism.* The force of their conclusions (and what was at stake in them) remained most readily evident in the work that was to be the founding text of this school: Peter Laslett's *World We Have Lost,* published in 1965 and revisited and revised in 1983. The book was the result of work that he began in the late 1950s and that he presented to a mass audience through a series of radio broadcasts made through the Third Programme of the British Broadcasting Corporation.[3]

The phrase "a one-class society" in Peter Laslett's broadcast title alerts one to the original context of these works, a context that plunges one into a world of *political* issues for which one is unlikely to be prepared but which at points break the surface. Laslett's book was a forthright rejection of the false and misleading picture, as he put it, of extended families in "the world we have lost," a view attributed by him to the historians he criticized, and of the supposed "welfare- and support-providing household" in that world for "the victims of age, sickness, bereavement or want."[4] The terms Laslett uses here catch the polemical political context in which his research figured. These terms—"the victims of age, sickness, bereavement or want"—ostensibly directed at the seventeenth century, also had a ready currency in postwar Britain, in the language of the postwar welfare state created by the reforming Labour government of 1945, which figured directly in the last of Laslett's broadcasts.

The immediate political context for Laslett's research in the late 1950s lay in the conservative election victories of 1951 and of (with increased majorities) 1955 and 1959, and in the widely shared expectation at the time that Britain would take off on the road to economic individualism, repairing the wrong turn represented by the welfare state. The welfare state itself was not at issue: its popular support at the time of Laslett's broadcasts in 1960 was widespread. The force of Laslett's conclusions was rather directed to the place that had been occupied, in his view, by the "extended" families of preindustrial England in the writings of the historians he characterized in *The World We Have Lost* as Marxist, historians who regarded a socialist management of the economy as the necessary adjunct of the welfare state. The account of English history he was criticizing was one in which the loss in the sixteenth and seventeenth centuries of the "extended" family was a measure of the misery that was to come under capitalism—to which the creation of the postwar welfare state was the socialist response.

Laslett's rejection of the myth of the "extended" family was an implicit rebuttal of the historical basis for the socialist implications of welfare politics, from which Britain seemed now to be turning. His broadcasts in 1960 closed with an attack on the Soviet Union and the regimes of Eastern Europe. As he later put it, when *The World We Have Lost* first appeared in 1965: "in tending to look backwards in this way, in diagnosing the difficulties as the outcome of something which has indeed been lost to our society, those concerned with social welfare are suffering from a false understanding of ourselves in time."[5]

What was at issue in Laslett's seminal work was not only the friendship created by kinship in the past but also the place of friendship between individuals and communities in postwar Britain. This debate, begun in the politics of postwar Europe, was to continue influencing the rapidly changing world of the 1960s and 1970s, where the wider attraction of this group of Cambridge historians lay in the reassurance they now appeared to provide, in the face of the new social relationships emerging as an incidental by-product of the political upheavals of the 1960s, most noticeably in the advent of feminism. Crucial to that reassurance was the prescriptive judgment implicit in the assertion these historians made, that the conjugal family had always "constituted the ordinary, expected, *normal* framework of domestic existence," as Laslett put it in 1972.[6] It addressed a disturbing possibility. If the conjugal family had been a product of modernity, as the Marxism they were criticizing seemed to imply, in the gathering crisis of late modernity it now appeared all too possible that it might disappear with it. In the eyes of their opponents, historians such as Laslett had sought to undermine the basis for a socialist management of the economy that a generation of historians had sought to justify in historical perspective, and it was this that created much of the bitterness of the subsequent debate. In 1970s Britain the appeal of their conclusions was that they seemed rather to shore up and buttress the *sexual* politics that an older orthodoxy no longer seemed able to sustain. Later this group of historians perhaps unwittingly were to provide much of the historical underpinning for the political program to defend an unchanging "traditional" family based on marriage that was to emerge in the 1980s, with the election victory in 1979 of Margaret Thatcher and the agenda of radical conservative reaction on which her government embarked, a program that would also provide a basis for the opposition to the popular Labour government elected in 1997.

The standoff between the historians identified with Peter Laslett and their opponents disguised the extent to which historians associated with him, such as Alan Macfarlane, had themselves emerged from a tradition shaped by Marxist historiography and were equipped by his revision of an

earlier orthodoxy to defend the pivotal role of the conjugal family. Both
groups of historians were in fact equally adapting the programmatic view
of the nineteenth-century historians such as William Stubbs, who had argued that proprietary landholding (i.e., based on the conjugal family) un-
derlay the distinctive development of English constitutional institutions (as
in Stubbs's "Systems of Landholding in Mediaeval Europe"). While their
socialist opponents emphasized the dynamic element in this account, historians such as Alan Macfarlane have rather emphasized its underlying continuity, but both were adapting the same account.

For the Victorian constitutional historians, their Marxist inheritors, and
the Cambridge critics of those Marxist historians alike, the interpretative crux
in their accounts has been the conjugal family; each declined to attribute any
shaping role in English history to ritual kinship other than marriage. Two
ever-expanding implications followed. The first was to exclude any such
shaping role to the wider friendship between households that ritual kinship
created. The line that these historians held in the years that followed, Marxist and neoliberal alike, was characteristically either to ignore the formal
bonds of friendship—by excluding them from their interpretive account—
or to diminish their significance on equally a priori grounds: in the one case
by identifying them with backward economic and social conditions, and in
the other by recognizing them only as an extension of biological kinship.
The wider historiographical point was that, in denying this role within an
English context (because of the pivotal role of England in their wider historiography of the rise of modernity that I mentioned earlier), they were
denying it also within their account of modernity itself—and of the future.

Breaking the Ice

Alan Macfarlane's response in his review of Lawrence Stone's *Family, Sex,
and Marriage in England* demonstrated the degree to which the tensions that
had animated a quarrel for a generation were still very much alive. Yet the
beginning of the 1980s was to be a turning point. The tacit political context
of this quarrel was the cause of the marked reluctance of historians more
generally to become involved in it, despite the mounting evidence of the inadequacy of the parameters of the debate. The basis for a less programmatic
view had been laid down (in fact if not in perception) in the 1940s, in the
work in France of Jean Leclercq and in England of the great medievalist
Kenneth McFarlane. Leclercq pointed to the wide scope of the "spiritual"
friendship and kinship of medieval Europe, and McFarlane's criticism of
the idea of a "bastard feudalism" similarly led him to stress the dynamic role

played by the formal friendship of the household. One can trace in the writings of each of these historians the extent to which they recognized that in the societies they were describing the good of kinship was perceived to lie in its ability to create friendship and that historically kinship has been formed not only by blood but also by ritual, by promise, and by obligation. In more anthropological terms, one might say that all kinship is in the strict sense of the word "artificial" and the product of human agency and that, where friendship is given a formal and objective character by ritual and oath, it can signify as kinship. In this Leclercq and McFarlane were exploring potential definitions of the family and kinship that extended beyond the conjugal unit, and in doing so began to open up the forms of friendship in which it has been embedded: McFarlane in the household and Leclercq in forms of ritual kinship other than marriage.

McFarlane wrote two seminal papers on "bastard feudalism."[7] His pervasive influence lay primarily, however, in his teaching and lectures as a fellow of Magdalen College, Oxford, especially in the monumental Ford Lectures of 1953. His papers and lectures were left for publication by his pupils. Jean Leclercq's work was similarly introduced to a British audience by a set of lectures he gave at Oxford in 1977.[8]

In the 1980s the wider implications of this work became apparent. As the political orthodoxies of the postwar years began to lose their hold, a concern with the uncertain ethics of friendship began to reassert itself in areas as diverse as philosophy, sociology, literary criticism, and the history of art. This reassessment would touch social history also. The reserve that had prevailed there since the 1940s was broken in 1980 by an article by Miranda Chaytor in *History Workshop Journal,* a journal of socialist and feminist historians, in which she criticized the dominant trends in the history of the family for leaving unexplored the content of social relations both within households and between them.[9] Despite Wrightson's irenic response, the strength of the reaction from Rab Houston and Richard Smith (all in the same journal) indicated what was at stake and explains much of the earlier reticence.[10] Chaytor's article opened the way, and criticisms similar to those she had voiced were subsequently to be developed by Barbara Hanawalt, David Cressy, Naomi Tadmor, A. Hassell Smith, Rosemary O'Day, and Diana O'Hara.[11] This book contributes to these doubts from its own distinctive viewpoint.

The description of the family in these studies—set within a frame of kin, friends, and neighbors—does not support the conviction fundamental to the historians who followed Peter Laslett (with their Victorian predecessors), that there was a great gulf in this respect between England and its continental neighbors. Markedly similar conclusions appear, for example, for corresponding Italian settings in Diane Hughes, D. V. and Francis Kent, Ronald Weissman, and Francesco Benigno.[12] As in the English context, studies of patronage into the "moral economy" of friendship were made in a French context by Kettering.[13]

The papers that followed Chaytor's had their parallels in a medieval context in studies of friendship and friendship networks that recognized these networks as instruments for political stability and located them firmly within the concerns of medieval theology and philosophy. Fundamental to this context was the steady extension of the work of Kenneth McFarlane and Jean Leclercq: McFarlane's work was extended by historians such as J. M. W. Bean and Mervyn James (and less directly Jean-Louis Flandrin), Leclercq's work by historians such as Brian McGuire and John Bossy. A recent commentary on the extensive subsequent literature shaped by McFarlane's work is Michael Hicks's *Bastard Feudalism*. Important works by Bossy on which I have drawn are *Christianity in the West* and *Peace in the Post-Reformation*. These were accompanied by a number of detailed studies.[14] They in turn paved the way for the important collection of papers edited by Julian Haseldine, *Friendship in Medieval Europe*, which contains extensive bibliographical guides to earlier work. The anthology contained a paper by Peter Burke that followed a number of similarly detailed studies on sixteenth- and seventeenth-century Europe.[15] The 1980s also saw two important studies that reassessed the political role of figures such as Piers Gaveston and George Villiers, whom the Victorian historians and their successors had dismissed.[16]

This book seeks to draw on and extend these works. It also owes two debts of a somewhat different kind. One is to the intellectual stimulus of Peter Brown's work, even though the mechanism he describes in *Cult of the Saints* and *Power and Persuasion* are outside my temporal frame. I also owe a considerable personal debt to my discussion over many years with Michel Rey, who was a member of the seminar of Jean-Louis Flandrin. His pioneering thesis was left incomplete at the time of his early death, but his papers were later published by Anne-Sophie Perriaux.[17] My chapter on the body of the friend first appeared in our joint names in recognition of my debt to him and as a tribute to his memory.[18]

The confidence in these studies over the last twenty years disguises the limited impact that they have had on the historians I have characterized as following in the approach of Peter Laslett or of the Marxist historians for the 1950s and in particular on the influence this older work has continued to exercise outside the academy. In large measure this debate is yet to be engaged. Let me therefore lay out where that as yet unresolved debate is likely in my opinion to take place.

The critical question will be the adequacy of the sources that have been deployed. The sources that have shaped the conclusions of the school of historians that have followed in the wake of Peter Laslett have been preeminently parish registers, manorial and estate records, parish account books, and taxation records; other sources (such as diaries or wills) have been consistently read in their light. These are the records of officials that have been preserved by their successors and are therefore relatively readily accessible in record offices across the country. But the unaddressed critical question in these sources is the extent to which such officials ever sought to regulate or recognize the formal ties of friendship that kinship created beyond the conjugal family. If they did not do so, and that is indeed the argument of this book, the argument from *silence* that has been built on the basis of sources such as these will scarcely appear convincing. They are rather, then, the unwitting instrument of the historian's abiding temptation, of looking only where the light is brightest. A corresponding criticism could also be made of the studies by historians such as Lawrence Stone or Anthony Fletcher. In an analogous manner the sources that have shaped their works have been the conduct books, exemplary sermons, and early medical and humoral theory, readily available in collections of sixteenth- and seventeenth-century printed books: that is, prescriptive literature that stressed the link between the governance of the household and the governance of the state. The error that, I would suggest, has been made by both sides in this sustained and unresolved debate has been to *replicate* (rather than critically to question) the strategies—of regulation and prescription—of which these books and records are the surviving material trace: they have been mistaken as transparent windows on the past.

Converging Streams

Within this broader frame, the disparate and often difficult evidence bearing on the detailed mechanisms of friendship has been brought together in a number of converging lines of research, which I review below. These are more circumscribed areas than the broad developments I have reviewed in this afterword, but they have played at points a critical role. In some cases they are also likely to play an instrumental role in the controversy that will follow in the wake of this book. In the 1990s they converged with the studies of a new generation of literary critics and with studies of political thought.

Three of these have concerned forms of ritual kinship that subsisted alongside and overlapped with that formed by a betrothal, and created wider bonds of friendship in a similar manner. One form was created by baptism (and its analogues such as fosterage).[19]

A second such area of research has been on the ritual kiss of peace. The classic treatise on the kiss of peace was (and remains) that of the thirteenth-century canonist William Durandus, "De Pacis Osculo."[20] Its place in traditional Christianity was described by John Bossy, while Joseph Jungmann provides the technical study.[21] L. Edward Phillips is illuminating on the anthropological perspective, while Colin Buchanan is indispensable on the modern revival of the kiss.[22] Much work remains to be done on the kiss of peace—it is potentially a key to the history of friendship more widely—and I am inclined to think that both Buchanan and Phillips underestimate the continued use of the kiss of peace after 1000: it was the social *significance* of the kiss, not its redundancy, that made its use rare and potentially momentous when employed.

A third such area has been the friendship constituted by the sworn brotherhood, which I argue in this book became increasingly associated in the Latin West with the Eucharist (and overlapped with the friendship established by baptism). This research has been much more fraught and contested than that concerned with baptism and the kiss of peace. Initially the presence of sworn brotherhood was more apparent to literary critics than to historians because of its presence in Middle English literature, although their discussions remained within the programmatic framework set by the constitutional historians of the nineteenth century, until the arrival of a new generation of "historicist" literary critics. When Laurens Mills discussed sworn brotherhood, he followed the lead the Victorian historians had given by assuming that the phenomenon must have derived in the distant past from a symbolic blood-brotherhood.[23] The same view was taken by Leach in his edition of *Amis and Amiloun*, as it was by the historian Maurice Keen.[24] Baldwin was later to do the same, as was Strohm, who placed his discussion of sworn brotherhood in terms of the "bastard feudalism" of the Victorian and Marxist historians.[25] Yet these studies by literary critics (and those of an earlier generation) grasped the importance (and complexities) of the subject.[26] Mills crucially grasped the conventional and rhetorical nature of the references to friendship in the literature of the English Renaissance (a point that I develop in my approach in chapter 2). Strohm pointed out that sworn brotherhood was perceived to touch on fidelity in all its ramifications and that the suspicions of connivance and self-advancement that sworn brotherhood aroused placed this at stake, a point I pick up in chapter 3 of this book. Baldwin also highlighted the moral ambiguities of sworn brotherhood, but the influence of these studies remained limited by their historical framework and restricted within disciplinary boundaries.

Sworn Friendship

John Boswell's *Same-Sex Unions in Premodern Europe* was to be a catalyst when it was published in 1994. His controversial thesis was that the Greek *adelphopoiesis*—literally a rite "for the making of brothers" or "sisters"—had functioned in the past as what we would today recognize as a homosexual marriage, a thesis that indirectly was addressed to the recognition of homosexual partnerships today and touched similarly contested definitions of the family that had underlaid earlier debates. Boswell's book was intended to be provocative. His failure to deal with the slippery definitional problems was compounded by the equivalent fault of his critics. Brent Shaw's radically unhistorical definition of marriage in an early response to Boswell was not applied later in his own writing on ritual brotherhood in Roman and post-Roman society, where the same definition would have substantially have been met.[27] Shaw's paper remained within the programmatic view of the nineteenth-century constitutional historians, and with evident discomfort he dismissed evidence that conflicted with that view, on a priori grounds, as "an exception," "singular," "occasional"—or simply as "irregular."[28]

Boswell's inadequate grasp of the Greek and Slavonic liturgical texts undermined much of the influence his study could have had,[29] and the reactions to it replayed—on a stage that now extended far beyond England—similar contemporary tensions akin to those that had underlaid Peter Laslett's early work and the later reaction to Miranda Chaytor's revisionist piece in *History Workshop Journal*. As tempers cooled, two major objections to the way Boswell handled his evidence stood out clearly, both of which are right. One is that the expected ideals of the rite would not have comprehended sexual intercourse. The other is that his thesis disguises the fact that the rite did not preclude the individuals involved also being married. Yet the matter will not rest confidently there, for the problem that remained is that an unqualified rejection of Boswell's thesis in these terms is itself open to the same kind of criticism. It reduces the range of what we recognize today as being sexual to the narrow question of sexual intercourse, and it glosses over the historical disparity that, in the past, marriage has been one, as it is not in modern society, among several forms of what one might call voluntary kinship: kinship created not by blood but by ritual or a promise. The claim that the relationships blessed by this rite were sexual and akin to marriage *and* the claim that they were not both involve an unsettling degree of anachronism. The question Boswell's book prompted for me was, however, different than that Boswell asked. While he was engaged by the similarity that he believed he could detect between such a rite and modern marriage, I was struck by how *different* it was from modern friendship; it is that historical disparity that I have sought to pursue in this book.

At a conference in 1996, the Byzantinist Margaret Mullett said, "We still do not know what brother-making means."[30] Late in the 1990s this would begin to take shape. Boswell rightly grasped that the theology of the *adelphopoiesis* turned on peace-making,[31] a point substantially overlooked by his critics, but one that potentially placed the rite in its context in intellectual history. He remained unaware of the corresponding Catholic rite, the *Ordo ad fratres faciendum* that had been edited by the learned Dominican O. Antonin Zaninović some years before.[32]

The scholarly basis for the study of ritual brotherhood in the Latin West was laid down by two important studies, one of which appeared at the same time as John Boswell's book, the other as a response to it. The first of these was Pierre Chaplais's *Piers Gaveston,* which drew attention to the studies of sworn friendship undertaken by antiquaries since the seventeenth century, begun by Charles Du Fresne Du Cange and the learned Dominican scholar Jacques Goar. The second was the symposium on ritual brotherhood that Elizabeth A. R. Brown edited in the journal *Traditio* (and to which she contributed a piece on medieval Europe).[33] The paper by Claudia Rapp in this collection grasped the analogous social role fulfilled by the various forms of ritual kinship, of which the *adelphopoiesis* was only one part, a point I have argued in this book is as relevant to the Latin West as to Greek and Slavonic cultures. Rapp was developing the insight in the pioneering paper of Evelyn Patlagean in *Annales* in 1978 that first pointed to the telling significance of the "confusion" in the terminology of ritual brotherhood, a view I develop also in this book. Brown's magisterial introductory survey to the symposium as a whole provided the scholarly basis for drawing together much of the extensive work on sworn friendship that up to that point had been fragmented among historians, literary critics, folklorists, and ethnographers.

Friendship and Homosexuality

Two other lines of research were to coincide with these studies. One concerned the difficult conceptual problems raised by a historical approach to homosexuality. This began with questioning the historical background to the ethical anxieties about homosexuality, in John Boswell's *Christianity, Social Tolerance, and Homosexuality.* As I explain in the introduction, *The Friend* revisits

the ethical ground first essayed in Boswell's study in the very different circumstances prevailing now, more than twenty years later. A similarly pioneering work in terms of female friendship was Lillian Faderman's *Surpassing the Love of Men*. Its contemporary counterparts are Valerie Traub, *The
Renaissance of Lesbianism*, and Martha Vicinus, *Intimate Friends*. Despite its title,
the conceptual framework of Traub's book is as much about friendship as
that of Vicinus's book; each can be used for the bibliographical guides they
represent to work that has appeared since Faderman's book.

My own book *Homosexuality in Renaissance England*, first published in 1982,
touched this ground. For reasons I explain in the introduction, *The Friend* is
in a substantial sense the second volume to that study; and in 1990 I published a paper in *History Workshop Journal* that made a first attempt at my
emerging conclusion, in which I explored the common terrain potentially
occupied by the "sodomite" and the male friend. The considerable support
the paper received persuaded me that I was on the right track. Alan Stewart's *Close Readers* was in part a response to this paper; in it he explored the
ends that the common terrain might be made to serve within the defensive
rhetoric of humanist friendship. In my chapter "Friends and Enemies," I revisit that paper in response to Stewart's book. It continues the discussion
between us.

My principal aim here is not to dwell on the widely recognized support
for one aspect of what would become this book. It is, rather, in the controversy that this book will prompt, to discuss the likely significance of two
bodies of work (currently unassociated) that are likely to figure in this controversy. The first concerns masculinity and male homosexuality. The second concerns female homosexuality. Both, I shall argue, raise wider issues
than might at first be apparent.

In the 1990s two book-length studies appeared that sought, while accepting the conclusion in my 1990 paper, to square the findings of that paper with a more familiar view of a "revolutionary" seventeenth century—
emerging out of the crisis into modernity—by relegating its conclusions to
an obsolescent past. In effect they sought to square them with the historiography criticized in this afterword.

The fullest of these discussions was Michael B. Young's *James VI and I*,
which argues that the language employed between King James I and the
duke of Buckingham exceeded the normal bounds of male friendship; that
James treated Buckingham as if he thought of him not as a man but as a *boy:*
and that by the end of the seventeenth century a significant change in this
respect had come about, from such age-structured pederastic relationships
involving an a older man and an adolescent to relationships involving two

adult men. This view has also been proposed in a more nuanced and historical form by Randolph Trumbach.[34]

The second of the two responses to my paper was in Anthony Fletcher's *Gender, Sex, and Subordination in England, 1500–1800*. Fletcher's argument is that men's acutely felt anxiety in sixteenth- and seventeenth-century England about women's sexual voraciousness was solved by the positive values ascribed to women in more modern conceptions of gender, the rise of which his book sets out to chart. He argues also that men's anxieties about the vulnerability of male friendship to a charge of homosexuality were similarly solved by English society's coming to understand homosexuality in gendered terms.[35]

In chapter 5 I set out my radical objections to the way both Young and Fletcher have handled their apparent evidence: the criticism that they have replicated the assertions on which they draw without a critical judgment on the tacit strategies these assertions were designed to fulfill. There is also an intractable factual problem with Fletcher's view on the vulnerability to a charge of homosexuality: in the greatly *increased* rather than diminished impact of the hostility to homosexuality evident in eighteenth-century England, Fletcher is unable to explain a murderous persecution on a scale that England had never before seen (which I described in *Homosexuality in Renaissance England*), which Fletcher excises from the account he gives.[36] That excision is perhaps one of the most telling points about his account.

The limited extent to which female homosexuality impinged on the accounts by Young and Fletcher is countered in the studies by Traub and Vicinus. An important development in charting the history of female homosexuality has taken place in nineteenth-century studies since Lillian Faderman's book appeared. This was the publication of the sexual passages in the diaries of Anne Lister (whom I discuss at length in chapter 6). These appeared in two important selections of passages from her diaries, Helena Whitbread's *I Know My Own Heart* and Jill Liddington's *Female Fortune*. The guide to the vast diaries and other manuscripts on which these books draw is the *Anne Lister Research Directory*, by Ros Westwood, Pat Sewell, and Jill Liddington. These four historians are some of the principal figures among a group of historians in the West Riding of Yorkshire who have studied and edited the Lister manuscripts. In the discussion below I refer to these co-operating scholars as the Calderdale group of historians.

The differences between the work of these historians and my own is marked but should not be overstated. In particular, the questions I pursued owe much to the persuasively argued juxtaposition Liddington makes in *Female Fortune* between Halifax and Shibden Hall's rural traditionalism in the early part of the nineteenth century. My contribution here supports and draws on that distinction as much as it sounds a critical note. I also owe much, on a personal level, to Jill Liddington's unstinting generosity in her discussions with me of my emerging conclusions.

Yet the doubts I voice here return—albeit in a new form—to concerns that were first entertained by studies that preceded those of the Calderdale historians. The first of these earlier researchers was the antiquary John Lister (the inheritor of Shibden Hall), who first published passages from the Lister diaries in the Halifax *Guardian* between 1887 and 1892. In the 1930s Muriel Green catalogued and transcribed the correspondence. In the 1960s Phyllis Ramsden and Vivien Ingham carried out the crucial work of systematically listing the contents of the diaries. Any historian today owes a massive debt to this work, and I acknowledge this unreservedly, even as I raise some radical questions about the contemporary form these studies have taken.

The question I tacitly revisit in my discussion of Anne Lister in this book is the inclusion of these sexual passages in the published selections from the diaries. My point here is not the propriety or otherwise of doing so, although judging by her use of code Lister herself would not have countenanced this. The point is that, given the vast extent of the diaries, any selection can only be a tiny proportion of the whole. A passage in the *Anne Lister Research Directory* added to these developing doubts. It acknowledged Lister's religion as a "research gap."[37] In the selections from the diaries by Whitbread and Liddington, Lister appears as a sexual radical in a religious context (that is, implied in the terms that Liddington uses).[38] In itself this is not improbable. One is dealing with the 1820s and 1830s—not the 1430s. But the point is open to question. On the one hand are the sexual passages. On the other hand is a research gap in Lister's religion. Could the appearance of this sexual radicalism merely be the result of this research gap, of not reading the one with the other? Could it be derived, not from what was included, but from what was *excluded*?

The question that drew me is whether Lister shared the tenacious traditional religious culture that I followed in this book. The difficulty is that, if this is the case, it would not be most apparent from the Lister manuscripts. This religious culture had always been a markedly *material* rather than documentary culture, associated with the sites and rites of a traditional Christianity. The place to look to find the answer would be Halifax Parish Church and (in view of the events of Easter Day 1834 that Liddington included in her selection from the diaries) in Holy Trinity Church in Goodramgate, York. The answers I found there, as my account makes clear, could not to me have been plainer: Anne Lister *did* share that traditional and tenacious religious culture.

Earlier generations of antiquaries in Halifax had a minute interest in the symbolic geography of buildings such as Halifax Parish Church. In that sense I am merely returning to an approach of that kind. Yet the portrait of Lister's sexuality that emerges from the frame of her religion, I acknowledge, is markedly less modern, less radical. It is likely that it will be bitterly controverted. Let me therefore say where I think the judgment will eventually have to rest.

Once the arguments ad hominem and for the preeminence of documentary as opposed to material culture have been laid aside, the issue is likely to crystallize on a point of critical historical judgment on the evidence. Can one distinguish a change during Lister's life? Should one distinguish between her intentions in solemnizing her promise of mutual faith with Mariana Belcombe in July 1821 and her union with Ann Walker in 1834? The terms Lister uses in 1821 have an antiquity to my mind beyond any serious argument, and I have taken them as illuminating her intentions both in 1821 and in 1834. But it may be argued that one should rather *distinguish* the two, that what Lister had in mind in 1834, across what would be much of her lifetime, was something new, fundamentally different—and recognizably modern. Let me therefore say now, plainly, that I regard such a distinction as paper thin. It eludes the critical point that a union between two *families* (the point at the heart of my argument) was as much at issue in 1834 as in 1821. More: to see the inadequacy of such an argument with one's own eyes, one need only visit Holy Trinity Church, Goodramgate, now almost exactly as Lister and Walker saw it and with the same striking antiquity: one (as I recount in the book) that directly reflects the nature of their union in 1834.

In this I am not denying the sexual nature of Lister's friendships, as my account makes plain. The question I raise instead is whether these passages, without their conservative religious frame, occlude the ethical uncertainty that *all* friendship was perceived to have within this moral tradition. The wider point, of course, is whether their effect also occludes that ethical uncertainty today.

The responses Lister and Walker made to that ethical uncertainty do not transfer directly to our world, but I would propose that the justification within a wider frame for my attempted recovery of those responses is the awesome import of that last gesture by Walker for her friend and for the family that had embraced her. Before such a gesture as this, the stars stop in their courses, and water heaven with their tears.

Friendship and the New Literary Criticism

If one line of research concerned the conceptual difficulties raised by the history of homosexuality, a second line of research would eventually arrive at the workings and rhetoric of male friendship in the sixteenth century and was the questioning of sixteenth-century humanism by a recent generation of historicist literary critics. It is here that the work of social historians would converge with a new generation of literary critics and with the history of political thought.

A prelude to this was the difficulty presented by Christopher Marlowe's play *Edward II.* Some critics read the relationship of Edward II and Piers Gaveston in the play as homosexual and Marlowe's treatment as an affirmation of humane values.[39] Others—in marked contrast—read it as an obscenity, apparently with equally persuasive evidence.[40] The assumption that the play *did* deal with an openly homosexual relationship was effectively left unquestioned on both sides of this argument. A neglected early clue was the importance of caricature in the writings of Marlowe, which T. S Eliot pointed to in 1919.[41] Equally overlooked was Laurens Mills's discussion of the role of friendship.[42] The basis of Mills's work was his dissertation, completed in 1925, the importance and originality of which went largely unrecognized because of its incongruence with the dominant historiography. The challenge to the adequacy of that historiography among historians in the 1980s found its counterpart among literary critics in a historicist reading of Marlowe's play.[43]

The debate over Marlowe's *Edward II* proved to be the beginning of a wider move. John Barrell alighted on the same ambivalent workings of male friendship in the context of northern humanism in his "Editing Out." Lisa Jardine's *Erasmus, Man of Letters* was the seminal work that focused the critical questioning of the rhetoric of humanism. Similar conclusions about the workings of male friendship were arrived at by M. J. Ailes from a medieval standpoint[44]—an indication of the extent to which these workings operated in the manuscript as well as in the print culture discussed by Jardine, a point I develop in this book. Jardine's book was quickly followed by Lorna Hutson's *The Usurer's Daughter* and Alan Stewart's *Close Readers.* Laurie Shannon's *Sovereign Amity* extended these studies into the history of political thought.

At the same time David Wootton placed friendship within a broad context of political and intellectual history, first by his discussion of Montaigne, and subsequently by his studies of Thomas More.[45] The defining moment would come with Jacques Derrida's *Politiques de l'amitié,* which drew together those uncertain ethics of friendship that had unmistakably reasserted themselves by this point at the end of the twentieth century: in areas as diverse as social history, sociology, literary criticism, and philosophy.

The emerging work I have followed in this afterword has been no easy path. Much has been at stake. The break this work made with an earlier programmatic view rooted in nineteenth-century historiography enabled it to describe a social cohesion that had an evident continuing vitality, and that description has challenged a dominant view of English history that has identified the changes of the sixteenth century as a watershed. But that debate, as I have argued, was itself only a proxy war. The questioning of that narrative indirectly has articulated some of the most contested issues about the potential shape and direction of postwar society. It still does. It is from this still emerging work that this book has set out, to recover the shape of a history for which a previous orthodoxy had—and still has—no place.

Chapter One

1. Düll, Luttrell, and Keen, "Faithful unto Death." My thanks to the Istanbul Arkeoloji Müzeleri Müdürlügü for their assistance in supplying me with a detailed photograph of the monument. On their careers and families, see Charles Young, *Neville Family*; McFarlane, *Lancastrian Kings*; Clanvowe, *Works*, 25–27.

2. Boutell, *Boutell's Heraldry*, 20, 38 (fig. 64), 159 (fig. 324), and compare 146, 154; Hope, *Stall Plates*, 21; Blackburne and Bond, *St George's Chapel*, 36.

3. Boutell, *Boutell's Heraldry*, 134–139. The Trotton brass is illustrated in Macklin, *Brasses of England*, 145.

4. Boswell, *Same-Sex Unions*.

5. London, British Library, Harleian MS 2259, fol. 27v. On Richard Strangways, see London, "Medieval Treatises."

6. *Amis and Amiloun*, 101.

7. McFarlane, "Business-Partnership."

8. *Romance of Guy of Warwick . . . 14th-Century Version*, 280–281; *Romance of Guy of Warwick . . . 15th-Century Version*, 135; Henry of Huntingdon, *Historia Anglorum*, 185.

9. Düll, Luttrell, and Keen, "Faithful unto Death," 175.

10. Boutell, *Boutell's Heraldry*, 116.

11. Hector and Harvey, *Westminster Chronicle*, 480–481. I made the translation given here.

12. Cicero, *De Senectute, De Amicitia*, 188–189.

13. Bartlett, *Gerald of Wales*.

14. Petrie, *Christian Inscriptions*, 2:61–62 and plate 35 (Dicul and Maelodran), 70 and fig. 77b (Ultan and Dubthach), 60–61 and plate 34 (Diarmait and Mac Cois). Compare 1:48–49, plate 28, and 2:24, 26, plates 17 and 18. My thanks to Robert Tobin for pointing out to me the monument to Diarmait and Mac Cois, and to Mark Cashman for visiting the site for me and photographing the monument.

15. Bodleian Library, Laud MS 720, fol. 224v, "De argumento nequitiae et novo desponsationis genere." I have given the collated transcription as in Gerald of Wales, *Opera*, 5:167.

16. In Michaud and Poujoulat, *Collection des Mémoires*, ser. 1, 2:444, 457.

17. As in the contemporary twelfth-century Magdalen and "Ely" pontificals given in *Manuale*. The Holy Trinity mass is also specified for betrothal in the three great late-medieval manuals:

York (*Manuale,* 29), Sarum (*Manuale,* appendix, 21), and Hereford (*Manuale,* appendix, 119). See also Stevenson, *Nuptial Blessing.*

18. *Cartulary of Oseney Abbey,* 4:1; *English Register of Oseney Abbey,* 5 ("Robert Doyly and Roger of Iuory").

19. Anglo-Saxon Chronicle E, in Plummer, *Saxon Chronicles Parallel,* 1:29; *Anglo-Saxon Chronicle,* 152.

20. Chaplais, *Piers Gaveston,* with Hamilton, *Piers Gaveston.*

21. I have given Chaplais's transcription as in *Piers Gaveston,* 13. See also Haskins, "Civil Wars of Edward II," 75.

22. *Amis and Amiloun,* 101.

23. *Vita Edwardi Secundi,* 7, 17, 28.

24. *Annales Paulini* in Stubbs, *Reigns of Edward I and Edward II,* 1:263.

25. Public Record Office, C54, 124, membrane 13d.

26. Guillaume de Jumièges, *Gesta Normannorum Ducum,* 109, "sumi nexu amoris."

27. For Worcester, see Anglo-Saxon Chronicle D, in Plummer, *Saxon Chronicles Parallel,* 2:152, and Florentii Wigorniensis, *Monachi Chronicon,* 178. For Peterborough, see Anglo-Saxon Chronicle E. For Durham, see *Historia Ecclesiae Dunhelmensis* in *Symeonis Monachi,* 1:219, and *Historia Regum* in 2:174–175. For Malmesbury, see William of Malmesbury, *De Gestis Regum Anglorum* 1:219.

28. *Laȝamons Brut:* Octa and Ebissa, Iuore and Yuni, Cadwalan and Edwine, Dunwale and Stater and Rudauc.

29. Henry of Huntingdon, *Historia Anglorum,* 185.

30. Florentii Wigorniensis, *Monachi Chronicon;* Hart, "Early Section of the *Worcester Chronicle.*"

31. *Annales Paulini* and possibly *Vita Edwardi Secundi.*

32. *Chronicon de Lanercrost,* 210.

33. The term "wedded" is that used in the romance *Athelston* and in Brie's transcription of the Dublin manuscript of the widely read Middle English *Brut* chronicle; see *Brut,* part 1, p. 120. Other common forms were "wed brother" or "sworn brother." The Latin terms are those employed in the above chronicles and register.

34. The traces of their oral counterparts, as Tessa Watt describes them (*Cheap Print and Popular Piety*), in the context of sworn brotherhood can be seen in Layamon's *Brut; Floris and Blancheflour; King Horn; Adam Bell, Clim of the Clough, and William of Cloudesly; Bewick and Graham;* and *Amys and Amylion.*

35. *Bewick and Graham,* in Child, *English and Scottish Popular Ballads,* part 7, pp. 147, 148.

36. Bodleian Library, Laud MS 720, 16.

37. Thompson, *Folktale,* 111 ff.

38. *Laȝamons Brut,* 3:295–296, 2:181, 265, 341. In *Brut,* translated by Rosamund Allen, 234, "wedbrother" is inappropriately translated as "blood-brother," elsewhere employing the more appropriate translation of "sworn brother" for the same term.

39. McFarlane, *Lancastrian Kings,* 183.

40. See Chaucer, *Complete Works,* for the *Knightes Tale* (at 4:33–34, 46), the *Shipmannes Tale* (4:168), the *Freres Tale* (4:362), and the *Pardoners Tale* (4:311, 314). See also Hermann, "Dismemberment, Dissemination, Discourse." V. A. Kolve's penetrating study of the theology of the *Freres Tale* in "Man in the Middle" touches on the conclusions of this study. The friars were preachers, and the *Freres Tale* is in the form of an *exemplum* used to illustrate a sermon. Kolve identified in the *Freres Tale* the same theology of grace that I argue was present in the eucharistic rite discussed in this study, but in word rather than sacrament, with the preacher's call that closes the tale.

41. McFarlane, "Business-Partnership," 291–292.

42. *Story of Genesis and Exodus,* 24, 44.

43. *Amys and Amylion*, edited by Le Saux, 32.

44. "Thy brother / Y-sworn full deep, and each of us till other [deeply sworn, and each of us pledged to the other], / That never, for to die in the pain [though we should die by torture for it], / Till that the death depart shall us twain [till that death shall part us two] / Neither of us in love to hinder other, / Ne in none other case, my leve [dear] brother; . . . We will meddle [mingle] us each with other / That no man, be he never so wroth [angry], / Shall have that one of two but both / at once, all beside his leave [without asking his leave], / Come we a-morwe or on eve, / Be we cried or still y-rouned" (*Hous of Fame* in Chaucer, *Complete Works*, 3:62, and the *Knightes Tale*, 4:33–34). The modern wording is by Skeat from this edition or by Cawley from his edition of the *Canterbury Tales.*

45. Other monuments on joint tombs lack inscriptions and might not be the parent and child or the brothers or sisters by blood that one would otherwise assume them to be. These include the brass of a franklin and a priest in the church of St. John the Baptist, Shottesbrooke, Berkshire, c. 1370, in Waller and Waller, *Monumental Brasses*, plate at 1370 43 Edw III; Morley, *Monumental Brasses of Berkshire*, 174, 177, 179; and Beaumont, *Ancient Memorial Brasses*, 43; two ladies, Narborough, Norfolk, c. 1400, in *Monumental Brasses: The Portfolio Plates*, no. 100; two priests, Great Marlow, Buckinghamshire, c. 1475, in *Monumental Brasses: The Portfolio Plates*, no. 204; two franklins, King's Somborne, Hampshire, c. 1380, in Macklin, *Brasses of England*, 59; and Page, *History of Hampshire*, 4:478–479; the "Civilian and wife" in *Monumental Brasses: The Portfolio Plates*, no. 57, to which compare *Portfolio of the Monumental Brass Society*, vol. 1 (June 1894 to December 1899), part 6 (December 1896), plate 1.

46. *Laʒamons Brut*, 1:177 (with 3:225, 465), and *Layamon's Brut*, ed. Hall, 96, 139, with the comments by Hall at line 692.

47. *Amis and Amiloun*, 101.

48. Shaw, "Ritual Brotherhood," 329, 350, 354.

49. McFarlane, "Business-Partnership," 290–291.

50. Boswell, *Same-Sex Unions*, 281, 188.

51. Pollock and Maitland, *History of English Law*, 31.

52. A powerful criticism of the usefulness to historians of the notion of "feudalism" is Elizabeth Brown, "Tyranny of a Construct."

53. McFarlane, "Business-Partnership," 291.

54. Shaw, "Groom of One's Own?"

55. McFarlane, "Business-Partnership," 309.

56. *Chronica Monasterii de Melsa*, 2:355; Hamilton, *Piers Gaveston*, 16, 109. I share the skepticism of Elizabeth Brown and J. S. Hamilton about Chaplais's doubts on this point. See Brown, "Ritual Brotherhood in Western Medieval Europe," 379–380; Hamilton, "Menage à Roi." See also Poos, "Heavy-Handed Marriage Counsellor"; Bossy, *Christianity in the West*, 18–19; Bossy, "Godparenthood," 194–201. Also pertinent here are Rocke, *Forbidden Friendships*, 108–109, 170–172; Rapp, "Ritual Brotherhood," 324–325; Kretzenbacher, "Serbische-orthodoxe 'Wahlverbrüderung,'" 163–183.

57. Michaud and Poujoulat, *Collection des Mémoires*, 457; McFarlane, "Business-Partnership," 309.

58. The point is well made by Jordan, "Romance of the Gay Couple," 301–310.

Chapter Two

1. British Library, Additional MS 64875, fols. 164–171v, from which the quotations below are taken. The manuscript is calendared in Royal Commission on Historical Manuscripts, "Twelfth Report: Appendix," part 1, 1:89–91. It is partly transcribed in Farmer, "Fulke Greville and Sir John Coke," 218–219; and in Rees, *Fulke Greville*, 22–25, with a photograph of part of Fulke Gre-

ville's letter. The Latin letter at fol. 164 was apparently enclosed with Greville's letter at 166–167v, in a parcel formed by fols. 165–165v (which carries the endorsement I refer to below). A copy of John Coke's reply is at fols. 168–171v. The manuscripts were preserved among the papers at Melbourne Hall, Derbyshire, and are now in the British Library. I am grateful for the assistance of the honorary archivist at the hall, Mr. Howard Usher. See also Aubrey, *Brief Lives*, 2:249; Rees, "Fulke Greville's Epitaph on Sidney," 47–51; Wilson, "Two Names of Friendship," 70–72; Michael Young, *Servility and Service*. The version of Shakespeare's twenty-ninth sonnet in the epigraph for this chapter is that presented by Barrell, "Editing Out," 20–21, for the reasons he gives in that essay.

2. British Library, Lansdowne MS 24, fol. 196v. My transcription differs from that in the note in Stow, *Survey of London*, 2:349.

3. The remains of the shrine of St. Erkenwald (and the memorial to Nicholas Bacon and his wives mentioned below) are shown in the contemporary engravings by Wenceslaus Hollar. See Pennington, *Etched Work of Wenceslaus Hollar*, 342, 348; Dugdale, *History of Saint Paul's Cathedral*, plates facing pp. 74 and 50. On their position, see Cook, *Old S. Paul's Cathedral*, 46–47.

4. Greville, *Prose Works*, 5.

5. Robertson, "Sidney and Bandello," 326–328 and plate 11.

6. Greville, *Prose Works*, 4. See also Rebholz, *Life of Fulke Greville*, and Duncan-Jones, *Sir Philip Sidney*. For Philip Sidney's will, see Sidney, *Miscellaneous Prose*, 149.

7. Jardine, *Erasmus*; Maurer, "Poetical Familiarity"; Swett, "Honor, Reciprocity, and Companionship." Each of these studies arrives at conclusions about the familiar letter that are comparable to those I set out in this chapter. A partly differing approach is adopted by Bergeron in *King James and Letters of Homoerotic Desire*. A major study of humanist epistolography is Najemy, *Between Friends*.

8. Ungerer, *Spaniard in Elizabethan England*, especially the letters in the first volume; Pérez, *Ad Comitem Essexivm*, Epistola 75, and in *Cartas de Antonio Perez*, British Library 246/i/8.

9. Wootton, "Francis Bacon."

10. Ungerer, *Spaniard in Elizabethan England*, 1:299.

11. For a copy of John Coke's reply, see British Library, Additional MS 64875, fols. 168–171v.

12. Greville, *Prose Works*, xxxvi–xl.

13. British Library, Lansdowne MSS 12, fol. 217; 107, fol. 170; 12, fols. 217–217v; 21, fol. 26; 36, fol. 212v (also 12, fols. 117–117v; 23, fols. 179–179v; 25, fol. 135; 31, fol. 40; 107, fols. 170–170v; 36, fols. 212–213; 107, fols. 168–168v; 61, fol. 170). These are discussed in Alan Smith, *Servant of the Cecils*, 22, 70, 92–96.

14. British Library, Additional MSS, Evelyn Correspondence, 12, items 1224–1246.

15. Bacon, *Letters and the Life*, 4:139–140, 144–145, 7:286–287, 428–431, 542.

16. Kinder, *Casiodoro de Reina*, 25–26, 95–97. See also McFadden, *Antonio del Corro*, 165 ff., 392.

17. Rees, *Fulke Greville*, 46. For the support Philip Sidney gave in this, see Duncan-Jones, *Sir Philip Sidney*, 197.

18. Duncan-Jones, *Sir Philip Sidney*, 224.

19. Bacon, *Harmony of the Essays*, 32–33.

20. Greville, *Prose Works*, xiii.

21. Rebholz, *Life of Fulke Greville*, 96, 197; Michael Young, *Servility and Service*, 9–18, 34.

22. Wilson, "Two Names of Friendship," 70, 80.

23. British Library, Lansdowne MS 107, fol. 168.

24. Gruenfelder, "Electoral Patronage," 557.

25. British Library, Harleian MS 285, fol. 173; also in Dudley, *Correspondence*, 33.

26. Adams, "Gentry of North Wales," 138, 147.

27. East Sussex Record Office, PAR 232/1/1/1, fol. 20 (and 23v, 28).

28. Cornwallis, "Of Friendship and Factions," in his *Essayes* (1600–1601), E2, E4, E6. See also Wootton, "Francis Bacon"; Charles Smith, "Sententious Theory," 170.

29. Cornwallis, *Essayes* (1600–1601), E3v.

30. Duncan-Jones, *Sir Philip Sidney*, 22–23.

31. Ungerer, *Spaniard in Elizabethan England*, 2:47–48.

32. Ibid, 1:327, 472–473.

33. Pérez, *Ad Comitem Essexivm*, Epistola 34. The words "vestre" and "amicitie" have an accent mark below the letter not reproduced here.

34. Rebholz, *Life of Fulke Greville*, 197–198; Michael Young, *Servility and Service*, 35–38. Michael Young rightly describes Fulke Greville's letter of 1615 as "a peace-offering" and a reconciliation.

35. The reading is "faythefully" and not "fully," as in Michael Young, *Servility and Service*, 37.

36. In the afterword I acknowledge the considerable debt I owe here to the intellectual stimulus of Peter Brown.

37. Michael Young, *Servility and Service*, 203 n. 46.

38. Nashe, *Works*, 1:159.

39. Barrell, "Editing Out," 30, 34.

40. McLoughlin, "*Amicitia* in Practice," 165–181; Haseldine, "Friendship and Rivalry"; Haseldine, "Language of *Amicitia*"; Haseldine, "Love, Separation"; Southern, *Saint Anselm*, 67–76; Cowdrey, "Pope Gregory VII"; Robinson, "Friendship Network"; Waddell, "Exegesis of a Letter."

41. *Adambel Clym of the Cloughe and Wyllyam of Cloudesle*; *History of Adam Bell*.

42. Puttenham, *Arte of English Poesie*, 83–84.

43. Walter Scott's view on the date of *Bewick and Graham* is given in *Minstrelsy of the Scottish Border*, 267. See also the comments by Francis James Child in the introduction to his edition of *Bewick and Graham* in Child, *English and Scottish Popular Ballads*, part 7, pp. 144–145.

44. *Annales Paulini* in Stubbs, *Reigns of Edward I and Edward II*, 1:258.

45. *Amys and Amylion*, 32; Chaucer, *Complete Works*, 4:33; *Romance of Guy of Warwick . . . 15th-Century Version*, 134, 284; *Romance of Guy of Warwick . . . 14th-Century Version*, 574–575.

46. *Amis and Amiloun*, cix–cx. I owe this point to a suggestion of Helen Cooper.

47. British Library, Additional MS 64875, fol. 170v.

48. Rubin, *Corpus Christi*, 293.

49. Pocock, *Ancient Constitution*.

50. Clanvowe, *Works*, 35–53.

51. Richard Harvey, "Lamb of God," 176–180; preface to Robert Greene's *Menaphon*, in Nashe, *Works*, 3:311–325; Hutson, *Thomas Nashe in Context*, 198–199.

52. Gabriel Harvey, *Fovre Letters and Certeine Sonnets*, 44; Nashe, *Works*, 1:303; Gabriel Harvey, *Works*, 2:77–78.

53. Gabriel Harvey, *Works*, 2:16, on which see Nashe, *Works*, 5:89–90. For Gabriel Harvey and the household of the earl of Leicester, see Jardine and Grafton, "Studied for Action."

54. Cornwallis, "Of Loue," in *Essayes* (1600–1601), D8v.

55. Cornwallis, *Essayes . . . Newlie corrected*. The emblematic interpretation here is in contrast to the supposition in William Hunt, "Sir William Cornwallis," *Dictionary of National Biography*, 12:244, and O'Donoghue and Hake, *Engraved British Portraits*, 1:494, that the second figure was Sir Charles Cornwallis (the father of William Cornwallis); and to that of Hind, Corbett, and Nor-

ton, *Engraving in England*, vol. 3, who suggested that the second figure was a double portrait of William Cornwallis himself.

Chapter Three

1. Wood, *History and Antiquities*, 23; Bott, *Monuments in Merton College*, 58–59, and plan 2 following p. 12; Garrod, *Ancient Painted Glass*. Two saints are depicted on a similar "bracket" monument in the brass illustrated in Macklin, *Brasses of England*, 74. On the paintings on the stalls (now lost), see Wood's comment in *Life and Times*, 1:309. On the first name, see Bennett, "Spiritual Kinship." On the use of "godbrother" (and "godsister") in these terms, see *Oxford English Dictionary*, 6:643, 647; and on the wider usage than these entries alone would indicate, Llinos Beverley Smith, "Fosterage, Adoption, and God-Parenthood," 30, on the phrases "anglice godbrother and godsister" and "frater spiritualis" from the courts of the diocese of Hereford, 1507–1509. On name giving and the saint's name as that of the saint as *patrinus*, see Bossy, *Christianity in the West*, 17; Bossy, "Godparenthood," 196. The epigraph for this chapter is from John 19:25–27, New English Bible.

2. Carlson, *Marriage and the English Reformation*, 124; *Amys and Amylion*, 32; *Floris and Blancheflour*, 45; *Romance of Guy of Warwick . . . 14th-Century Version*, 280; *Story of Genesis and Exodus*, 44; *Bewick and Graham* in Child, *English and Scottish Popular Ballads*, part 7, pp. 146, 147. Also relevant here is Pedersen, "Did the Medieval Laity Know the Canon Law Rules on Marriage?" in which the answer is that they did.

3. *Athelston*, 67–68.

4. *Floris and Blancheflour*, 45.

5. *Romance of Guy of Warwick . . . 14th-Century Version*, 280, 306.

6. Manuscript D in Plummer, *Saxon Chronicles Parallel*, 2:152, in the one case, and the Laud Manuscript in the other, 2:153.

7. *Vita Edwardi Secundi*, 28.

8. Chaplais, *Piers Gaveston*, 13; *Amis and Amiloun*, 101.

9. Painter, *Palace of Pleasure*, fol. 336v.

10. Greene, *Life and Complete Works*, 13:88.

11. Chaplais, *Piers Gaveston*, 33.

12. Rapp, "Ritual Brotherhood," 319, 323.

13. Peter Brown, *Cult of the Saints*, 12–22.

14. Norfolk Record Office, Consistory Court Wills, 32, Wight. The date is given in Farrow and Millican, *Index to Wills*, 1:216. "Bulleyne" is the form used in William Jekkes's will. The more familiar form is of course "Boleyn." My thanks to Dr. Eamon Duffy for this reference (and to the Norfolk Record Office for a copy of the will).

15. Gonville and Caius, MS 614/767, pp. 174–175. There is a transcription in Caius, *Annals*, 233. See also Venn, *Biographical History*, 1:142–143, 151; Brooke, *Gonville and Caius*, 114.

16. MacCulloch, "Henry Chitting's Suffolk Collections," 113–114.

17. *Amis and Amiloun*, 109–110.

18. Edward VI, *First Prayer-Book*, 212, 244. The phrase was included in the institution narrative in the second Edwardian liturgy of 1552 and retained in subsequent English revisions, including those of 1559 and 1604.

19. On John Gostlin and Thomas Legge (here and below), see Venn, *Biographical History*, 3:64–69, 74–85, 169, and plates before pp. 164, 169; Brooke, *Gonville and Caius*, 79 ff., 104 ff.; Caius, *Annals*, where the passage on the memorial of Legge is at pp. 213–214. My thanks to Jean Wilson for pointing out to me the memorial to Gostlin's friendship with Legge. On the religious tensions in the college, see in particular Venn, *Early Collegiate Life*, 80–103, 146–150.

20. Brooke, *Gonville and Caius*, 80 n. 3. The inscription I quote appears to be too integral a part of the monument to have been added in 1626.

21. British Library, Harleian MS 7031/243, a copy made by the antiquary Thomas Baker from a contemporary manuscript account. My transcription differs in some respects from that of Venn, *Biographical History*, 3:78–79.

22. Moran, *Catholic Archbishops of Dublin*, 1:446 (in the appendix); McCarthy, *Irish Church History*, 1:122; Bossy, "Counter-Reformation," 155–169.

23. Venn, *Biographical History*, 3:65.

24. Brooke, *Gonville and Caius*, 92.

25. Venn, *Biographical History*, 3:75.

26. Greene, *Frier Bacon and frier Bongay*, H1r. For contemporary analogies to Greene's two scholars, see O'Day, "Room at the Top," 37; O'Day, *Family and Family Relationships*, 73, 281; Venn, *Biographical History*, xiii.

27. Gonville and Caius, MS 614/767, p. 157, with a transcription in Caius, *Annals*, 214.

28. Gonville and Caius, MS 614/767, p. 175, with a transcription in Caius, *Annals*, 233.

29. *Amis and Amiloun*, 109.

30. The manuscript described in James, *Descriptive Catalogue*, 2:199–201, is said to have been given to the college by William Moore. It contains among other items the text of Middle English romances including *Athelston*. The nineteenth-century catalogue of the manuscripts in the university contains a fourteenth-century manuscript of the Latin *Amys and Amylion*; see Luard and Hardwick, *Catalogue of the Manuscripts*, 4:380–383.

31. Bodleian Library, Tanner MS 72, fol. 14r–v. Godfrey Goodman printed a transcription (which differs from my own) in his *Court of King James the First*, 2:379. James O. Halliwell printed a version in his *Letters of Kings of England*, 2:236. There are versions in modern spelling and layout in Akrigg, *Letters of King James VI and I*, 431–432, and Bergeron, *King James*, 173–175 (with a photograph of fol. 14v). I have read Goodman's "pullet" and Halliwell's "billet" as "p^{rst}," that is, with Akrigg and Bergeron as "present." The sheet was folded back so that fol. 14r or its reverse side—the open edges of fol. 14r and 14v being bound together into the volume—would have formed the outer membrane of the letter; both lack any sign of a seal or direction (as I discuss below). William Oldys added the annotation to fol. 14r that I mention below.

32. National Library of Scotland, Advocates MS 33.1.7, vol. 22, no. 77. "For them" has been deleted after "word." There are versions in modern spelling in Williamson, *George Villiers*, 243 (from the later copy in British Library, Harleian MS 6987, fol. 225v), and Bergeron, *King James*, 183–184.

33. Cardwell, *Canons of 1604*; Herbert, "Countrey Parson," 3:174. Herbert adds "afore and after harvest, and the beginning of Lent."

34. *Oxford English Dictionary*, s.v. "marriage," definition 2b.

35. Cornwallis, "Of Loue," in *Essayes* (1600–1601), D8v; Chaucer, *Complete Works*, 3:62.

36. Lockyer, *Buckingham*, 197–198, 233. Akrigg, *Letters of King James VI and I*, 431–432, dates James's letter as "December 1623?" although he adds that D. Harris Wilson "was quite possibly correct" in dating the letter as December 1624 (445). The argument Akrigg makes at p. 432—that the reference to physical separation may be an indirect reference to Buckingham's return from Spain—could apply to 1624. Williamson, *George Villiers*, 121, 243, tentatively dated Buckingham's letter to 1622 on the grounds that in the letter the purchase of New Hall appears recent. Bergeron, *King James*, 173, 183, followed Akrigg in dating James's letter (and Williamson in dating Buckingham's letter). Bingham adopted the same dating as Lockyer in her *James I of England*, 205.

37. Lockyer, "English *Valido?*" 50; Lockyer, *James VI and I.*

38. Gardiner, *History of England*, 5:184.

39. Lockyer, *Buckingham*, 193.

40. On the uncertainty of observers at this point, see ibid., 198.

41. I have taken the annotation on fol. 14r as that of the eighteenth-century antiquary William Oldys.

42. Bergeron, *King James*, 160. On the public context of the letters between James I and the duke of Buckingham, see Jonathan Goldberg, *James I*, 143. Akrigg's comments on James's use of a secretary and of his own hand are in *Letters of King James VI and I*, 24, 26–27.

43. National Library of Scotland, Advocates MS 33.1.7, vol. 22, no. 87; also in Williamson, *George Villiers*, 259; Bergeron, *King James*, 210.

44. Bingham, *James I of England*, 205; McElwee, *Wisest Fool in Christendom*, 275.

45. Chamberlain, *Letters*, 2:430; Lockyer, *Buckingham*, 119–120, 461. I have given the date in the style of Chamberlain's contemporary letter, written later that day.

46. British Library, Harleian MS 6987, fol. 42r; also in Akrigg, *Letters of King James VI and I*, 401, and Bergeron, *King James*, 159. James uses the term "Christen gosseppe" at British Library, Lansdowne MS 1236, fol. 64v; also in Akrigg, 387, and Bergeron, 150. Compare Lockyer, *Buckingham*, 152: James describes himself as *Buckingham's* gossip—"thy perpetuall gosseppe"—not as that of the child (as its godfather), in the sense adverted to by the *Oxford English Dictionary*, s.v. "gossip," definition 1d. Akrigg is evidently alert to the issue and more cautious at pp. 402 and 447.

47. On Buckingham's dukedom, see Lockyer, *Buckingham*, 154–155.

48. British Library, Lansdowne MS 1236, fol. 64v; also in Akrigg, *Letters of King James VI and I*, 387, and Bergeron, *King James*, 150; Harleian MS 6987, fols. 141r and 188r; also in Akrigg, 423, 441, and Bergeron, 172, 178.

49. On this see Flandrin, *Families in Former Times*, 4–10.

50. Macpherson, Caley, and Illingworth, *Rotuli Scotiae*, 2:75.

51. Boutell, *Boutell's Heraldry*, 140, 154; Friar, *New Dictionary of Heraldry*, 115–116.

52. O'Hara, "Ruled by My Friends"; Tadmor, "'Family' and 'Friend' in *Pamela.*"

53. MacCulloch, "Henry Chitting's Suffolk Collections," 103–105, 113–114, 125; MacCulloch, *Suffolk and the Tudors*, 118.

54. McFarlane, *Lancastrian Kings*, 176, 172, 232.

55. Raine et al., *Wills and Inventories*, 38–42.

56. Parsons, *Salle*, 182–183; Sidney, *Miscellaneous Prose*, 149.

57. Laing, *Early Metrical Tales*, 2.

58. Maddern, "Best Trusted Friends," 112; Hanham, *Celys*, 9–10.

59. Cox, *Parish Registers*, 49–58.

60. Hanham, *Celys*, 64, 69–70, 9, 93–94, 99; Maddern, "Best Trusted Friends," 106; O'Day, "Room at the Top," 37; O'Day, *Family and Family Relationships*, 73, 87, 281; Cox, *Parish Registers*, 51.

61. Cox, *Parish Registers*, 55.

62. Hanham, *Celys*, 93.

63. Hamilton, *Piers Gaveston*, 29–30.

64. *Bewick and Graham*, in Child, *English and Scottish Popular Ballads*, part 7, p. 147.

65. Lander, "'Family,' 'Friends,' and Politics."

66. Hamilton, *Piers Gaveston*, 100–102.

67. McFarlane, "Business-Partnership," 290, 310.

68. Hamilton, *Piers Gaveston*, 100.

69. Cambridge, Trinity College, MS O.3, fol. 58r. The *Amice Christi Johannes* is the penultimate item on the roll. I have followed the transcription given in the second edition of R. L. Greene, *Early English Carols*, 55, with the abbreviations as expanded there. Other variants of this genre are on pp. 55–58. The comments on Oxford, Bodleian MS Eng. Poet. e.1., associated with Beverley Minster are on pp. 317–318. On the date of the manuscript in Trinity College Cambridge, see p. 327. I have followed Davies in *Medieval English Lyrics*, 157, in glossing "may" as virgin. A recent work on the much discussed connection between the religious lyric and preaching is Siegfried Wenzel, *Preachers, Poets, and the Early English Lyric*. The manuscripts of the preaching notebooks of the friars are discussed by Rosemary Woolf in appendix A to her important work *The English Religious Lyric in the Middle Ages*. For her discussion of the scene with John at the foot of the cross, see pp. 221–222. On the popularity of this lyric, see Greene, *Early English Carols*, 366; Stevens, *Mediaeval Carols*, 117.

70. The question I pose here was prompted by Peter Brown's *Cult of the Saints*.

71. The three scenes are at John 13:23, 18:28–19:16, and 19:25–27. The quotation from Christ's farewell discourse is from John 14:27 and 15:15. The translation is from the Jerusalem Bible. The reference to the disciple "quem diligebat Iesus" [whom Jesus loved] is John 13:23.

72. From the introduction to Grisdale, *Three Middle English Sermons*, xxv.

73. I am grateful to John Bossy for pointing this out to me.

74. *Story of Genesis and Exodus*, 24, 44.

75. Greene, *Early English Carols*, 57.

76. Grisdale, *Three Middle English Sermons*, 47.

77. Greene, *Early English Carols*, 56 (if "Prynce" is vocative as "Amice"). It is possible that "the Prynce of Pees" in the version I quote above is also vocative and addressed to John as himself the Prince of Peace as Christ's friend, but there I think it is on balance more probable that "Prey" is transitive and has a personal object (in Christ), seeking John's intercession.

78. Greene, *Early English Carols*, 56.

79. Florentius Wigorniensis, *Monachi Chronicon*, 1:178.

80. Henry of Huntingdon, *Historia Anglorum*, 185.

81. 1 Samuel 18:3–4, 20:41–42, 23:18; 2 Samuel 1:26.

82. William of Malmesbury, *De Gestis Regum Anglorum*, 210; Haskins, "Civil Wars of Edward II," 75; Florentius Wigorniensis, *Monachi Chronicon*, 178–179; 1 Samuel 20:41–42, "et osculantes se alterutrum . . . Dixit ergo . . . Vade in pace"; Henry of Huntingdon, *Historia Anglorum*, 185.

83. Cornwallis, "Of Loue," in *Essayes* (1600–1601), D8r–D8v.

84. *Adam Bell, Clim of the Clough, and William of Cloudesly*, in Child, *English and Scottish Popular Ballads*, part 5, pp. 25, 26.

85. Michaud and Poujoulat, *Collection des Mémoires*, ser. 1, 2:444, 456.

86. Bodleian Library, Laud MS 720, fol. 224v, with the transcription in Gerald of Wales, *Opera*, 5:167.

87. "Tunc ingrediantur in Ecclesiam" and "et post intrent omnes in Ecclesiam" in the contemporary "Ely" and Magdalen pontificals, *Manuale*, 160, 162. On the church door, see Bossy, *Christianity in the West*, 14, 21, 25; Bradley, "Quem Aspicientes Viverunt."

88. *Amys and Amylion*, 32.

89. Elizabeth Brown, "Ritual Brotherhood in Western Medieval Europe," 361. The Slavonic rites are discussed with a translation in Woods, "Same-Sex Unions." Translations of the Greek rites are given by Boswell in *Same-Sex Unions*, 291–306, 311–323, 327–341, 345–363. I discuss the reactions to John Boswell's book more fully in the afterword. While my views here can be attrib-

uted only to myself, the generous comments of Archimandrite Ephrem on an earlier draft have helped me to avoid some potential pitfalls. I also owe a considerable debt to Dr. Wendy Bracewell for drawing to my attention the study by O. Antonin Zaninović, discussed below, and for her translation of the study.

90. Boswell, *Same-Sex Unions*, 296, 304, 314, 317, 322, 331, 339, translates "proskyno" here as "kissing," as does Woods, "Same-Sex Unions," 339, with the equivalent term used in the Old Church Slavonic. Robin Darling Young's reservations about Boswell's translation, in "Gay Marriage," 48, are shared by Archimandrite Ephrem, who proposes the less explicit translation of "venerate" in his review of John Boswell's book (53). A "kiss," of course, need not be an actual *osculum oris.* Zaninović (see below) documents the use of the kiss of peace. The present conditions in Croatia have not enabled me to consult the original manuscript, and my edition must be provisional on this.

91. Rapp, "Ritual Brotherhood," 323.

92. I have employed the transcription in Zaninović, "Dva Latinska spomenika," 715–716. Zaninović gives the manuscript's reference in the library of the church of St. John in Trogir as manuscript missal no. 5.

93. Woods, "Same-Sex Unions," 339.

94. Carlson, *Marriage and the English Reformation*, 125–126, 133–134.

95. *Chronicon de Lanercrost*, 210.

96. From the Slavonic *Euchologion Sinaiticum* translated by Woods, "Same-Sex Unions," 338–340.

97. As for example in Vatican Library, Barberini Gr. MS 336, for which see Strittmatter, "Barberinum S. Marci," and the *Euchologion Sinaiticum*, which Ephrem discusses in his review of Boswell's book (52).

98. Vasey, "Family and the Liturgy."

99. Rubin, *Corpus Christi*, 336 and passim.

100. The troubled history of the Greek canon law on the *adelphopoiesis* is set out in Rapp, "Ritual Brotherhood." That among Catholics using the corresponding Latin rite is set out (inter alia) in Wendy Bracewell's as yet unpublished paper on ritual brotherhood on the frontiers of the *triplex confinium*, which will be a major contribution to the subject.

101. From the "Nicene" Creed, used in the mass before the Reformation and in the later reformed Order for the Administration of the Lord's Supper, or Holy Communion, of 1559 (and in subsequent revisions).

102. I owe this understanding of the "sacrifice" in the mass to Bossy, "Mass as a Social Institution."

103. "The Kiss of the Crusaders," BBC Radio 4, broadcast 12 June 1999, transcript.

104. Franklyn and Tanner, *Encyclopaedic Dictionary of Heraldry*, 1.

105. Shakespeare, *Shake-Speares Sonnets*, C1.

106. Martial, *Martial, Book XI*, 25 (text), 118–121 (commentary); Virgil, *Virgil*, 2:362, book 12, line 932; Dryden, *Poems*, 3:1423; Virgil, *Aeneid*, 287. See also Orgel, *Impersonations*, 56–57.

107. Barrell, "Editing Out," 12.

Chapter Four

1. I am grateful to Christ's College for the access I have been given to this monument and its inscription, signed "JOSEPHUS CATTERNS / Londinensis / sculpsit." See Royal Commission on Historical Monuments, *An Inventory of the Historical Monuments in the City of Cambridge*, part 1, 28–32 and plates 96 and 98–99. Detailed commentary, transcriptions, and translations (which I have not necessarily followed) are in Malloch, *Finch and Baines*; Wilson, "Two Names of Friendship,"

71–79. The quotation in the epigraph for this chapter is a translation of the words of institution in the canon of the mass.

2. British Library, Sloane MS 3329, fols. 5r–6v; also in Malloch, *Finch and Baines,* 75, and Wilson, "Two Names of Friendship," 73.

3. Sévigné, *Lettres,* 2:197; North, *Lives,* 2:422.

4. With some reluctance, I have followed the transcription "sacros" of Malloch and Wilson rather than the obscure "saeros."

5. Taylor, *Whole Works,* 1:69–98, with quotations from 86 and 91. The editions of *A Discourse of Friendship* (entitled *A Discourse of the Nature, Offices, and Measures of Friendship, with Rules of conducting It* when in 1657 it was published separately from his *Polemical Discourses*) are discussed in Gathorne-Hardy and Williams, *Bibliography of the Writings of Jeremy Taylor,* 82–86. A recent discussion of the *Discourse* is Askew, *Muskets and Altars,* 182–190.

6. This is shown in Royal Commission on Historical Monuments, *An Inventory of the Historical Monuments in the City of Cambridge,* plate 96, but had evidently been removed when I visited the chapel in the summer of 2000.

7. Marshall and Marshall, *Latin Prayer Book of Charles II.* The edition I have used is the *Liturgia seu Liber Precum Communium,* D6r, F5v.

8. Taylor, *Whole Works,* 1:98. The quotation attributed to Solomon seems rather an echo of Cicero, *De Amicitia* 9.29.

9. John Ward, *Professors of Gresham College,* 227. One can see this relationship at work in Finch's and Baines's roles in the matter of Mr. Uvedale, as in Royal Commission on Historical Manuscripts, *Report on the Manuscripts of the Late Allan George Finch,* 2:70–71, and in the two letters to Finch from the earl of Winchilsea asking that Baines should come to him to act as his "secretary" (473, 448–449).

10. The classic anthropological account of gift giving is Mauss, *The Gift.* This has been utilized in understanding sixteenth-century friendship by Zemon Davis, "Beyond the Market"; Heal, *Hospitality in Early Modern England;* and Hutson, *Usurer's Daughter.*

11. Weldon, *Court and Character of King James,* 102–103 (modernized quotation). Three editions of Anthony Weldon's book were published in 1650, and a fourth was published in 1651. I have quoted from the edition of 1650 catalogued in the British Library as 610.a.32. All four editions differ in spelling and punctuation, and the 1651 edition contains some alterations and additional material not contained in the earlier editions; these appear to be of an editorial nature. If Anthony Wood is correct, all four editions were published after Weldon's death: Wood, *Athenae Oxonienses,* 2:868. I have emended the apparent misprint "naturall" (in line with other editions). Page 103 of Weldon is misprinted as "130". "Slabbering" (spelled "slabboring" in Weldon) means "to wet." "Let" means "to allow to go." I have used "Villiers" rather than the "Villers" used in the text.

12. Spenser, *Works,* 1:7 (modernized quotation).

13. Aubrey, *Brief Lives,* 2:248.

14. D'Avenant, *Dramatic Works,* 1:119–120.

15. Peck, *Northampton,* 30 (modernized quotation).

16. Trokelowe and Blaneford, *Chronica Monasterii S. Alabani,* 65. See also Hamilton, *Piers Gaveston,* 47.

17. Weldon, *Court and Character of King James,* 97–98 (modernized quotation). I have used "Humphrey" rather than "Humfrey," which is the spelling in the text.

18. Bacon, "Of Followers and Friends," B4v.

19. Peck, *Northampton,* 36 (modernized quotation).

20. On the great houses, see Girouard, *Life in the English Country House*; Mertes, *English Noble Household*; Johnson, *Housing Culture*.

21. Peck, "Benefits, Brokers, and Beneficiaries," 109–127.

22. Paston, *Letters and Papers*, 617 (modernized quotation). "Radcliffe": Radclyff.

23. Cambridge, Sidney Sussex College, Ward papers, "Some passages of the synod of Dort" (modernized quotation).

24. Evelyn, *Diary*, 647 (modernized quotation).

25. Hanham, *Celys*, 47. "My Lord of St. John" was Sir John Weston, prior of St. John of Jerusalem in England.

26. Chamberlain, *Letters*, 2:80 (modernized quotation).

27. Public Record Office, State Papers, 14/65, fol. 78 (modernized quotation), calendared (without the term "bedfellow") in Public Record Office, *Calendar of State Papers, Domestic Series, of the Reign of James I.* "Unrespectively" means "disrespectfully."

28. Lambeth Palace Library, MS 653, fol. 318 (modernized quotation), also in Ungerer, *Spaniard in Elizabethan England*, 1:219, where he rightly corrects the transcription by James Spedding that I followed in *Homosexuality in Renaissance England*, 49.

29. Chapman, *Comedies*, 161–167, 213.

30. Laud, *Works*, 3:170. I have followed the translation in Prynne, *Breviate of the Life of William Laud*, 6 (modernized quotation); compare Carlton, *Archbishop William Laud*, 152.

31. Longleat House, Portland Papers, 2, fol. 44r (modernized quotation). Transcriptions are given in Public Record Office, *Calendar of the Manuscripts of the Marquis of Bath, Preserved at Longleat, Wiltshire*, 2:71. There is a later copy at British Library, Harleian MS 6987, fol. 214r–v, which Williamson transcribed for his *George Villiers*, 235, and which Bergeron transcribed for his version in *King James*, 179. Compare Lockyer, *Buckingham*, 22.

32. Starkey, *English Court*. See also Starkey, "Representation through Intimacy," 187–224.

33. O'Day, "Room at the Top," 34.

34. Cuddy, "Revival of the Entourage," 185–186.

35. *Amis and Amiloun*, 105.

36. *Romance of Guy of Warwick . . . 15th-Century Version*, 261; *Romance of Guy of Warwick . . . 14th-Century Version*, 521.

37. Lyly, *Complete Works*, 1:199.

38. Bacon, "Of Followers and Friends," 5v (B5v).

39. Chetham Society, *Remains Historical & Literary*, 23–27.

40. Percy, *Regulations and Establishment*.

41. Ross, "Historical Accounts of Elizabeth Berkeley," 91–92.

42. Fletcher and Upton, "'Monastic Enclave' or 'Open Society'?" 1–9.

43. P. J. P. Goldberg, *Women, Work, and Life Cycle*, 313, 317–318; Clark and Clark, "Social Economy of the Canterbury Suburbs," 79–80; Keene, *Medieval Winchester*, 1:388; Pythian-Adams, *Desolation of a City*, 203. In France such groups of women continued into the eighteenth century; see Hufton, "Women without Men," 361–362.

44. Hobsbawm, "Tramping Artisan," 34–63; Leeson, *Travelling Brothers*.

45. Roberts, "Women and Work," 86–102.

46. The Metsys portraits and Thomas More's letter are discussed in Campbell et al., "Quentin Matsys," 716–725; Trapp, "Postscript to Matsys," 434, 437; Jardine, *Erasmus*, 27–39; Wootton, "Friendship Portrayed," 28–47. The text of More's letter is in Eramus, *Opvs Epistolarvm*, 3:105–107.

47. Erasmus, *Parabolae sive Similia*, ordo 1, vol. 5, pp. 87–88. The translation is by Craig R. Thompson, *Collected Works of Erasmus*, 23:130.

48. Erasmus, *Opvs Epistolarvm*, 3:106.

49. Jardine, *Erasmus*, 31.

50. Wootton, "Friendship Portrayed," 47, 42.

51. The reading is that given by Alfred Woltmann in 1868 (with "Anverpiae" as possibly "Anverpiis"). The writing has since been overpainted and obscured. On this see Campbell et al., "Quentin Matsys," 718.

52. Erasmus, *Opvs Epistolarvm*, 3:107, as above employing Jardine's translation in *Erasmus*, 28. Campbell et al., "Quentin Matsys," 719 n. 34, describe the resemblance of the writing on the panel to Erasmus's own hand as "compelling."

53. As, for example, it does in Juvenal's thirteenth satire. See *Juvenal and Persius*, 256–257.

54. British Library, Additional MS 64875, fol. 165v, the direction on the outer cover of the letter.

55. Robinson, "Friendship Network," 9.

56. Allen, "Erasmus's Money," 142–144; Thomas More as in *Complete Works*, vol. 3, part 2:422; Campbell et al., "Quentin Matsys," 720, 724.

57. Erasmus, *Opvs Epistolarvm*, 2:255. The translation is from Erasmus, *Correspondence*, 3:308.

58. The manuscript of More's letter and the published editions are discussed in More, *Complete Works*, 3/2:66; Campbell et al., "Quentin Matsys," 717.

59. Cambridge University Library, MS Dd. 3.63, fol. 35r. See Peck, *Northampton*, 30–40, though I have not wholly followed the transcription at p. 39.

60. British Library, Harleian MS 6987, fol. 23r. See below regarding this manuscript.

61. Public Record Office, State Papers, 78/37, fol. 49r, in Ungerer, *Spaniard in Elizabethan England*, 1:424–425. Pérez included the letter in his *Ad Comitem Essexivm*, 42r–42v, as Epistola 60, where "Nauntonum" is reduced to "N::::," "celet et ambiat" is altered to "seruet, & celet," and the second "amicam" is altered to "amicum."

62. Hatfield House, Cecil Papers, 134, fol. 71 (modernized quotation here, in contrast to the later quotations below). There is a deletion between "thing" and "be" in the later quotation from this manuscript. A sentence from this letter was included by Peck, *Northampton*, 214.

63. British Library, Lansdowne MSS 21, fol. 26 and 12, fol. 217 (modernized quotation).

64. British Library, Additional MSS, Evelyn Correspondence, JE/A/12, item 1229 (modernized quotation). The words "to be" have been deleted before "a statue," and I have omitted the character before "friend." My thanks to Douglas Chambers for this reference.

65. As at National Library of Scotland, Advocates MS 33.1.7, vol. 22, no. 87.

66. The letter is at British Library, Harleian MS 6987, fols. 153r–154v (and see below on this manuscript).

67. The most recent statement of this approach is Michael Young, *James VI and I*, which I discuss in the next chapter. On the courts of Henry VIII and Queen Elizabeth in this regard, see Jonathan Goldberg in *Sodometries*, 29–61. On Christopher Marlowe, see chapter 5. For John Donne and Richard Crashaw, see Rambuss, "Pleasure and Devotion," 253–279.

68. Kinder, *Casiodoro de Reina*, 25–26, 95–97. See also McFadden, *Antonio del Corro*, 165 ff., 392. One can see the expressions added to the biblical text in Corro's paraphrase of Romans 1:26–27 in Corro (Antonius Corranus), *Dialogvs Theologicvs* (London, 1574), rendered into English as *A Theological Dialogve* (London, 1575), and in both his *Dialogvs in Epistolam D. Pauli ad Romanos* (Frankfurt, 1587) and *Epistola Beati Pavli Apostoli ad Romanos* (London, 1581), in which Corro gathered his lectures together for publication.

69. Bacon, *Letters and the Life*, 4:139–140, 144–145, 7:286–287, 428–431, 542, although Spedding's transcriptions need to be treated with caution.

70. Augustine, *Confessions*, translated by Tobie Matthew, 108–109.

71. Public Record Office, State Papers, 78/37, fol. 49v, the verso of the sheet not given in Ungerer, *Spaniard in Elizabethan England*, 1:424–425. On the permission he obtained when he visited England to practice Catholicism, see 1:145. The Inquisition's charges of sodomy are set out in Salvá and Sainz de Barando, *Documentos Relativos a Antonio Perez*, 224–236, 255–259, 400–401; Marañon, *Antonio Pérez*, 1:306–309; vol. 2, appendix, no. 26; 1:310–311. The independent nature of much of this evidence is striking.

72. James VI (and I), *Basilikon Dôron*, 37–38. I have transliterated the title, which was in Greek capitals. Buggery was usually excluded from a general pardon: Sharpe, *Crime in Seventeenth-Century England*, 147, 257.

73. Taylor, *Whole Works*, 7:127. See also Askew, *Muskets and Altars*, 182–190, a version of a paper prepared by the author for the working party that produced the report *Homosexual Relationships*. See also Lyly, *Complete Works*, 1:280, which is an addition Lyly made during his paraphrase of Plutarch, for which see *Plutarch's Moralia*, 1:54–55.

74. Prynne, *Breviate of the Life of William Laud*, 6, to which compare p. 29.

75. The ethical context for which I argue here may go some way to explaining the "ostentatio genitalium" described by Leo Steinberg in *Sexuality of Christ.*

76. British Library, Harleian MS 6987, fols. 23r–24v. Williamson gave a version in *George Villiers*, 290–291, and Bergeron gives another in *King James*, 186. The layout of fol. 23r given here is not (other than in very broad terms) an accurate facsimile of its layout in the manuscript. Part of fol. 24v would have formed the outer cover for the letter. There are a number of (to me at least) now indecipherable deletions, which I have not noted in this transcript beyond the comment I add. The marked rhetorical distance left in the manuscripts between the text of this letter (and that in the note immediately following) and the signatures and (in this letter) the postscript suggests that these were not drafts or purely contrived items. This conclusion is supported by their provenance: an endorsement on each of these letters in the handwriting of William Oldys, the antiquary and secretary of Edward Harley, the second earl of Oxford, identifies these letters as part of a collection given by William Stratford, canon of Christ Church, Oxford, who died in 1729; but the seals on letters in this collection both from and to James (in the one case MS 6987, fols. 9r–10v, and in the other MS 6987, fols. 19r–20v) indicate that some (at least) of these letters were not a contemporary collection. The manuscripts of the first and second earls of Oxford were subsequently acquired by the British Museum.

77. British Library, Harleian MS 6987, fols. 153r–154v. See the version in Williamson, *George Villiers*, 309–310; Bergeron, *King James*, 192–193. Part of fol. 154v would have formed the outer cover for the letter. See the previous note on this manuscript. At some points in this letter my transcription has to make a judgment on characters obscured by the binding of the volume or a nearby deletion. I have supplied the apparently overlooked "is" (as Bergeron does also) but have not included deletions in the transcription itself.

78. Painter, *Palace of Pleasure*, 256v–8 (modernized quotation). "Accounted" was spelled "accompted"; see *Oxford English Dictionary*, s.v. "account . . . v." "Mids" is now obsolete in English, meaning "the middle." "Sith" is used in the now archaic sense of "seeing that." The 1566 edition (fols. 336v–338v) differs in some textual respects.

79. P. J. P. Goldberg, "Women in Fifteenth-Century Town Life," 108–109, 123; P. J. P. Goldberg, *Women, Work, and Life Cycle.*

80. Perceptively discussed by Rowe, "Female Body Politics." I am persuaded by Rowe that *Athelston* is a political fable.

81. *Amis and Amiloun*, 105–107. The corresponding account in the Middle English version is *Amys and Amylion*, ed. Le Saux, 95–104.

Chapter Five

1. The epigraph for this chapter is Luke 22:47–48 (from the New English Bible). I am grateful to Dr. Judith Champ for drawing my attention to this monument (and for the information she kindly provided) and to the Venerable English College for permission to inspect the monument and to photograph it. I am of course solely and entirely responsible for the comments here. The monument is now on the left-hand wall of the present church, near the altar wall, behind the priests' benches. The inscription was included by Vincenzo Forcella in *Iscrizioni delle Chiese*, 7:175. Several of the inscriptions in the chapel appear to be later copies, including the inscription to John Seton evidently intended to accompany the monument to Nicholas Morton, included in Forcella, *Iscrizioni delle Chiese*, 174. The monument to Morton is clearly, however, not a later copy. The present church dates from 1888 and was built following damage and disrepair of the earlier building. The monument to Morton appears to have been preserved on a wall of the college (where it was seen by Forcella). On the church, see Williams, *Venerable English College . . . History;* Williams, *Venerable English College . . . Guide*, 19–24, with an illustration of Durante Alberti's picture on p. 20; Champ, *English Pilgrimage to Rome;* and the following items in the serial *The Venerabile* (Exeter): Cartmell, "Church of St. Thomas of the English"; Shutt, "Plan of the College in 1630"; Hay, "Pilgrims and the Hospice"; Laird, "College Church"; Matus, "Reordering of the Church"; Whinder, "Iconography of the College Church." The transcription is from the monument itself, where I have not preserved the marks separating the individual words, the spacing, or the marks of abbreviation. My transcription also does not preserve the compressed *L* and *O* of "ANGELO" and *Q* and *E* of "ROMAQ". DOM: the most usual reading would be "Deo Optimo Maximo." On Robert Morton and his visits to the college and studies there, see "The Librarian" in *Venerabile* 4 (1928–1930): 382–383, with a reproduction of the entry in the *Liber Ruber* 5 (1930–1932): 173; 7 (1934?): 238. The Blessed Robert Morton was beatified by Pope Pius XI in 1929.

2. The translation is in the vernacular form used in England at the time.

3. Pagitt, *Heresiography*, 139.

4. Perkins, *Workes*, vol. 3, part 2:532, from his *Godly and Learned Exposition vpon the Whole Epistle of Jude* (modernized quotation). On the association of popery with sodomy, see Bray, *Homosexuality in Renaissance England*, 19–20.

5. Michael Young, *James VI and I*, 70, 71, 153, 154.

6. Anthony Fletcher, *Gender, Sex, and Subordination*, 27, 50–51, 58, 401–402.

7. Shepard, *Works*, 1:28; Rainolds, *Th'overthrow of the stage-playes*, 10, 32 (modernized quotations). See also Bray, *Homosexuality in Renaissance England*, 16; Kinder, *Casiodoro de Reina*, 28, 29, 105, 107, 109.

8. Harris, *Destruction of sodome*, 9.

9. Public Record Office, State Papers, 12/151, fols. 100–102, 103–104v, 109–109v, 113–113v, 118–119v, calendared in Public Record Office, *Calendar of State Papers, Domestic Series of the Reigns of Edward VI, Mary, Elizabeth, James I*, 2:38–40; British Museum, Cotton MSS, Titus C VI, 5 ff.; Coke, *Twelfth Part of the Reports*, 37. The explanation given in this section of the nature of the "sodomite" in Elizabethan England is set out more fully in Bray, *Homosexuality in Renaissance England*, 13–32.

10. Pagitt, *Heresiography*, 138–139.

11. Persons, "Domesticall Difficulties," 155, 147, 148; Bossy, *English Catholic Community*, 25–27.

12. Harris, *Destruction of sodome*, 34.

13. Hatfield House, Cecil Papers, 83, fol. 62. The letters from Piers Edmonds at 90, fols. 76

and 77, contain more information about him. They are calendared in Royal Commission on Historical Manuscripts, *Calendar of the Manuscripts of the Most Hon. the Marquis of Salisbury, Preserved at Hatfield House, Hertfordshire*, part II, pp. 93–94. I have emended the "called Called" of the text and omitted the illegible (or deleted) word that follows.

14. Marlowe, *Complete Works*, 2:56 ff., 36–38, 46; Cambridge University Library MS Dd. 3.63, fol. 35; and see Peck, *Northampton*, 38–40.

15. Marlowe, *Complete Works*, 2:16–17, 15, 29; Ungerer, *Spaniard in Elizabethan England*, 1:490–493; Pérez, *Ad Comitem Essexivm*, Epistola 61, which is also in Ungerer, 1:475.

16. Marlowe, *Complete Works*, 2:20, 22, 88.

17. Marlowe, *Complete Works*, 2:29; Giles Fletcher, *Christ's Victory and Triumph*, 117; Bray, *Homosexuality in Renaissance England*, 16, 53, 66, 126.

18. Gaveston's Italian tastes are emphasized in Marlowe, *Complete Works*, 2:16, 35, and his foreign origins at 2:21, 22. On the assumed connection between these and sodomy, see Bray, *Homosexuality in Renaissance England*, 75–76.

19. Marlowe, *Complete Works*, 2:90–93. I accept the arguments for the view that the murder of Edward was enacted in full view of the audience but my point holds good even if Marlowe felt he could go no further than to allude to it in the references we see in the text.

20. I. M. [Gervase Markham?], *Gentlemanly Profession of Seruingmen*, C1–C1v.

21. Marlowe, *Complete Works*, 2:20.

22. John Ernest Neale, "Elizabethan Political Scene," 161.

23. Byrne, *Lisle Letters*, 3:1–35; Darell, *Short Discourse*, 124 (modernized quotation).

24. John Ernest Neale, "Elizabethan Political Scene," 153; Peck, *Northampton*, 59.

25. Bray, *Homosexuality in Renaissance England*, 14–15, 29–30, 49, 54, 72, 121; Kinder, *Casiodoro de Reina*, 27–37, 58–59, 99–120; Herrup, *House in Gross Disorder.*

26. Barrow, *Plaine Refvtation*, 252.

27. British Library, Harleian MS 6848, fols. 185r–186v; Harleian MS 6853, fols. 307r–308v, with quotations from 185r and 185v. There is a transcript by C. F. Tucker Brooke in *Life of Marlowe*, 98–100. On the identity of Richard Baines, see Kuriyama, "Marlowe's Nemesis," 343–360. For a perceptive analysis of Baines's allegations, see Jonathan Goldberg, "Sodomy and Society," 371–378.

28. British Library, Harleian MS 646, fols. 59r–59v. There is a transcript in Hearne, *Historia Vitae et Regni Ricardi II*, 385–388, appendix.

29. Hutson, *Usurer's Daughter*; Stewart, *Close Readers.*

30. Stewart, *Close Readers*, 127

31. Hutson, *Usurer's Daughter*, 112

32. My discussions on this point in this chapter and the last are set out more fully in Bray, *Homosexuality in Renaissance England*, especially 58–80.

33. Traub, "(In)significance of 'Lesbian' Desire," 150–169; Traub, "Perversion of 'Lesbian' Desire," 19–49; Traub, *Renaissance of Lesbianism.*

34. Bacon, *Harmony of the Essays*, 38–39.

35. Aubrey, *Brief Lives*, 1:67.

36. *Trve and Perfect Relation*, B2r–B3r, B4v, Bbb3v, Aaa2r, Aaa2v.

Chapter Six

1. Wood, *Life and Times*, 1:199, 309. The translation of *The Wanderer* at the opening of this chapter is from Chadwick, *Anglo-Saxon and Norse Poems*, 11. The quotation from W. H. Auden's "Wanderer" is from his *Collected Poems*, 62. On the Anglo-Saxon poem, see Conner, *Anglo-Saxon Exeter.*

2. Wood, *History and Antiquities*, 26–27; Bott, *Monuments in Merton College*, 21–22, 109; Bertram et

al., "Lost Brasses of Oxford," 224–225, 227, 235–237, 251; *Registrum Annalium Collegii Mertonensis,* 10 (where Hamsterley and Harper are linked together in 1483), 136 (Hamsterley's provision for the stalls), 367 (the death of Thomas Harper), 480 (Hamsterley's chantry). There are detailed entries for Hamsterley and Harper in Emden, *Biographical Register of the University of Oxford,* 2:864–865, 878–879. See also Martin and Highfield, *History of Merton College,* 141–143. The sixteenth-century inscription is from Wood. The later inscription follows the reconstruction in Bott and the valuable paper by Bertram and his colleagues, since the inscription itself is now in fragments. My thanks to Diarmaid MacCulloch for drawing my attention to this monument.

3. Torr, "Oddington Shroud Brass," 231.

4. Garrod, *Ancient Painted Glass,* 10–12; Bott, *Monuments in Merton College,* 8.

5. Bott, *Monuments in Merton College,* 8, 59; Henderson, *Merton College,* 218.

6. Girouard, *Life in the English Country House,* 122–123, 136–143, 189, 219.

7. Green, "University and Social Life," 322–327, 330–331.

8. Leicestershire Record Office, DG7, box 4985, partly calendared in Royal Commission on Historical Manuscripts, *Report on the Manuscripts of the Late Allan George Finch,* 2:128–130.

9. Day, *English Secretorie,* part 2, p. 123; Rambuss, *Spenser's Secret Career,* 43.

10. The cenotaph to Granville Piper and Richard Wise is in the north aisle of the church of St. Mary Magdalene, Launceston, near the pulpit. I am grateful for the access I was granted to inspect the monument. The quotations from the inscription in this chapter are from my own transcription. On the cenotaph and the families of Granville Piper and Richard Wise, here and below, see Gilbert, *County of Cornwall,* 1:30, 2:237, 331, 503–504, plates 19 and 25. The situation of the Piper burial place is indicated by the terms used in the Piper monuments and their location (now dispersed) when Gilbert saw them. The transcriptions given in Gilbert's (nevertheless valuable) account are not fully accurate, and the same is the case with the transcriptions in Polsue and Lake, *Parochial History,* 3:68, 90–91. See also Peter and Peter, *Histories of Launceston,* 325–326, 401, 403; Robbins, *Launceston,* 69, 264; Pevsner, *Cornwall,* 97 and plate 41; Pevsner, *North Somerset and Bristol,* 103; Wilson, "Ethics Girls," 87. The controversy surrounding the erection of the monument (and the situation of the Piper family pew) is referred to in Rendell, *Launceston,* 30–31. I am most grateful to Miss Rendell for the further information she kindly provided in correspondence and to Jean Wilson for first drawing this monument to my attention.

11. Archenholz, *Picture of England,* 1:128; Grosley, *Tour to London,* 1:40; La Rochefoucauld, *Frenchman in England,* 25; La Rochefoucauld and La Rochefoucauld, *Innocent Espionage,* 199.

12. Archenholz, *Picture of England,* 2:103–104; Mirabeau, *Letters,* 1:189.

13. *Satan's Harvest Home,* 51.

14. Saint-Evremond, *Works,* 2:265–266; Levine, *Between the Ancients and the Moderns,* 111–158.

15. Locke, *Two Treatises of Government,* 336–337.

16. Stubbe, *Discoverie of a gaping gulf,* B7v.

17. Bossy, "Some Elementary Forms of Durkheim," 3–18.

18. Locke, *Two Treatises of Government,* 343, 348.

19. Kant, *Metaphysics of Morals,* 215 ff. The quotation depends both on Gregor's translation, p. 217, and on Derrida, "Politics of Friendship," note 7.

20. McCracken, "Exchange of Children," 303–313.

21. *Statutes at Large,* 26 George. II cap. 33, 7:525–528. I have employed the contemporary pamphlets on the act bound together as British Library Tracts 1705. Henry Stebbing, *An Enquiry into the Force and Operation of the Annulling Clauses in a late Act for the better preventing of Clandestine Marriages, with Respect to Conscience,* is item 3 in this collection, with my quotations from pp. 13, 15, and 21. James Tunstall, *A Vindication of the Power of States to prohibit Clandestine Marriages under the Pain of Ab-*

solute Nullity . . . in Answer to The Rev. Dr. Stebbing's Dissertation, is item 8, with quotations from pp. 57 and 23. See also Outhwaite, *Clandestine Marriage in England.*

22. Trumbach, *Sex and the Gender Revolution,* 1:377–378, 471.

23. I described this change in *Homosexuality in Renaissance England.* A comparable thesis (both to the cognitive dissonance I described in this book and its subsequent transformation) is put forward in the context of female friendship in Valerie Traub's *Renaissance of Lesbianism in Early Modern England,* following her earlier articles, "The (In)significance of 'Lesbian' Desire" and "The Perversion of 'Lesbian' Desire."

24. I have looked at the depositions in the London Metropolitan Archives of Sara Cunningham (Diocese of London, Depositions, DL C 240, fols. 137v–138r), Jane Jones (fols. 138r–138v) and Phoebe Horton (fols. 138v–139r), and at the "personal answers" of Amy Poulter (DL C 196, fols. 26v–28v). The entry in the Marylebone parish register is at P89/MRY1/1, fol. 120 (the second entry in the left-hand column). This is a later transcript of the register apparently made from the original when it had been damaged by fire, as calendared in *Registers of Marriages of St. Mary le Bone,* 1:83. Patricia Crawford and Sara Mendelson provide transcriptions, with some small differences from my own (together with other relevant records and a commentary), in their "Sexual Identities in Early Modern England," 362–377, and in Mendelson and Crawford, *Women in Early Modern England,* 248–249. On the Poulter (or "Pulter") family (and Amy Poulter's death), see Clutterbuck, *County of Hertford,* 3:517–518. There are entries for Arabella Hunt in Hawkins, *Science and Practice of Music,* 564, 761; Smith, Stephen, and Lee, *Dictionary of National Biography,* 28:263; Ashbee and Lasocki, *Biographical Dictionary of English Court Musicians,* 1:612–614; Sadie, *New Grove,* 11:872. For Marylebone old church, see Cherry and Pevsner, *London,* 602; Lindsay, *Hogarth,* 85; Quennell, *Hogarth's Progress,* 132. From the viewpoint of the historians concerned with economic individualism that I discuss in the afterword, see Bouton, "Itching after Private Marryings?" 15–34; Bouton, "Clandestine Marriages in London," 191–210. My thanks to Patricia Crawford and Sara Mendelson for their generous discussions with me of this incident.

25. Carlson, *Marriage and the English Reformation.* Pedersen, "Medieval Laity," is very good here.

26. Congreve, "On Mrs. Arabella Hunt Singing," 465. Epigram from Congreve, *Works,* 3:250. Kneller's portrait with Congreve's epigram are reproduced in Crawford and Mendelson, "Sexual Identities in Early Modern England."

27. Brayley, *Abbey Church of St. Peter,* 2:185–186, 246; John Preston Neale, *Westminster Abbey,* 67; Royal Commission on Historical Monuments, *An Inventory of the Historical Monuments in London,* 1:39; *Westminster Abbey: Official Guide,* 59; Pevsner, *London 1: The Cities of London and Westminster,* 437. There is an illustration of part of the monument in *Westminster Abbey: The Monuments,* 15, 120, and plate 33, though the text is too despairing on what can be known about Mary Kendall. The main part of the inscription (with some small differences from my transcription and a commentary) is given in Wilson, "Two Names of Friendship," 78, 83, which first drew my attention to this monument. A discussion (with a photograph) of this monument in the context of female friendship is in Traub, *Renaissance of Lesbianism,* 70–72.

28. *Marriage, Baptismal, and Burial Registers,* with extensive notes, at 193 (a son of the earl of Ranelagh), 237 (the countess of Ranelagh), 264 (James Kendall), 267 (Mary Kendall with a note on Captain Charles Kendall), 273 (the earl of Ranelagh), 356 (Lady Catharine Jones), and 392 (Lady Elizabeth Jones).

29. Carte, *James Duke of Ormonde,* 2:451; Smith, Stephen, and Lee, *Dictionary of National Biography,* 30:154–156.

30. Wilson, "Ethics Girls."

31. The quotations here and below from 1 Corinthians (in the English translation of 1611 in use in the Church of England at the time) are from 1:24, 11:23–26, 13:9–10, 12–13, 15:20, 23.

32. On the monument, see Rawlinson, *City and Cathedral-Church of Hereford*, 98–99; Willis, *Survey of the Cathedrals*, 2:529–530, with the plan between pp. 489 and 499; Duncumb, *Collections*, 1:548; plan in Havergal and Walker, *Hereford Cathedral Church*; Havergal, *Fasti Herefordenses*, the plan of the cathedral and p. 40 (including note 2); Havergal, *Monumental Inscriptions*, 8, 14; Royal Commission on Historical Monuments, *An Inventory of the Historical Monuments in Herefordshire*, 1:112; Pevsner, *Herefordshire*, 163, though not "1669 and 1691"; Aylmer and Tiller, *Hereford Cathedral*, 121. I have not attempted to judge between the dates for Benson's death. The date of Croft's death shown on his ledger stone is 18 May 1691, that of Benson on his as 24 August 1691 (followed in the Royal Commission on Historical Monuments volume from 1931). Rawlinson and Duncomb each gave the date of Benson's death, as transcribed from the ledger stone, as 24 August 1692. Havergal gives 1692 in *Fasti Herfordenses*, 40. Bannister gives the dates as "within a year of one another, in 1691–2," *Cathedral Church of Hereford*, 102 n. Moir, *Deans of Hereford Cathedral Church*, 42, describes the dates as "within a year of each other." Aylmer and Tiller, *Hereford Cathedral*, 121, describe Benson's death as "fifteen months" after the death of Croft on 18 May 1691 (the date of Benson's death on his ledger stone is cut off in the illustration). My thanks to Diarmaid MacCulloch for drawing this monument to my attention.

33. 2 Samuel 1:23, "Saul et Jonathas amabiles et decora in vita sua, in morte quoque non sunt divisi" (as in Aylmer and Tiller, *Hereford Cathedral*, 121 n. 71). *Amys and Amylion* as quoted in Caius, *Annals*, discussed above in chapter 3.

34. Moir, *Deans of Hereford Cathedral Church*, 40–42, which rightly describes the monument as "a symbol of the reconciliation between dean and bishop on the vexed problem of episcopal visitation." For a timetable for the visitation, which took almost a year to complete, compare Aylmer and Tiller, *Hereford Cathedral*, 117 n. 46, to Bannister, *Cathedral Church of Hereford*, 102. On the episcopal visitation of the cathedral (and on Bishops Scory and Beauclerk and the occupation of Hereford by Colonel Birch), see Smith, Stephen, and Lee, *Dictionary of National Biography*, 13:105–107; Bannister, *Cathedral Church of Hereford*, especially 86–88, 104–107, 176–180, compared with the now indispensable Aylmer and Tiller, *Hereford Cathedral*, especially 91–95, 100–103, 110, 116–121, 130–135.

35. The original setting of the monument (and of the bishop's throne) is shown in the plan in Willis, *Survey of the Cathedrals*, and referred to in the terms used by Rawlinson and Duncomb. The moving of the ledger stones is described by Havergal, *Fasti Herefordenses*, 40 n. 2, and is shown in his plan. See also Merewether, *Statement of the condition*, 49, and plates 6 and 7.

36. Ramsden, "Anne Lister's Journal," 1–13; Lister, *I Know My Own Heart*; Lister, *No Priest but Love*; Lister, *Female Fortune*; Liddington, *Presenting the Past*; Liddington, "Beating the Inheritance Bounds," 260–274; Anderson, "Anne Lister Papers," 190–192; Westwood, Sewell, and Liddington, *Anne Lister Research Directory*. These defined the direction of this work on Anne Lister. My thanks to Randolph Trumbach, who first suggested to me the importance of Lister's diary in the context I discuss here.

37. Lister, *Female Fortune*, 62.

38. Ibid., 63.

39. Ibid., 94.

40. Ibid., 100, 268.

41. Lister, *I Know My Own Heart*, 159.

42. Ibid., 160.

43. Ibid., 177–178.

44. Ibid., 154.

45. Lister, *Female Fortune*, 93.

46. Ibid., 93, 95.

47. On Holy Trinity Church, Goodramgate, see Knowles, "East Window," 1–24; Gibson, "Stained and Painted Glass of York," 172–177; Royal Commission on Historical Monuments, *An Inventory of the Historical Monuments in the City of York*, 5:5–9, and plates 9, 16, 34, 45, 46, 56; Routh, "Gift and Its Giver," 109–121; H.E.C.S., *Holy Trinity Church*. There are contemporary descriptions of Holy Trinity as Lister and Walker would have seen it, in *Strangers' Guide through the City of York*, 108; and Whellan and Co., *History and Topography*, 1:560–561. My thanks to the admirable Churches Conservation Trust and their representative Naomi Tummons for the access I was given to the church and for Tummons's generous discussion of the church and its stained glass.

48. The inscriptions are partly damaged. I have followed the transcriptions in Royal Commission on Historical Monuments England, *An Inventory of the Historical Monuments in the City of York*, 5:8.

49. Routh, "Gift and Its Giver," 110–111.

50. Ibid., 112.

51. Knowles, "East Window," 4–5.

52. Ibid., 9–10.

53. H.E.C.S., *Holy Trinity Church*, 2.

54. Knowles, "East Window," was presumably unaware of this line of interpretation in his judgment at p. 23.

55. Routh, "Gift and Its Giver."

56. H.E.C.S., *Holy Trinity Church*, 6–7.

57. There are translations of *De Spiritali Amicitia* (which I have partly followed) in *Aelred of Rievaulx: Spiritual Friendship*, translated by Mary Eugenia Laker, and in Talbot, *Christian Friendship*. My discussion has been greatly assisted by McEvoy, "Notes on the Prologue." McGuire, *Brother and Lover*, provides an introduction to the large (and growing) studies of Aelred. My discussion here revisits that in Boswell, *Christianity, Social Tolerance, and Homosexuality*, 221–226.

58. Aelred, *De Spiritali Amicitia*, 348.

59. Ibid., 345 ff., with the quotation at 347–348.

60. Anselm of Canterbury, *Cur Deus Homo*, 130–131. On Anselm, see Bossy, *Christianity in the West*, 3 ff.

61. Aelred, *De Spiritali Amicitia*, 287. I have followed the translation by McEvoy, "Notes on the Prologue," 398.

62. Aelred, *De Spiritali Amicitia*, 301; McEvoy, "Notes on the Prologue," 402.

63. Augustine, *Confessions* 4.9.4; 1:38. Aelred expands Augustine's formulation by reading it in the light of 1 John 4:16 as Augustine (necessarily then) had expanded Tobit 13:18 in reading it in the light of Matthew 5:44.

64. McEvoy, "Notes on the Prologue," 404.

65. Aelred, *De Spiritali Amicitia*, 289.

66. Derrida, *Politiques de l'amitié*. I have used the translation by George Collins, *Politics of Friendship*.

67. Aelred, *De Spiritali Amicitia*, 303.

68. Ibid., 345; Cicero, *De Amicitia* 102, in *De Senectute, De Amicitia*, 208.

69. Aelred, *Liber de Speculo Caritatis*, 57 ff.

70. Derrida, *Politics of Friendship*, 276.

71. Aelred, *Liber de Speculo Caritatis*, 64–65. I have retained Talbot's translation of this exuber-

ant passage (except to employ "you" and "your" rather than "thy" and "thine"), from *Christian Friendship*, 129.

72. Aelred, *De Spiritali Amicitia*, 307; "four" is based on the fourfold "in."

73. Lister, *Female Fortune*, 164.

74. Ibid., 11.

75. On Anne Lister's godparents, see Ramsden, "Anne Lister's Journal," 6.

76. Lister, *Female Fortune*, 9.

77. Ibid., 12–13, 19.

78. Edward VI, *First Prayer-Book*, 294, 300. This work will be cited below as the Book of Common Prayer.

79. Lister, *Female Fortune*, 3. On Shibden Hall, see Pevsner, *Yorkshire*, 239; Westwood and Brown, *Shibden Hall Halifax*. I am grateful to the staff at Shibden Hall and to Polly Salter, the social history officer, for the access I was given to Shibden Hall (and for Polly Salter's alerting me to the discovery of Anne Lister's gravestone).

80. Lister, *Female Fortune*, 203.

81. On Halifax Parish Church, see Watson, *Parish of Halifax*, 330–394; Savage, "Halifax Parish Church . . . Architecture"; Savage, "Halifax Parish Church . . . Woodwork"; Crossley, *Monumental and Other Inscriptions*; Hanson, "Evolution of the Parish Church"; Bretton, "Heraldry"; Bretton, "Halifax Parish Church"; Pevsner, *Yorkshire*, 229–230; Crabtree and Washington, *Halifax Parish Church*. My thanks to the Rev. Pauline Millward and the volunteer helpers at the church for assisting with my visit.

82. Lister, *Female Fortune*, 21, "Our burying place is in the south chapel, at the west end, next to the constable's pews"—the "south chapel" would be the Holdsworth Chapel, comparing Watson's comment in 1775 (*Parish of Halifax*, 358), "There are two chapels within this church, one on the north side, and the other on the south."

83. Hargreaves, "Georgian and Early Victorian Church," 59, 67.

84. Lister, *I Know My Own Heart*, 242.

85. Some of the monuments in Wiveton church (not including that of Catherine Jennis and Anne Fleming) are described in Pevsner and Wilson, *Norfolk*, 728–729; and two pamphlets, the first by J. N. G. (whom I take to be Mrs. J. N. Gordon), *St. Mary the Virgin, Wiveton*, and the second by Butler-Stoney, *Wiveton St Mary, the Virgin*. There are brass rubbings from the church in Countryside Commission, *Wiveton Village*.

86. Lister, *I Know My Own Heart*, 163.

87. Lister, *Female Fortune*, 143–144, 156, 221–222, 273.

88. Kendall, "Two Halifax Ladies of Quality," 138.

89. Lister, *I Know My Own Heart*, 210. An important early discussion of Lady Sarah Ponsonby and Miss Eleanor Butler was Faderman, *Surpassing the Love of Men*, 120–125. More recently on their friendship as a marriage (and as a family that could transcend social distinctions), see Vanita, *Sappho and the Virgin Mary*, 111–119.

90. The first collect after the Litany beginning "We humbly beseech thee, O Father, mercifully to look upon our infirmities," etc., and the collects for the third and fourth Sundays after Epiphany quoted here.

91. Lister, *Female Fortune*, 89.

92. Liddington, "Anne Lister . . . Her Diaries," 52.

93. Ruggiero, *Boundaries of Eros*, 113, 189.

94. In Peter Damian, *Die Briefe*, 1:284–330. My discussion here is a dialogue with Jordan, *In-*

vention of Sodomy, 45–66 and passim; Jordan, *Silence of Sodom.* My thanks for his generous discussion of my work.

95. Jordan, *Invention of Sodomy,* 1 and passim.

96. Peter Damian, *Die Briefe,* 1:328.

97. My quotations from Jordan here and below are from *Invention of Sodomy,* 44, 161, and *Silence of Sodom,* 115.

98. Aelred, *De Spiritali Amicitia,* 313.

99. Augustine, *Confessions* 2.2.2, 3.1.1; 1:16, 23.

100. Aelred, *De Spiritali Amicitia.*

101. Peter Damian, *Die Briefe,* 1:298.

102. Latham, *Revised Medieval Latin Word-List,* 443. This judgment must be provisional on the eventual entry in the developing *Dictionary of Medieval Latin from British Sources.*

103. Bray, *Homosexuality in Renaissance England,* 70–74, and, on subsequent studies, 116, to which I would now add Boes, "On Trial for Sodomy."

104. Lister, *Female Fortune,* 86.

105. Ibid., 92–93.

106. Ibid., 93.

107. Crucial here in understanding the diaries is Liddington, *Presenting the Past,* with the quoted comment at p. 57.

108. Lister, *Female Fortune,* 61.

109. Ibid., 122. The authoritative analysis (on which I have drawn) is Liddington, "Beating the Inheritance Bounds," and *Female Fortune,* 27–38.

110. The plans are reproduced in Westwood and Brown, *Shibden Hall Halifax,* 49–51.

111. Lister, *I Know My Own Heart,* 159.

112. Cox, *Parish Registers,* 57, 53.

113. Lister, *FemaleFortune,* 283.

114. Lister, *I Know My Own Heart,* 216.

115. This transcription is provisional: more of the inscription could I think be legible under more suitable conditions for transcription.

116. Lister, *FemaleFortune,* 235–241.

117. Scott, *Minstrelsy of the Scottish Border,* 267; Child, *English and Scottish Popular Ballads,* part 7, p. 144, on Scott's text and the continuing appearance of the ballad *Bewick and Graham.*

118. Brand, *Newcastle upon Tyne,* 2:261; Brockett, *Glossary of North Country Words,* 52.

119. The legal report is given in Orth, *Combination and Conspiracy,* 113. I have also drawn here on the discussions in Cole, *Attempts at General Union,* 70–74, 127–136; Oliver, "Tolpuddle Martyrs," 5–12; E. P. Thompson, *Making of the English Working Class,* 556–561; Marlow, *Tolpuddle Martyrs.* The cordwainers' ceremony I refer to below is described in Oliver's paper. The wool combers' ceremony is in *Character, Objects & Effects of Trades' Unions,* 66–73, and in Cole, *Attempts at General Union,* 187–192. The clothiers' ceremony is described by E. P. Thompson, *Making of the English Working Class,* 558–560, and characterized as such in *Character, Objects & Effects of Trades' Unions,* 73. My earlier chapters arguably substantiate the suggestions—which at the time might have seemed somewhat improbable—by Oliver, "Tolpuddle Martyrs," 9, and by E. P. Thompson, *Making of the English Working Class,* 557, that the rituals of early nineteenth-century trade unionism drew in some way on the medieval confraternities: the tenacity of the enduring link lies in my conclusions (which I share with Oliver) on the real and continuing substance of the religious element in these ceremonies.

120. E. P. Thompson, *Making of the English Working Class,* 908.

121. Cole, *Attempts at General Union*, 187–188, 190–191, 192.

122. E. P. Thompson, *Making of the English Working Class*, 558.

123. Marlow, *Tolpuddle Martyrs*, 47.

124. E. P. Thompson, *Making of the English Working Class*, 556.

125. Marlow, *Tolpuddle Martyrs*, 46.

Chapter Seven

1. Newman's instructions on his burial are in the Birmingham Oratory Archives, BOA A29 3, p. 5, in a notebook in Newman's handwriting of instructions written in view of death to Father William Neville, the first-named executor in Newman's will (which is in BOA A5). On the origin of the notebook, see Newman's letter of 14 November 1878, which I discuss below. The instructions of 23 July 1876 are on pp. 5 and 7 of this manuscript (headed "Text" and "Private for William," i.e., William Neville) with the facing pp. 4 and 6 together with 8 (the verso p. 7) containing notes. Neville included the note of 23 July 1876 in Newman, *Meditations and Devotions*, 611. It is partly transcribed in Newman, *Letters and Diaries*, 28:89–90, which shows Newman's later addition of "Card." Although I am of course solely responsible for my conclusions here, in the discussion that follows I have been assisted by the generous comments of Gerard Tracey, the archivist of the Newman manuscripts at the Birmingham Oratory, who pointed out to me the significance of the pencil sketch by Newman's instructions for his burial that I discuss below, and the important paper by Tolhurst, "Blessed and Ever Enduring Fellowship." I share Father Tolhurst's view that Newman intended that "friendship is that glimpse of a deeper communion" (428), and my historical perspective supports his view that Newman's theology should be understood here with Eamon Duffy's studies of medieval Catholicism (433).

2. I have transliterated (without accents) the Greek characters Newman employs here for the two Greek words "eikôn" and "skia" [image and shadow].

3. Tristram, *Newman and His Friends*, 221–222.

4. Birmingham Oratory, BOA CL 1875, to Lord Blachford, 31 May 1875, calendared in Newman, *Letters and Diaries*, 27:305. Here and below, "CL" indicates an early copy of a manuscript made when collections were being put together for a biography of Newman (in some cases his letters are extant only in this form). Where I have seen the original holograph manuscript, this is noted. Where I consulted a photograph in the Birmingham Oratory Archives of a manuscript held elsewhere, this is also noted.

5. To Lady Henry Kerr, 18 June 1875, in Newman, *Letters and Diaries*, 27:321.

6. I have quoted from the photograph in the Birmingham Oratory Archives of the letter, calendared in Newman, *Letters and Diaries*, 27:308.

7. To Miss Holmes, 13 June 1875, Birmingham Oratory, BOA PC 58 (no item number), calendared in Newman, *Letters and Diaries*, 27:319; to Mrs. Athy, 27 June 1875, BOA ML 1875, calendared in Newman, *Letters and Diaries*, 27:325, from copy letter; to Lady Herbert of Lea, 13 June 1875, BOA PC 164, item 17, calendared in Newman, *Letters and Diaries*, 27:319; to G. D. Boyle, 7 June 1875, BOA CL 1875, calendared in Newman, *Letters and Diaries*, 27:315; to Ambrose Phillipps de Lisle, 5 June 1875, BOA CL 1875, calendared in Newman, *Letters and Diaries*, 27:313. See also the photographs in the Birmingham Oratory Archives of the letters to William Robert Brownlow, 7 June 1875, calendared in Newman, *Letters and Diaries*, 27:315, from copy letter; and to William Leigh Junior, 5 June 1875, calendared in Newman, *Letters and Diaries*, 27:313.

8. To Emily Bowles, 22 June 1875, Birmingham Oratory, BOA PC 14, item 25, calendared in Newman, *Letters and Diaries*, 27:324.

9. To the Hon. Mrs. Maxwell-Scott, 3 June 1875, in Newman, *Letters and Diaries*, 27:310.

10. I have quoted from the photograph in the Birmingham Oratory Archives of the letter to Agnes Wilberforce, 18 June 1875, calendared in Newman, *Letters and Diaries*, 27:322.

11. To Lady Henry Kerr, 18 June 1875, in Newman, *Letters and Diaries*, 27:322.

12. I have quoted from the photographs in the Birmingham Oratory Archives of the letter to Mrs. Henry Wilberforce, 26 May 1875, calendared in Newman, *Letters and Diaries*, 27:304; and to Robert Monteith, 8 June 1875, calendared in Newman, *Letters and Diaries*, 27:317; and from the copy letter to Lord Blachford, 31 May 1875, BOA CL 1875, calendared in Newman, *Letters and Diaries*, 27:306.

13. To Emily Bowles, 12 January 1878, in Newman, *Letters and Diaries*, 28:300.

14. To Mrs. Wilberforce, 18 January 1878, in Newman, *Letters and Diaries*, 28:303.

15. Quoted in Tristram, *Newman and His Friends*, 115. See also, on Joseph Gordon, 108–116; on Ambrose St. John, 221–231; on Edward Caswall, 235–239; on William Neville, 239–243; and on their burial at Rednal near Newman, 218–219. There is a photograph of the altar in Newman's room facing p. 168 (and in Martin, *John Henry Newman*, 134).

16. To R. W. Church, 14 November 1878, in Newman, *Letters and Diaries*, 28:421.

17. Newman, *Apologia pro Vita Sua*, 252.

18. Newman, *Parochial and Plain Sermons*, 4:211–218, from June 1837; Newman, *Sermons*, 1:368; Tolhurst, "Blessed and Ever Enduring Fellowship," 426, 455.

19. Cicero, *De Officiis* 3.17.69, with the note in Cicero, *Obligations*, 192.

20. Newman, *Letters and Diaries*, 6:95; Tolhurst, "Blessed and Ever Enduring Fellowship," 427.

21. Newman, *Letters and Diaries*, 6:102.

22. Newman, *Parochial and Plain Sermons*, 7:211; Tolhurst, "Blessed and Ever Enduring Fellowship," 426.

23. Newman, *Meditations and Devotions*, 602; Tolhurst, "Blessed and Ever Enduring Fellowship," 436.

24. Hume, "Note" (February 1995). Cardinal Hume's "Note" expanded his "Observations on the Catholic Church's Teaching concerning Homosexual People," prepared in 1993, and should be read in its entirety with the later expanded version published in his *Created Design*, 20–24. My thanks to Richard Cunliffe for assistance with this documentation.

25. The awareness of Aelred at the Birmingham Oratory in Newman's time is reflected in the study of Aelred by John Dobree Dalgairns that appeared in Newman's *Lives of the English Saints* as discussed by Roden, "Aelred of Rievaulx," 85–99.

26. Pope, *Iliad of Homer*, 23:75–92.

27. Birmingham Oratory, BOA A1, edited by Tolhurst, "Blessed and Ever-Enduring Fellowship," 440–453.

28. On Newman's room, see Tolhurst, "Blessed and Ever-Enduring Fellowship," 424, 440.

29. Wilfrid Ward, *Life of John Henry Cardinal Newman*, 1:21–22.

30. I have quoted from the photograph in Birmingham Oratory Archives of the letter to Robert Monteith, 8 June 1875, calendared in Newman, *Letters and Diaries*, 27:317.

31. Birmingham Oratory, BOA OL 1875, item 78b, calendared in part in Newman, *Letters and Diaries*, 27:301 n. 1.

32. Newman, *Apologia pro Vita Sua*, 213.

33. Newman, *Historical Sketches*, 3:313–335.

34. Ingram, *Memorials of Oxford*, 1:19–20, 32.

35. *Times* (London), 24 June 1861, 12; 27 June 1861, 12; 28 June 1861, 10.

36. [Newman], *Loss and Gain*, 11–14.

37. Pope John Paul II to Archbishop Vincent Nichols, *Tablet* 255 (2001): 290.

38. The text of Pope John Paul's speech was posted on the official Vatican website. Before his visit Pope John Paul II would have been briefed by the prefect of the Congregation for the Oriental Churches, at that time Cardinal Patriarch Ignace Moussa I Daoud, himself a Syrian Catholic.

39. Robin Darling Young, "Gay Marriage," 43.

Afterword

1. *Tablet*, 4 August 2001, 1108–1109, with an editorial on p. 1103.

2. The study of this group of historians within the Communist Party is Kaye, *British Marxist Historians*, especially 9–18.

3. The broadcasts were "The World We Have Lost: Peter Laslett on 'The Sovereignty of the Family,'" no. 1619, 7 April 1960; "The World We Have Lost: A One-Class Society," no. 1620, 14 April 1960; "The World We Have Lost: Social Change and Revolution," no. 1621, 21 April 1960. They were published in *The Listener and B.B.C. Televison Review* 63 (January–June 1960): 607–609, 657–660, 699–701.

4. Laslett, *World We Have Lost: Further Explored*, 91, 92.

5. Laslett, *World We Have Lost*, 1st ed., 236.

6. Laslett and Wall, *Household and Family in Past Time*, preface, italics mine.

7. McFarlane, "Bastard Feudalism"; McFarlane, "Parliament and 'Bastard Feudalism.'"

8. Leclercq, *Monks and Love.*

9. Chaytor, "Household and Kinship."

10. Wrightson, "Household and Kinship," 152–158; Houston and Smith, "New Approach to Family History?" 120–131.

11. Hanawalt, *Ties That Bound;* Cressy, "Kinship and Kin Interaction"; Tadmor, "'Family' and 'Friend' in *Pamela*"; A. Hassell Smith, "Labourers in Late Sixteenth-Century England"; O'Day, *Family and Family Relationships;* O'Hara, *Courtship and Constraint.*

12. Hughes, "Urban Growth"; Kent, *Household and Lineage;* Kent and Kent, *Neighbours and Neighbourhood;* Weissman, *Ritual Brotherhood in Renaissance Florence;* Benigno, "Southern Italian Family."

13. Kettering, "Gift-Giving and Patronage" and "Friendship and Clientage," following her *Patrons, Brokers, and Clients.*

14. Wormald, *Lords and Men in Scotland;* McLoughlin, "*Amicitia* in Practice"; Haseldine, "Friendship and Rivalry"; Haseldine, "Language of *Amicitia*"; Haseldine, "Love, Separation."

15. Burke, "Humanism and Friendship"; Peck, *Northampton;* Peck, "Benefits, Brokers, and Beneficiaries"; Lytle, "Friendship and Patronage in Renaissance Europe"; Heal, *Hospitality in Early Modern England;* Wilson, "Two Names of Friendship." Jean Wilson's paper and our subsequent correspondence were crucial for me in reflecting on the tomb monuments that punctuate the argument of this book.

16. Lockyer, *Buckingham;* Hamilton, *Piers Gaveston.*

17. Rey, *L'Amitié à la Renaissance.*

18. Bray and Rey, "Body of the Friend."

19. An important early technical work was Bailey, *Sponsors at Baptism and Confirmation,* and more recently Lynch, *Godparents and Kinship in Early Medieval Europe.* John Bossy's works, including "Godparenthood," laid the foundations for the later illustrations of godparenthood's practical deployment in studies by Hanham, *Celys;* Maddern, "Best Trusted Friends"; Llinos Beverley Smith, "Fosterage, Adoption, and God-Parenthood."

20. In Durandus, *Rationale Divinorum Officiorum,* 309–311.

21. Bossy, "Mass as a Social Institution"; Jungmann, *Mass of the Roman Rite*, 2:321–332.

22. Phillips, *Ritual Kiss*; Buchanan, *Kiss of Peace*. In *Tablet*, 1 July 2000, 892, I commented on the Pelagian form that the kiss of peace has taken in the modern liturgy.

23. Mills, *One Soul in Bodies Twain.*

24. Keen, "Brotherhood in Arms," 1–17.

25. Baldwin, "*Amis and Amiloun*," 353–365; Strohm, *Social Chaucer*, especially 95–102.

26. Gerould, "Social and Historical Reminiscences."

27. Shaw, "Groom of One's Own?"; Shaw, "Ritual Brotherhood," especially 336–337 (Chramnesindus and Sicharius) and 343 (Macliavus and Bodicus).

28. Shaw, "Ritual Brotherhood," 340, 351, 353.

29. Ephrem, review of *Same-Sex Unions*, 50–55; Woods, "Same-Sex Unions," 338–342.

30. Haseldine, *Friendship in Medieval Europe*, 167.

31. Boswell, *Same-Sex Unions*, 199–202.

32. Zaninović, "Dva Latinska spomenika."

33. Elizabeth Brown, "Symposium," 261–381.

34. Michael Young, *James VI and I*, 148–153; Trumbach, "Gender and the Homosexual Role"; Trumbach, "Sex, Gender, and Sexual Identity." Also, on a different point, as my references in chapter 6 indicate, I am much indebted there to my discussions with Professor Trumbach of his studies of traditional Christian marriage practices.

35. Anthony Fletcher, *Gender, Sex, and Subordination*, 405–407, 101, 204, 96.

36. Ibid., 339.

37. Westwood, Sewall, and Liddington, *Anne Lister Research Directory*, 18–19.

38. Lister, *Female Fortune*, 67.

39. For example, Brodwin, "Edward II"; Boyette, "Wanton Humour"; Huebert, "Tobacco and Boys and Marlowe."

40. For example, Sanders, *Dramatist and the Received Idea*, 121–142; Godshalk, *Marlovian World Picture*, 59 ff., a view more recently revisited by Cartelli, *Marlowe, Shakespeare*, 121–135.

41. Eliot, "Christopher Marlowe," 118–125.

42. Mills, "Meaning of Edward II."

43. Shepherd, *Marlowe*, 197–207; Jonathan Goldberg, "Sodomy and Society"; Archer, "Marlowe and the Observation of Men," 67–94. The ambiguity in the play was referred to briefly but perceptively by Anne Barton in a review of my *Homosexuality in Renaissance England*, 18.

44. Ailes, "Medieval Male Couple," 214–237.

45. Wootton, "Levellers," 83–84; Wootton, "Friendship Portrayed"; Wootton, "Francis Bacon."

Adambel Clym of the Cloughe and Wyllyam of Cloudesle. London, n.d.

Adams, S. L. "The Gentry of North Wales and the Earl of Leicester's Expedition to the Netherlands, 1585–1586." *Welsh History Review* 7 (1974–1975): 129–147.

Aelred of Rievaulx. *Aelred of Rievaulx: Spiritual Friendship.* Translated by Mary Eugenia Laker. Introduced by Douglass Raby. Kalamazoo, MI: Cistercian Publications, 1977.

———. *De Spiritali Amicitia.* In *Aelredi Rievallensis Opera Omnia,* vol. 1, *Opera Ascetica,* edited by A. Hoste and C. H. Talbot, 279–350. Turnhoult: Brepols, 1971.

———. *Liber de Speculo Caritatis.* In *Aelredi Rievallensis Opera Omnia,* vol. 1, *Opera Ascetica,* edited by A. Hoste and C. H. Talbot, 1–161. Turnhoult: Brepols, 1971.

Ailes, M. J. "The Medieval Male Couple and the Language of Homosociality." In *Masculinity in Medieval Europe,* edited by D. M. Hadley, 214–237. London: Longman, 1999.

Akrigg, G. P. V. *Letters of King James VI and I.* Berkeley: University of California Press, 1984.

Allen, P. S. "Erasmus's Money and Rings in 1534." *Bodleian Quarterly Record* 2 (1917–1919): 142–144.

Amis and Amiloun. Edited by Eugen Kölbing. Heilbronn: Gebr. Henninger, 1884.

Amis and Amiloun. Edited by MacEdward Leach. London: Early English Text Society, by H. Milford, Oxford University Press, 1937.

Amys and Amylion. Edited by Françoise H. M. Le Saux. Exeter: University of Exeter Press, 1993.

Anderson, Olive. "The Anne Lister Papers." *History Workshop Journal,* no. 40 (fall 1995): 190–192.

The Anglo-Saxon Chronicle. Edited by G. N. Garmonsway. London: Dent, 1953.

Anselm of Canterbury. *Cur Deus Homo.* In *S. Anselmi Cantuariensis Archiepiscopi Opera Omnia,* edited by Franciscus Salesius Scmitt, 2:37–133. Edinburgh: T. Nelson, 1946.

Archenholz, Johann Wilhelm von. *A Picture of England.* London: E. Jeffery, 1789.

Archer, John Michael. "Marlowe and the Observation of Men." In *Sovereignty and Intelligence: Spying and Court Culture in the English Renaissance,* edited by John Michael Archer, 67–94. Stanford: Stanford University Press, 1993.

Ashbee, Andrew, and David Lasocki, comps. *A Biographical Dictionary of English Court Musicians, 1485–1714.* Aldershot: Ashgate, 1998.

Askew, Reginald. *Muskets and Altars: Jeremy Taylor and the Last of the Anglicans.* London: Herndon, 1997.

Athelston: A Medieval English Romance. Edited by A. McI. Trounce. London: Oxford University Press, 1951.

Aubrey, John. *"Brief Lives," Chiefly of Contemporaries, Set Down by John Aubrey, Between the Years 1669 and 1696.* Edited by Andrew Clark. Oxford: Clarendon Press, 1898.

Auden, W. H. "The Wanderer." In *Collected Poems,* 62. London: Faber and Faber, 1976.

Augustine. *Confessions.* Edited by James J. O'Donnell. Oxford: Oxford University Press, 1992.

———. *The Confessions of the Incomparable Doctovr S. Augustine.* Translated by Tobie Matthew. [Rouen]: n.p., 1620.

Aylmer, Gerald, and John Tiller, eds. *Hereford Cathedral: A History.* London: Hambledon Press, 2000.

Bacon, Francis. *A Harmony of the Essays, etc. of Francis Bacon.* Edited by Edward Arber. London: n.p., 1871.

———. *The Letters and the Life of Francis Bacon.* Edited by James Spedding. London: Longman, Green, et al., 1861–1874.

———. "Of Followers and Friends." In *Essayes, Religious Meditations, Places of Perswasion and disswasion, Seene and allowed.* London: H. Hooper, 1597.

Bailey, Derrick Sherwin. *Sponsors at Baptism and Confirmation: An Historical Introduction to Anglican Practice.* London: SPCK, 1952.

Baldwin, Dean R. "*Amis and Amiloun:* The Testing of *treupe.*" *Papers on Language and Literature* 16 (1980): 353–365.

Bannister, Arthur T. *The Cathedral Church of Hereford: Its History and Constitution.* London: SPCK, 1924.

Barrell, John. "Editing Out: The Discourse of Patronage in Shakespeare's Twenty-Ninth Sonnet." In *Poetry, Language, and Politics,* 18–43. Manchester: Manchester University Press, 1998.

Barrow, Henry. *A Plaine Refvtation of M. G. Giffardes Reprochful Booke, Entituled a Short Treatise against the Donatists of England.* In *The Writings of Henry Barrow, 1590–1591,* edited by Leland H. Carlson, 25–331. London: George Allen and Unwin, 1966.

Bartlett, Robert. *Gerald of Wales, 1146–1223.* Oxford: Clarendon Press, 1982.

Barton, Anne. Review of *Homosexuality in Renaissance England* by Alan Bray. *London Review of Books* 5, no. 15 (18–31 August 1983): 18–19.

Beaumont, Edward T. *Ancient Memorial Brasses.* London: Henry Milford, Oxford University Press, 1913.

Benigno, Francesco. "The Southern Italian Family in the Early Modern Period: A Discussion of Co-residential Patterns." *Continuity and Change* 4 (1989): 165–194.

Bennett, Michael. "Spiritual Kinship and the Baptismal Name in Traditional European Society." In *Principalities, Powers, and Estates: Studies in Medieval and Early Modern Government and Society,* edited by L. O. Frappell, 1–13. Adelaide: Adelaide University Union Press, 1979.

Bergeron, David M. *King James and Letters of Homoerotic Desire.* Iowa City: University of Iowa Press, 1999.

Bertram, Jerome, and other members of the Oxford University Archaeological Society. "The Lost Brasses of Oxford." *Transactions of the Monumental Brass Society* 11 (1969–1975): 219–252.

Bingham, Caroline. *James I of England.* London: Weidenfeld and Nicolson, 1981.

Blackburne, Harry W., and Maurice F. Bond. *The Romance of St George's Chapel, Windsor Castle.* Windsor: Oxley and Son, 1976.

Boes, Maria R. "On Trial for Sodomy in Early Modern Germany." In *Sodomy in Early Modern Europe,* edited by Thomas Betteridge, 27–45. Manchester: Manchester University Press, 2002.

Bossy, John. *Christianity in the West, 1400–1700.* Oxford: Oxford University Press, 1985.

———. "The Counter-Reformation and the People of Catholic Ireland, 1596–1641." In *Historical Studies: Papers Read before the Irish Conference of Historians, Dublin, 27–30 May 1969,* vol. 8, edited by Thomas Desmond Williams, 155–169. Dublin: Gill and Macmillan, 1971.

————. *The English Catholic Community.* London: Darton, Longman, and Todd, 1975.

————. "Godparenthood: The Fortunes of a Social Institution in Early Modern Christianity." In *Religion and Society in Early Modern Europe, 1500–1800,* edited by Casper von Greyerz, 194–201. London: German Historical Institute, 1984.

————. "The Mass as a Social Institution, 1200–1700." *Past and Present,* no. 100 (August 1983): 29–61.

————. *Peace in the Post-Reformation.* Cambridge: Cambridge University Press, 1998.

————. "Some Elementary Forms of Durkheim." *Past and Present,* no. 95 (May 1982): 3–18.

Boswell, John. *Christianity, Social Tolerance, and Homosexuality: Gay People in Western Europe from the Beginning of the Christian Era to the Fourteenth Century.* Chicago: University of Chicago Press, 1980.

————. *Same-Sex Unions in Premodern Europe.* New York: Random House, Villard Books, 1994.

Bott, Alan. *The Monuments in Merton College Chapel.* Oxford: Blackwell, 1964.

Boutell, Charles. *Boutell's Heraldry.* Edited by J. P. Brooke-Little. London and New York: F. Warne, 1990.

Bouton, Jeremy. "Clandestine Marriages in London: An Examination of a Neglected Urban Variable." *Urban History* 20 (1993): 191–210.

————. "Itching after Private Marryings? Marriage Customs in Seventeenth-Century London." *London Journal* 16 (1991): 15–34.

Boyette, Purvis E. "Wanton Humour and Wanton Poets: Homosexuality in Marlowe's Edward II." *Tulane Studies in English* 22 (1977): 33–50.

Bradley, S. A. J. "'Quem Aspicientes Viverunt': Symbolism in the Early Medieval Church Door and Its Ironwork." *Antiquaries Journal* 68 (1988): 223–237.

Brand, John. *The History and Antiquities of the Town and County of the Town of Newcastle upon Tyne . . .* London: B. White and Son, 1789.

Bray, Alan. "Homosexuality and the Signs of Male Friendship in Elizabethan England." *History Workshop Journal,* no. 29 (spring 1990): 1–19. Reprinted in *Queering the Renaissance,* edited by Jonathan Goldberg, 40–61. Durham, NC: Duke University Press, 1994.

————. *Homosexuality in Renaissance England.* New York: Columbia University Press, 1995. Originally published London: Gay Men's Press, 1982.

Bray, Alan, and Michel Rey. "The Body of the Friend: Continuity and Change in Masculine Friendship in the Seventeenth Century." In *English Masculinities, 1660–1800,* edited by Tim Hitchcock and Michèle Cohen, 65–84. London: Longman, 1999.

Brayley, Edward W. *The History and Antiquities of the Abbey Church of St. Peter, Westminster.* Illustrated by John P. Neale. London: J. P. Neale, 1818–1823.

Bretton, R. "The Heraldry of the Halifax Parish Church." *Transactions of the Halifax Antiquarian Society* (1931): 29–72.

————. "Halifax Parish Church." *Transactions of the Halifax Antiquarian Society* (1967): 72–91.

Brockett, John Trotter. *A Glossary of North Country Words, with their etymology, and affinity to other languages; and occasional notices of local customs and popular superstitions.* Newcastle-upon-Tyne: E. Charnley, 1829.

Brodwin, Leonora L. "Edward II: Marlowe's Culminating Treatment of Love." *English Literary History* 31, no. 2 (1964): 139–155.

Brooke, C. F. Tucker. *The Life of Marlowe and the Tragedy of Dido Queen of Carthage.* New York: Gordian Press, 1966.

Brooke, Christopher N. L. *A History of Gonville and Caius College.* Woodbridge, Suffolk: Boydell, 1985.

Brown, Elizabeth A. R. "Ritual Brotherhood in Western Medieval Europe." *Traditio* 52 (1997): 357–381.

————. "The Tyranny of a Construct: Feudalism and Historians of Medieval Europe." *American Historical Review* 79 (1974): 1063–1088.

————, ed. "Ritual Brotherhood in Ancient and Medieval Europe: A Symposium." *Traditio* 52 (1997): 261–381.

Brown, Peter. *The Cult of the Saints: Its Rise and Function in Latin Christianity.* London: SCM, 1981.

————. *Power and Persuasion in Late Antiquity: Towards a Christian Empire.* Madison: University of Wisconsin Press, 1992.

Brut. Translated by Rosamund Allen. London: Dent, 1992.

The Brut, or the Chronicles of England. Edited by Friedrich W. D. Brie. London: K. Paul, Trench, Trübner for the EETS, 1906–1908.

Buchanan, Colin. *The Kiss of Peace.* Bramcote, Nottinghamshire: Grove Books, 1982.

Burke, Peter. "Humanism and Friendship in Sixteenth-Century Europe." In *Friendship in Medieval Europe*, edited by Julian P. Haseldine, 262–274. Thrupp, Stroud: Sutton, 1999.

Butler-Stoney, Richard. *Wiveton St Mary, the Virgin.* From notes by Mrs. J. N. Gordon. Drawings by Hugh Holbeach. N.p. 1987. Pamphlet.

Byrne, Muriel St. Clare, ed. *The Lisle Letters.* Chicago: University of Chicago Press, 1981.

Caius, John. *The Annals of Gonville and Caius College.* Edited by John Venn. Cambridge: Cambridge Antiquarian Society, 1904.

Campbell, Lorne, Margaret Mann Phillips, Hubertus Schulte Herbrüggen, and J. B. Trapp. "Quentin Matsys, Desiderius Erasmus, Pieter Gillis, and Thomas More." *Burlington Magazine* 120 (1978): 716–725.

Cardwell, Edward. *The Canons of 1604 XXI.* Vol. 1 of *Synodalia: A Collection of Articles of Religion, Canons, and Proceedings of Convocations in the Province of Canterbury, from the Year 1547 to the Year 1717.* Oxford: University Press, 1842.

Carlson, Eric Josef. *Marriage and the English Reformation.* Cambridge, MA: Blackwell, 1994.

Carlton, Charles. *Archbishop William Laud.* New York: Routledge and Kegan Paul, 1987.

Carte, Thomas. *A History of the Life of James Duke of Ormonde, from his Birth in 1610, to his Death in 1688 . . . to which is added . . . in another volume, A very valuable Collection of Letters.* London: J. J. and P. Knapton, 1735–1736.

Cartelli, Thomas. *Marlowe, Shakespeare, and the Economy of Theatrical Experience.* Philadelphia: University of Pennsylvania Press, 1991.

Cartmell, Joseph. "The Church of St. Thomas of the English." *Venerabile* 3 (1926–1928): 31–40.

Cartulary of Oseney Abbey. Edited by H. E. Slater. Vol. 4. Oxford: Clarendon Press for the Oxford Historical Society, 1934.

Chadwick, Norah Kershaw, ed. and trans. *Anglo-Saxon and Norse Poems.* Cambridge: University Press, 1922.

Chamberlain, John. *The Letters of John Chamberlain.* Edited by Norman E. McClure. Philadelphia: American Philosophical Society, 1939.

Champ, Judith. *The English Pilgrimage to Rome: A Dwelling for the Soul.* Leominster: Gracewing, 2000.

Chaplais, Pierre. *Piers Gaveston: Edward II's Adoptive Brother.* Oxford: Clarendon Press, 1994.

Chapman, George. *The Plays of George Chapman: The Comedies.* Edited by Allan Holaday. Urbana: University of Illinois Press, 1970.

Character, Objects & Effects of Trades' Unions, with Some Remarks on the Law concerning Them. London, 1834.

Chaucer, Geoffrey. *Canterbury Tales.* Edited by A. C. Cawley. London: Dent, 1958.

————. *The Complete Works of Geoffrey Chaucer.* Edited by Walter W. Skeat. Oxford: Clarendon Press, 1894.

Chaytor, Miranda. "Household and Kinship: Ryton in the Late 16th and Early 17th Centuries." *History Workshop Journal*, no. 10 (autumn 1980): 25–60.

Cherry, Bridget, and Nikolaus Pevsner. *London: 3, North West.* London: Penguin, 1991.

Chetham Society. *Remains Historical & Literary Connected with the Palatine Counties of Lancaster and Chester* 31 (1853): 23–27.

Child, Francis James, ed. *The English and Scottish Popular Ballads.* Boston: Houghton, Mifflin, 1882–1898.

Chronica Monasterii de Melsa . . . Edited by Edward Augustus Bond. London: Longman, Green, Reader, and Dyer, 1866–1868.

Chronicle of the Grey Friars of London. Edited by John Gough Nichols. London: Camden Society, 1852.

Chronicon de Lanercost, M.CC.I–M.CCC.XLVI. e codice Cottoniano . . . Edited by Joseph Stevenson. Edinburgh: n.p., 1839.

Cicero. *Cicero on Obligations (De Officiis).* Edited by P. G. Walsh. Oxford: Oxford University Press, 2000.

———. *De Senectute, De Amicitia, De Divinatione.* Edited by William Armistead Falconer. London: Heinemann; New York: G. P. Putnam's Sons, 1923.

Clanvowe, John. *Works of Sir John Clanvowe.* Edited by V. J. Scattergood. Cambridge: D. S. Brewer; Totowa, NY: Rowman and Littlefield, 1975.

Clark, Peter, and Jennifer Clark. "The Social Economy of the Canterbury Suburbs: The Evidence of the Census of 1563." In *Studies in Modern Kentish History,* edited by Alec Detsicas and Nigel Yates, 79–80. Maidstone: Kent Archaeological Society, 1983.

Clutterbuck, Robert. *The History and Antiquities of the County of Hertford.* London: Nichols, Son, and Bentley, 1815–1827.

Coke, Edward. *The Twelfth Part of the Reports of Sir Edward Coke, Kt. of divers resolutions and judgments given upon solumn arguments . . .* London: T. R. for Henry Twyford et al., 1656.

Cole, G. D. H. *Attempts at General Union: A Study in British Trade Union History, 1818–1834.* London: Macmillan, 1953.

Congreve, William. "On Mrs. Arabella Hunt Singing." In *The Works of Congreve: Comedies, Incognita, Poems,* edited by F. W. Bateson, 465. London: Davies, 1930.

———. *The Works of William Congreve.* London: J. and R. Tonson, S. Draper, 1753.

Conner, Patrick W. *Anglo-Saxon Exeter: A Tenth-Century Cultural History.* Woodbridge, Suffolk: Boydell, 1993.

Cook, G. H. *Old S. Paul's Cathedral: A Lost Glory of Mediaeval London.* London: Phoenix House, 1955.

Cornwallis, William. *Essayes.* London: Mattes, 1600–1601.

———. *Essayes by Sr William Cornwallyes, the younger, knight. Newlie corrected.* London: Thomas Harper for I. M., 1632.

Corro, Antonio del. *Dialogvs in Epistolam D. Pauli ad Romanos.* Frankfurt, 1587.

———. *Dialogvs Theologicvs.* London, 1574. Translated as *A Theological Dialogve.* London, 1575.

———. *Epistola Beati Pavli Apostoli ad Romanos.* London, 1581.

Countryside Commission. *Wiveton Village.* Wiveton: n.d.

Cowdrey, H. E. J. "Pope Gregory VII and the Anglo-Norman Church and Kingdom." *Studi Gregoriani per la Storia della "Libertas Ecclesiae"* 9 (1972): 77–174.

Cox, J. Charles. *The Parish Registers of England.* London: Methuen, 1910.

Crabtree, Selwyn, and Geoffrey Washington. *Halifax Parish Church: St. John the Baptist.* Plan by Norman Tatham. Halifax, 1994.

Crawford, Patricia, and Sara Mendelson. "Sexual Identities in Early Modern England: The Marriage of Two Women in 1680." *Gender and History* 7 (1995): 362–377.

Cressy, David. "Kinship and Kin Interaction in Early Modern England." *Past and Present*, no. 113 (November 1986): 38–69.

Crossley, E. W. *The Monumental and Other Inscriptions in Halifax Parish Church.* Leeds: John Whitehead, 1909.

Cuddy, Neil. "The Revival of the Entourage: The Bedchamber of James I, 1603–1625." In *The English Court: From the Wars of the Roses to the Civil War,* edited by David Starkey. London: Longman, 1987.

Darell, Walter. *A Short Discourse of the Life of Seruingmen.* London, 1578. Reprinted in *Studies in Philology* 31 (1934): 115–132.

D'Avenant, William. *The Dramatic Works of Sir William D'Avenant.* Edited by James Maidment and W. H. Logan. Edinburgh: W. Paterson, 1872–1874.

Davies, R. T. *Medieval English Lyrics: A Critical Anthology.* London: Faber and Faber, 1963.

Day, Angell. *The English Secretorie; or, plaine and direct Method, for the enditing of all manner of Epistles or Letters . . .* London, 1592.

Derrida, Jacques. "The Politics of Friendship." *Journal of Philosophy* 85 (1998): 632–644.

———. *Politics of Friendship.* Translated by George Collins. London: Verso, 1997.

———. *Politiques de l'amitié.* Paris: Editions Galilée, 1994.

Dictionary of Medieval Latin from British Sources. Edited by R. E. Latham and D. R. Howlett. London: Oxford University Press for the British Academy, 1975–.

Dryden, John. *The Poems of John Dryden.* Edited by James Kinsley. Oxford: Oxford University Press, 1958.

Dudley, Robert. *Correspondence of Robert Dudley, Earl of Leycester, during His Government of the Low Countries, in the Years 1585 and 1586.* Edited by John Bruce. London: J. B. Nichols for the Camden Society, 1844.

Dugdale, William. *The History of Saint Paul's Cathedral, in London, from Its Foundation: Extracted out of original charters, records, ledger-books, and other manuscripts.* London: Lackington, Hughes, Harding, et al., 1818.

Düll, Siegrid, Anthony Luttrell, and Maurice Keen. "Faithful unto Death: The Tomb Slab of Sir William Neville and Sir John Clanvowe, Constantinople 1391." *Antiquaries Journal* 71 (1991): 174–190.

Duncan-Jones, Katherine. *Sir Philip Sidney: Courtier Poet.* New Haven: Yale University Press, 1991.

Duncumb, John. *Collections towards the History and Antiquities of the County of Hereford.* Hereford: E. G. Wright, 1804–1812.

Durandus, Gulielmus. *Rationale Divinorum Officiorum.* Naples: Josephus Bibliopola, 1859.

Edward VI. *The First Prayer-Book of Edward VI, Compared with the Successive Revisions of the Book of Common Prayer.* Oxford: J. Parker, 1877.

Eliot, T. S. "Christopher Marlowe." In *Selected Essays,* 118–125. London: Faber and Faber, 1951.

Emden, A. B., ed. *A Biographical Register of the University of Oxford to A. D. 1500.* Oxford: Clarendon Press, 1957–1959.

The English Register of Oseney Abbey, by Oxford, Written about 1460. Edited by Andrew Clark. London: K. Paul, Trench, Trübner for the EETS, 1913.

Ephrem, Archimandrite. Review of *Same-Sex Unions in Premodern Europe* by John Boswell. *Sourozh*, no. 59 (February 1995): 50–55.

Erasmus, Desiderius. *Collected Works of Erasmus.* Translated by Craig R. Thompson. Toronto: University of Toronto Press, 1974–.

———. *The Correspondence of Erasmus.* Translated by R. A. B. Mynors and D. F. S. Thomson. Toronto: University of Toronto Press, 1975–.

———. *Opvs Epistolarvm Des. Erasmi Roterodami.* Edited by P. S. and H. M. Allen. Oxford: Clarendon Press, 1906–1958.

———. *Parabolae sive Similia.* In *Opera Omnia Desiderii Erasmi Roterodami,* vol. 5, edited by J. C. Margolin. Amsterdam: North-Holland, 1969–.

Evelyn, John. *The Diary of John Evelyn.* Edited by E. S. de Beer. London: Oxford University Press, 1959.

Faderman, Lillian. *Surpassing the Love of Men: Romantic Friendship and Love between Women from the Renaissance to the Present.* London: Women's Press, 1985.

Farmer, Norman, Jr. "Fulke Greville and Sir John Coke: An Exchange of Letters on a History Lecture and Certain Latin Verses on Sir Philip Sidney." *Huntington Library Quarterly* 33 (1969–1970): 218–219.

Farrow, Margaret A., and Percy Millican, eds. *Index to Wills Proved in the Consistory Court of Norwich and Now Preserved in the District Probate Registry at Norwich.* London: British Record Society by S. Austin and Sons, 1945–1950.

Flandrin, Jean-Louis. *Families in Former Times: Kinship, Household, and Sexuality.* Translated by Richard Southern. Cambridge: Cambridge University Press, 1979.

Fletcher, Anthony. *Gender, Sex, and Subordination in England, 1500–1800.* New Haven: Yale University Press, 1995.

Fletcher, Giles. *Christ's Victory and Triumph in Heaven and Earth, Over and After Death.* Edited by Will T. Brooke. London: Griffith, Farran, Okeden, and Welsh, 1888.

Fletcher, John M., and Christopher A. Upton. "'Monastic Enclave' or 'Open Society'? A Consideration of the Role of Women in the Life of an Oxford College Community in the Early Tudor Period." *History of Education* 16 (1987): 1–9.

Florentius Wigorniensis. *Monachi Chronicon ex Chronicis.* Edited by Benjamin Thorpe. Vol. 1. London: English Historical Society, 1848.

Floris and Blancheflour. Edited by A. B. Taylor. Oxford: Clarendon Press, 1927.

Forcella, Vincenzo. *Iscrizioni delle Chiese e d'altri Edificii di Roma dal Secolo XI Fino ai Giorni Nostri.* Rome: Tip. Delle scienze matematiche e fisiche, 1869–1884.

Franklyn, Julian, and John Tanner, eds. *An Encyclopaedic Dictionary of Heraldry.* Oxford: Pergamon, 1970.

Friar, Stephen, ed. *A New Dictionary of Heraldry.* Sherborne: Alphabooks, 1987.

Gardiner, Samuel R. *History of England from the Accession of James I to the Outbreak of the Civil War, 1603–1642.* New ed. London: Longmans, Green, 1884–1891.

Garrod, H. W. *Ancient Painted Glass in Merton College, Oxford.* London: Oxford University Press, 1931.

Gathorne-Hardy, Robert, and William Proctor Williams. *A Bibliography of the Writings of Jeremy Taylor to 1700.* Dekalb: Northern Illinois University Press, 1971.

Gerald of Wales. *Giraldi Cambrensis Opera.* Vol. 5. Edited by James F. Dimock. London: Longman, 1867.

Gerould, G. H. "Social and Historical Reminiscences in the Middle English Athelston." *Englische Studien* 36 (1905–1906): 193–208.

Gibson, Peter. "The Stained and Painted Glass of York." In *The Noble City of York,* edited by Alberic Stacpoole et al., 172–177. York: Cerialis Press, 1972.

Gilbert, C. S. *An Historical Survey of the County of Cornwall to which is added a complete Heraldry of the same, with numerous Engravings.* Plymouth: J. Congdon, 1817–1820.

Girouard, Mark. *Life in the English Country House: A Social and Architectural History.* New Haven: Yale University Press, 1978.

Godshalk, William L. *The Marlovian World Picture.* The Hague: Mouton, 1974.

Goldberg, Jonathan. *James I and the Politics of Literature: Johnson, Shakespeare, Donne, and Their Contemporaries.* Baltimore: Johns Hopkins University Press, 1983.

———. *Sodometries: Renaissance Texts, Modern Sexualities.* Stanford: Stanford University Press, 1992.

———. "Sodomy and Society: The Case of Christopher Marlowe." *Southwest Review* 69 (1984): 371–378.

Goldberg, P. J. P. "Women in Fifteenth-Century Town Life." In *Towns and Townspeople in the Fifteenth Century,* edited by John A. F. Thomson, 107–128. Gloucester: Alan Sutton, 1988.

———. *Women, Work, and Life Cycle in a Medieval Economy.* Oxford: Clarendon Press, 1992.

Goodman, Godfrey. *The Court of King James the First.* London: R. Bentley, 1839.

Green, V. H. H. "The University and Social Life." In *The History of the University of Oxford,* vol. 5, *The Eighteenth Century,* edited by L. S. Sutherland and L. G. Mitchell, 309–358. Oxford: Clarendon Press, 1986.

Greene, Richard Leighton, ed. *The Early English Carols.* Oxford: Clarendon Press, 1977.

Greene, Robert. *The Honorable Historii of frier Bacon and frier Bongay.* London: Edward White, 1594.

———. *The Life and Complete Works of Robert Greene.* Edited by Alexander B. Grosart. London: printed for private circulation only, 1881–1886.

Greville, Fulke. *The Prose Works of Fulke Greville, Lord Brooke.* Edited by John Gouws. Oxford: Clarendon Press, 1985.

Grisdale, D. M., ed. *Three Middle English Sermons from the Worcester Chapter Manuscript F.10.* Leeds: T. Wilson for the School of English Language in the University of Leeds, 1939.

Grosley, Pierre Jean. *A Tour to London, or New Observations on England and its Inhabitants.* Translated by Thomas Nugent. London: Lockyer Davis, 1772.

Gruenfelder, John K. "The Electoral Patronage of Sir Thomas Wentworth, Earl of Stafford, 1614–1640." *Journal of Modern History* 49 (1977): 557–574.

Guillaume de Jumièges. *Gesta Normannorum Ducum.* Edited by Jean Marx. Rouen: A. Lestringat; Paris: A. Picard, 1914.

Halliwell, James O. *Letters of Kings of England.* Edited by J. S. Brewer. London: R. Bentley, 1846.

Hamilton, J. S. "Menage à Roi: Edward II and Piers Gaveston." *History Today* 49, no. 6 (June 1999): 26–31.

———. *Piers Gaveston, Earl of Cornwall, 1307–1312: Politics and Patronage in the Reign of Edward II.* Detroit: Wayne State University Press, 1988.

Hanawalt, Barbara A. *The Ties That Bound: Peasant Families in Medieval England.* New York: Oxford University Press, 1986.

Hanham, Alison. *The Celys and Their World: An English Merchant Family of the Fifteenth Century.* Cambridge: Cambridge University Press, 1985.

Hanson, T. W. "The Evolution of the Parish Church, Halifax: From 1455 to 1530." *Transactions of the Halifax Antiquarian Society* (1917): 181–204.

Hargreaves, J. A. "The Georgian and Early Victorian Church in the Parish of Halifax, 1740–1851." *Transactions of the Halifax Antiquarian Society* (1990): 44–82.

Harris, John. *The destruction of sodome: A sermon.* London, 1628.

Hart, Cyril. "The Early Section of the *Worcester Chronicle.*" *Journal of Medieval History* 9 (1983): 251–315.

Harvey, Gabriel. *Fovre Letters and Certeine Sonnets.* Edited by G. B. Harrison. Edinburgh: Edinburgh University Press, 1966.

————. *The Works of Gabriel Harvey.* Edited by Alexander B. Grosart. [London]: for private circulation only, 1884.

Harvey, Richard. "Lamb of God." In Thomas Nashe, *The Works of Thomas Nashe,* vol. 5, edited by Ronald B. McKerrow, revised by F. P. Wilson, 176–180. Oxford: Blackwell, 1966.

Haseldine, Julian P. "Friendship and Rivalry: The Role of *Amicitia* in Twelfth-Century Monastic Relations." *Journal of Ecclesiastical History* 44 (1993): 390–414.

————. "Love, Separation, and Male Friendship: Words and Actions in Saint Anselm's Letters to His Friends." In *Masculinity in Medieval Europe,* edited by D. M. Hadley, 238–255. London: Longman, 1999.

————. "Understanding the Language of *Amicitia:* The Friendship Circle of Peter of Celle (c. 1115–1183)." *Journal of Medieval History* 20 (1994): 237–260.

————, ed. *Friendship in Medieval Europe.* Stroud: Sutton, 1999.

Haskins, George L. "A Chronicle of the Civil Wars of Edward II." *Speculum* 14 (1939): 73–81.

Havergal, Francis T. *Fasti Herefordenses and Other Antiquarian Memorials of Hereford.* Edinburgh: P. Clark, 1869.

————. *Monumental Inscriptions in the Cathedral Church of Hereford.* Illustrated by Robert Clarke. London: Simpkin, Marshall, 1881.

Havergal, Francis T., and J. Severn Walker. *Ground Plan of Hereford Cathedral Church.* Hereford, 1865.

Hawkins, John. *General History of the Science and Practice of Music.* A new edition, with the author's posthumous notes. London: Novello, Ewer, 1875.

Hay, George. "Pilgrims and the Hospice." *Venerabile* 19 (1958–1960): 329–339.

Heal, Felicity. *Hospitality in Early Modern England.* Oxford: Clarendon Press, 1990.

Hearne, Thomas. *Historia Vitae et Regni Ricardi II . . .* Oxford: Sheldonian Theater, 1729.

H.E.C.S. *Holy Trinity Church Goodramgate, York.* Revised by G. Wilson. Churches Conservation Trust, 2000.

Hector, L. C., and Barbara F. Harvey, eds. *The Westminster Chronicle.* Oxford: Clarendon Press, 1982.

Henderson, Bernard W. *Merton College.* London: F. E. Robinson, 1899.

Henry of Huntingdon. *Historia Anglorum.* Edited by Thomas Arnold. London: Longman, 1879.

Herbert, George. "A Priest to the Temple, or the Countrey Parson his Character and Rule of Holy Life." In *The Complete Works in Verse and Prose of George Herbert,* edited by Alexander B. Grosart. London: printed for private circulation [Robson], 1874.

Hermann, John P. "Dismemberment, Dissemination, Discourse: Sign and Symbol in the *Shipman's Tale.*" *Chaucer Review* 19 (1984–1985): 302–337.

Herrup, Cynthia B. *A House in Gross Disorder: Sex, Law, and the Second Earl of Castlehaven.* Oxford: Oxford University Press, 1999.

Hicks, Michael. *Bastard Feudalism.* London: Longman, 1995.

Hind, A. M., Margery Corbett, and Michael Norton. *Engraving in England in the Sixteenth and Seventeenth Centuries.* Cambridge: University Press, 1952–1964.

The History of Adam Bell, Clim of the Clough and William of Cloudesly. Glasgow: Robert Sanders, 1668.

Hobsbawm, E. J. "The Tramping Artisan." In *Labouring Men: Studies in the History of Labour,* 34–63. London: Weidenfeld and Nicolson, 1964.

Homosexual Relationships: A Contribution to Discussion. London: CIO for the General Synod Board for Social Responsibility, 1979.

Hope, W. H. St. John. *The Stall Plates of the Knights of the Order of the Garter, 1348–1485.* Westminster: A. Constable, 1901.

Houston, Rab, and Richard Smith. "A New Approach to Family History?" *History Workshop Journal,* no. 14 (fall 1982): 120–131.

Howell, James. *Epistolae Ho Elianae: Familiar Letters Domestic & Forren, Partly Historical, Political, Phylosophical*. London, 1645.

Huebert, Ronald. "Tobacco and Boys and Marlowe." *Sewanee Review* 92, no. 2 (1984): 206–224.

Hufton, Olwen. "Women without Men: Widows and Spinsters in Britain and France in the Eighteenth Century." *Journal of Family History* 9 (1984): 355–376.

Hughes, Diane O. "Urban Growth and Family Structure in Medieval Genoa." *Past and Present*, no. 66 (February 1975): 3–28.

Hume, Basil. *Created Design: Some Pastoral Guidelines for the Care of Lesbian and Gay People*. [London?]: Catholic AIDS Link, 1997.

———. "A Note on the Teaching of the Catholic Church concerning Homosexual People." *Briefing* 25, no. 3 (16 March 1995).

Hutson, Lorna. *Thomas Nashe in Context*. Oxford: Clarendon Press, 1989.

———. *The Usurer's Daughter: Male Friendship and Fictions of Women in Sixteenth-Century England*. London: Routledge, 1994.

I. M. [Gervase Markham?]. *A Health to the Gentlemanly Profession of Seruingmen*. London: W. W., 1598.

Ingram, James. *Memorials of Oxford*. London: J. H. Parker, 1837.

James VI (and I). *BASILIKON DŌRON devided into three Bookes*. Edinburgh, 1596.

James, M. R. *A Descriptive Catalogue of the Manuscripts in the Library of Gonville and Caius College*. Cambridge: University Press, 1907.

Jardine, Lisa. *Erasmus, Man of Letters: The Construction of Charisma in Print*. Princeton: Princeton University Press, 1993.

Jardine, Lisa, and Anthony Grafton. "'Studied for Action': How Gabriel Harvey Reads His Livy." *Past and Present*, no. 129 (November 1990): 30–78.

J. N. G. [Mrs. J. N. Gordon]. *St Mary the Virgin, Wiveton*. N.p., n.d. Pamphlet.

Johnson, Matthew. *Housing Culture: Traditional Architecture in an English Landscape*. London: UCL Press, 1993.

Jordan, Mark D. *The Invention of Sodomy in Christian Theology*. Chicago: University of Chicago, 1997.

———. "A Romance of the Gay Couple." *GLQ* 3 (1996): 301–310.

———. *The Silence of Sodom: Homosexuality in Modern Catholicism*. Chicago: University of Chicago Press, 2000.

Jungmann, Joseph A. *The Mass of the Roman Rite: Its Origins and Development*. New York: Benziger, 1951–1955.

Juvenal and Persius. Edited by G. G. Ramsay. London: Heinemann, 1918.

Kant, Immanuel. "On the Most Intimate Union of Love with Respect to Friendship." In *The Metaphysics of Morals*, translated by Mary J. Gregor, 215–217. Cambridge: Cambridge University Press, 1996.

Kaye, Harvey J. *The British Marxist Historians: An Introductory Analysis*. New York: Polity Press, 1984.

Keen, Maurice. "Brotherhood in Arms." *History* 47 (1962): 1–17.

Keene, Derek. *Survey of Medieval Winchester*. Oxford: Clarendon Press, 1985.

Kendall, Mrs. "Two Halifax Ladies of Quality." *Transactions of the Halifax Antiquarian Society* (1918): 117–138.

Kent, D. V., and Francis W. Kent. *Neighbours and Neighbourhood in Renaissance Florence: The District of the Red Lion in the Fifteenth Century*. Locust Valley, NY: J. J. Augustin, 1982.

Kent, Francis W. *Household and Lineage in Renaissance Florence: The Family Life of the Capponi, Ginori, and Rucellai*. Princeton: Princeton University Press, 1977.

Kettering, Sharon. "Friendship and Clientage in Early Modern France." *French History* 6 (1992): 139–158.

————. "Gift-Giving and Patronage in Early Modern France." *French History* 2 (1988): 131–151.

————. *Patrons, Brokers, and Clients in Seventeenth-Century France.* New York: Oxford University Press, 1986.

Kinder, Arthur Gordon. *Casiodoro de Reina: Spanish Reformer of the Sixteenth Century.* London: Tamesis, 1975.

Knowles, John A. "The East Window of Holy Trinity Church, Goodramgate, York." *Yorkshire Archaeological Journal* 23 (1926): 1–24.

Kolve, V. A. "'Man in the Middle': Art and Religion in Chaucer's *Friar's Tale.*" *Studies in the Age of Chaucer* 12 (1990): 5–46.

Kretzenbacher, Leopold. "Serbische-orthodoxe 'Wahlverbrüderung' zwischen Gläubigenwunsch and Kirchenverbot von heute." *Südost-Forschungen* 38 (1979): 163–183.

Kuriyama, Constance B. "Marlowe's Nemesis: The Identity of Richard Baines." In *A Poet and a Filthy Play-Maker: New Essays on Christopher Marlowe,* edited by Kenneth Friedenreich, Roma Gill, and Constance B. Kuriyama, 343–360. New York: AMS Press, 1988.

Laing, David. *Early Metrical Tales including the History of Sir Egeir, Sir Gryme, and Sir Gray-Steill.* Edinburgh: W. D. Laing, 1826.

Laird, Anthony. "The College Church." *Venerabile* 24 (1967–1968): 28–38, 159ff., 258–268.

Lander, J. R. "'Family,' 'Friends,' and Politics in Fifteenth-Century England." In *Kings and Nobles in the Later Middle Ages: A Tribute to Charles Ross,* edited by Ralph A. Griffiths and James Sherborne, 27–40. New York: St. Martin's Press, 1986.

La Rochefoucauld, François de. *A Frenchman in England 1784: Being the "Mélanges sur l'Angleterre."* Edited by Jean Marchand. Translated by S. C. Roberts. Cambridge: University Press, 1933.

La Rochefoucauld, François de, and Alexandre de La Rochefoucauld. *Innocent Espionage: The La Rochefoucauld Brothers' Tour of England in 1785.* Edited by Norman Scarfe. Woodbridge, Suffolk: Boydell, 1995.

Laslett, Peter. *Family Life and Illicit Love in Earlier Generations: Essays in Historical Sociology.* Reprint, with corrections. Cambridge: Cambridge University Press, 1980.

————. *The World We Have Lost.* London: Methuen, 1965.

————. *The World We Have Lost: Further Explored.* London: Methuen, 1983.

Laslett, Peter, and Richard Wall, eds. *Household and Family in Past Time: Comparative Studies in the Size and Structure of the Domestic Group over the Last Three Centuries in England, France, Serbia, Japan, and Colonial North America, with Further Materials from Western Europe.* Cambridge: University Press, 1972.

Latham, R. E., ed. *Revised Medieval Latin Word-List from British and Irish Sources.* London: Oxford University Press, 1965.

Laud, William. *The Works of the Most Reverend Father in God, William Laud, D.D., Sometime Lord Archbishop of Canterbury.* Edited by William Scott and James Bliss. Oxford: J. H. Parker, 1847–1860.

Lazamons Brut: A Poetical Semi-Saxon Paraphrase of the Brut of Wace . . . Edited by Frederic Madden. London: Society of Antiquaries of London, 1847.

Layamon's Brut: Selections. Edited by Joseph Hall. Oxford: Clarendon Press, 1924.

Leclercq, Jean. *Monks and Love in Twelfth-Century France: Psycho-historical Essays.* Oxford: Clarendon Press, 1979.

Leeson, R. A. *Travelling Brothers: The Six Centuries' Road from Craft Fellowship to Trade Unionism.* London: Allen and Unwin, 1979.

Levine, Joseph M. *Between the Ancients and the Moderns: Baroque Culture in Restoration England.* New Haven: Yale University Press, 1999.

"The Librarian." *Venerabile* 4 (1928–1930): 382–383.

Liddington, Jill. "Anne Lister of Shibden Hall, Halifax (1791–1840): Her Diaries and the Historians." *History Workshop Journal*, no. 35 (spring 1993): 45–77.

———. "Beating the Inheritance Bounds: Anne Lister (1791–1840) and Her Dynastic Identity." *Gender and History* 7 (1995): 260–274.

———. *Presenting the Past: Anne Lister of Halifax (1791–1840)*. Hebden Bridge, West Yorkshire: Pennine Pens, 1994.

Lindsay, Jack. *Hogarth: His Art and His World*. London: Hart-Davis MacGibbon, 1977.

Lister, Anne. *Female Fortune: Land, Gender, and Authority: The Anne Lister Diaries and Other Writings, 1833–1836*. Edited by Jill Liddington. London: Rivers Oram, 1998.

———. *I Know My Own Heart: The Diaries of Anne Lister, 1791–1840*. Edited by Helena Whitbread. New York: New York University Press, 1992.

———. *No Priest but Love: Excerpts from the Diaries of Anne Lister, 1824–1826*. Edited by Helena Whitbread. Otley: Smith Settle, 1992.

Liturgia seu Liber Precum Communium, et Administrationis Sacramentorum Aliorúmque . . . London: E. Jones, 1703.

Locke, John. *Two Treatises of Government*. Edited by Peter Laslett. Cambridge: University Press, 1960.

Lockyer, Roger. *Buckingham: The Life and Political Career of George Villiers, First Duke of Buckingham, 1592–1628*. London: Longman, 1981.

———. "An English *Valido*? Buckingham and James I." In *For Veronica Wedgwood These: Studies in Seventeenth-Century History*, edited by Richard Ollard and Pamela Tudor-Craig, 45–58. London: Collins, 1986.

———. *James VI and I*. London: Longman, 1998.

London, H. Stanford. "Some Medieval Treatises on English Heraldry." *Antiquaries Journal* 33 (1953): 169–183.

Luard, Henry Richards, and Charles Hardwick, eds. *A Catalogue of the Manuscripts Preserved in the Library of the University of Cambridge*. Cambridge: University Press, 1856–1867.

Lyly, John. *The Complete Works of John Lyly*. Edited by R. W. Bond. Oxford: Clarendon Press, 1902.

Lynch, Joseph H. *Godparents and Kinship in Early Medieval Europe*. Princeton: Princeton University Press, 1986.

Lytle, Guy Fitch. "Friendship and Patronage in Renaissance Europe." In *Patronage, Art, and Society in Renaissance Italy*, edited by F. W. Kent and Patricia Simons with J. C. Eade, 47–61. Canberra: Humanities Research Centre Australia, 1987.

MacCulloch, Diarmaid. "Henry Chitting's Suffolk Collections." *Proceedings of the Suffolk Institute of Archaeology and History* 34 (1977–1980): 113–114.

———. *Suffolk and the Tudors: Politics and Religion in an English County, 1500–1600*. Oxford: Clarendon Press, 1986.

Macfarlane, Alan. *The Culture of Capitalism*. Oxford: Blackwell, 1987.

———. *The Family Life of Ralph Josselin: A Seventeenth-Century Clergyman: An Essay in Historical Anthropology*. Cambridge: University Press, 1970.

———. *Marriage and Love in England: Modes of Reproduction, 1300–1840*. Oxford: Blackwell, 1986.

———. *The Origins of English Individualism: The Family, Property, and Social Transition*. Oxford: Blackwell, 1978.

———. Review of *Family, Sex, and Marriage in England, 1500–1800*, by Lawrence Stone. *History and Theory* 18 (1979): 103–126.

Macklin, Herbert W. *The Brasses of England*. London: Methuen, 1907.

Macpherson, David, I. Caley, and W. Illingworth, eds. *Rotuli Scotiae in Turri Londinensi et in Domo Capitulari Westmonasteriensi Asservati.* London: G. Eyre and A. Strahan, 1814–1819.

Maddern, Philippa. "'Best Trusted Friends': Concepts and Practices of Friendship among Fifteenth-Century Norfolk Gentry." In *England in the Fifteenth Century: Proceedings of the 1992 Harlaxton Symposium,* edited by Nicholas Rogers, 100–117. Stamford: P. Watkins, 1994.

Malloch, Archibald. *Finch and Baines: A Seventeenth-Century Friendship.* Cambridge: University Press, 1917.

Manuale et Processionale ad Usum Insignis Ecclesiae Eboracensis. Edited by W. G. Henderson. Durham: Andrews for the Surtees Society, 1875.

Marañon, Gregorio. *Antonio Pérez: El Hombre, el Drama, la Epoca.* Madrid: Espasa-Calpe, 1948.

Marlow, Joyce. *The Tolpuddle Martyrs.* London: Deutsch, 1971.

Marlowe, Christopher. *The Complete Works of Christopher Marlowe.* Edited by Fredson Bowers. Cambridge: Cambridge University Press, 1981.

The Marriage, Baptismal, and Burial Registers of the Collegiate Church or Abbey of St. Peter, Westminster. Edited by Joseph L. Chester. London: n.p., 1876.

Marshall, Charles, and William W. Marshall. *The Latin Prayer Book of Charles II, or An Account of the Liturgia of Dean Durel . . .* Oxford: J. Thornton, 1882.

Martial. *Martial, Book XI: A Commentary.* Edited by N. M. Kay. London: Oxford University Press, 1985.

Martin, Brian. *John Henry Newman: His Life and Work.* London: Chatto and Windus, 1982.

Martin, G. H., and J. R. L. Highfield. *A History of Merton College, Oxford.* Oxford: Oxford University Press, 1997.

Matus, Ray. "The Reordering of the Church of St. Thomas of Canterbury, Venerable English College, Rome." *Venerabile* 27 (1979–1982): 80–83.

Maurer, Margaret. "The Poetical Familiarity of John Donne's Letters." In *The Power of Forms in the English Renaissance,* edited by Stephen Jay Greenblatt, 183–199. Norman, OK: Pilgrim Books, 1982.

Mauss, Marcel. *The Gift: Forms and Functions of Exchange in Archaic Societies.* Translated by Ian Cunnison. New York: Norton, 1967.

McCarthy, Daniel, ed. *Collections on Irish Church History from the MSS of the Late V. Rev. Laurence F. Renehan, President of Maynooth College.* Dublin: C. M. Warren, 1861.

McCracken, Grant. "The Exchange of Children in Tudor England: An Anthropological Phenomenon in Historical Context." *Journal of Family History* 8 (1983): 303–313.

McElwee, William. *The Wisest Fool in Christendom: The Reign of King James I and VI.* London: Faber and Faber, 1958.

McEvoy, James. "Notes on the Prologue of St. Aelred of Rievaulx's *De Spiritali Amicitia,* with a Translation." *Traditio* 37 (1981): 396–411.

McFadden, William. *The Life and Works of Antonio del Corro (1527–1591).* Ph.D. thesis. Queen's University of Belfast, 1953.

McFarlane, Kenneth B. "Bastard Feudalism." *Bulletin of the Institute of Historical Research* 20 (1943–1945): 161–180. Reprinted in *Fifteenth Century: Collected Essays by K. B. McFarlane,* 1–22. London: Hambledon Press, 1981.

———. "A Business-Partnership in War and Administration, 1421–1445." *English Historical Review* 78 (1963): 290–310.

———. *Lancastrian Kings and Lollard Knights.* Oxford: Clarendon Press, 1972.

———. "Parliament and 'Bastard Feudalism.'" *Transactions of the Royal Historical Society,* ser. 4, 26

(1944): 53–79. Reprinted in *Fifteenth Century: Collected Essays by K. B. McFarlane*, 23–43. London: Hambledon Press, 1981.

McGuire, Brian Patrick. *Brother and Lover: Aelred of Rievaulx.* New York: Crossroad, 1994.

McLoughlin, John. "*Amicitia* in Practice: John of Salisbury (c. 1120–1180) and His Circle." In *England in the Twelfth Century: Proceedings of the 1988 Harlaxton Symposium*, edited by Daniel Williams, 165–181. Woodbridge, Suffolk: Boydell, 1990.

Mendelson, Sara, and Patricia Crawford. *Women in Early Modern England, 1550–1720.* Oxford: Clarendon Press, 1998.

Merewether, John. *A Statement of the condition and circumstances of the Cathedral Church of Hereford ...* Hereford: W. H. Vale, 1842.

Mertes, Kate. *The English Noble Household, 1250–1600.* Oxford: Blackwell, 1988.

Michaud, J. F., and J. J. F. Poujoulat, eds. *Nouvelle Collection des Mémoires pour servir à l'Histoire de France.* Ser. 1, vol. 2. Lyon: Guyot, 1851.

Mills, Laurens J. "The Meaning of Edward II." *Modern Philology* 32, no. 1 (1934–1935): 11–31.

————. *One Soul in Bodies Twain: Friendship in Tudor Literature and Stuart Drama.* Bloomington, IN: Principia Press, 1937.

Mirabeau, Honoré Gabriel Riquetti de. *Mirabeau's Letters during his Residence in England ...* London: E. Wilson, 1832.

Moir, Arthur L. *The Deans of Hereford Cathedral Church.* Hereford: A. L. Moir, 1968.

Monumental Brasses: The Portfolio Plates of the Monumental Brass Society, 1894–1984. Woodbridge, Suffolk: Boydell, 1988.

Moran, Patrick Francis. *History of the Catholic Archbishops of Dublin since the Reformation.* Vol. 1. Dublin: J. Duffy, 1864.

More, Thomas. *The Complete Works of St. Thomas More.* New Haven: Yale University Press, 1963–.

Morley, H. T. *Monumental Brasses of Berkshire, 14th to 17th Century ...* Reading: Electric Press, 1924.

Morton, A. L. *A People's History of England.* London: V. Gollancz, 1938.

Najemy, John M. *Between Friends: Discourses of Power and Desire in the Machiavelli-Vettori Letters of 1513–1515.* Princeton: Princeton University Press, 1993.

Nashe, Thomas. *The Works of Thomas Nashe.* Edited by Ronald B. McKerrow. Revised by F. P. Wilson. Oxford: Blackwell, 1966.

Neale, John Ernest. "The Elizabethan Political Scene." In *The Age of Catherine de Medici, and Essays in Elizabethan History*, 145–170. London: J. Cape, 1971.

Neale, John Preston. *The History and Antiquities of Westminster Abbey.* London: Willis and Sotheran, 1856.

Newman, John Henry. *Apologia pro Vita Sua.* Edited by Martin J. Svaglic. Oxford: Clarendon Press, 1967.

————. *Historical Sketches.* London: B. M. Pickering, 1872.

————. *John Henry Newman Sermons, 1824–1843.* Edited by Placid Murray. Oxford: Clarendon Press, 1991–1993.

————. *The Letters and Diaries of John Henry Newman.* Vol. 6. Edited by Gerard Tracey. Oxford: Clarendon Press, 1984.

————. *The Letters and Diaries of John Henry Newman.* Vol. 27. Edited by Charles Stephen Dessain and Thomas Gornall. Oxford: Clarendon Press, 1975.

————. *The Letters and Diaries of John Henry Newman.* Vol. 28. Edited by Charles Stephen Dessain and Thomas Gornall. Oxford: Clarendon Press, 1975.

[————]. *Loss and Gain.* London: J. Burns, 1848.

————. *Meditations and Devotions of the Late Cardinal Newman.* Edited by W. P. Neville. New York and London: Longmans, Green and Co., 1893.

———. *Parochial and Plain Sermons.* New edition. Preface by W. J. Copeland. London: Rivingtons, 1868.

———. Review of *Memorials of Oxford* by James Ingram. *British Critic* 24 (1838): 133–146.

North, Roger. *The Lives of the Right Hon. Francis North, Baron Guilford, . . . the Hon. Sir Dudley North, . . . and the Hon. and Rev. Dr John North.* London: H. Colburn, 1826.

O'Day, Rosemary. *The Family and Family Relationships, 1500–1900: England, France, and the United States of America.* Basingstoke: Macmillan, 1994.

———. "Room at the Top: Oxford and Cambridge in the Tudor and Stuart Age." *History Today* 34 (February 1984): 31–38.

O'Donoghue, Freeman, and Harry M. Hake. *Catalogue of Engraved British Portraits Preserved in the Department of Prints and Drawings in the British Museum.* London: Trustees of the British Museum, 1908–1925.

O'Hara, Diana. *Courtship and Constraint: Rethinking the Making of Marriage in Tudor England.* Manchester: Manchester University Press, 2000.

———. "'Ruled by My Friends': Aspects of Marriage in the Diocese of Canterbury, c. 1540–1570." *Continuity and Change* 6 (1991): 9–41.

Oliver, W. H. "Tolpuddle Martyrs and the Trade Union Oaths." *Labour History* 10 (May 1966): 5–12.

Orgel, Stephen. *Impersonations: The Performance of Gender in Shakespeare's England.* Cambridge: Cambridge University Press, 1996.

Orth, John V. *Combination and Conspiracy: A Legal History of Trade Unionism, 1721–1906.* Oxford: Clarendon Press, 1991.

Outhwaite, R. B. *Clandestine Marriage in England, 1500–1850.* London: Hambledon Press, 1995.

Page, William, ed. *A History of Hampshire and the Isle of Wight.* Westminster: A. Constable, 1900–1912.

Pagitt, Ephraim. *Heresiography, or A Description of the Heretickes and Sectaries . . .* London: William Lee, 1674.

Painter, William. *The Palace of Pleasure.* London: Thomas March, 1575.

Parsons, Walter L. E. *Salle: The Story of a Norfolk Paris: Its Church, Manors, and People.* Norwich: Jarrold and Sons, 1937.

Paston, John. *Paston Letters and Papers of the Fifteenth Century.* Edited by Norman Davis. Oxford: Clarendon Press, 1971.

Patlagean, Evelyn. "Christianization and Ritual Kinship in the Byzantine Area." In *Ritual, Religion, and the Sacred: Selections from the Annales, Économies, Sociétés, Civilisations,* vol. 7, edited by Robert Forster and Orest Ranum. Baltimore: Johns Hopkins University Press, 1982. Translated from the French of *Annales Économies, Sociétés, Civilisations* 33 (1978): 625–636.

Peck, Linda Levy. "Benefits, Brokers, and Beneficiaries: The Culture of Exchange in Seventeenth Century England." In *Court, Country, and Culture: Essays on Early Modern British History in Honor of Perez Zagorin,* edited by Bonnelyn Young Kunze and Dwight D. Brautigam, 109–127. Rochester, NY: University of Rochester Press, 1992.

———. *Northampton: Patronage and Politics at the Court of James.* London: Allen and Unwin, 1982.

Pedersen, Frederik. "Did the Medieval Laity Know the Canon Law Rules on Marriage? Some Evidence from Fourteenth-Century York Cause Papers." *Mediaeval Studies* 56 (1994): 111–152.

Pennington, Richard. *A Descriptive Catalogue of the Etched Work of Wenceslaus Hollar, 1607–1677.* Cambridge: Cambridge University Press, 1982.

Percy, Henry Algernon. *The Regulations and Establishment of the Household of Henry Algernon Percy . . .* Edited by Thomas Percy. London: W. Pickering, 1827.

Pérez, Antonio. *Ant. Perezii ad Comitem Essexivm, singularem Angliae Magnatem, & ad Alios Epistolarvm, Centuria vna.* Paris, 1603.

Perkins, William. *The Workes of that Famous and Worthie Minister of Christ in the Vniversitie of Cambridge.* Cambridge: John Legate, 1609.

Persons, Robert. "A Storie of the Domesticall Difficulties in the Englishe Catholike cause." In the Catholic Record Society, *Miscellanea: II.* London: Catholic Record Society, 1906.

Peter, Richard, and Otho Bathurst Peter. *The Histories of Launceston and Dunheved in the County of Cornwall.* Plymouth: W. Brendon and Son, 1885.

Peter Damian. *Die Briefe des Petrus Damiani.* Edited by Kurt Reindel. Munich: Monumenta Germaniae Historiae, 1983.

Petrie, George. *Christian Inscriptions in the Irish Language.* Edited by Margaret Stokes. Dublin: University Press for Royal Historical and Archaeological Association of Ireland, 1872 and 1878.

Pevsner, Nikolaus. *Cornwall.* Revised by Enid Radcliffe. Harmondsworth: Penguin, 1970.

———. *Herefordshire.* Harmondsworth: Penguin, 1963.

———. *London 1: The Cities of London and Westminster.* Revised by Bridget Cherry. Harmondsworth: Penguin, 1973.

———. *North Somerset and Bristol.* Harmondsworth: Penguin, 1958.

———. *Yorkshire: The West Riding.* Revised by Enid Radcliffe. Harmondsworth: Penguin, 1967.

Pevsner, Nikolaus, and Bill Wilson. *Norfolk 1: Norwich and North-East.* Harmondsworth: Penguin, 1997.

Phillips, L. Edward. *The Ritual Kiss in Early Christian Worship.* Cambridge: Grove Books, 1996.

Plummer, Charles, ed. *Two of the Saxon Chronicles Parallel, with Supplementary Extracts from Others.* Oxford: Clarendon Press, 1892.

Plutarch. *Plutarch's Moralia.* Translated by Frank Cole Babbitt. London: Heinemann, 1927–1969.

Pocock, J. G. A. *The Ancient Constitution and the Feudal Law: A Study of English Historical Thought in the Seventeenth Century.* Cambridge: University Press, 1957.

Pollock, Frederick, and Frederic William Maitland. *The History of English Law before the Time of Edward I.* Cambridge: University Press, 1898.

Polsue, Joseph, and William Lake. *A Complete Parochial History of the County of Cornwall compiled from the best Authorities & corrected and improved from actual Survey.* Truro: W. Lake, 1867–1872.

Poos, L. R. "The Heavy-Handed Marriage Counsellor: Regulating Marriage in Some Later-Medieval English Local Ecclesiastical Court Jurisdictions." *American Journal of Legal History* 39 (1995): 291–309.

Pope, Alexander. *The Iliad of Homer, Books X–XXIV.* Edited by Maynard Mack. Twickenham Edition of the Poems of Alexander Pope, vol. 8. London: Methuen, 1967.

Prynne, William. *A Breviate of the Life of William Laud.* London: M. Sparke, 1644.

Public Record Office. *Calendar of State Papers, Domestic Series of the Reigns of Edward VI, Mary, Elizabeth, James I.* London, 1956.

———. *Calendar of State Papers, Domestic Series, of the Reign of James I.* Vol. 2. London, 1857–1859.

———. *Calendar of the Manuscripts of the Marquis of Bath, Preserved at Longleat, Wiltshire.* Vol. 2. London, 1904–1980.

Puttenham, Richard or George. *The Arte of English Poesie.* Edited by Gladys Doidge Willcock and Alice Walker. Cambridge: University Press, 1936.

Pythian-Adams, Charles. *Desolation of a City.* Cambridge: Cambridge University Press, 1979.

Quennell, Peter. *Hogarth's Progress.* London: Collins, 1955.

Raine, James, William Greenwell, John Crawford Hogdson, and Herbert Maxwell Wood, eds. *Wills and Inventories Illustrative of the History, Manners, Language, Statistic, &c., of the Northern Counties of England from the Eleventh Century Downwards.* London: J. B. Nicholas for the Surtees Society, 1835.

Rainolds, John. *Th'overthrow of the stage-playes, by the way of controversie betwixt D. Gager and D. Rainoldes, wherein all the reasons that can be made for them art notably refuted* . . . Middlebruigh: Richard Schilders, 1599.

Rambuss, Richard. "Pleasure and Devotion: The Body of Jesus and Seventeenth-Century Religious Lyric." In *Queering the Renaissance,* edited by Jonathan Goldberg, 253–279. Durham, NC: Duke University Press, 1994.

———. *Spenser's Secret Career.* Cambridge: Cambridge University Press, 1993.

Ramsden, Phyllis M. "Anne Lister's Journal, 1817–1840: An Unusual and Valuable Contemporary Record." *Transactions of the Halifax Antiquarian Society* (1970): 1–13.

Rapp, Claudia. "Ritual Brotherhood in Byzantium." *Traditio* 52 (1997): 286–326.

Rawlinson, Richard. *The History and Antiquities of the City and Cathedral-Church of Hereford* . . . London: R. Gosling, 1717.

Rebholz, Ronald A. *The Life of Fulke Greville, First Lord Brooke.* Oxford: Clarendon Press, 1971.

Rees, Joan. *Fulke Greville, Lord Brooke, 1554–1628: A Critical Biography.* Berkeley: University of California Press, 1971.

———. "Fulke Greville's Epitaph on Sidney." *Review of English Studies,* n.s., 19 (1968): 47–51.

The Registers of Marriages of St. Mary le Bone, Middlesex, 1668–1754, and of Oxford Chapel, Vere Street, St. Mary le Bone, 1736–1754. Edited by W. Bruce Bannerman and R. R. B. Bannerman. London: n.p., 1917–1927.

Registrum Annalium Collegii Mertonensis, 1483–1521. Edited by H. E. Salter. Oxford: Clarendon Press for the Oxford Historical Society, 1923.

Rendell, Joan. *Launceston: Some Pages in History.* Truro: Landfall, 1993.

Rey, Michel. *L'Amitié à la Renaissance: Italie, France, Angleterre, 1450–1650.* Edited by Anne-Sophie Perriaux. Florence: European University Institute, 1999.

Robbins, Alfred F. *Launceston: Past and Present: A Historical and Descriptive Sketch.* Launceston: Walter Weighell, 1888.

Roberts, Michael. "Women and Work in a Sixteenth-Century English Town." In *Work in Towns, 850–1850,* edited by Penelope J. Corfield and Derek Keene, 86–102. Leicester: Leicester University Press, 1990.

Robertson, Jean. "Sidney and Bandello." *Library,* ser. 5, 21 (1966): 326–328. In *Transactions of the Bibliographical Society,* ser. 3, vol. 21.

Robinson, I. S. "The Friendship Network of Gregory VII." *History* 63 (1978): 1–22.

Rocke, Michael. *Forbidden Friendships: Homosexuality and Male Culture in Renaissance Florence.* Oxford: Oxford University Press, 1996.

Roden, Frederick S. "Aelred of Rievaulx, Same-Sex Desire, and the Victorian Monastery." In *Masculinity and Spirituality in Victorian Culture,* edited by Andrew Bradstock, Sean Gill, Anne Hogan, and Sue Morgan, 85–99. Houndmills: Macmillan, 2000.

The Romance of Guy of Warwick: The First or 14th-Century Version. Edited by Julius Zupitza. London: K. Paul, Trench, Trübner for the EETS, 1883–1891.

The Romance of Guy of Warwick: The Second or 15th-Century Version. Edited by Julius Zupitza. London: N. Trübner for the EETS, 1875–1876.

Ross, C. D. "Historical Accounts of Elizabeth Berkeley, Countess of Warwick." In *Transactions of the Bristol and Gloucestershire Archaeological Society* 70 (1951): 91–92.

Routh, Pauline E. Sheppard. "A Gift and Its Giver: John Walker and the East Window of Holy Trinity, Goodramgate, York." *Yorkshire Archaeological Journal* 58 (1986): 109–121.

Rowe, Elizabeth Ashman. "The Female Body Politics and the Miscarriage of Justice in *Athelston.*" *Studies in the Age of Chaucer* 17 (1995): 79–98.

Royal Commission on Historical Manuscripts. *Calendar of the Manuscripts of the Most Hon. the Marquis of Salisbury, Preserved at Hatfield House, Hertfordshire.* London, 1906.

———. *An Inventory of the Historical Monuments in Herefordshire.* London, 1931–1934.

———. *An Inventory of the Historical Monuments in London.* Vol. 1. London, 1924–1930.

———. *An Inventory of the Historical Monuments in the City of Cambridge.* Part 1. London, 1959.

———. *An Inventory of the Historical Monuments in the City of York.* Vol. 5. London, 1962–.

———. *Report on the Manuscripts of the Late Allan George Finch, Esq. of Burley-on-the-Hill, Rutland.* Vols. 1 and 2. London, 1904–1957.

———. "Twelfth Report: Appendix." Part 1. *The Manuscripts of the Earl of Cowper, K.G., preserved at Melbourne Hall, Derbyshire.* London, 1887–1889.

Rubin, Miri. *Corpus Christi: The Eucharist in Late Medieval Culture.* Cambridge: Cambridge University Press, 1991.

Ruggiero, Guido. *The Boundaries of Eros: Sex Crime and Sexuality in Renaissance Venice.* New York: Oxford University Press, 1985.

Sadie, Stanley, ed. *The New Grove Dictionary of Music and Musicians.* London: Grove, 2001.

Saint-Evremond, Charles de Marguetel de Saint-Denis de. *The Works of Monsieur de Saint-Evremond, made English from the French Original.* Edited by Pierre des Maizeaux. London: J. and J. Knapton et al., 1728.

Salvá, Manuel, and Pedro Sainz de Barando. *Documentos Relativos a Antonio Perez, Secretario que fué de Felipe II.* In *Colleción de Documentos Inéditors para la Historia de España,* vol. 12. Madrid: Academia de la Historia, 1848.

Sanders, Wilbur. *The Dramatist and the Received Idea: Studies in the Plays of Marlowe and Shakespeare.* Cambridge: University Press, 1968.

Satan's Harvest Home, or the Present State of Whorecraft, Adultery, Fornication, Procuring, Pimping, Sodomy, and the Game at Flatts. London: printed for the editor, 1749.

Savage, Canon. "The Halifax Parish Church: Features of Its Architecture." *Transactions of the Halifax Antiquarian Society* (1906): 165–175.

———. "Halifax Parish Church: The 17th Century Woodwork." *Transactions of the Halifax Antiquarian Society* (1908): 351–395.

Scott, Walter. *Minstrelsy of the Scottish Border.* London: T. Legg. et al., 1839.

Sévigné, Marie de Rabutin-Chantal de. *Lettres de Madame de Sévigné.* Paris: Furne, 1860.

Shakespeare, William. *Shake-Speares Sonnets. Neuer before Imprinted.* 1609. Reprinted, London: Noel Douglas Replicas, 1926.

Shannon, Laurie. *Sovereign Amity: Figures of Friendship in Shakespearean Contexts.* Chicago: University of Chicago Press, 2001.

Sharpe, J. A. *Crime in Seventeenth-Century England: A County Study.* Cambridge: Cambridge University Press, 1983.

Shaw, Brent D. "A Groom of One's Own?" *New Republic,* July 1994. Electronic MS.

———. "Ritual Brotherhood in Roman and Post-Roman Society." *Traditio* 52 (1997): 327–355.

Shepard, Thomas. *The Works of Thomas Shepard, First Pastor of the First Church . . .* Boston: Doctrinal Tract and Book Society, 1853.

Shepherd, Simon. *Marlowe and the Politics of Elizabethan Theatre.* Brighton: Harvester Press, 1986.

Shutt, Francis J. "A Plan of the College in 1630." *Venerabile* 12 (1944–1946): 48–50.

Sidney, Philip. *Miscellaneous Prose of Sir Philip Sidney.* Edited by Katherine Duncan-Jones and J. A. Van Dorsten. Oxford: Clarendon Press, 1973.

———. *The Poems of Sir Philip Sidney.* Edited by William A. Ringler, Jr. Oxford: Clarendon Press, 1962.

Smith, A. Hassell. "Labourers in Late Sixteenth-Century England: A Case Study from North Norfolk." *Continuity and Change* 4, no. 1 (1989): 11–52; no. 3 (1989): 367–394.

Smith, Alan G. R. *Servant of the Cecils: The Life of Sir Michael Hickes, 1543–1612*. London: J. Cape, 1977.

Smith, Charles G. "Sententious Theory in Spenser's Legend of Friendship." *English Literary History* 2 (1935): 165–191.

Smith, George, Leslie Stephen, and Sidney Lee, ed. *Dictionary of National Biography*. London: Oxford University Press, 1885–1901.

Smith, Llinos Beverley. "Fosterage, Adoption, and God-Parenthood: Ritual and Fictive Kinship in Medieval Wales." *Welsh History Review* 16 (1992–1993): 1–35.

Smith, Richard M. *Land, Kinship, and Life-Cycle*. Cambridge: Cambridge University Press, 1984.

Southern, R. W. *Saint Anselm and His Biographer: A Study of Monastic Life and Thought, 1059–c. 1130*. Cambridge: University Press, 1963.

Spenser, Edmund. *The Works of Edmund Spenser: A Variorum Edition*. Edited by Edwin Almiron Greenlaw, Charles Grosvenor Osgood, and Frederick Morgan Padelford. Baltimore: Johns Hopkins Press, 1947.

Starkey, David. "Representation through Intimacy: A Study in the Symbolism of Monarchy and Court Office in Early-Modern England." In *Symbols and Sentiments: Cross-Cultural Studies in Symbolism*, edited by I. M. Lewis, 187–224. London: Academic Press, 1977.

———, ed. *The English Court: From the Wars of the Roses to the Civil War*. London: Longman, 1987.

The Statutes at Large: From Magna Charta to 4 George III (1763–1764): From the Twentieth Year of the Reign of King George the Second to the Thirtieth Year of the Reign of King George the Second. Edited by Owen Ruffhead. London: Basket, 1764.

Stebbing, Henry. *An Enquiry into the Force and Operation of the Annulling Clauses in a late Act for the better preventing of Clandestine Marriages, with Respect to Conscience*. London: M. Cooper, 1754.

Steinberg, Leo. *The Sexuality of Christ in Renaissance Art and in Modern Oblivion*. 2d edition. Chicago: University of Chicago Press, 1996.

Stevens, John E., ed. *Mediaeval Carols*. London: Stainer and Bell, 1952.

Stevenson, Kenneth. *Nuptial Blessing: A Study of Christian Marriage Rites*. London: Alcuin Club, SPCK, 1982.

Stewart, Alan. *Close Readers: Humanism and Sodomy in Early Modern England*. Princeton: Princeton University Press, 1997.

Stone, Lawrence. *The Family, Sex, and Marriage in England, 1500–1800*. London: Weidenfeld and Nicolson, 1977.

The Story of Genesis and Exodus, an Early English Song, about A.D. 1250. Edited by Richard Morris. London: Trübner for the EETS, 1865.

Stow, John. *A Survey of London*. Edited by Charles L. Kingsford. Oxford: Clarendon Press, 1908.

The Strangers' Guide through the City of York, and its Cathedral . . . York: Bellerby, 1846.

Strittmatter, Anselm. "The 'Barberinum S. Marci' of Jacques Goar: Barberinianus graecus 336." *Ephemerides Liturgicae*, n.s., 7 (1933): 329–367.

Strohm, Paul. *Social Chaucer*. Cambridge, MA: Harvard University Press, 1989.

Stubbe, John. *The discoverie of a gaping gulf whereinto England is like to be swallowed by another French marriage, if the Lord forbid not the banes, by letting her Maiestie see the sin and punishment thereof*. London: H. Singleton for W. Page, 1579.

Stubbs, William. *Constitutional History of England in Its Origin and Development*. Oxford: Clarendon Press, 1874–1878.

———. "Systems of Landholding in Mediaeval Europe." In *Lectures on Early English History*, edited by Arthur Hassall. London: Longmans, Green, 1906.

————, ed. *Chronicles of the Reigns of Edward I and Edward II*. London: Longman, 1882–1883.

Swett, Katharine W. "'The Account between Us': Honor, Reciprocity, and Companionship in Male Friendship in the Later Seventeenth Century." *Albion* 31, no. 1 (spring 1999): 1–30.

Symeonis Monachi Opera Omnia. Edited by Thomas Arnold. London: Longman, 1882–1885.

Tadmor, Naomi. "'Family' and 'Friend' in *Pamela*: A Case-Study in the History of the Family in Eighteenth-Century England." *Social History* 14 (1989): 289–306.

Talbot, Hugh. *Christian Friendship, by Saint Ailred of Rievaulx*. London: Catholic Book Club, 1942.

Taylor, Jeremy. *The Whole Works of the Right Rev. Jeremy Taylor*. Edited by Reginald Heber. Revised by Charles Page Eden. London: Longmans, 1854.

Thompson, E. P. *The Making of the English Working Class*. Harmondsworth: Penguin, 1968.

Thompson, Stith. *The Folktale*. New York: Dryden, 1951.

Tolhurst, James. "A Blessed and Ever Enduring Fellowship: The Development of John Henry Newman's Thought on Death and the Life Beyond." *Recusant History* 22 (1994–1995): 424–457.

Torr, V. J. B. "The Oddington Shroud Brass and Its Lost Fellows." *Transactions of the Monumental Brass Society* 7 (1934–1942): 225–235.

Trapp, J. B. "A Postscript to Matsys." *Burlington Magazine* 121 (July 1979): 434–437.

Traub, Valerie. "The (In)significance of 'Lesbian' Desire in Early Modern England." In *Erotic Politics: Desire on the Renaissance Stage*, edited by Susan Zimmerman, 150–169. New York: Routledge, 1992.

————. "The Perversion of 'Lesbian' Desire." *History Workshop Journal*, no. 41 (spring 1996): 19–49.

————. *The Renaissance of Lesbianism in Early Modern England*. Cambridge: Cambridge University Press, 2002.

Tristram, Henry. *Newman and His Friends*. London: John Lane, 1933.

Trokelowe, John de, and Henry Blaneford. *Joannis de Trokelowe, et Henrici de Blaneford, Monachorum S. Albani, Chronica Monasterii S. Alabani*. Edited by Henry Thomas Riley. London: Longmans, Green, Reader, and Dyer, 1886.

A Trve and Perfect Relation of the whole proceedings against the late most barbarous Traitors, Garnet a Iesuite, and his Confederats. London: Robert Barker, 1606.

Trumbach, Randolph. "Gender and the Homosexual Role in Modern Western Culture: The 18th and 19th Centuries Compared." In *Homosexuality, Which Homosexuality? International Conference on Gay and Lesbian Studies*, edited by Dennis Altman, 149–169. London: Gay Men's Press, 1989.

————. *Sex and the Gender Revolution*. Vol. 1. *Heterosexuality and the Third Gender in Enlightenment London*. Chicago: University of Chicago Press, 1998.

————. "Sex, Gender, and Sexual Identity in Modern Culture: Male Sodomy and Female Prostitution in Enlightenment England." In *Forbidden History: The State, Society, and the Regulation of Sexuality in Modern Europe: Essays from the Journal of the History of Sexuality*, edited by John C. Fout, 89–106. Chicago: University of Chicago Press, 1992.

Tunstall, James. *A Vindication of the Power of States to prohibit Clandestine Marriages under the Pain of Absolute Nullity . . . in Answer to The Rev. Dr. Stebbing's Dissertation*. London: J. and J. Rivington, 1755.

Ungerer, Gustav. *A Spaniard in Elizabethan England: The Correspondence of Antonio Pérez's Exile*. London: Tamesis, 1974–1976.

Vanita, Ruth. *Sappho and the Virgin Mary: Same-Sex Love and the English Literary Imagination*. New York: Columbia University Press, 1996.

Vasey, Michael. "The Family and the Liturgy." In *The Family in Theological Perspective*, edited by Stephen C. Barton, 169–185. Edinburgh: T. and T. Clark, 1996.

Venn, John, et al. *Biographical History of Gonville and Caius College, 1349–1897.* With supplements by E. S. Roberts, Edward John Gross, and others. Cambridge: University Press, 1897–1912.

———. *Early Collegiate Life.* Cambridge: W. Heffer, 1913.

Vicinus, Martha. *Intimate Friends: Same-Sex Love between Women, 1780–1920.* Forthcoming.

Virgil. *The Aeneid of Virgil.* Translated by C. Day Lewis. London: Hogarth, 1952.

———. *Virgil.* Edited by I. Rushton Fairclough. London: Heinemann, 1918.

Vita Edwardi Secundi, Monachi cuiusdam Malmesberiensis. Edited by Noël Denholm-Young. London: Nelson, 1957.

Waddell, Chrysogonus. "Notes towards the Exegesis of a Letter by Saint Stephen Harding." In *Noble Piety and Reformed Monasticism,* edited E. Rozanne Elder, 10–39. Kalamazoo, MI: Cistercian Publications, 1981.

Wall, Richard, Jean Robin, and Peter Laslett, eds. *Family Forms in Historic Europe.* Cambridge: Cambridge University Press, 1983.

Waller, J. G., and L. A. B. Waller. *A Series of Monumental Brasses, from the Thirteenth to the Sixteenth Century.* London: Nichols, 1864.

Ward, John. *The Lives of the Professors of Gresham College . . .* London: J. Moore, 1740.

Ward, Wilfrid. *The Life of John Henry Cardinal Newman, Based on His Private Journals and Correspondence.* London: Longmans, Green, 1912.

Watson, John. *The History and Antiquities of the Parish of Halifax, in Yorkshire.* London: T. Lowndes, 1775.

Watt, Tessa. *Cheap Print and Popular Piety, 1550–1640.* Cambridge: Cambridge University Press, 1991.

Weissman, Ronald F. E. *Ritual Brotherhood in Renaissance Florence.* New York: Academic Press, 1981.

Weldon, Anthony. *The Court and Character of King James.* London: R. I. and J. Wright, 1650.

Wenzel, Siegfried. *Preachers, Poets, and the Early English Lyric.* Princeton: Princeton University Press, 1986.

Westminster Abbey: Official Guide. London: Dean and Chapter of Westminster, 1977.

Westminster Abbey: The Monuments. Photographs by Joe Whitlock Blundell. Introduced by John Physic. London: Murray, 1989.

Westwood, Rosalind, and Pete Brown. *Shibden Hall Halifax: A Visitor's Guide.* Calderdale Leisure Services, 1998.

Westwood, Rosalind, Pat Sewell, and Jill Liddington. *Anne Lister Research Directory: An Introduction to the Sources.* Calderdale Leisure Services, 1997.

Whellan, T., and Co. *History and Topography of the City of York and the North Riding of Yorkshire.* Vol. 1. Beverley: J. Green for the publishers, 1857.

Whinder, Richard. "The Iconography of the College Church." *Venerabile* 31 (1996–1999): 70–76.

William of Malmesbury. *Willelmi Malmesbiriensis Monachi De Gestis Regum Anglorum.* Edited by William Stubbs. London: Eyre and Spottiswoode for HMSO, 1887–1889.

Williams, Michael E. *The Venerable English College, Rome: A History, 1579–1979.* London: Associated Catholic Publications, 1979.

———. *The Venerable English College, Rome: An Illustrated Guide.* [London: Associated Catholic Publishers,] 1999.

Williamson, Hugh Ross. *George Villiers, First Duke of Buckingham: Study for a Biography.* London: Duckworth, 1940.

Willis, Browne. *A Survey of the Cathedrals of York, Durham, Carlisle, Chester, Man, Lichfield, Hereford, Worcester, Gloucester, and Bristol . . .* London: R. Gosling, 1727–1730.

Wilson, Jean. "Ethics Girls: The Personification of Moral Systems on Early Modern English Monuments." *Church Monuments* 13 (1998): 87–105.

———. "'Two Names of Friendship, but One Starre': Memorials to Single-Sex Couples in the Early Modern Period." *Church Monuments* 10 (1995): 70–83.

Wiveton Village. Wiveton, n.d. Pamphlet.

The Women-Hater's Lamentation. London: n.p., 1707.

Wood, Anthony A. *Athenae Oxonienses: An Exact History of All the Writers and Bishops . . .* Edited by Philip Bliss. London: Rivington, 1813–1820.

———. *The History and Antiquities of the Colleges and Halls in the University of Oxford.* Edited by John Gutch. Oxford: Clarendon Press, 1786.

———. *The Life and Times of Anthony Wood, Antiquary, of Oxford, 1632–1695, Described by Himself.* Edited by Andrew Clark and Llewelyn Powys. Oxford: Oxford Historical Society at the Clarendon Press, 1891–1900.

Woods, Constance. "Same-Sex Unions or Semantic Illusions?" *Communio* 22 (summer 1995): 338–342.

Woolf, Rosemary. *The English Religious Lyric in the Middle Ages.* Oxford: Clarendon Press, 1968.

Wootton, David. "Francis Bacon: Your Flexible Friend." In *The World of the Favourite*, edited by J. H. Elliott and L. W. B. Brockliss, 184–204. New Haven: Yale University Press, 1999.

———. "Friendship Portrayed: A New Account of Utopia." *History Workshop Journal*, no. 45 (spring 1998): 28–47.

———. "The Levellers." In *Democracy: The Unfinished Journey*, edited by John Dunn, 71–89. Oxford: Oxford University Press, 1992.

Wormald, Jenny. *Lords and Men in Scotland: Bonds of Manrent, 1442–1603.* Edinburgh: J. Donald, 1985.

Wrightson, Keith. "Household and Kinship in Sixteenth Century England." *History Workshop Journal*, no. 12 (fall 1981): 152–158

Wrightson, Keith, and David Levine. *Poverty and Piety in an English Village: Terling, 1525–1700.* New York: Academic Press, 1979.

Young, Charles R. *The Making of the Neville Family in England, 1166–1400.* Woodbridge, Suffolk: Boydell, 1996.

Young, Michael B. *James VI and I and the History of Homosexuality.* Basingstoke: Macmillan, 2000.

———. *Servility and Service: The Life and Work of Sir John Coke.* Woodbridge, Suffolk: Boydell for the Royal Historical Society, 1986.

Young, Robin Darling. "Gay Marriage: Reimagining Church History." *First Things* 47 (1994): 43–48.

Zaninović, O. Antonin. "Dva Latinska spomenika o sklapanju pobratimstva u Dalmaciji." *Zbornik za narodni život i običaje Južnih Slavena* 45 (1971): 713–724.

Zemon Davis, Natalie. "Beyond the Market: Books as Gifts in Sixteenth-Century France." *Transactions of the Royal Historical Society* 33 (1983): 69–88.

INDEX